Men as Women, WOMEN AS MEN

Translated from the German by John L. Vantine

Men as Women, WOMEN AS MEN

Sabine Lang

Changing Gender in Native American Cultures

University of Texas Press *Austin*

Printed in the United States of America
First edition, 1998

Requests for permission to reproduce material from this work should be sent to
Permissions, University of Texas Press, P.O. Box 7819,
Austin, TX 78713–7819.

♾The paper used in this publication meets the minimum requirements of American National Standard for Information Sciences—Permanence of Paper for Printed Library Materials, ANSI Z39.48-1984.

Library of Congress Cataloging-in-Publication Data

Lang, Sabine.
[Männer als Frauen, Frauen als Männer. English]
Men as women, women as men : changing gender in Native American cultures / Sabine Lang ; translated from the German by John L. Vantine.
p. cm.
Includes bibliographical references and index.
ISBN 0-292-74700-4 (cloth : alk. paper).—
ISBN 0-292-74701-2 (paper : alk. paper)
1. Indians of North America—Sexual behavior. 2. Indians of North America—Social life and customs. 3. Sex role—Cross-Cultural studies. 4. Homosexuality—Cross-cultural studies. 5. Transvestism—Cross-cultural studies. I. Title.
E98.S48L3613 1998
305.3'08997—dc21 97-34759

To my parents

Contents

List of Maps, Tables, and Figures

MAPS†

†*(Map of North America after Driver 1961, California Map after Kroeber 1925)*

TABLES

FIGURES

Preface

When the German version of this book was published in 1990, the most exhaustive works about those people in Native American cultures commonly referred to as "berdaches" in anthropological literature—that is, people who partially or completely take on the culturally defined role of the other sex and who are classified neither as men nor as women, but as genders of their own in their respective cultures—were Callender and Kochems' 1983 article, "The North American Berdache," Walter Williams' book, *The Spirit and the Flesh* (1986b), and the anthology *Living the Spirit,* edited by Gay American Indians and Will Roscoe (1988). What was still missing was a monographic work taking into account all the available written sources and the great diversity expressed in them. Callender and Kochems' contribution to the subject came closest to accomplishing this task, yet, since it was an article and not a book, its scope necessarily had to be limited. Williams' book, on the other hand, was the first monograph on the North American "berdache," as well as similar phenomena in cultures outside North America. Williams (1986b:4), however, explicitly "focuses on those societies which, at least aboriginally, provided berdaches a respected status." While this is a legitimate approach, it results in a one-sided picture of the role and status of "berdaches" in Native American cultures, leaving the reader with the impression that being a "berdache" in those cultures was a universal, timeless, and blissfully primeval experience (cf. Jacobs, Thomas, and Lang, 1997a).

As I point out in more detail in the introductory chapters to follow, the present book attempts to demonstrate and discuss the great variety of roles and statuses that have been subsumed under the term "berdache." In some Native American cultures, for example, male-bodied "berdaches" traditionally (that is, in the pre-reservation and early reservation periods) were held in high esteem as medicine persons endowed with special powers, but in other cultures their roles and statuses apparently were far more secular and less esteemed. Although "berdaches" of both sexes were certainly not universally highly revered individuals to whom special supernatural potential was attributed, they seem at least to have been *accepted* in almost all Native American cultures in which they have been reported to exist. The present book was written to explore these roles—their cultural construction, expression, and context—in depth and in detail. Such an "encyclopedic" work on the subject in English is still lacking, although since 1990 a few articles (such as Fulton and Anderson 1992; Jacobs and Cromwell 1992; Roscoe 1994; Schnarch 1992) and two monographs (Roscoe 1991, on the famous Zuni *lhamana*, Wewha, and Trexler 1995) have appeared in print.

When I presented some of the results of my research during the annual meeting of the American Anthropological Association in 1991, Theresa J. May, assistant director and executive editor of University of Texas Press, became interested in my work. We agreed that I should find a translator and funding to pay him or her, and then submit a translated version of *Männer als Frauen, Frauen als Männer* to be considered for publication by University of Texas Press. Funds for the translation were made available by the California Institute of Contemporary Arts, and John L. Vantine, who is a linguist as well as an anthropologist specializing in Plains archaeology and anthropology, agreed to translate the book into English. When going through the translation after it was finished, I made minor changes wherever I felt that there was need for a small addition or clarification. Substantively, the text corresponds to the German original.

This book is an ethnohistoric work about the past. While doing library research and writing the dissertation, however, I became interested in the present. Thus, my work on the North American "berdache" has continued since I completed the German version of this book, *Männer als Frauen, Frauen als Männer*. In 1992 and 1993, I embarked on a fieldwork project on gender variance—defined by Jacobs and Cromwell (1992:63) as "cultural expressions of multiple genders (i.e., more than two) and the opportunity for individuals to change gender roles and identities over the course of their lifetimes"—in contemporary Native American communities (Lang 1996). Some of the results of this research have already been published (e.g., Lang 1994, 1995, 1996, 1997a), and the bulk of the results, including lengthy excerpts from taped conversations, will be published as a monograph.

Soon after I started to talk to Native American people about the research I was planning to conduct, two things became apparent. First, in most Native American communities both on and off the reservations, the roles and statuses explored in the present book had disappeared by the 1930s or 1940s (with some exceptions, such as the *winkte* interviewed by Williams in the early 1980s and some people I interviewed who identified with the gender variance traditions of their respective cultures). Second, many Native Americans have become increasingly disenchanted with the term "berdache." Williams (1986b:9f.), whose book circulates widely among Native American gays, lesbians, and people who identify themselves as being of a gender other than woman or man within cultural constructions of multiple genders, has pointed out that the word "berdache" derives from an Arab term that means "male prostitute" or "catamite" (Angelino and Shedd 1955).

I also learned that the term "two-spirit" (or "two-spirited") has come into general use in the urban Native American gay and lesbian communities. According to Anguksuaq (in press), the term originated in 1989 during an international/intertribal gathering of gay and lesbian Native Americans. Native American lesbians and gays have long been struggling to find an identity and self-identifying terms appropriate to them—terms reflecting both their sexual orientation and their specific ethnic heritage (Gay American Indians and Roscoe 1988; Jacobs, Thomas, and Lang 1997a; Lang 1994, 1995). Since those individuals usually called "berdaches" in anthropological writings often entered into relationships with partners of the same (biological) sex, many urban gay and lesbian Native Americans have come to view themselves as continuing the traditions of gender variance that once existed in most Native American cultures (see Burns 1988). The term "two-spirit" reflects the combination of masculinity and femininity that was often attributed to males in a feminine role and females in a masculine role in the tribal societies. In the tribal societies, however, such a combination of the masculine and the feminine manifested itself in very tangible ways, whereas contemporary Native American gays and lesbians regard the combination of masculine and feminine potentials as a more abstract, "spiritual" quality inherent, or inborn, in homosexual individuals. Hence, I suppose, the term "two-spirited" and not "two-gendered."

"Two-spirit"/"two-spirited" originally referred to (1) those people referred to as "berdaches" in the literature, (2) modern Native Americans who identify with these "alternative" roles and gender statuses, and (3) contemporary Native American lesbians and gays. Tietz (1996:205) has pointed out that the term has meanwhile come to encompass an entire host of roles, gender identities, and sexual behaviors—namely,

- contemporary Native American/First Nations people who are gay or lesbian;
- contemporary Native American/First Nations alternative genders;
- the traditions of institutionalized gender variance and alternative sexualities in Native American/First Nations (tribal) cultures;
- traditions of gender variance in other cultures;
- transvestites, transsexuals, and transgendered people; and
- drag queens and butches.

The contemporary two-spirit identities are discussed in some detail elsewhere, both by self-identified Native American two-spirited people and by Native and non-Native anthropologists (Jacobs, Thomas, and Lang 1997b). For the present book, the issue of terminology is of primary importance. When I wrote my dissertation in German, I used the term "berdache," which I defined as "a person of physically unambiguous sex who voluntarily and permanently takes on the culturally defined activities and occupations of the opposite sex, and who has a special (ambivalent) gender status assigned to him/her by his/her culture" (Lang 1990:10). Like many anthropologists before me, I used "berdache" as a term well known and long established in anthropology, and—also like many anthropologists (and even Native American writers) before me, I am sure—with no intention of implying that the roles of males in a woman's role or females in a man's role in Native American cultures resemble those of Arab "kept boys" or "prostitutes." Yet, with the new awareness on the part of both anthropologists and Native Americans of the word's original meaning, I agree that it is time to find more appropriate terminology.

In 1993 and 1994, two conferences on the North American "berdache," organized by Sue-Ellen Jacobs (University of Washington), Wesley Thomas (Navajo, University of Washington), and myself, convened non-Native and Native anthropologists as well as self-identified two-spirited community activists. The goal of the conferences was to discuss matters of representation and terminology, a discussion which we felt had too long been dominated by White anthropologists and historians, without Native American participation. Although the submitted papers reflected a variety of scholarly and autobiographical concerns (Jacobs, Thomas, and Lang 1997b), the discussion during both conferences centered largely on terminology. We all agreed that the term "berdache" was no longer appropriate. If it is ill-chosen for referring to males, it is downright absurd when used to refer to females. But which term, or terms, should replace it? My suggestion to replace "berdache" with the descriptive terms "womanly male" (for male-bodied "berdaches") and "manly female" (for female-bodied "berdaches") was met with little enthusiasm, especially by the Native American participants, one of whom discarded the terms as "too sterile." Instead, it finally was agreed upon to replace "berdache" with "two-spirit" (see Jacobs and Thomas 1994). It was further agreed upon that, whenever we needed to use the term "berdache" in our writings (for example, when referring to earlier sources), the word should be put into quotation marks.

Some time has elapsed since the two conferences were held, and I have had ample opportunity to reflect on the best way to rephrase the term in the present book. When I gave the manuscript to the translator, I asked him just to translate the word as it was; I would decide about terminology as I went through the translation before mailing it to the publisher.

For several reasons, I did not replace "berdache" with "two-spirit," but usually used other terms instead. Most importantly, a scholarly work needs clarity. Like "berdache," "two-spirit" has come to encompass a variety of different identities and roles. In the following, however, it is necessary to distinguish clearly among various categories of people whose roles and statuses are not identical, and often, as far as can be ascertained, were also not considered identical in traditional/tribal Native American cultures. Moreover, "two-spirit" is a term that originated under very specific historical circumstances and that started out with a very specific meaning. In its original meaning, it encompasses contemporary gay and lesbian Native Americans as well as people, both in the old tribal cultures and in the present, who identify themselves as being of a gender other than man or woman, such as the Navajo *nádleehé,* the Shoshoni *tainna wa'ippe,* or the Lakota *winkte.* In that meaning, Native American gays/lesbians of today and the alternatively gendered people of the tribal cultures are viewed as essentially identical. This view, however, is not even unanimously shared in Native American communities, especially by people who are still familiar with the traditions of gender variance in their cultures and who will often, for various reasons (Lang, 1997a), view gays and lesbians as different from *winkte, tainna wa'ippe,* and so on.

The term and concept of "two-spirit" is of great importance to contemporary gay and lesbian/two-spirited people. In urban Native American gay and lesbian communities, it has led to the development, and strengthening, of specifically Native American lesbian and gay identities and roles. On a political level, within the context of the interaction of these communities with the Indian communities at large, the interpretation of contemporary gays and lesbians as continuing the once culturally accepted traditions of gender variance will hopefully lead to greater acceptance. For scholarly purposes, however, replacing "berdache" with "two-spirit" would blur differences as well as changes that have occurred in the course of time that, within the historical contexts outlined in the present book, cannot be ignored. Another problem is that "two-spirit" is a term that, as conference participants also agreed, is not supposed to be translated into Native American languages because it can assume meanings not intended by those who in the late 1980s coined the English term. If translated into Navajo, "two-spirit" means someone who is neither living nor dead (Wesley Thomas, information shared during the 1994 conference), a state of being that is dreadful to Navajo people given their attitude toward the dead. Traditional Navajos on the reservation would probably be horrified if someone identified himself or herself as such a person. If translated into Shoshoni, "two-spirit" assumes the meaning "ghost" (Clyde Hall, information shared during the 1994 conference). According to Will Roscoe (personal communication, 1992), the Zuni translation of "two-spirit" would be "witch."

In the following, the term "berdache" (in quotation marks) will be used whenever direct reference is made to earlier sources. Otherwise, those who in anthropological writings have been termed male "berdaches" will be referred to by their traditional names, such as *nadle* (Navaho), *winkte* (Lakota), and so on, or by the term *women-men* (or, for female "berdaches," *men-women).* Readers who are familiar with the subject will notice that the use of the term *men-women* is in direct contrast to some anthropological writings—such as Fulton and Anderson (1992) or Roscoe (1991)—in which males in a woman's role are called "men-women." Linguistically, however, and also in the context of the cultures under discussion, it makes much more sense to put the *chosen* gender first, and the gender corresponding to the sex of birth second. In this choice I follow Bleibtreu-Ehrenberg (1984), who titled her book on males who take up the culturally defined feminine role *Der Weibmann* (The Woman-Man). Also, within the context of constructions of multiple genders, the sex of birth is invariably less important than the gender chosen by a person who decides to take up the culturally defined role of the "other" sex. When I discussed the matter of terminology with Sue-Ellen Jacobs and Wesley Thomas, and then with the translator of the present book, John L. Vantine, we all agreed that "woman-man" is a more fitting designation for males taking up the woman's role than is "man-woman." For the same reasons, "man-woman" is the most suitable term for females in a man's role.

Moreover, the terms woman-man and man-woman are purely descriptive, and do not carry any preconceived meaning. They also generally reflect the terminology employed in Native American cultures themselves. There, wherever institutionalized gender variance (and special gender statuses for people who were neither men nor women) existed or still exists, the terms for males in a woman's role and females in a man's role usually indicate that they were seen as combining, in one way or another, the masculine and feminine genders.

Also important is the use of the personal pronouns for referring to women-men and men-women, respectively. At the 1993 conference "The 'North American Berdache,'" Evelyn Blackwood noted that "white anthropologists have tended to study those two-spirit/berdache who physically have our own sex and then refer to them by the pronoun appropriate to their physical sex, but not their gender . . . Consequently, we are reproducing our own cultural models on two-spirit/berdache gender." Yet which pronoun is appropriate to their gender? What Blackwood probably meant is that women-men and men-women should be referred to by the pronoun appropriate for persons who fulfill the *gender role* chosen by them. That would mean that women-men should be referred to as "she," and men-women as "he." However, since women-men and men-women are within their cultures viewed as neither men nor women, but as intermediate genders of their own, neither the feminine nor the masculine pronoun is really appropriate. In the present book, I decided upon a course that would recognize the importance of local cultural context as well as gender role (how one is seen, how one behaves) and gender identity (how one experiences oneself). In the main, I use the pronoun that corresponds to chosen gender. In many cases, however, I use the pronoun that most aptly fits the particular circumstance.

In recent anthropological literature, the term "gender variance" has been employed both to refer to the *phenomenon* itself (people expressing the desire to live in the culturally defined role of the other sex; see, e.g., Williams 1986b) and to the *institutionalization* of the phenomenon (by means of cultural constructions of multiple genders; see, e.g., Jacobs and Cromwell 1992). The term used in the German version of the present work was *Geschlechtsrollenwechsel* (gender role change), referring to the process of exchanging the gender role culturally ascribed to one's sex of birth for the gender role of the other sex. When talking about gender variance in the sense of institutionalized systems of multiple genders, the term *institutionalisierter Geschlechtsrollenwechsel* (institutionalized gender role change) is used. This terminology is maintained in the English translation.

One last remark about terminology. In the following, "Indian" and "Native American" are used interchangeably. The general usage in anthropological writings in the United States now seems to be to more or less exclusively employ the term "Native American." In the German original of this book I used "Indian," mostly because there is no German word that corresponds to "Native American," and "Native American" cannot easily and directly be translated into German. When translated into German, it becomes the verbal monstrosity *nordamerikanische Ureinwohner/innen* (aboriginal inhabitants of North America). When talking to Native Americans on and off the reservations, however, I have noticed that some prefer to refer to themselves as Native American, others as Indian. Thus, in the English translation I have not given preference to either term over the other.

PART ONE

Introduction, Background, and Definitions

Chapter ONE

INTRODUCTION

HISTORICAL BACKGROUND

The changing of gender roles—the adoption, for the most varied reasons, of the culturally defined social role of the opposite biological sex—has been reported worldwide for numerous cultures and for all historic periods. In Greek mythology, Thetis hides her son Achilles, whose death before Troy has been prophesied, by disguising him as a girl at the court of King Lycomedes on the island of Scyrus. But in order to win him for the military campaign, Odysseus resorts to a ruse which, in modified form, was also used by North American Indians in order to determine whether a boy really was a "berdache": he has a spear and a shield brought into the women's room, and orders the war trumpet blown. Achilles reaches for the weapons and thus gives himself away as a man (Ranke-Graves 1960, 2:271; Schwab 1986:354).

The Amazons of antiquity were described as an entire nation of women who pursued male occupations (Hammes 1981; Herodotus 1971:292ff.). Change of gender roles for a lifetime was found among some men of the Scythians, and according to Herodotus, the young women of the neighboring Sarmatians led the life of warriors until they had killed an enemy; only then were they permitted to marry. But even as married women, they went on the hunt dressed as men, whether alone or in the company of their husbands, and they accompanied the men in war (see Herodotus 1971:294; Hammond 1882:339ff., 1891:107ff.). Gender role change also occurred in ancient Rome (Green 1974:4ff.), and the female pope Joan has gone down in the history of the European Middle Ages as a spectacular, if isolated, case (Fiocchetto 1988:212; Green 1974:6).

In later centuries, reports are encountered over and over again con-

Map 1. Tribes Investigated for This Study

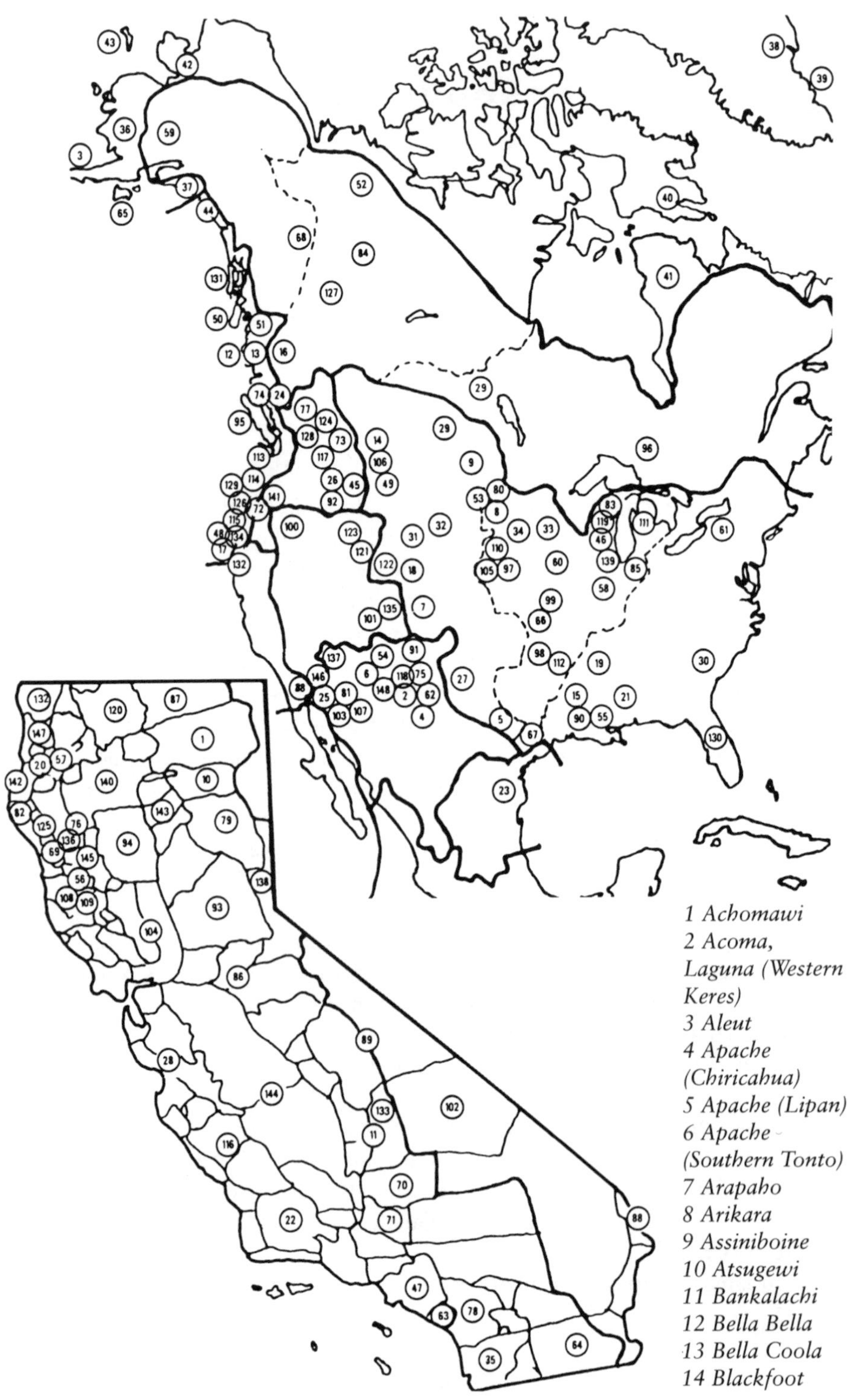

15 Caddo
16 Carrier
17 Chetco River
18 Cheyenne
19 Chickasaw
20 Chilula
21 Choctaw
22 Chumash
23 Coahuiltecan
24 Coast Salish
25 Cocopa
26 Coeur d'Aléne
27 Comanche
28 Costanoan
29 Cree
30 Creek
31 Crow
32 Lakota (Teton)
33 Dakota (Santee)
34 Dakota (Yankton)
35 Diegueño
36 Eskimo (Alaska)
37 Eskimo (Chugach)
38 Eskimo (Ammassarlik)
39 Eskimo (Akerniaq)
40 Eskimo (Baffin Land)
41 Eskimo (Hudson Bay)
42 Eskimo (Máhlemut)
43 Eskimo St. Lawrence)
44 Eyak
45 Flathead
46 Fox
47 Gabrielino
48 Galice Creek
49 Gros Ventre (Atsina)
50 Haida
51 Haisla
52 Hare
53 Hidatsa
54 Hopi
55 Houma
56 Huchnom
57 Hupa
58 Illinois
59 Ingalik
60 Iowa
61 Iroquois
62 Isleta
63 Juaneño
64 Kamia (Tipai)
65 Kaniagmiut
66 Kansa
67 Karankawa
68 Kaska
69 Kato
70 Kawaiisu
71 Kitanemuk
72 Klamath
73 Kutenai
74 Kwakiutl
75 Tewa-Pueblos
76 Lassik
77 Lillooet
78 Luiseño
79 Maidu
80 Mandan
81 Maricopa
82 Mattole
83 Menomini
84 Métis (Canada)
85 Miami
86 Miwok
87 Modoc
88 Mohave
89 Mono (Californian Paiute)
90 Natchez
91 Navajo
92 Nez Percé
93 Nisenan (Southern Maidu)
94 Nomlaki (Central Wintun)
95 Nootka
96 Ojibwa
97 Omaha
98 Osage
99 Oto
100 Paiute (Northern)
101 Paiute (Southern)
102 Panamint
103 Papago
104 Patwin (Southern Wintun)
105 Pawnee (Skidi Band)
106 Piegan
107 Pima
108 Pomo (Northern, Kalekau)
109 Pomo (Northern, Clear Lake)
110 Ponca
111 Potawatomi
112 Quapaw
113 Quileute
114 Quinault
115 Rogue River (Oregon Shasta)
116 Salinan
117 Sanpoil
118 San Felipe etc. (Eastern Keres)
119 Sauk
120 Shasta
121 Shoshoni-Bannock
122 Shoshoni (Wind River)
123 Shoshoni (Lemhi)
124 Sinkaietk (Southern Okanagon)
125 Sinkyone
126 Siuslaw
127 Slave
128 Thompson
129 Tillamook
130 Timucua
131 Tlingit
132 Tolowa
133 Tübatulabal
134 Tututni
135 Ute
136 Wailaki
137 Walapai
138 Washo
139 Winnebago
140 Wintun
141 Wishram
142 Wiyot
143 Yana
144 Yokuts
145 Yuki
146 Yuma
147 Yurok
148 Zuni

Kamia = Tipai; Tewa: San Juan, Santa Clara, San Ildefonso, Tesuque, Nambé; Eastern Keres: Cochití, San Felipe, Santo Domingo, Sia, Santa Ana; Métis: the example in this book is from Liard River, Canada.

cerning persons in Europe (see Dekker and Van de Pol 1990; Green 1974:7ff.) and in the United States (Katz 1985) who lived successfully in the social role of the opposite sex, and who frequently went unrecognized for a long time.

With the broadening of horizons during the Age of Discovery, it became apparent that gender role change was also to be found in numerous cultures outside of Europe, often even in institutionalized form (Bullough 1976; Greenberg 1988; Karsch-Haack 1911; Williams 1986b:252ff.). The *hijras* of India (Nanda 1986), the Samoan *faafafine* (Munroe and Munroe 1987:60), the Tahitian *mahus* (Williams 1986b:255ff.), and the Siberian "soft men" (Bogoraz 1907:449ff.; Williams 1986b:252ff.) are additional examples of this.

In the ethnographic literature, however, the best-known example is that of the North American "berdaches" who constitute the subject of this book. A listing of sources within the framework of the GAI (Gay American Indians) history project reveals "berdaches" and other alternative gender roles in 133 Indian groups (Gay American Indians and Roscoe 1988:217ff.; Roscoe 1987).

In our own culture, gender role change appears in the form of transsexualism. Transsexuals aspire not only to the role but also to the gender status of the opposite sex. Usually they desire a new classification of their persons not as ambivalent (transsexual) but rather as unambiguous and definite. In these cases hormonal, surgical, and legal measures such as a change of personal status and of name are intended to facilitate the adjustment of the physically actual to the subjectively felt sex (see Benjamin 1966; Burchard 1961, Green 1974; Green and Money 1969; Hamburger 1954a, 1954b; Kessler and McKenna 1977; Pauly 1974; Schicketanz et al. 1989).

Not least because of their appearance in numerous groups and because of the comparatively rich and comprehensive source material do the North American "berdaches" seem particularly appropriate for the investigation of gender role change in extra-European cultures. Regionally, the present work embraces the entire North American subcontinent from the Mexican border southwest of the United States to Alaska in the northernmost part of the hemisphere, and along with the Indian groups, also includes the Inuit (see Map 1).

THE NORTH AMERICAN "BERDACHES"

The designation "berdache" originally comes from the Arabic-speaking region, where *bardaj* or *barah* meant "kept boy," "male prostitute," "catamite" (Angelino and Shedd 1955:121). "Berdache" is the French adaptation of these terms and was first used by eighteenth-century

French travelers, who mainly applied the word to supposedly "passive homosexual" Native American males who were transvestites and who fulfilled the culturally defined role of a woman (see Angelino and Shedd 1955:121f.).

In the course of time, very different phenomena came to be referred to by the designation "berdache": transvestism (cross-dressing), effeminacy, the carrying out of female tasks and activities, entering into homosexual relationships, and intersexuality (Angelino and Shedd 1955: 122ff.). Around the beginning of this century, the term was extended to females who had taken on the social role of a man. Emphasis on the choice of sexual partners was particularly long-lasting, so that the designations "berdache" and "homosexual" frequently appear as synonymous, but the terms "berdache" and "transvestite" often occur as synonymous as well (see Angelino and Shedd 1955:122ff.).

However, so many variant expressions of gender role change exist that such equations turn out to make little sense: males in the social role of a woman enter into marriages with women; males in a masculine role have sexual relations with non-"berdache" men; and transvestism (cross-dressing) proves to be as readily dispensable a component of any gender role change as homosexual behavior (Angelino and Shedd 1955: 122ff.). With this in mind, Angelino and Shedd suggested a definition of "berdache" which is based on such persons' social (gender) role:

> In view of the data we propose that berdache be characterized as an individual of a definite physiological sex (male or female) who assumes the role and status of the opposite sex, and who is viewed by the community as being of one sex physiologically but as having assumed the role and status of the opposite sex. (1955:125)

Thirty years later, in light of more recent investigations and the results of his own fieldwork, Williams proposed another definition: "Briefly, a berdache can be defined as a morphological male who does not fill a society's standard male role, who has a nonmasculine character. This type of person is often stereotyped as effeminate, but a more accurate characterization is androgyny" (1986b:2). At the basis of this definition lies the observation, also attested to both by numerous primary sources and by Native American terms for women-men and men-women, of "gender mixing." Gender mixing represents a combination of masculine and feminine gender statuses instead of a genuine change from "one" gender into "the" other. Consequently, gender mixing is often expressed by a combination of the feminine gender role with the masculine gender role (see Callender and Kochems 1986). As will be shown in what follows, this combination is not uniform, and comprises a spectrum from quasi-masculine to quasi-feminine role makeup and organization (*Ausgestaltung*).

The entire adoption of the feminine gender role by males, which lies at the basis of Angelino and Shedd's (1955) definition, is found here as well, but it no more leads to the ascription of a feminine gender status (i.e., the gender status of "woman") than does a "mixed" gender role.

In this connection, the distinction between gender category and gender status is significant: the gender category is based on the biological distinction between males and females, whereas the gender status, as culturally defined, can be either masculine (man) or feminine (woman), but can also entail and hold open other possibilities:

> At the gender-category level, classification as not-male necessarily means being classified as female, and vice versa. At the level of gender status, however, definition as not-man is not equivalent to identification as woman . . . because status depends on the cultural construction of gender. While women are, by definition, not-men, other social groups within a society may consist of males whose gender status is that of not-men but who are also defined as not-women. Gender-mixing statuses . . . are an example. (Callender and Kochems 1986:166)

This view, shared by Whitehead (1981), Kessler and McKenna (1977), and Martin and Voorhies (1975), assumes at the outset that, beyond a purely masculine or feminine socially defined gender membership, other, "supernumerary genders" (Martin and Voorhies) can also exist which can be characterized as gender mixing.

Within the framework of this view, investigations of nonmasculine or nonfeminine genders in other cultures no longer need to be limited by the polarization of sex/gender membership so characteristic of Western culture—a polarization that in fact shapes gender role change in Western culture. Because the category "gender mixing" does not exist in the West, transsexuals strive for complete identification with the opposite sex, even to the extent of a new, surgically constructed physical definition of their sex (see Benjamin 1966; Green 1974; Green and Money 1969; Kessler and McKenna 1977:26).

In Western culture, the social pressures to conform to a nonambivalent gender status are great. Gender status is not defined as in Callender's and Kochems' cross-cultural notion: if you are a man but do not so identify yourself, you must try to be accepted as a woman; likewise for a woman who does not identify herself as such. Within this pattern of thinking, there is no place for the ambivalence of androgyny.

Prevailing uses of the term "berdache" reflect this inflexibility as well as the distortions that can result from imposing gender polarity on non-Western cultures. Williams pointed out, for example, that the application of the term "berdache" to females who effect a change in gender roles is inappropriate because the word originally derives from a term for male prostitutes, as well as because females in the role of hunters and warriors would also be conceptualized in Native American cultures as being different from male "berdaches." He therefore suggested the term "Amazons" (1986b:11). This does not appear to be the optimal solution, however, because historically, Amazons are distinctly associated with the warlike element of the masculine role: the ancient sources emphasize above all the Amazons' warlike fighting spirit (see Hammes 1981). In Native North America, however, this warlike component appears in connection with women who go to war without either giving up the feminine role or transforming their feminine gender status into an ambivalent one (see Chapter 17).

What terminology, then, is appropriate? As noted in the Preface, Native Americans and anthropologists alike have rejected the term "berdache" as inappropriate for persons of either sex; in the following, it will be retained only in references to earlier sources. For reasons also outlined in the Preface, those individuals who were referred to as male "berdaches" in the earlier anthropological writings will usually be termed "women-men" in this book; females in a masculine role who occupy a nonfeminine gender status in their respective tribes will be termed "men-women." And, as noted, I will also use the Native American terms for these individuals.

The designation "gender role change" will serve as a higher level generic term for various kinds of crossing over culturally defined gender roles, usually including the entrance into an ambivalent gender status. At the same time, I assume along with Callender and Kochems (1986:166) that a change of gender roles does not imply a change of gender status from "man" to "woman" or vice versa. (For the definition of "status" and of "role" used in this study, see Chapter 4). Following Callender and Kochems (1986:168), I will define gender role change using four features which in turn form the basis for defining an alternative gender status ("gender mixing"). However, unlike Callender and Kochems, I will refer to persons of both sexes. Furthermore, I will call *ambivalent gender status* what they designate as "gender-mixing status" (see Chapter 4).

Gender role change may include the following characteristic features:

1. partial or complete transvestism (cross-dressing);
2. the expression of culturally defined characteristic behavior patterns of the opposite sex;
3. the carrying out of activities that are culturally assigned to the opposite sex;
4. no sexual relations with persons who occupy the same gender status as the person in question.

Transvestism may not appear at all, and would seem to be the most dispensable component of gender role change and ambivalent gender status (see Callender and Kochems 1986:168). Further, modes of behavior and occupations that belong to the standard gender role of one's own sex can be retained, along with the practice of behavioral modes and activities of the opposite sex. The most important characteristic of gender role change is the preference for the occupations and activities of the opposite sex (Callender and Kochems 1986:176; Whitehead 1981:85f.). The following definition of women-men and men-women (as opposed to those who cross gender role boundaries without having a special assigned status in their own culture) combines the elements of gender role change and gender status change: A woman-man or a man-woman is a person of usually physically unambiguous sex who voluntarily and permanently takes on the culturally defined activities and occupations of the opposite sex, and who has a special (ambivalent) gender status assigned to him or her by his or her culture. The following are distinguished in Native American cultures from women-men and men-women ("berdaches"):

- persons who have sexual relations with members of their own sex without carrying out a change of gender roles;
- persons who wear the clothing of the opposite sex (transvestites) without carrying out a change of gender role (e.g., in certain ritual situations);
- feminine men and masculine women who retain their gender status;
- "warrior women" and other persons who cross gender role boundaries without, by so doing, exchanging their gender status for an ambivalent one; and
- men who because of a failure in the warrior role are forced as a humiliation to wear women's clothing, and occasionally also to take on the womanly role (although these men actually want the masculine role and occasionally rehabilitate themselves by undertaking some daredevil act of war on their own; see Bossu's example from the Illinois, 1962:82).

Hermaphrodites and intersexuals were usually integrated into the woman-man/man-woman statuses because their physical ambivalence was regarded as comparable to the ambivalence (due to the discrepancy between physical sex and lived-out gender role) manifested by non-intersexual women-men and men-women (see Chapter 8). The above list of exceptions should not be taken as absolute. The distinction between gender role change and gender role crossing is not qualitative, but rather quantitative. When sources give details concerning persons to whom an ambivalent gender status has been assigned by the members of an ethnic group, such "emic" classifications and their culturally specific backgrounds must be considered. The definition suggested here has the advantage of taking into account the wide range of statuses formerly referred to as "berdache." It seems reasonable to include examples of *gender role crossing* in the present study. Gender role crossing refers to people who take up some elements of the culturally defined role of the other sex but at the same time largely retain the standard gender role culturally assigned to their own sex. Unlike the majority of women-men or men-women, they do not take up the gender role of the other sex more or less completely. In many places, gender roles are more flexible than has long been assumed (see Blackwood 1984). Yet there is scarcely any information available concerning the degree or point in gender role crossing beyond which a person was classified as a woman-man or man-woman (see Parsons 1939b: 38 and 38 n. on the delimitation of gender role crossing and woman-man/man-woman statuses among the Pueblos). A comparison of women-men and men-women with persons who cross over into the role of the opposite sex without being so classified can help to illuminate the statuses of women-men and men-women within a broader cultural context.

FOCUS OF THIS BOOK

Although "berdaches" (primarily women-men) have been the subject of in-depth investigations by Callender and Kochems (1983), Trexler (1995), and Williams (1986b), a thorough, detailed, and systematic reappraisal of the available published sources of information is still lacking. The present study is intended to fill this gap and constitutes an expansion of the above-named investigations. At the same time, however, it is also intended as a close reexamination of statements and of theoretical reflections encountered in these and other works on the subject.

The primary emphasis of the present study is on the traditional status (i.e., the status as held in the tribal societies and in the early reservation period) of women-men and men-women in Native American cultures in North America. For a discussion of more recent and to some extent homosexual/gay self-definitions by members of widely differing Native American groups, the reader should consult Williams (1986b). In his detailed investigation of the "berdache" phenomenon, Williams dealt mainly with those groups in which women-men enjoyed high standing as recipients of especially potent latent spiritual power. He also analyzed the changes that the "berdache" roles and statuses underwent within processes of acculturation. However, he heavily emphasized the sexual aspect of the institution as a culturally approved opportunity for same-sex relationships. By contrast, the present study takes into consideration all groups from which a "berdache" status has (to my knowledge) ever been reported, irrespective of the prevailing attitude toward women-men and men-women within the respective groups, and whether or not a spiritual component existed (although when present, the latter has naturally been taken into account).

The study which in its approach most closely resembles my own is that of Callender and Kochems (1983), who also adduced the entire corpus of available information in order to arrive at definitive statements concerning the "berdache" status. However, because that study is in essay form, many questions of detail had to remain unanswered. Among other things, the present study is intended to address some of these questions, so that, against the background of a broader cultural context, more differentiated statements can be made. In the other most recent work on this topic (Kenny 1988; Midnight Sun 1988; Trexler 1995; Whitehead 1981), the body of data has been applied selectively, partly in order to support preconceived theoretical standpoints. Because of this, the authors mentioned have not done justice to the complexity of the topic. For example, Whitehead's argument (see Chapter 3) is acceptable only if one accepts her equation:

male : female :: culture : nature

and shares her view that a universal gender hierarchy necessarily results from it.

Finally, investigations of gender role change among females and of female homosexuality have been scarce up to now (but see Allen 1981, 1986; Blackwood 1984; Whitehead 1981; Williams 1986b:233ff.). The present volume, by using the entire corpus of data on men-women and women-men, will contribute to this relatively unexplored area of study.

Primarily, this investigation focuses on working out the relationship of gender role, as it is lived out and experienced by the woman-man or man-woman, to the sexual role differentiation customary in each of the respective groups for which data have been reported. The goal is to determine the kind and degree of gender role change and at the same time to pursue the question of the gender status of the women-men/men-women. In connection with this, my point of departure is recent theoretical approaches to problems of gender status which depart from the concept of two polarized gender statuses. Instead, these approaches demonstrate that a change of gender status is more likely to result in an ambivalent status than in the status of the opposite sex: it will be shown in the case of the women-men/men-women and related phenomena that "gender mixing" takes place, not "gender crossing" (Callender and Kochems 1986; Kessler and McKenna 1977; Martin and Voorhies 1975; Whitehead 1981; Williams 1986b). This viewpoint will also make it possible to recognize the alternative gender status constructions that exist in non-European societies, and, by examining the experiences of persons who live in such mixed roles, to come to grips with these constructs. A two-part preliminary question, therefore, is this: which North American Indian cultures developed an ambivalent gender status? For the groups where it existed, how was/is the content structure of this status actually worked out and enacted by individuals making use of the gender roles? It is also necessary to determine whether persons described in the literature as "berdaches" actually were/are women-men or men-women, according to the definition provided above. If they are not, it is important to determine whether they were classified as "berdaches" in the sources by anthropologists or other writers on the basis of the sex/gender concepts of the ethnographer or of the consultant. In addition, it is crucial to consider how men-women and women-men might have been associated with particular social phenomena. For example, the Navajo connected *nadle* (women-men and men-women; in more recent literature also spelled *nádleehé,* see Thomas, 1997) with intersexuality, whereas some Shoshoni-speaking groups associated them with infertility.

Women-men's and men-women's relationships with partners as an expression of gender role and gender status also require examination. Among other things, it is necessary to investigate the extent to which classifications such as "homosexual" or "heterosexual" are applicable to women-men and men-women, or whether such classifications instead represent projections of Western categories upon non-Western cultural phenomena.

The motivation for gender role change constitutes an additional topic of investigation, and it is important to distinguish between what consultants said about this topic and what outside observers reported. All too often, ethnographers and other observers speculated about etiology in terms of unsubstantiated ideas based on prevailing Western psychiatric and psychological models (such as overprotective mothers, weak masculine identity, latent homosexuality, etc.).

Another question that needs to be addressed is the nature of the special spiritual powers sometimes attributed to women-men (and, though to a lesser extent, to men-women) on account of their gender ambivalence. What special tasks were assigned to them? Are these tasks associated with the feminine or masculine role domain? Furthermore, given that these powers have by no means been universally granted to the women-men, in which cultural context(s) were they regarded as being spiritually gifted?

Because the sources have focused almost exclusively on women-men, much of the present discussion focuses on them. Part 3 deals with the available source materials relating to females in a masculine role. Gender role crossing, which has been observed much more frequently among women than among men (e.g., in the form of "warrior women," manly-hearted women, etc.), will also be discussed, even though gender role crossing is, as noted, not the same as gender role change.

The present book, therefore, first of all examines the componential organization of gender role as executed by women-men and men-women: what feminine and masculine role components, respectively, are lived out? Are there differences between transvestite and nontransvestite women-men and men-women? Apart from everyday and specialized activities, what behavior patterns or attributes could possibly signal that the person who adopted these has or will effect a change of gender role and gender status? What is the relationship of women-men and men-women, who are ambivalent because of a discrepancy between biological sex and behavior, to hermaphrodites or intersexuals, who manifest a sexual ambivalence that is purely biological?

This book also addresses the consequences of gender role change. To what specialized occupations or ritual activities were women-men and/or men-women entitled on the basis of their special gender status? On the other hand, which of these activities or occupations were, by contrast, seen as constituent aspects of a feminine or masculine role? These questions are especially instructive for drawing conclusions regarding the gender status of women-men and men-women, for example, in cases in which they carry out occupations otherwise reserved for members of their own biological sex. In other cases, it is necessary to ask whether an activity possibly devolved upon the woman-man or man-woman less because of any inherent special powers than because the activity in question was chosen by the woman-man or man-woman as an additional component of his or her chosen opposite-sex role.

Relationships of marriage or of partnership with persons of the same biological sex can also be an expression of gender role change. These relationships, as well as relationships with partners of the opposite sex are discussed in Chapter 11. The central question is, to what extent were relationships with partners of the same biological sex, but not of the same gender, actually comparable to those relationships classified in Western culture as homosexual, as some authors have asserted (see Chapter 3)? A further issue for investigation here is the degree to which sexual relations between partners of the same biological sex and of the same gender might have corresponded to the definition of homosexuality currently valid in Western culture. In addition, the cultural background of the promiscuity frequently attributed to women-men will also be discussed.

The actual process of carrying out a change of gender role is likewise a topic of the present inquiry. What motives lie at the basis of a person's taking on the role of the opposite biological sex? How was entry into a new gender status legitimized and, if necessary, culturally standardized? Did visions provide occasions in an individual's life for an abrupt turning point from one gender status to another, or did they only legitimate a process of change that had been under way for a long time? How did the social environment react to signs of a gender role change, or to those persons who entered into an ambivalent gender status?

Another important goal of the present study is to determine how it becomes possible for individual persons in the Native American cultures investigated to cross over or even to abandon completely the standard gender role of their sex in a culturally acceptable and often even institutionalized form. One factor is surely the construction of alternative gender statuses in addition to the standard masculine and feminine ones. Western culture does not admit entry into gender ambivalence; it recognizes only a polarization into male and female, masculine and feminine. Ambivalent individuals consequently have to choose one or the other of these poles. Furthermore, in extreme cases (e.g., among transsexuals), this leads to a situation in which individuals actually feel out of place in their own bodies, and consequently attempt by surgical means to adjust their "wrong" bodies to their "right" sexual identity. This constitutes a gender crossing in the sense of Callender and Kochems (1986), as well as a change in gender status and probably even in terms of gender categories. Transsexuals in Western culture do not wish for a "berdache" status for themselves, but rather a nonambivalent gender status: "There're only two alternatives in society. You're either a man or a woman. If I don't feel like a woman then it's got to be the other way" (female-to-male transsexual, in Kessler and McKenna 1977:112). In other cultures, quite obviously, there are more than two alternatives. The present study is intended to show how gender status alternatives can in fact be formulated culturally.

A comparison of research results pertaining to women-men as opposed to men-women also makes it possible to arrive at distinctions about the cultural acceptance or institutionalization of gender role change and gender role crossing. In particular, the biologistic explanatory pronouncement of Whitehead (1981; and see below, Chapter 3) requires close examination: were female "berdaches" essentially rarer than male ones because the female bodily functions made access to male areas of life impossible? This explanatory statement is not acceptable if one does not agree with the structuralist equation, first formulated by Ortner (1974) and later asserted by Whitehead, that female is to male as nature is to culture, together with the assumption deriving from it of a universal dominance of man (Culture) over woman (Nature) (see Ortner 1974: 67ff.). The discussion in the literature regarding the existence of male dominance in Native American cultures has not yet been concluded.

However, several authors have justifiably come out against the sweeping assumption of such a dominance (see Albers and Medicine 1983; M. N. Powers 1986; Weist 1980). Above and beyond this, it can be shown that crossing beyond the boundaries of their gender role was easier for women than it was for men, and that in such cases women did not have to take on an alternative gender status permanently (see Chapter 17). The present study likewise seeks explanations for this differential flexibility with regard to gender roles. For example, could the higher incidence of women-men possibly be connected with the fact that there existed more gender role alternatives for women than for men? (see, e.g., Kehoe 1983:66, on Blackfoot women). And how does this variability relate to a possible gender hierarchy?

Before proceeding to investigate male and female gender role change, I first need to discuss several topic-specific problems regarding the source materials and then present a critical account of the contemporary state of research as well as previous theoretical approaches to the topic. After these preliminaries, I will describe the mutual interconnection of gender identity, gender role, and gender status. These relationships are crucial to the approach taken in the present work, which constitutes a study of women-men and men-women against the background of culturally defined gender roles and gender statuses, with special reference to aspects of gender role change among members of North American Indian nations.

Chapter **Two**

Early Sources: Missionaries and Traders, Physicians and Ethnologists

THE MISSIONARIES AND TRADERS: ACCOUNTS OF SODOMITES AND HERMAPHRODITES

The primary sources on gender role change in Native American cultures go from the time when the Spanish first explored the southern parts of the subcontinent to the 1980s. The earliest known source is that of Cabeza de Vaca (1555), who after the failure of the Narváez Expedition, together with three other survivors fought his way from present-day Louisiana through to Culiacán (1528–1538). The most recent source as of this writing is the anthology *Living the Spirit* (Gay American Indians and Roscoe 1988), put together by members of the organization GAI (Gay American Indians). Between these time points exist many reports concerning gender role change and homosexual behavior which show great diversity both in quality and in quantity. In scope, these reports range from succinct observations such as "There were berdaches" (Kroeber 1932:272) to the comprehensive essay by Devereux (1937) on the Mohave *alyha* and *hwame.* For the most part, the references are restricted to brief tabulations (in the *Anthropological Records*) or to short paragraphs in the monographs on the respective tribes.

Unfortunately, if the quantity of these reports is considerable, the quality is variable at best. In the eyes of European observers, the institution of gender role change was tainted from the very beginning with the stigma of sexual perversion. Most women-men and men-women maintained sexual relations or even marriages with partners of the same sex. Most of the earlier chroniclers were missionaries, conquistadors, traders, or other persons who were rooted in Christian ideas of morality (see Kessler and McKenna 1977:30). Within the framework of these moral ideas, homosexual behavior was very severely judged (Romans 1.26; see Ranke-Heinemannn 1988:334ff.; Romans 1962:26), and the Spanish administration of justice punished "sodomy" as a crime that stood directly after heresy and crimes against the person of the king (Guerra 1971:221).

Not all of the early writers, however, foregrounded the same-sex love life of the women-men (men-women were usually not described in the early sources). Where this subject was foregrounded, however, it tended to eclipse detailed description of other aspects of gender role change. With reference to the Illinois, for example, Hennepin (1699:61) stressed the "sin . . . that is committed against nature" and represented the institution as though it functioned to produce partners for male homosexual relationships. On the other hand, Marquette (1959:129), whose attitude toward the Illinois (in contrast to Hennepin's and also Liette's [1962:112f.]) was positive, did not mention same-sex relationships at all, and provided a detailed and positive description of the "berdache" institution.

Other eighteenth-century authors limited themselves to lumping (male) Native Americans of a tribe together and characterizing them as "sodomites" without any further discussion of gender role change (e.g., Bossu 1962:169; Romans 1962:70). Such sources are not useful for an investigation of the institution of gender role change, although they may offer at least some usable data. Many authors failed to place women-men in their total cultural context, and their reports nearly always contain value judgments. Moreover, it appears to have seemed to them improper to give much attention to this topic. Most of the early reports are very brief, and, apart from taking note of the "unnatural" sexual life of the women-men, they at most provide short descriptions of the men's, women's, or specialists' occupations carried out by them (e.g., Cabeza de Vaca 1555:36; Dumont 1753:249ff.; Henry 1897:163f.; Liette 1962: 112f.; Tanner 1830:305ff.). Nonjudgmental and detailed descriptions such as those by Denig (1961:187f.) from the 1850s are extremely rare.

THE PHYSICIANS: ANTHROPOMETRIC SURVEYS OF "BERDACHES"

Physicians, who were interested in women-men from a medical perspective, were another early source. Hammond (1882), an eminent nineteenth-century neurologist (L. A. White 1943:324), and Holder (1889) examined and took anthropometric measurements of the genitals and physique of *bate* (women-men) among the Crow, and also of *mujerados* at Acoma and Laguna. Their purpose was to establish neurological or physiological causes of the women-men's effeminization. In their supplementary ethnographic statements, these authors also emphasized the same-sex relationships of the *bate* and of the *mujerados*. Furthermore, Hammond (1882:447f.) offered an etiology for the evident genital atrophy that he established for the *mujerados* he examined. However, according to modern medical and cultural anthropological knowledge, this etiology is untenable (Parsons 1918, 1929; L. A. White 1943: 324; see also below, Chapter 8). Hammond, who was a specialist in the field of sexual impotence, was probably misinformed intentionally on this matter by his consultants, just as in other cases consultants lied to visitors out of animosity or lied to them to please them (see example below). His references to artificial effeminization resulting from excessive riding and masturbation fit only too well into his deliberations on the origin of impotence, the "Disease of the Scythians" (1882).

THE ETHNOLOGISTS: ANXIETIES AND TABOOS

It is clear that from the earlier ethnographic reports to the present, consultants have given researchers the answers which the consultants thought they wanted to hear, sometimes denying the existence of "berdaches" altogether. This has, of course, made assessment of the traditional attitudes of individual Indian groups toward women-men and men-women more difficult (see Kroeber 1940:209, n. 4). A Paiute consultant candidly told Stewart (1941:440) that there weren't any *tüvasa* ("berdaches") in his group "because our Indians were good and taught their children right." This problem could be even worse for female ethnologists whose informants have taken over the "White" notion that sexual topics are not suitable for female ears. Landes (1968:153) reported that she was not told details concerning the marriages of Santee Dakota *winkta* because such things were held to be "too bawdy for polite ears."

The value-laden association of women-men with "homosexuals" characteristic of the earliest sources persisted as investigation of the phenomenon passed into the hands of the science of ethnology or anthropology at the end of the nineteenth century. What earlier had been "the sin of sodomy" (cf. Liette 1962:112) now became a "frame of mind, which seems to have a congenital or psychological basis well recognized by the psychiatrist" (Kroeber 1925:46). The stigma of sin was followed closely by the stigma of abnormality.

As Williams (1986b:11f.) has pointed out, measured by the wealth of data that ethnologists have compiled in the last hundred years, astonishingly little has been written about the "berdache" traditions. It is possible that the consultants were either aware of the ethnographers' prejudice against "berdaches" as "homosexuals," or that in the process of acculturation, the consultants themselves had acquired this prejudice (see Lurie 1953:708; Williams 1986b:187ff.). Or, as Williams has suggested, it may be that ethnographers excised information about "berdaches":

> Few of them have felt genuinely comfortable in writing about sexual variance. . . . On more than one occasion I have interviewed anthropologists who have written ethnographies on specific tribes, but whose books do not mention berdaches. When I specifically ask them about it, they often will admit to knowing about it. When I have asked them why this information was not included in their book, some have seemed rather proud to say, "Such things don't interest me." (Williams 1986b:12)

Thus it is likely that, for many Native American cultures, more detailed information concerning "berdaches" slumbers on today in archives or in ethnographers' personal field notes. Reading the primary sources, one actually gets the impression, also noted by Blackwood, that most anthropologists "have been affected by or accepted the prejudices of Western society toward homosexual behavior, and consequently have not considered the study of homosexuality to be a legitimate pursuit" (Blackwood 1986:2f.). For example, Evans-Pritchard published his essay on homosexual behavior among the Azande in 1970, almost thirty years after the appearance of his other publications on this tribe (Carrier 1986:xii). In the United States, at least, the academic climate apparently did not encourage treatment of this topic even in the mid-1980s:

> A sad comment on our times is that many anthropologists have collected empirical data on homosexual behavior . . . but have never published it partly because of their fear of being stigmatized and partly because anthropological journals have rarely accepted articles dealing with homosexuality . . . graduate students of anthropology may still be reluctant to study homosexuality as a dissertation topic because of the problems it often brings with members of their graduate committees and because they fear it may limit their future employability. (Carrier 1986:xii)

Thus, in addition to whatever culturally inscribed bias ethnographers (or their consultants) may have experienced, they also faced professional stricture. In 1975, the executive board of the American Anthropological Association voted "not to endorse anthropological research on homosexuality across national borders" (Williams 1986b:13). Although this decision was later revoked, it makes clear the magnitude of the problems—which exist down to the present—involved in a treatment of homosexual behavior and gender role change, which is often equated with it. These problems, of course, have left their mark upon the sources. When Williams presented a paper on "berdaches" at a history conference in 1980, "I was scolded by a leading historian. . . . He bluntly told me that if I pursued this topic I would threaten my scholarly reputation. Later, when I asked him to write another letter of recommendation, he refused with a homophobic comment" (Williams 1986b:8).

Fear of contact may also be the reason why, with few exceptions, ethnographers have not tried to interview women-men and men-women themselves. Admittedly, the early ethnographers for the most part still had personal contact with "berdaches" and, as Williams has established, were more impartial than later authors (see Williams 1986b:12; examples include Stevenson, Parsons, Underhill, Mead, and Landes). It is also true that, in most cases, "berdaches" either had in fact disappeared in many tribes or had at least become invisible by the 1930s, at the latest (Jacobs 1968:30; Williams 1986b:185ff.). Williams was the first one who, in the early 1980s, visited a series of Indian reservations and discovered that traditions of gender role change still existed—even if in a changed form—and interviewed women-men (Williams 1986a, 1986b). The personal accounts of a number of women-men published by that author are the only sources that permit us to draw conclusions pertaining to the gender identity of these persons. It is gender identity in particular, however, that is an indispensable factor in, for example, cross-culturally classifying relationships as "homosexual" or "heterosexual"—or as neither or both.

In general, anthropologists took up the topic of "berdache" gingerly and treated it as briefly as possible. This is especially true of the *Anthropological Records* publication series. Gifford, for example, restricted himself to three single items of information: "Berdaches admitted," "Males as Females," and "Females as Males" (1940:137). The items reported by other authors in this series—for example, Voegelin (1942), Steward (1941), and Stewart (1942)—are more numerous. In most of these sources, however, it is apparent that the questions asked were from a standard repertoire focused on the aspects of gender role change which were familiar at that time: the wearing of clothing of the opposite sex, the choice of partners of the same sex, the incidence of "berdache shamans," the performance of tasks of the opposite sex (which were not further specified), and the attitude of the group toward "berdaches." The available information, however, is minimal, and hardly adequate for satisfactory answers even to these questions. The terminology chosen frequently derived from the vocabulary of psychiatry: "sexual pervert, sodomite" (Stewart 1942:298), "male homosexuals" (Hoebel 1960: 77), "homosexual intercourse with normal man" (Driver 1939:372), "inverts" (Lowie 1935:48), "transvestite," "homosexual," "victims of biological homosexuality" (Hassrick 1982:135f.). Clearly, this kind of reporting is based on an estimation of gender role change as a psychiatric problem. Because of this, any cultural anthropological investigation against the background of the individual cultural context was considered either impossible or unnecessary. The first studies which foregrounded gender role change and its cultural background without viewing the phenomenon from a psychological/psychiatric perspective began to appear, with one exception (Jacobs 1968), only in the mid-1970s (Blackwood 1984; Callender and Kochems 1983, 1986; Kessler and McKenna 1977; Martin and Voorhies 1975; Whitehead 1981). This is true not only of the literature on the North American "berdache," but also of the literature on gender role change and homosexual behavior in general (see Carrier 1986:xii).

Evaluation of the sources is also problematic because the phenomenon as presented in the literature is characterized by an extraordinary lack of unity; many different forms of gender role change, gender role crossing, femininity, and so forth, are subsumed under the heading "Berdaches." Thus, a statement ascertaining the mere presence of "berdaches" in a group without supplementary information pertaining to the structural constituency and actual manifestation of this status simply cannot be evaluated. At the same time, however, it is necessary to define the status of "berdache" in an unambiguous way (Angelino and Shedd 1955) and also to distinguish it both from other forms of gender role crossing and from homosexual behavior between two partners, neither of whom holds the status of woman-man or man-woman.

MEN-WOMEN: NONEXISTENT? OR NOT REPORTED?

The general state of the sources with regard to female "berdaches" is even more scanty than for male ones. This also holds true for female homosexual behavior. Regarding homosexual behavior by women, Blackwood (1986:8) has attributed this to the fact that traditional ethnographers dealt almost exclusively with the normative role for women, and within the context of this role they assumed heterosexual behavior as self-evident and a matter of course. Furthermore, "anthropological work . . .[was] done predominantly by males, talking to male informants about male activities" (Blackwood 1986:8). For the ethnographers, female homosexual behavior remained to a large extent invisible, especially as the women involved were likely to be married to men (Blackwood 1986:10). Blackwood's argument, however, does not explain why men-women should have been invisible to male researchers. When interacting with the men of a given tribe, these researchers in all likelihood encountered females in a man's role. Naturally, such females associated with the men and not with the women. Hall (1992) pointed out to me that men-women were possibly so convincing in their masculine role that they were not recognizable as females to nineteenth-century male researchers. Yet gender role change among females was still more conspicuous than homosexual behavior among women, and was sometimes reported (see Part 3). On closer examination, however, numerous examples prove to be cases not of female gender role change involving a change of gender status, but rather of women who in no way sought a complete role change, and who for the most varied reasons crossed beyond their female gender role. In other cases, it is not a matter of an institutionalized form of gender role change such as was usual among women-men. Instead, it is a matter of individual persons who took on the male role and a quasi-male status due to a combination of cultural and individual factors (see Chapter 14).

CONCLUSIONS AND PROSPECTS

In conclusion, there exist numerous references to gender role change in the ethnographic and historical sources. However, in terms of providing detailed information, and especially details concerning the cultural contexts of the "berdache" institution, the sources are very inconsistent and are often limited to "stock" aspects. Exemplary exceptions are Parsons' (1916) investigation of the Zuni *lhamana*; Grinnell's (1962) study of the Cheyenne *heemaneh'*; D. G. Mandelbaum's (1940) work on the Plains Cree; Landes' work on the Santee Dakota (1968) and the Prairie Potawatomi (1970); Denig's (1961) report on the Crow *bate*; Williams' (1986a, 1986b) interviews with Oglala Lakota *winkte*; Stevenson (1904); Schaeffer (1965); Devereux (1937); Hill (1935), and Osgood (1958). In these works, the componential structure and manifestation of the women-men's status are presented in such detail that the information is suitable for a thorough examination. Hassrick's account (1982) is likewise detailed, but is so heavily permeated by ethnocentric judgments that it can be evaluated and used only in combination with other sources (see M. N. Powers 1986: 14ff.).

The extraordinarily negative attitude of Euro-American culture toward homosexual behavior has hindered ethnographers for a long time in obtaining relevant information and has prevented gender role change from receiving the space that it deserves in descriptive and theoretical treatises. Furthermore, as Blackwood has noted, the long unquestioned and unanalyzed treatment of gender role change and "homosexuality" as equivalent has only very recently been challenged, finally allowing these phenomena to be depathologized and made available for an investigation in the framework of cultural structures:

> Most anthropologists based their evaluation of homosexual practices in other cultures on the deviance model of psychology and sociology, assuming that heterosexuality represented the norm for sexual behavior, and, therefore, homosexuality was abnormal or deviant behavior. Such evaluations were often in direct contrast to the meaning or value attached to homosexual behavior in the culture studied. (1986:3)

In addition, viewing the statuses of women-men and men-women from standpoints other than those common in Western culture (perversion, deviance) became possible only after the gender constructs of our own culture were called into question. As Kessler and McKenna (1977:33) stated, "Coming to a village with the concept of two genders, the observer sees two genders and understands the berdache phenomenon on those terms." At the same time, the possibility of an ambivalent gender status (different from both the gender statuses of "men" and "women") calls into question the assumption that same-sex relationships with women-men or men-women correspond to homosexual relationships as defined in Western culture (see Chapter 11). Likewise, behavior cannot be seen as deviant if a culture integrates it by means of a defined and accepted status (see Benedict 1934). I will follow up on this in the following chapters. One thing should be kept firmly in mind: the centuries-old view of the institution of "berdache" as equivalent to "homosexuality," together with the stigmatization of homosexual behavior—first as sinful and later as abnormal—is reflected in the sources by the often judgmental and nearly always meager information they contain. Moreover, the pertinent statements in the available sources differ greatly in quality as well as in scope. This factor creates additional difficulties for an adequate investigation of gender role change. For example, most ethnographers reported on the sex of the women-men's and men-women's partners, but only one (Devereux 1937) described an imitation of physiological patterns of the opposite sex. If it is simply maintained that male "berdaches" did "women's work," one cannot determine the degree to which they may have retained masculine role components. Similarly, it is difficult if not impossible to evaluate the bare statement—without supplementary comment—that women-men or men-women were "shamans": were they religious practitioners or healers because quite specific androgynous powers inhered in them? Or did women-men, for example, take up the task within the context of their chosen feminine gender role? Where both sexes are active in different areas of the healing profession, in which area do women-men or men-women specialize? Such interpretative problems are inherent in the sources, and the present work will have to take them into account. I agree with Williams' conclusion that the time is ripe for renewed fieldwork on the topic of gender role change and homosexual behavior: "The published reports and documents that are known have been examined and reexamined; what is now needed is more field work to see if further answers can be found" (1986b:4). Likewise, the field would benefit if any anthropologists who have obtained data pertaining to gender role change and homosexual behavior within the context of their field researches, but who have never published these, would follow the example set by Evans-Pritchard.

Chapter THREE

Twentieth-Century Research

KARSCH-HAACK ON THE "SAME-SEX LIFE OF PRIMITIVE PEOPLES"

The first detailed documentation of (male) gender role change and homosexual behavior among North American Indians is contained in Karsch-Haack's (1911) extensive work, *The Same-Sex Life of Primitive Peoples* (Das gleichgeschlechtliche Leben der Naturvölker). In it, the author cited all the sources on this subject which had appeared up to that time. Karsch-Haack was quite obviously influenced by Magnus Hirschfeld's theory of "*sexuelle Zwischenstufen*" (intermediate stages in terms of gender, a theory Hirschfeld formulated in 1914 based on theories appearing earlier). Karsch-Haack collapsed under the category of same-sex relationships all possible manifestations of these gender variations, from friendships between men (1911:328) that seemed to smack of homoeroticism, to reports of "sodomy," to dances which could have homoerotic interpretations, to North American "berdaches" and "hermaphrodites" (1911:307f.). However, Karsch-Haack did differentiate the various kinds of nonmasculinity more thoroughly than most of the later authors (1911:307f.).

CULTIC TRANSVESTITES: BAUMANN AND BLEIBTREU-EHRENBERG

The topic of gender role change was not taken up again in the German-language cultural anthropological literature until Baumann treated it from the standpoint of the anthropology of religion, first in an essay (1950) and soon afterward in a monograph (1955). He perceived gender role change so strongly within a religious frame of reference that he tended to conceptualize it as a strictly religious phenomenon (Baumann

1955:14). He claimed that even those cases which at first appeared to be profane were actually grounded in religion (1955:14). As far as North America is concerned, this claim is not supported. From a wealth of North American examples documenting woman-man statuses, Baumann selected just exactly those few which corresponded to the "cultic transvestites" he was investigating (1955:21).

Signorini (1972:158) criticized Baumann's cultural historical approach as theoretically inadequate. As obsolete as Baumann's assignment of different kinds of transvestism to various forms of cultural and economic organization may be (see Signorini 1972:157f.), however, his perspective nonetheless remains helpful if one sees it within the context of the total culture. Especially in regard to a tribe like the Navajo (see Chapter 5), the concept of increasing human potency by uniting masculine and feminine components is indispensable for interpreting the cultural position of the *nadle.* And it is precisely the ambivalence of this status in terms of masculinity and femininity which also appears to be significant for an examination of the status of other supernaturally legitimated women-men.

With the exception of Baumann (see also Pytlik 1983), only Bleibtreu-Ehrenberg (1970, 1984) within the German-speaking regions dealt with gender role change, again focusing on males. Like Baumann, Bleibtreu-Ehrenberg discussed North American examples only marginally, foregrounding religious, "cultic" aspects of the phenomenon. Bleibtreu-Ehrenberg (1970:221) characterized transvestism and the assumption of the role of the opposite sex as correlates of men's participation in areas of shamanism dominated by women. In her view, these were caused either by psychic factors (identification with the opposite sex) or by problems with the male role in cultures which did not allow an intermediate solution as an alternative to the roles of the two sexes. In this, of course, she stands in direct conflict with American approaches. Bleibtreu-Ehrenberg emphasized the male transvestite's self-modeling after the woman (1970:207) and occasionally also after a goddess worshipped by female cultic attendants (1970:209).

Much influenced by the cultural historical school of thought (see Hunter and Whitten 1976:111) as well as psychiatric explanatory models, Bleibtreu-Ehrenberg theorized an integration of psychically deviant personality types against the background of religious notions, and above all of specialized religious activities dominated by women. In connection with these, and in the context of efforts to compensate for personal role conflicts, transvestite shamans were supposedly enabled to carry out "outstanding shamanistic accomplishments" (Bleibtreu-Ehrenberg 1970:222; see also her 1984 *Der Weibmann* [The Woman-Man]).

Because of her theoretical orientation, Bleibtreu-Ehrenberg tended to fixate on the "cultic" aspect of gender role change, which led to a selective and sometimes uncritical use of the data sources. This in turn offers little in the way of starting points for an analysis of gender role change in North America, where this practice was often profane or secular. To postulate a "cultic" element in the phenomenon, even when this element is not verifiable, is neither justifiable nor tenable in connection with a systematic investigation of the available data. Bleibtreu-Ehrenberg (1970:221) did, however, precede American authors in characterizing homosexual behavior as a component of the feminine role rather than as a motivation for gender role change.

COWARDLY WARRIORS AND MOMMA'S BOYS

Generally, the "berdache" phenomenon has been conceptualized in two ways: as a form of social failure and as institutionalized homosexuality. In the "failure" paradigm, women-men are seen as individuals who are not in a position to adapt themselves to the masculine role prescribed by their culture. The women-men of the Plains are usually cited as an example. In this approach, it is assumed that they are incapable of taking on the warrior role because they lack the necessary personality structure (see, e.g., Erikson 1949:183f.; Forgey 1975:10; Hoebel 1958:589; Linton 1936:480; Mead 1970:260f.; Mirsky 1937a:416f.; Opler 1965:111). This view is also particularly characteristic of Hassrick (1982:135f., 1989:133f.), who sees women-men as "sissies" and who builds a psychological approach into his interpretation of the phenomenon: women-men are victims of excessive maternal love. According to Hassrick, some mothers attempt to protect their sons from "what might be considered the senseless dangers of aggressive warfare" (1989:135; see also Forgey 1975: 10f.).

It must be noted, however, that within North America, the appearance of women-men is in no way restricted to warlike groups. Furthermore, Callender and Kochems (1983:448) have already made the relevant point that, for men who rejected the warrior's life for themselves, other role alternatives, along with the woman-man status, were also available. While it is true that men who were failures as warriors occasionally were forced to wear women's clothing, these men did not count as "berdaches" (Callender and Kochems 1983:448). Moreover, the high standing that women-men enjoyed among the Plains tribes, in particular, argues against such a negative definition of their status. This stands in contrast to the attitudes toward men who defined themselves as warriors, but who then were not able to fulfill this role within the masculine status (see Callender and Kochems 1983:448). And finally, women-men

did go to war—just as did some women—in a number of tribes (see Chapter 5).

The problem of the "failure" approach probably lies, inter alia, in the fact that the women-men's ambivalence in both role and status is overlooked. The associative linkage: "berdache" = failure = woman = inferior is especially clear in Hassrick's (1982:135) account, in which the status of the *winkte* and that of the woman are equally misjudged. That Lakota men did not like to be called "heart of a woman" in council meetings (Hassrick 1989:133) is less likely to mean that women were regarded as inferior than that the warrior's role was sharply set off from the woman's role (see DeMallie 1983): a warrior clearly held the status of "man." Because the Lakota *winkte* (upon whom Hassrick's interpretations are based) were culturally defined as "non-men," the norms valid for the masculine role were therefore not applied to them.

In contrast to Hassrick (1982:136), who characterized women-men among the Oglala as deviants who were avoided, Hoebel stressed their integration into the structures of their respective cultures, although, like Hassrick, he also saw them as failures in terms of the warrior role. Furthermore, on the basis of Benedict's (1934:74) definition of the abnormal, Hoebel (1958:589) concluded that "Plains Indian berdaches, while relatively rare, were not abnormal personalities, because they were supported by their culture."

Within the framework of a supposed institutionalized deviance, Le Vine ascribed a dual function to the "berdache" status: first, that of providing a "regular place in the social structure for those who might otherwise rebel against it"; and second, "reminding others that the price of deviation is to be stigmatized as not entirely acceptable in all social contexts" (Le Vine 1973:142). In all these points of departure, women-men are characterized as socially deviant if not psychically abnormal.

INSTITUTIONALIZED HOMOSEXUALITY

The second starting point in the American anthropological literature interprets the "berdache" tradition as institutionalized homosexuality, whether innate or acquired within the framework of individual personality development. Kroeber saw women-men as representatives of a "set of psychiatric phenomena, those of sexual inversion," which "certain primitives accept with equanimity and provide a social channel for" (1940:210). Blackwood has designated this interpretation the "homosexual niche theory," which is based on the assumption that homosexual individuals exist in every culture who then "take on the role in their culture which allows the expression of a homosexual nature" (1986:4). "The homosexual" here appears as a transcultural phenomenon. Kroeber saw advantages for both the individual and the society in cultural institutions such as that of the "berdache" status, because no emotional distress arises for the supposedly innately "homosexual" individual, and his social environment does not experience him as a threat: "A status of adjustment is achieved instead of one of conflict and tension" (1940: 210)—"born a male, he became accepted as a woman socially" (1940: 209; see also Kiev 1964:21; Benedict 1934:64; Minturn, Grosse, and Haider 1969:303; Stewart 1960; Werner 1979; Ford and Beach 1968; Katz 1985).

Kardiner's explanation of the absence of "homosexuality and transvestism" among the Comanche as a function of the ideal of masculinity among the Plains tribes illustrates some of the problems resulting from overgeneralization: "Passive attitudes of any kind on the part of the male would have destroyed the society, as long as the economy depended on enterprise and prowess" (1945:88). What Kardiner ignored is the fact that the "berdache" was especially accepted and respected in the Plains tribes except the Comanche. The absence of this institution among the Comanche can therefore be explained only with difficulty by the emphasis on a certain masculine personality structure which was, after all, present in all of the Plains tribes.

Like other authors of her time, Benedict viewed the institution of the "berdache" as a culturally accepted niche for homosexual males (or males with what she called "weak sexual endowment") (1934, 1949), but in response to the prevailing emphasis on pathology, she pointed out that "normal" and "abnormal" are relative categories: "Normality . . . is culturally defined. It is primarily a term for the socially elaborated segment of human behavior in any culture; and abnormality, a term for the segment that that particular civilization does not use" (Benedict 1934: 73). She found that some persons who are classified in Western culture as abnormal are accepted in other cultures, sometimes being assigned important roles (1934:60f.), and that "many of our culturally discarded traits are selected for elaboration in different societies" (1934:64). It is unfortunate that Benedict's exposition did not open the way for a cultural anthropological—in place of a psychological—interpretation of the "berdache" phenomenon.

Continuing the psychologically/psychoanalytically oriented tradition, Forgey theorized that women-men served as a cushioning or absorption mechanism to handle some men's compulsive homosexual drives and desires. In Forgey's view, the "custom of berdache . . . provided an outlet for aggressive homosexuality," an "escape mechanism for individuals who would otherwise become anti-social . . . an outlet for aggressive homosexual tendencies even in men who were not themselves berdaches" (1975:10). In the "ultra-masculine" Plains culture, Forgey proposed, the "berdache" institution both prevented aggressions from being directed against men who otherwise would have been "total misfits" and reduced "in-group hostility," thereby strengthening the stability of the group (1975:13f.). Such theories cannot be verified or falsified by cultural anthropological methods. Certainly, however, Forgey's construct is hardly tenable outside of the Plains culture, because many groups which had women-men statuses were not "ultra-masculine." The martial ideal of masculinity on the Plains seems to have been particularly fascinating to ethnologists, many of whom made it the basis of numerous explanations for the "berdache;" in so doing, they completely overlooked the women-men among the less warlike groups.

CROSS-CULTURAL STUDIES

In several cross-cultural studies, observations made among North American Indian groups seem to have determined the formulation of hypotheses, the testing of which was based on worldwide samples. Downie and Hally investigated the hypothesis that gender role change frequently occurs in association with a strictly defined masculine role, so that "transvestism" (here meaning gender role change) could be interpreted as an escape route from a stifling masculine role: ". . . therefore, it was hypothesized that the strict sex-role differentiation would be correlated with presence of transvestism, and conversely, low sex-role differentiation with absence of transvestism" (Downie and Hally 1961:2). The investigation results, however, showed exactly the opposite: in the sample (and according to the index chosen by the authors), gender role change turned up with a higher probability in societies with a lower degree of gender role differentiation (1961:8). The authors concluded that ". . . societies that tolerate the performing of the same roles by men and women will also tolerate a role that men can assume in which they function essentially as women" (1961:11). Munroe, Whiting, and Hally (1969) replicated this investigation using a larger sample and a different index of gender role differentiation. These authors also found that "transvestism" (gender role change) was not associated with higher gender role differentiation (1969:88). They reasoned that the degree of change necessary for the individual in weakly differentiating societies was lower and more easily tolerable. Institutionalized gender role change, therefore, was more likely in these societies than in those with strongly differentiated gender roles (1969:89): " . . . the institution tends to appear wherever there are few sex distinctions, i.e., whenever there are few inhibiting sociocultural factors" (1969:90).

The following cultural features served as indices of "sex distinctions" in the study by Munroe, Whiting, and Hally (1969): residence rules, unilinear kinship groups, the terms of address for father's brother and mother's brother, the kinship terminology for cousins, the succession to positions of authority, eating arrangements (men and women separated or together), and the presence or absence of men at the birth of a child (1969:88). Whether one accepts their results depends, among other things, on whether one regards the indices chosen as definitive for culturally determined gender differences. In each case, one can think of indices that define gender role differences from other viewpoints—for example, in terms of the flexibility or rigidity of these roles.

In a later study, Munroe and Munroe investigated the relationship between male-dominated subsistence (men responsible for obtaining food) and "male transvestism." All twenty-four societies in which male transvestism (again meaning gender role change) showed up "were determined by male predominance in subsistence" (1977:307f.), in relation to which "the quantitative contribution of males, not the degree of task differentiation from females, is predictive of male transvestism" (1977:308). Thus institutionalized gender role change, according to Munroe and Munroe's study, occurs either in connection with a strongly male-dominated subsistence or in connection with weakly differentiated gender roles (1977:308; see also Munroe, Whiting, and Hally 1969). Once again, gender role change is seen as a flight from the burdensome masculine role, this time not from the warlike component, but instead from the tasks of the provider. However, from the cultural anthropological standpoint, it is questionable whether, among North American groups (the cross-cultural studies were based on a worldwide sample), the female area of responsibility for certain tasks actually represented an enticing alternative to the male responsibility for securing subsistence. Even in societies with male-dominated subsistence, the burden of the everyday tasks (including feminine contributions to subsistence, such as time-consuming gathering activities) and of processing the products acquired by the men (such as game animals) usually devolved onto the women (see Niethammer 1985:156f.).

Munroe (1980) has also dealt with gender role change in a cross-cultural study conducted within the framework of psycho-cultural analysis. Starting with the hypothesis that both "transvestism" and couvade equally constitute a response to inadequate masculine identification, he investigated the possible occurrence of both institutions in the same group(s) at the same time. It turned out that the couvade and gender role change did not occur together (1980:52). The author interpreted both institutions psychologically: the couvade practiced by the men "indicates identification with the female role at a fundamental psychic stratum" (1980:54) and is to be accounted for by fixation on the mother in early childhood (1980:50). Supposedly, this fixation on the mother was lacking in groups with institutionalized transvestism (gender role change), where weak gender role differentiation instead created identity problems for the men (1980:55). Consequently, according to Munroe, the couvade was found among the corresponding groups as an opportunity for all men to act out their female identification, whereas transvestism appeared only among a few individuals, who at the same time acted "as a kind of foil, providing contrastive role-definition for men whose sense of differentiation from women is relatively weak, but whose desire to act out the role of women is probably not overriding" (1980:58). This interpretation turns out to be problematic, however, if one does not share Munroe's assumption that the desire for demarcation from the opposite sex is universally present (see Callender and Kochems 1986; Kessler and McKenna 1977).

The data for Native American groups with institutionalized gender role change show clearly differentiated gender roles (see, e.g., DeMallie 1983 on the Dakota; in general, see Niethammer 1985:93,155 f.). The Inuit, by contrast, who did not have "berdaches" in the sense defined above for Native American cultures (even though certain traditions of "third genders" existed within the shamanic traditions [see Saladin d'Anglure 1992 and Goulet 1982]), formulated gender roles clearly, but carried them out in everyday life with extraordinary flexibility (see Giffen 1930).

Female gender role change cannot be integrated into such "flight-from-masculinity" interpretations. Furthermore, in North America, female—but not male—gender role change appeared with significantly greater frequency precisely in those regions with very pronounced male dominance in the subsistence area (see Chapter 15).

Extending Munroe's (1980) investigation, Gray and Ellington (1984) assumed as their starting point that couvade and transvestism "are related in differing manners to the frequency of male homosexual behavior exhibited in society" (1984:55). The authors hypothesized that when the couvade was present, there would be a low occurrence of homosexual behavior, because "the expression of the feminine role by males in situations outside is threatening to the psychological well-being of all males"; by contrast, homosexual behavior should be frequent when transvestism (gender role change) was also present, because the gender roles were not sharply differentiated in such cultures, and men in them were not psychically threatened by (male) homosexual behavior (1984: 58f.). According to these authors, homosexual behavior and gender role change constitute circumstantial evidence of a male identity problem, namely, of a feminine identity on the part of men (1984:62). Both of the hypotheses were confirmed by their cross-cultural study (1984:59f.). Again in this case, however, the hypotheses were based on psychological and not on cultural anthropological formulations of the question.

At least as far as North America is concerned, the connection between the couvade and gender role change is more complicated than it might seem. Many California tribes, for example, showed evidence of the existence of women-men as well as of a so-called *semi-couvade* (Hunter and Whitten 1976:94)—not in the form of a masculine childbed, but rather in the form of dietary prescriptions as well as other prohibitions and regulations for the father. Among these tribes are, inter alia: the Yurok (Kroeber 1925:45); the Yuki (Kroeber 1925:180); the Pomo (1925:254: "The father observed a mild couvade, *as among so many Californian tribes*" [emphasis mine]); the Shasta (1925:299); the Achomawi (1925:313); the Maidu (1925:402); the Juaneño (1925:647); the Luiseño (1925:688: "The usual Californian semicouvade was in force") and Diegueño (1925:720; see also Kroeber 1925:840 for general information). It is also very possible that such an association or co-occurrence of the semicouvade with the "berdache" institution also existed outside of California. For the purposes of the present investigation, however, this question was not pursued.

In regard to homosexuality, Minturn, Grosse, and Haider (1969:303) assumed psychological factors similar to those of the previously cited authors. Collapsing gender role change as well as transvestism under the category of homosexuality, these authors concluded the following: if homosexuality (homosexual behavior) and "adolescent segregation in same-sex groups" were mutually associated, this is to be explained by the fact that these same-sex groups prevented heterosexual activities. The authors theorized that homosexuality and rape are negatively correlated when a passive sexual behavior predominates among men. When homosexual behavior and rape both occur frequently, these behaviors are positively correlated with "sexual anxiety" (1969:307).

Werner (1979) tested various hypotheses pertaining to the genesis and cultural integration of homosexual behavior within the framework of a cross-cultural study, although—in view of earlier one-dimensional models—he called for a more broadly applied theoretical framework for investigation.

The cross-cultural studies on homosexual behavior and gender role change (the latter being subsumed under homosexuality) are briefly summarized in Broude (1981:651f.). These works are not very helpful for investigating gender role change among North American Indians, though, because of their (for the most part) strongly psychologically oriented hypothesis formation and explanatory approaches and indices. These studies are nevertheless important for showing how the investigation of gender role change has generally been shaped in the cultural anthropological literature. However, the cross-cultural validity of Western psychological paradigms has neither been called into question, nor been replaced by cultural anthropological hypotheses in the studies outlined above.

CULTURE AND SEXUAL BEHAVIOR: MORE RECENT APPROACHES FROM MEAD TO THAYER

Apart from the inclusion of North American examples in the cross-cultural studies mentioned above, Kroeber's call, issued as early as 1940, for a "synthetic work" (1940:209) on the institution of the "berdache" remained virtually unheard during following decades. Angelino and Shedd (1955) were the first to propose a nonambiguous definition of "berdache" which was not based on discrete characteristics such as sexual orientation, hermaphroditism, cross-dressing, and (possibly) promiscuity. Instead, they proposed as a foundational criterion the adoption of the role and status of the opposite sex by a person of nonambiguous biological sex (1955:125). Like Benedict's (1934) earlier attempt, this one might also have led from a psychological to a cultural anthropological consideration of the phenomenon, but it remained to a great extent unnoticed.

With regard to the discussion of homosexual behavior and gender role change, Mead and Benedict were unique in deemphasizing etiology, instead stressing much more the embedding of such behavior in different cultural contexts, as Blackwood (1986:4) has noted:

> In considering "the homosexual," the emphasis in both their works . . . was on the failure of the individual to adjust; nevertheless, it was argued that cultural factors shaped the homosexual response. . . . Mead (1961) later pointed out that various individual personality cues combine with the cultural interpretation of sexuality to shape an individual's sex role.

It was primarily Mead who brought out the fact that, while sexual dimorphism does constitute an important "differentiating factor of human beings" (1961:1451) in all human societies, many cultures place at the disposal of each biological sex several gender role *alternatives*. She even conceptualized (male) gender role change as one of these alternative "sex careers" (1961:1451). The "berdache," whose personality did not allow him to conform to the cultural ideal of bravery, "might be assigned a transvestite role, to which he would then adjust by identifying, not with either warriors or women, but with other transvestites" (1961:1452). Mead was the first to underline the ambivalent status of the woman-man: socially, he became a "transvestite" (and therefore "berdache"), but not—as Angelino and Shedd (1955) assumed—a woman. At the same time, Mead also proposed that a broad spectrum of physical and psychic characteristics are available for the assignment of a gender role, and that different cultures vary in their selection of particular characteristics (1961:1454). Sexual behavior is regarded as "learned behavior" (1961:1454). Homosexual behavior as a form of sexual behavior contained in the human potential is likewise handled culturally, and if necessary, an institutionalized homosexual role is learned and acquired. The significance of Mead's explanatory observations regarding gender role change and homosexual behavior lies in the shift from seeing cultural structures as merely reactive—by integrating deviant personalities, for example—to seeing them as active, in that they shape human behaviors.

The first systematic working up and presentation of the source material pertaining to "berdaches" was carried out by Jacobs in 1968. At the time, Jacobs' way of tackling the problem was novel in that she examined the body of data as a whole in order to arrive at definite statements instead of using it selectively to illustrate preconceived theoretical ideas. Jacobs also discussed the undifferentiated application of the term "berdache" in the literature and then explored the spatial occurrence of gender role change, both Native American and cultural anthropological attempts to explain the phenomenon, and the componential organization and development (*Ausgestaltung*) of the woman-man's role, as well as attitudes toward "berdaches."

A similarly comprehensive working up of the data was undertaken by Callender and Kochems (1983). This investigation, like that of Jacobs (1968), was based on purely cultural anthropological formulations of the problem and considered Native American women-men and men-women in their own cultural context, thus questioning earlier, psychological, interpretations of the "berdache" phenomenon (Callender and Kochems 1983:454f.). A number of the results they reported are confirmed in the present study:

- The gender status of the "berdaches" is ambivalent (Callender and Kochems 1983:453f.).
- Homosexual behavior appears as a consequence, and not as a cause, of gender role change (1983:444).
- In the case of women-men and men-women, gender mixing is present.
- Women-men's ritual occupations, which are legitimized by visions, belong to a nonfeminine role domain (1983:454).

In a later essay, Callender and Kochems (1986) discussed in further detail the concept of gender mixing. They found that male "berdaches"—along with their equivalents in cultures outside of North America—do not change from a masculine into a feminine gender status (see below,

Chapter 4), but on the contrary occupy their own status, formed by combining the respective gender statuses of both sexes (1986:177). Nonmen are not classified as women, and male "berdaches" do not attempt "to achieve social recognition as females or to attain the gender status of women" (1986:166). This mixed gender status is made possible by a construction of gender membership, which, along with "masculine" (man) and "feminine" (woman), allows yet a third gender status (1986: 165). This status, however, is taken on by persons who are not characterized primarily by their (mostly same-sex) choice of sexual partners, but rather by their penchant for the activities and behavior of the opposite biological sex: "It would seem that, wherever gender-mixing statuses exist, choice of sexual object has less significance in gender construction than either occupation or dress and demeanor" (1986:176). Consequently, it is not "homosexuality" that is being institutionalized, but rather nonmasculinity or nonfemininity.

The one-sidedness of psychological approaches with an emphasis on the sexual aspects of the "berdache" status was also underscored by Thayer:

> A cultural institution must be dealt with in its own terms and cultural-historical context; descriptions of the berdache as "transvestites" . . . or "extreme introverts, transvestites, and homosexuals" . . . are not at all helpful. Such description focuses attention to the overt (genital) sexuality of the institution, the very aspect which ironically is the least predictable variable concerning their behavior . . . a psycho-functional explanation tends to *reduce* the institution to a socially acceptable form of perverted sexual activity, whereby all other aspects of the berdache's life . . . are irrelevant . . .[My] objection also concerns the position taken . . . that "emic" categories, or native values, are basically worthless in the face of the superior, "etic" analysis preferred by the researcher. (Thayer 1980:288f., emphasis in the original)

Thayer erred, however, in assuming that same-sex relationships are the least predictable aspect of the "berdache" status: most women-men and men-women enter into relationships with partners of the same biological sex (see below, Chapters 11, 16, and 19). These relationships, however, are not an indispensable part of the "berdache" role, and the woman-man's and man-woman's status is not acquired on the basis of homosexual behavior. To this extent, Thayer's critique of many authors' fixation on the sexual aspect of the "berdache" institution is thoroughly justified. Thayer also examined the Plains women-men in their religious context, describing their ambivalent status against the background of Douglas' reflections (1988) pertaining to the latent spiritual power and consequent dangerous nature of persons or things which cross over fixed categories or boundaries, in this case the boundaries of gender status (Thayer 1980:291f.).

CULTURE AGAINST NATURE: WHITEHEAD'S APPROACH

Whitehead (1981) studied the cultural context of the "berdache" institution in detail, also emphasizing gender mixing (1981:88). She defined the minimal elements of gender role change as "assuming part or most of the attire, occupation, and social—including marital—status of the opposite sex for an indeterminate period" (1981:85). She agreed with Callender and Kochems that occupation and behavior play a greater role in the construction of gender membership among North American Indian cultures than does the choice of partner.

Whitehead asserted that there has been no feminine counterpart to the masculine institution of the "berdache," explaining that "the anatomic-physical component of gender was more significant in the case of the female than in the case of the male, and is thus less easily counterbalanced by the occupational component" (1981:91). Thus, according to Whitehead, because of their bodily functions (menstruation), which are regarded as harmful, access to a masculine role has been denied women (1981:92). At the same time, the author interpreted the lack of a "berdache" status for females against the background of a "status asymmetry of the sexes in North America": "The man was everywhere considered superior to the woman. As in most hierarchical systems, downward mobility was more easily achieved than upward mobility" (1981:86). Such an estimation of the masculine status as superior to the feminine status in North American Indian cultures, however, contradicts the findings of a number of authors who have argued that women have more subtle power mechanisms at their disposal (e.g., Callender and Kochems 1983:455f.; Kehoe 1983; M. N. Powers 1986). Datan, though (1983:458), agreed with Whitehead, reasoning that such mechanisms would not necessarily rule out "unequal access to power."

Whitehead's theses are, in any case, provocative. She theorized that "gender . . . was heavily defined in terms of prestige-relevant occupations" (1981:102). Whitehead explained that occupational activities played a central role among Native American cultures in determining gender membership and that there was a sexual/gendered division of labor. The production of durable consumer goods was the responsibility of women and was an occupation that could lead to both prestige and prosperity. At the same time, according to Whitehead, male dominance was not pronounced, and the boundaries between the respective spheres of both sexes were consequently open. In Whitehead's view, "berdaches" could, by means of a gender role change, gain access to the prestige that accrued to female skills: "The ways of women could lead to material prosperity and social distinction and were so perceived" (1981:107).

> What seems to have been . . . disturbing to the culture—which means, for all intents and purposes, to the men—was the possibility that women, within their own department, might be onto a good thing. It was into this unsettling breach that the berdache institution was hurled. In their social aspect, women were complimented by the berdache's imitation. In their anatomic aspect, they were subtly ridiculed by his vaunted superiority. Through him, ordinary men might reckon that they still held the advantage that was anatomically given and inalterable. (1981:109)

To summarize very simply: according to Whitehead, the institution of the "berdache" is an opportunity for men to have access to domains in which the women were able to compete with them for prestige, economic well-being, and social influence, "a cultural compromise formation founded on an incipient, though never fully realized, collapse of the gender-stratification system" (1981:111). (This would, incidentally, mean that women-men are not to be found in societies with an intact gender hierarchy, because in those cases all paths to prestige are firmly in the hands of men.)

The most challenging critique of Whitehead came from Callender and Kochems (1983:455f.), who cast doubt on Whitehead's assumption of male superiority in North American Indian cultures, as well as on her biologistic rationale for the alleged nonexistence of female "berdaches" (see below, Part 3). One problem with her argumentation certainly lies in the fact that Whitehead described the gender hierarchy as being not very highly developed, with the result that the boundaries of the gender spheres were not vigorously defended. However, according to her own argument, these boundaries must have been sufficiently developed in order to permit gender role change in only one direction, namely into the feminine sphere.

At the same time, it remains unclear why biologically "impure" women could not carry out a gender role change, since they were frequently able to encroach into male role domains (e.g., as women who went to war). Moreover, the claim that women did not cross over is not supported by the available data—the phenomenon of men-women very definitely occurred, even if not as frequently as that of women-men (see below, Part 3). Also problematic is Whitehead's assertion, obviously based on Ortner (1974), of a culture-molding biologization of the woman (woman = nature, man = culture). In this view, woman/nature is universally subordinate to man/culture (see MacCormack's 1980:16f. critique as well as MacCormack and Strathern 1980). One might also argue that men could be "negatively biologized"—for example, as nonmenstruating and non-childbearing—which would not hinder encroachments into the feminine gender role, but which would bar males from entry into a gender status which is identical to that of females (see Chapter 4).

ADDITIONAL AND MIXED GENDER STATUSES: NEW POINTS OF DEPARTURE

In their investigation of the cultural construction of gender membership, Kessler and McKenna cited the "berdache" as an example to support their assertion that "gender is not constituted in universal ways" (1977: 27). At the same time, they differentiated the "berdache" phenomenon from transsexualism, in contrast to Benjamin (1966) and Green (1974). Kessler and McKenna argued that transsexualism in no way casts doubt on or otherwise calls into question the gender dichotomy, but instead strengthens and confirms it (1977:27, 112f.). After examining the data, the authors concluded that in many cultures, "the possibility of a third gender category, separate from male and female" does exist, and is expressed by means of a "third gender role" (1977:29). Their view, that the anthropologists' rootedness in their own categories of gender has for a long time stood in the way of understanding the "berdache" phenomenon, is confirmed by the anthropological literature on the subject, in which a male who wore women's clothing and who maintained relationships with men could under no circumstances be seen otherwise than as a homosexual or as a transsexual.

Some time before, Martin and Voorhies (1975:85f.) had already questioned the universal existence of only two culturally defined genders. These authors interpreted the male "berdache" as having "third gender status" (1975:92f., 99f.) and the female "berdache" in turn as having the status of a fourth gender (1975:96), concluding that "the relationship between biological sex and social gender is neither simple nor direct" (1975:105).

Martin and Voorhies also offered the example of the Navajo *nadle* to show how even three anatomically different sexes actually can be recognized. One gender status is created for each of the three sexes (1975: 106). Other societies—the Mohave, for example—recognize only two biological sex categories, but apply "the principle of biological sex to create four rather than two gender statuses . . . by the social device of allowing cross-sex transformations" (1975:106). Still other groups—for example, in the Plains—institutionalize only one "feminine-like gender status" for males, but have no status equivalent for females (1975:106).

J. Miller's (1974) symbolic interpretation of the transformation of the entire Delaware tribe into "women" is original, but offers little in the way of starting points for an interpretation of the institution of gender role change. In a further essay, Miller interpreted both left-handed bears and "berdaches" as standing equidistant between the sexes and therefore as mediators between nature and culture (J. Miller 1982). In doing so, Miller was following the structuralist equation of man and culture versus woman and nature that was proposed by Ortner (1974). Associating "left" with "female," Miller proposed that bears that were male-and-wild but left-handed functioned as mediators among the animals, and that the "berdaches"—because they were likewise between genders—functioned as mediators in the domain of humans (1982:285f.).

DeMallie (1983), in his essay "Male and Female in Traditional Lakota Culture," characterized the distinction between male and female as "the single most important attribute for defining an individual in Lakota culture" (1983:238), which results in a strict sexual division of labor and avoidance of female/feminine characteristics and activities on the part of men (1983:239f.). Against such a background, it seems to the author to be "the greatest tragedy that could befall a Lakota male . . . to become a winkte" (1983:243). He pointed out, however, that a male did not become a *winkte* because of cowardice, but rather on the basis of a special kind of supernatural power which possessed him, and on account of which the *winkte* was not held responsible for his conduct (1983: 245). According to DeMallie, for a boy to be called a woman or a *winkte* was the worst possible shame (1983:247). Hence, in DeMallie's interpretation, *winkte* are individuals who, although they are men, behave in a manner that is flagrantly unmanly according to the Lakota ideas of manliness and womanliness. Here the *winkte* do not appear as ambivalent on account of their status, but instead as masculine, and as a cautionary example for other men. This interpretation of the phenomenon is similar to those of Le Vine (1973), Forgey (1975), and Munroe (1980).

The recent anthology *Living the Spirit* (Gay American Indians and Roscoe 1988), assembled by members of the homosexual organization GAI (Gay American Indians), contains two essays on the topic of the "berdache." Maurice Kenny's (Mohawk) overview of the "berdache" tradition characterized the institution as an alternative for men who could not fulfill the "high Indian standards" for masculinity (1988:18) but who were nonetheless integrated and often respected (1988:20, 23f., 30). Perhaps motivated by the desire to interpret the woman-man phenomenon in a positive light, Kenny misinterpreted the sources in several instances. For example, the Mandan "dandies" which Catlin (1926) described should not (as Kenny asserted) be equated with "berdaches"; rather, they were fops who did not carry out a gender role change at all.

Also, Catlin did not describe the "Dance to the berdash" of the Sauk "admiringly" (Kenny 1988:22); he clearly regarded it as an oddity, and the institution as a whole with nothing but repugnance (Catlin 1926, 2: 244: "I should wish that it might be extinguished before it be more fully recorded"). All in all, this paper provides no new starting points for interpretation.

In the same anthology, Midnight Sun (Anishnabe [Ojibwa]) investigated the Mohave and Navajo women-men as well as the manly-hearted women of the Piegan against the background of the economic conditions in the individual tribes (Midnight Sun 1988). She stressed the necessity for a paradigm shift from the construction of gender membership and sexuality typical of Western culture to the "cultural construction of sex, gender and sexuality" as the starting point for an interpretation of alternative gender roles (1988:36). Midnight Sun approached the topic in "historical materialist terms": "[sex/gender systems] . . . are shaped, in part, to meet economic interests and reinforced and validated by the dominant ideology" (1988:45). Even the componential organization and development of the "berdache" status is seen against the background of the ethnic group's means of production. Thus, according to Midnight Sun, the flexible, non-male-dominated gender role formulation of the Navajo, which was based on horticulture, favored institutionalized gender role change. By contrast, the more rigid construction of gender roles among the Mohave (horticulture in combination with a stress on masculine warrior virtues) resulted in the devaluation of the *alyha* (women-men) and the *hwame* (men-women) (1988:46). The author interpreted the manly-hearted women as one of the few possibilities within the male-dominated status system for Plains women to gain prestige within the framework of certain "patterns of allocation and production" (1988:46f.).

These interpretations are problematic in light of Kehoe's (1983) description of the high status of Blackfoot women and the numerous opportunities existing in that society for women to acquire prestige. Moreover, if one follows the logic of Midnight Sun's explanation that the imitation of biological patterns of the opposite sex by women-men and men-women results from a rigid gender role construction, women-men's imitation of menstruation and pregnancy should occur not only among the Mohave, but also in numerous other groups (1988:46). Further, in her conclusions, Midnight Sun reduced the analytical framework to the economic means of production, thus falling into the same kind of one-sided interpretation which, with good reason, she had accused other authors of committing (1988:35). In discussing the three groups individually, however, she definitely considered aspects other than economic ones.

The most comprehensive and extensive description of the institution of the "berdache" so far is that of Williams (1986b), who dealt with the subject monographically in the framework of a historical investigation, supporting his presentation with his own fieldwork results, which are remarkably comprehensive. He concentrated on Native American cultures in which women-men were held in more or less high esteem. This restriction in focus was probably due to his stated purpose, which was "to examine how a culture can accommodate gender variation and sexual variation beyond man/woman opposites, without being threatened by it" (1986b:4f.). A drawback of this restriction is that it does not account for the full complexity of the phenomenon; there were, in fact, groups in which the "berdache" was not held in high esteem. After describing the traditional aspects of "berdache" status, Williams focused primarily on changes in the institution resulting from the pressure of dominating Anglo-American influences and also on the partial redefinition of the "berdache" tradition in the context of the Gay American Indians movement. He is also one of the few authors who, in addition, considered for female gender variance/gender role change. Although Williams described the "berdache" institution as the cultural integration of homosexual behavior, he largely escaped the temptation which has ensnared other homosexual authors—equating "the berdache" with "the homosexual" of our culture (e.g., Katz 1985) and thereby interpreting the data so that Indian communities appear as models for the integration of persons who, in the sense of Western culture's definition, are homosexual. Even homosexuality and "the homosexual" are, after all, cultural constructs (see McIntosh 1972; and see below, Chapter 11).

On the contrary, Williams clearly delineated the construction of an ambivalent gender status for women-men. In general, his work functions as a plea for the cultural acceptance of sexual diversity, and it represents the most sensitive representation up to now of "berdaches" in their own cultural context. The excerpts from interviews with women-men reproduced in it, as well as Williams' working out of common features—*and* differences—between the homosexual relationships that occur in Western culture and those that occur between women-men and men, all cast doubt on earlier interpretations. In addition, Williams' work underscores the necessity of a cultural anthropological perspective instead of a psychological perspective on gender role change.

INVESTIGATIONS OF MEN-WOMEN: A GAP IN RESEARCH

The studies discussed so far have been concerned almost exclusively with masculine gender role change and/or male homosexual behavior. Studies of gender role change on the part of females have scarcely been undertaken. Williams dedicated a chapter of his study to them under the designation "Amazons" (1986b:233f.) and also addressed gender role crossing, as opposed to gender role change, as, for example, by the warrior women of the Plains (Williams 1986b:243f.). Whitehead (1981:90f.) also considered female "berdaches" and, as noted, traced the essentially rarer occurrence of female gender role change to the physiological characteristics of women, whose menstruation is considered to be harmful for masculine activities. According to Whitehead, this made gender role change for the most part impossible for females—or at least permitted them access to masculine activities only after menopause, when they were too old to take up an active hunter's or warrior's life (1981: 92f.). Thus, Whitehead's theoretical reflections focused primarily on women-men.

Some of the reasons for the lack of sources on female homosexuality and gender role change on the part of women have been cited by Blackwood (1986:8f.). With respect to North American Indian cultures, the sources are characterized by a distorted picture of the life of women over a long period of time, based on ethnocentric paradigms (for discussion see DeMallie 1983; Kehoe 1983; Weist 1983). Added to this is a lack of data, resulting in large part from the fact that male ethnographers interviewed male consultants. Moreover, they frequently had only limited access to female consultants, who were often inhibited when answering questions in the ethnographers' presence (see Kehoe 1983:54f.).

While it is certain that female homosexuality remained mostly hidden, female gender role change and gender role crossing were visible to the ethnographers, and the sources definitely permit analysis and evaluation. This was first carried out by Blackwood (1984) after Allen (1981; see revised version in Allen 1986: 244–261) published a paper on Native American lesbians.

Stating that direct references to female homosexuality in North American Indian groups scarcely exist, Allen (1981:67) asserted that "simple reason dictates that lesbians did exist in tribal cultures, for they exist now" (1981:79), further proposing that "because they were tribal people, the terms on which they existed must have been the terms of tribal existence" (1981:79). Allen speculated that lesbian love was probably an integral part of Indian life, because women spent most of their time with other women. In addition, according to Allen, lesbian women probably maintained a spiritual relationship to a female goddess, in a fashion similar to male "berdaches" (1981:81f.). Allen did not discuss female gender role change. Her remarks concerning the social and spiritual position of women in North American groups appear to be plausible, although apart from the Lakota *koskalaka,* Allen provided no concrete examples either of alternative gender roles or of lesbian relationships among Native American women. In fact, Beatrice Medicine (1993) has recently challenged Allen's interpretation of the *koskalaka* as lesbians as linguistically and culturally inaccurate. According to Medicine, *koskalaka* means "young man" or "postpubescent male," and *wi koskalaka* means "young woman"; there is, according to Medicine, no term equivalent to "lesbian" in Lakota language.

Thus Allen's explanations are largely hypothetical and are not grounded in data on existing lesbian relationships. Further, to attribute the lack of information on Indian "medicine Lesbians" to a conspiracy on the part of patriarchal historiographers (1981:84f.) is certainly too simple an explanation, even if it might contain a small grain of truth. As Williams noted with regard to women-men, fieldwork is necessary. In particular, fieldwork on female gender role change and homosexual behavior is needed in order to go beyond basing hypotheses on mere speculation. Similarly, as necessary and justified as the increasing correction in recent years of the traditional picture of Native American women is, an exchange of the androcentric perspective for an unexamined "gynecocentric" perspective seems equally unserviceable.

Unlike Allen (1981, 1986), Blackwood (1984) based her study of Indian "cross-gender females" on the available data. Blackwood opposed Whitehead's (1981) biologistic approach, as well as Callender and Kochems' (1983, 1986) concept of a mixed gender status which does not admit the idea of a "complete social role reclassification" (p. 29). Blackwood theorized that the feminine gender *status* is exchanged for a masculine *status*. She attributed the possibility of female gender role change to an equal ranking of the gender roles in the groups concerned, combined with a mutually flexible openness of boundaries between the roles, as well as a kinship system in which marriages were not tied by means of the bride to a transfer of wealth or prestige (Blackwood 1984: 32f.). Because the marriage of a daughter was not a prerequisite for her family to obtain rank, a woman was able to put aside her feminine role and, in addition, as a "social male," could enter into marriage with a woman (1984:34). In particular, Blackwood emphasized the flexibility of the gender roles and did not ascribe a mixed gender status to the male "berdache" (as Callender and Kochems did), but rather a social membership in the chosen gender, a "social fiction of the cross-gender role despite the obvious physical differences, indicating the unimportance of biological sex to the gender role" (1984:41); this situation is thus favored by pronounced role variability of the genders/sexes.

Blackwood challenged Whitehead's interpretation, which was based on the assumed unequal valuation and standing of the sexes/genders. (Blackwood 1984:41). I agree with Blackwood's criticism, especially since recent works have painted a more positive picture of the feminine status in Native American cultures than did the more traditional—and even feminist—ones (see, e.g., Albers and Medicine 1983 for a differentiated picture of Plains Indian women's roles). As a result of this recent work, it is clear that the assumption of a general male dominance is just as untenable as the assumption of rigid, scarcely crossable gender roles. Whether the boundaries of these roles were actually as easily permeable as Blackwood represented them, however, is questionable; and against the background of Callender and Kochems' (1983, 1986) theoretical work as well as the results of the present study, I cannot agree that the gender status of the opposite sex could be taken on. Reflections on these questions stand at the center of the following chapter.

Chapter **FOUR**

GENDER IDENTITY, GENDER ROLE, AND GENDER STATUS

THE COMPONENTS OF GENDER

Gender—which may be characterized as the cultural meaning given to an individual's physical sex—has three basic components. *Gender identity* reflects a person's subjectively felt experience of being masculine, feminine, or ambivalent. *Gender role* is the observable expression of gender identity in the social context. And *gender status* is the social position of an individual with reference to the other members of her or his culture as a woman, man, or someone belonging to an additional gender status separate from both. An individual's gender status is determined by cultural factors such as the gender role performed and the gender identity experienced by her or him, but also by biological sex (see Callender and Kochems 1986:166).

> Gender role: everything that a person says and does, to indicate to others or to the self the degree in which one is male or female or ambivalent . . . Gender role is the public expression of gender identity, and gender identity is the private experience of gender role. (Money and Ehrhardt 1972:284)

This definition by the American sex researchers Money and Erhardt offers an appropriate point of departure for formulating the question of what a gender role change involves. For the investigation of this phenomenon among North American Indians, it is significant that, according to the definition cited, a change of gender role can lead to an ambivalence of this role and also to an ambivalent, nonmasculine but also nonfeminine status. Such a gender role would then be the expression of a gender identity that either hovers between the masculine and the feminine gender identities or that comprises both the masculine and feminine gender identities equally.

Because the concept of gender role refers to externally manifested behavior, it is easier to observe than is gender identity, which represents the subjective experience of an individual (see Money and Erhardt 1972:215f.). Certainly, conversation with individuals can give some insight into their gender identity; unfortunately, however, the number of researchers who have actually spoken with women-men or men-women is very small. Typically, ethnographers have had contact only with Native American consultants who were not men-women or women-men themselves.

Only in a few isolated cases did actual interviews take place. Hammond (1882), Holder (1889), and S. Powers (1877:132) were mainly interested in medical examinations of the women-men known to them. Stevenson (1904) and Parsons (1916, 1923, 1932) personally knew and interviewed Zuni *lhamana*. Reichard (1950) worked briefly with Klah, a well-known Navajo chanter, who apparently was classified as a *nadle* primarily because as a boy he had been emasculated during an attack by the Utes (Reichard 1950:141). Among the Klamath, Spier (1930) interviewed a woman-man *(tw!inna'ek)* who had been a transvestite but was no longer cross-dressing by the time Spier met her/him, and Voegelin (1942) interviewed a male among the Shasta who showed many characteristics of a "berdache." These authors did not establish anything about the subjectively felt gender identity of their women-men acquaintances, however. Further, the few observers who had direct contact sometimes seem to have misinterpreted what they saw. Hill (1935) attempted an interview with Kinipai, a Navajo *nadle* (see Figure 1). Because among the Navajo it was regarded as grossly impolite to mention the peculiarities of the *nadle,* Kinipai became very upset in the face of the questions that Hill put to her via the interpreter ("You do not mention to a person that they are nadle because you respect them, and they do not mention that they are nadle because they respect themselves" [1935:279]). Hill assessed Kinipai's confused, muddled, and disconnected answers as a sign of "maladjustment" (1935:278), although doubtless the cause was that Hill—in his zealous effort to obtain first-hand information about *nadle*—committed some faux pas that were perceived by Kinipai as shocking and as evidence that Hill did not respect her.

Williams (1986a, 1986b), who mainly interviewed self-identified Oglala *winkte,* stands out as a counterexample. Williams' interviews provide deeper insight into the subjective experience of gender identity on the part of women-men, conveying a strong sense of emotionally felt gender identity.

Gender role includes a wide variety of components by means of which a person communicates whether he or she is male, female, or ambivalent.

Kinipai, a Navajo nadle. (From Hill 1935:277, Fig. 1) Reproduced by permission of the American Anthropological Association from American Anthropologist *37, 1935.*

An obvious means of signaling femininity is for a male to take on the clothing, hair-style, adornments, and possibly body decoration (e.g., certain sex/gender-specific tattoos) of a woman. To this may be added a culturally defined sex/gender-specific body language (facial expressions, gestures, manner of sitting). Beyond this, there is found in all Native American cultures a more or less developed sexual/gendered division of labor (see Driver and Massey 1957:365 ff.). Thus, for example, femininity can additionally be signaled by a male's performing the activities assigned to the female sex/gender. In the area of language, femininity can be directly expressed verbally ("I am a woman"), or it may be expressed through forms of address, expression, or word choice that signal the sex/gender of the speaker. All of these external signals of gender membership have frequently been used in the context of gender role change. Gender ambivalence, on the other hand, can be expressed alone through the fact that physical sex and the gender role are not congruent. Gender ambivalence can, however, also be communicated through a combination of masculine and feminine role components.

Gender role also has components that cannot be copied because they are based on physiological functions. In numerous California Native groups, for example, a girl's femaleness is first brought to unique expression by a puberty ceremony which is connected with her menarche. After that, it is expressed each month through a several days' stay in the menstrual hut (see Kroeber 1925). Such a public observance of the first menstruation and of those following can also be found elsewhere throughout North America, to varying degrees, among other groups (Driver 1941, 1961:441ff.).

Menarche and the ceremonies connected with it appear to be *the* critical event which confers on a girl the *gender status* of a woman. The culturally prescribed behavior of the girl within the framework of this entrance into the feminine gender status is a constituent of the feminine role. Along with gender role and gender identity, gender status is the third component of a person's social gender membership. Hoebel characterized social status as follows:

> A status is the social position of an individual with reference to the other members of his society as determined by a specific attribute, cluster of attributes, or the generalized summation of all his attributes. Thus, every person has a number of statuses simultaneously. He has . . . as many statuses as there are recognized characteristics of the individual in his culture. Such characteristics are age, sex, bodily traits, and specific social experiences and affiliations. (1958:384)

Role is thus a complex of behavior patterns that are associated with, but are not identical to, status (see Hoebel 1958:385). It is in connection with gender role change that the distinction between *ascribed* and *achieved status* becomes significant (Hoebel 1958:386ff.; Linton 1936: 479, 115ff.). Gender is primarily an ascribed status, based on physical characteristics. Thus, the status "woman" cannot fundamentally be achieved by a biological male; at most, what can be achieved is the status of a male who has carried out a change of gender role. Thus, Linton (1936:480) classified the status of the "berdache" as an achieved status: "They wore women's costumes and carried on women's activities. At the same time they occupied a distinct status not exactly equivalent to that of women." Naturally, this is also true in reverse for gender role change on the part of females. Female physiology impedes not so much the encroachment by females into the masculine gender *role,* as assumed by Whitehead (1981), but rather the taking on of a masculine gender *status.*

Therefore, three components interact together in the cultural context of gender role change: gender identity as the subjective, felt perception of gender membership on the part of an individual; gender role as the outward expression of this perception; and gender status, which is the social position assigned to the individual by that person's culture. For women-men and men-women, this status takes on an ambivalent character. This becomes especially evident in all cases in which the terms for women-men and/or men-women in a given Native American culture have come down to us (see Tables 6 and 7 below). This is true even when the gender role acted out by an individual is oriented so closely on the role of the opposite sex that, to all outward appearances, there is no longer any recognizable difference. The members of the group can speak of a woman-man as "she" and address him as a female relative, but they will not designate him as a "woman" but rather as a "halfman-halfwoman" (*heemaneh*, Cheyenne; Grinnell 1962, 2:40), as someone who "feels impelled against his will to act the woman" (*miati*, Hidatsa; Dorsey 1894:516f), as a "woman pretender" (Ingalik; Osgood 1958: 261), or as someone who "imitates a woman" (*kupatke'tek*, Kutenai; Schaeffer 1965:217).

Thus, by use of the sources, it is possible to determine what status persons occupy who have carried out a gender role change, and the degree to which the performance of the gender role shows whether this individual is masculine ("man"), feminine ("woman"), or ambivalent. What cannot be ascertained is whether a person who copies the role of the opposite sex perfectly is in fact striving not for an ambivalent status, but rather for the same status as transsexuals in Western culture: not to be a "woman-man" but rather a "woman." It would be worthwhile and rewarding to investigate such a possible gap between individual feelings and the cultural constructions of gender status in Native American cultures, particularly in view of gender identity problems in Western culture. This would, however, require a number of Native American women-men and men-women autobiographies as a foundation.

PHYSIOLOGY AND GENDER STATUS

So, a status similar to that of the opposite sex cannot be ascribed, but only achieved on grounds of biologically based sexual dimorphism. The cultural expression of physiological functions can be key to the process by which individuals are assigned gender status.

An example of this are some Paiute and Shoshoni groups, in which persons who changed their gender role were referred to by the same word that was applied to infertile individuals of both sexes (Kelly 1932: 157; Steward 1943:385), although occasionally by another word that referred specifically to women-men (as a subcategory of infertile persons) (Steward 1941:353). For a girl, menarche represented the transition from infertility to fertility, while the status of "woman," in turn, required proof of fertility. If, however, a woman remained infertile, she entered into the status of *tü'basa* or *dü'bas*, a "sterile person"; the same was true of infertile men and occasionally of men-women. It is possible that a young male would have fallen under such a category after completing a change of gender role because he was infertile in his chosen role as a woman—that is, he was incapable of bearing children, regardless of his biological capacity to procreate. That the classification of women-men as "sterile" cannot have resulted from biological impotence is shown by an example that Steward cited, in which a male carried out a gender role change in his youth, but later resumed the masculine role and founded a family (Steward 1941:353). Yet inability to bear children does not seem to be the only factor involved in the "infertile" appellation. Many women-men in the Great Basin, for example, chose men as their partners, and so remained nonfertile even in the male domain. Nonbearing and nonprocreating in all probability seem to have been decisive for the assignment of men-women to the category "sterile."

The significance of physiological functions and their cultural expression within the framework of gender role is shown by the fact that in a few cases, women-men even simulated menstruation and childbirth, and in one case (among the Mohave), they also observed the regulations and prohibitions prescribed for women in connection with these events (see Devereux 1937; Essene 1942:65; Stewart 1942:298; see below, Chapter 8).

PARTNER CHOICE AS AN ASPECT OF GENDER ROLE

Partner choice is a central aspect of gender role (see Whitehead 1981:85). A person who undertakes a gender role change will usually look for a partner of the same biological sex. In contrast to Western homosexual relationships (two persons of the same gender identity, the same gender role, and the same gender status), women-men and men-women may also assume roles considered complementary in heterosexual marriage. Thus a male (or female) couple might marry and assume complementary gender roles. In any case, the majority of women-men sought male partners, and the majority of men-women sought female partners, whether for marriage-like relationships, for more fleeting partnerships, or for sexual contacts in general (see Chapter 11 and Part 3). Relationships with partners who are of the same sex as the woman-man or man-woman, but of a different gender, and whose gender role is complementary to that of the woman-man or man-woman, are taken up as an additional component of the role of the opposite sex.

AMBIVALENCE AND NONAMBIVALENCE OF ROLE AND STATUS

It is difficult to determine the degree of gender role change on the basis of the sources. Culturally defined gender roles consist of numerous single components, but the sources typically refer to only a few aspects, and not to the totality of the role of women-men or men-women in a given culture. Often, the sources contain only sweeping general statements concerning a male's change to feminine role behavior—for example, that he "lives like a woman," "dresses like a woman," or "performs women's work":

> They dress, talk, and live like women because they want to, and in their body they are men (Acoma; L. A. White 1943:325).
>
> . . . a few bucks who have the dress and manner of the squaws and who cohabit with other bucks (Hidatsa; Holder 1889:623).
>
> . . . wore women's clothing, followed feminine daily pursuits, lived with a man (Huchnom; Foster 1944:227).
>
> . . . wear women's clothes, do women's work (Hupa; Driver 1939:347).

Admittedly, the sources frequently specify feminine tasks which were performed by women-men. However, in all societies, the role of women is differentiated, apart from clothing and everyday activities, into a great number of single roles, so that it is usually not possible to ascertain the extent to which a male, within the framework of his gender role change, has brought to expression the *totality* of feminine role behavior. Despite the copying of a large number of feminine role components, it remains an open question whether this change actually expressed femininity, or rather—because of the omission of components—ambivalence. Gender status ambivalence can be deduced from the descriptive terms that were given to women-men and men-women (see Tables 6 and 7).

An ambivalence in both gender role and gender status is clearly recognizable when role components of both sexes are combined, and only a partial gender role change results. This is expressed in the case of males, for example, by feminine everyday activities, combined with special activities which are regarded as belonging to the masculine role domain, above all those of a ritual nature.

THE COMPONENTS OF GENDER ROLE

Gender role has been broken down into its main components in order to ascertain how (and to what extent) within the context of gender role change persons abandon their own role and assume components of the role of the opposite sex. Gender role contains the following components:

1. Everyday and religious activities as well as specialist occupations which are assigned to a man or a woman in the framework of the sexual/gendered division of labor.
2. Clothing which, on the basis of culturally determined dis-

tinguishing features, shows that the wearer is a man or a woman.

3. Body language that is culturally specified as feminine or masculine (e.g., folding under or crossing the legs while sitting, turning the tips of the feet inward by women, etc.).
4. Language forms which are culturally defined as masculine or feminine.
5. The keeping of culturally determined rules respecting physiologically based life crises (e.g., puberty fasting for boys, menarche ceremonies for girls).
6. Bonding with a partner of the biologically opposite sex or of "the other" (or another) gender as an economic and reproduction-oriented unit.

Gender status does not depend on whether all of the role components are fulfilled: for example, a woman does not lose her gender status if she temporarily or permanently lives separated, widowed, or as a single person. Likewise, infertile women or postmenopausal women are not classified as nonwomen. Even when postmenopausal women are culturally compared with men (and sometimes have access to masculine, and particularly ritual, activities not open to them before menopause; see, e.g., Niethammer 1985:335; Ray 1963:42f.; Shimkin 1947:319), they do not exchange their feminine gender status for an ambivalent one. Even the taking on of role components of the opposite sex does not necessarily lead to a reclassification into an ambivalent gender status: the "warrior women" are an example of this (see Chapter 17).

A person engaged in a gender role change has to orient him- or herself to the whole tangled network of gender-specific roles sketched above. The extent to which women-men, men-women, and certain other individuals in Native American cultures took over role components that were associated with the gender status of the opposite sex, and the extent to which they retained those of their own sex, is the subject of the following chapters.

SUMMARY

According to the definition cited at the beginning of this chapter, gender role is the expression of the gender identity (the subjective feeling of one's own gender membership) of an individual and represents the complex of culturally determined behavior patterns that are associated in a given culture with the corresponding gender status. On account of the incompleteness and many gaps in the data for the North American Indian groups, the gender identity of women-men and men-women cannot, in the main, be determined. In the few cases in which information pertaining to the gender identity of "berdaches" exists (e.g., Williams' Oglala informants), it can be seen that their gender role reflects an ambivalent, masculine-feminine gender identity.

Meanwhile, the components which in each case characterize the masculine and the feminine role are known, so that by using descriptions of gender role change, we can investigate the extent to which opposite-sex role components are integrated into a person's behavior and, if necessary, the extent to which components of the standard role culturally assigned to the biological sex of such a person are retained. Because of the sketchiness of the database, however, it is often not possible to draw conclusions about details of gender role makeup and organization, and it is therefore difficult to make general statements about whether, for example, all of the social roles associated with the feminine gender status were in fact actually filled by women-men. Descriptive terms which were applied to women-men and men-women in the individual Native American cultures do provide some information about the gender status achieved (or kept) in the course of a gender role change.

PART TWO

Gender Role Change by Males

Chapter **FIVE**

CROSS-DRESSING AND MIXED GENDER ROLES

"CROSS-DRESSING" AND "CROSS-ACTING"

TRANSVESTISM AND THE FEMININE GENDER ROLE

At first glance—and independently of gender role behavioral components—men's or women's clothing appears to signal the gender to which the wearer feels he or she belongs. Cross-dressing (transvestism) in the framework of a gender role change has been reported from a large number of Native American cultures (see Map 2). Most of the sources contain explicit information about whether male "berdaches" put on women's clothes. In some cases, the comments are less clear; for example, in early lists of the *Anthropological Records,* Gifford (1940:66) included as the only entries "Berdaches admitted," "Males as females," and "Females as males." The exact meaning of "Males as females" is left to the speculation of the reader. Driver's compilation (1937) poses similar problems. However, because the term "berdache" in the American scholarly literature is usually understood to refer to males in women's clothing, such unclear or ambiguous examples have—with reservations—been included in Map 2, but they are designated as "cross-dressing assumed."

Voegelin (1942:134), Essene (1942:31), and Steward (1941:312) expanded their lists to include the topical entry "Wear women's clothes." Steward's examples make it clear that, even in view of a heading such as "berdache" or "transvestite," cross-dressing can be assumed only with reservations. For several subgroups of the Nevada Shoshoni, the compilation indicates that "Male berdaches" do "woman's work" but do not wear women's clothing (Steward 1941:312).

Other examples (also included in Map 2, with reservations) include comments such as "Berdaches (men living as women) . . . had the natural desire to become women. . . . They were married to men. . . . The

Map 2. Gender Role Change and Cross-Dressing by Males

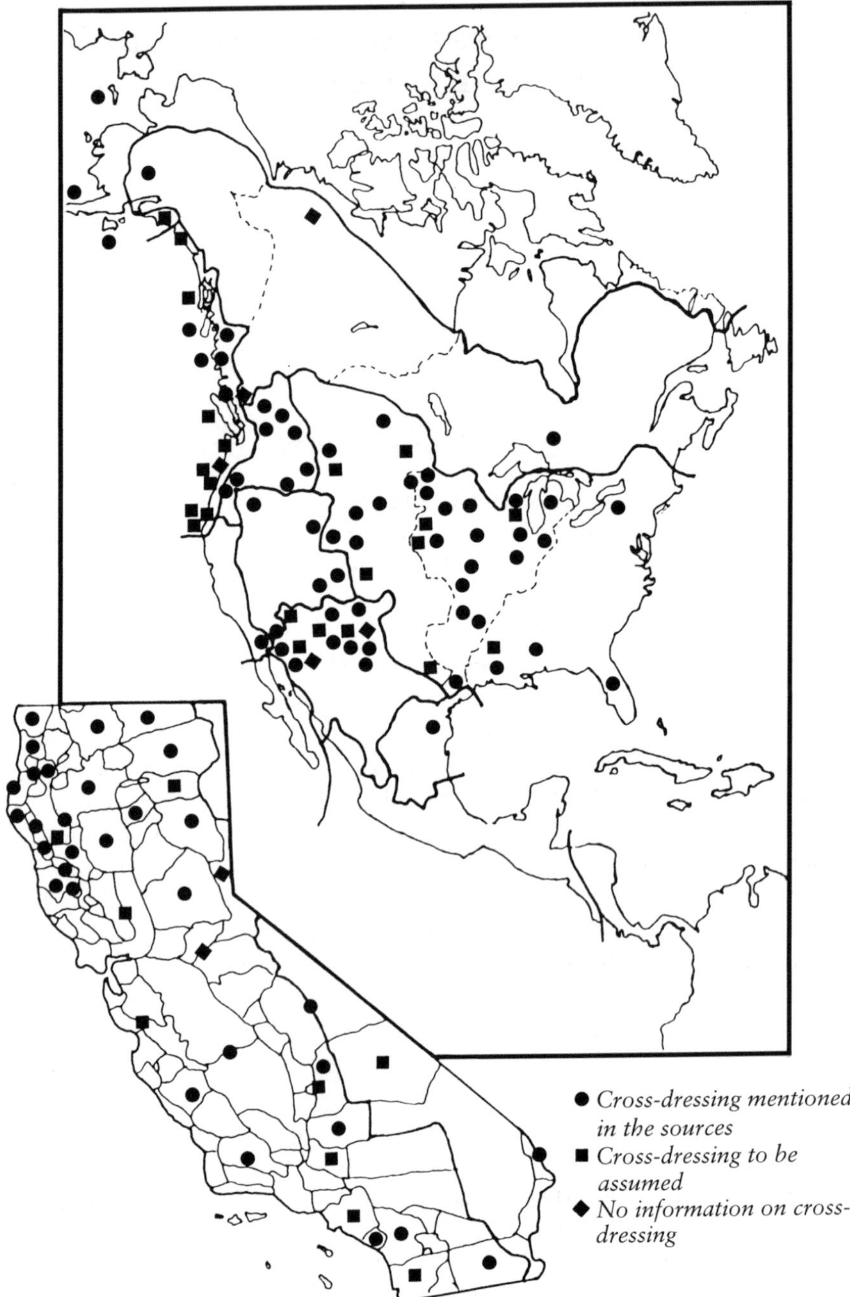

Arapaho declare that they never had any women that dressed and lived as men" (Kroeber 1902:19). Since Kroeber explicitly denied the existence of both gender role change *and* cross-dressing for females, however, it can be assumed that Arapaho *haxu'xan* (women-men) cross-dressed, especially since their gender role change was very pronounced. The Eyak provide a similar example. Under the heading "Transvestites and Witches," Birket-Smith and De Laguna (1938:206) described "men who lived like women, who did women's work and did not hunt." The heading ("transvestites") indicates cross-dressing even though the text does not expressly mention it.

The example of non-transvesting women-men among the Nevada Shoshoni demonstrates that the carrying out of feminine activities by males is not absolutely connected with transvestism. Conversely, the wearing of women's clothing by males is not always accompanied by "cross-acting"—that is, the assumption of feminine activities or behavior patterns. One Osage warrior, on the grounds of a vision experience, took on women's clothing and women's language but retained his role as a warrior (Fletcher and La Flesche 1911:132f.). Women's clothing served a nineteenth-century Piegan medicine man merely as an expression of his personal "medicine," by no means identifying him as a "berdache" (Schaeffer 1965:221f.).

In both tribes, there also existed alongside these cases fully developed masculine gender role change, including cross-dressing. Again, in other cases quite different in nature, women's clothing was put on, but certain aspects of the masculine role were retained along with feminine role behavior, for example by Coahuiltecan women-men (Cabeza de Vaca 1555:36). Navajo *nadle* performed both masculine and feminine tasks (Hill 1935:274f.); the Papago woman-man Shining Evening shared all women's tasks with the female members of her/his parents' household, but was described by her/his sister-in-law as "both a son and a daughter" to the widowed mother. Even her/his preference for the excessive consumption of whiskey appears more likely to belong to masculine role behavior, because Underhill's female consultant never mentioned that comparable alcoholic excesses (outside ritual contexts) were common among the Papago women (Underhill 1936:39, 43f., 51). Zuni *lhamana* took on women's clothing and feminine activities, but were—like every boy but hardly ever a girl—initiated into the *ko'tikili* (kachina cult), where they remained members throughout their lives (Parsons 1916: 527). In still other tribes, males carried out a gender role change at one point in their lives, but rescinded that change after several years had passed (Klamath, Spier 1930:53; Shoshoni, Steward 1941:253).

Even this limited number of examples shows that gender role change is anything but a unitary phenomenon. First of all, a distinction needs to be made between cross-dressing and "cross-acting," which refers to the adoption of activities, personality expressions, and so forth, that are culturally attributed to the opposite sex. The mere fact that a male wears women's clothing does not say anything about his role behavior, his gender status, or even his choice of partner—or about the circumstances leading to his adopting women's clothing. As a unitary phenomenon, the "berdache" quite obviously doesn't exist. Instead, there exists a great number of "cross-dressers" and "cross-actors" who act out their roles in different cultural contexts, at first glance showing only one commonality: they move to varying degrees away from the masculine toward the feminine role, which in turn usually leads to an ambivalence of their gender role.

For example, Four Bears, the Piegan medicine man already mentioned, crossed out of his masculine role within a certain cultural context—when he was performing very particular kinds of ritual acts (Schaeffer 1965:221f.). He did not hold the status of a "berdache," or woman-man: the women's clothes were an expression of his personal "medicine" pertaining to certain ritual acts. In other cases, masculine and feminine role components balanced each other out; the Navajo *nadle* should serve as an appropriate example. Aside from hunting and warfare, all masculine and feminine spheres of activity alike were open to them (Hill 1935:275). In other Native American cultures, males adopted the feminine gender role virtually in toto: among these are the Yuma boys described by Alarcón (1565:368), who received from birth onward a completely feminine upbringing, and also the Aleut *shupans,* who likewise were raised as girls and who mastered the feminine role to perfection (see Dall 1897:402f.).

In the following, I describe and discuss the various forms of gender role change. The point of departure is the existence or nonexistence of cross-dressing on the occasion of a partial or complete adoption of feminine role behavior on the part of males.

TRANSVESTISM AND THE MASCULINE GENDER ROLE

The combination of transvestism and masculine gender role is extremely rare. In one case, an Osage warrior had a vision in which he was told to take on the status of the *mixu'ga* (woman-man); a complete gender role change, however, did not result:

> There was a young man who had been out to fast many times. He had dreams which he thought were the kind that would make him a man of valor. He went on the warpath and took with him a number of followers. They found the enemy, defeated him, and returned with many trophies. On the way home, he got up to dance one night in honor of his victory. As

> he was dancing, brandishing his weapons and praising himself, an owl hooted near-by in the woods, and after each hooting the owl would say: "The leader is a mixu'ga!" The people listened in amazement, and at last the leader cried: "I have done that which a mixu'ga could never do!" However, on reaching his home the young leader dressed as a woman and spoke as a woman. He married and had children. He was successful as a warrior, but when about to go to war he discarded his women's clothing and dressed himself as a man. (Fletcher and La Flesche 1911:133)

The man follows the command of the apparition to the extent, therefore, that he adopts women's clothing and women's manner of speaking. Otherwise, he quite obviously remains faithful to the masculine role, fathers children, and continues to go to war. Moreover, in regard to the possibility that he pursued feminine activities, the sources do not say a word. His founding of a family allows us to suppose that he also continued to pursue masculine subsistence occupations. For one thing, the raising of corn and women's gathering activities can hardly have sufficed to nourish a family without the addition of meat to the diet. Further, it is difficult to imagine that the man would have been able to find a wife if he had not been in a position to contribute his share to subsistence acquisition. Because he kept his daily life (in women's clothing) and his warrior's life (in men's clothing) distinctly separate, we can more accurately speak of a *gender role split* than of a gender role change: the two roles—that of the warrior and the "woman's role" (with the latter restricted to a few aspects)—are not mixed, but instead are lived out in parallel.

Apart from this, the vision experience of this man is atypical. The standard vision of a *mixu'ga* among the Osage contained either an encounter with a female supernatural being or a variant of the Omaha standard vision, in which the visionary is supposed to choose between bow-and-arrow and a carrying-strap; on the basis of a cunning ruse on the part of the supernatural being that appears in the vision, he ends up with the carrying-strap (Fletcher and La Flesche 1911:132f.). This vision was obviously binding for a boy or a man. A psychic component also comes into play, because it can be assumed that a *mixu'ga* vision would not run counter to the wishes of the visionary. He then adopted the clothing and occupations of a woman for life (1911:132f.). Thus, the warrior's *mixu'ga* vision was in this sense atypical. Also, he had previously had a series of visions of a totally different kind which had granted him just the opposite, namely a dazzling career as a warrior. These earlier visions must have contained spirit helpers that were either so lucky or so strong that the young warrior could risk standing up to the *mixu'ga* vision not only verbally—"I have done that which a mixu'ga could never do!" (1911:133)—but also by his way of life. Among the Osage, *mixu'ga* quite obviously did not go to war. The man, meanwhile, could not totally disregard the command in his vision. So he partitioned his life into two gender roles. In his day-to-day life, he wore women's clothing and engaged in a woman's way of speaking; he also apparently assumed the status of a *mixu'ga,* notwithstanding the only partial nature of his gender role change. In this way, he satisfied the *mixu'ga* vision. In time of war, he took the warrior role, in men's clothing, and thus was able to pursue his real life's destiny, to which his earlier visions had led him. As an expression of gender identity, however, the lived-out gender role in this case was unambiguously masculine, because the feminine role was apparently limited to externals (speech, clothing) and did not include everyday activities of a woman within the sexual division of labor. The episode recorded by Fletcher and La Flesche also suggests that a *mixu'ga* vision did not necessarily lead to a complete gender role change if a man did not feel that the woman's role was entirely appropriate for him.

A further example of cross-dressing in spite of—and along with—masculine role behavior is the already-mentioned Piegan medicine man Four Bears (Schaeffer 1965:221f.). He led an everyday life as a husband and as the father of two sons, and he was also the chief of a local group and a "powerful shaman" (1965:221). Only the last-named social role included cross-dressing, and this, moreover, was not associated with feminine role behavior. The Moon Deity had bestowed on Four Bears great powers as a medicine man (this designation is used here for persons with supernatural powers in place of the term "shaman," which is frequent in the literature). His powers were bestowed on the condition that he would put on women's clothes during certain ritual activities. Dressed in "a woman's canvas dress, a leather belt studded with brass tacks, and two copper bracelets with elk-teeth," he then practiced his profession, which focused mainly on ensuring young men success in war expeditions (1965:222). Four Bears also invited the young men to suck at his breast in order to impart to them even more supernatural powers: "If you can stand to come to me, I will nurse you like a woman" (1965:222). While the warriors were away on raiding expeditions, he performed supporting rites in women's clothes and, from time to time, went out on horse-stealing forays dressed as a woman (1965:222). In contrast to this situation, examples can also be found among the Piegan, as among the Osage, of the complete adoption in everyday life of the feminine role by males, such as a woman-man named Piegan Woman, who, however—in addition to his everyday feminine role—also regularly went on the warpath (1965:223).

In the case of Four Bears, one cannot speak of a gender role change—he was no "berdache," and there is no indication that he was classified as such by the other members of his community. His gender role and gender identity remained within the male domain. In contrast to the Osage warrior described above who drew his "power" from visions which emphasized masculinity, but who received no supernatural powers, or "medicine," from the *mixu'ga* vision, Four Bears' cross-dressing was an *expression of his personal "medicine"*: the women's clothes that he wore are comparable to the medicine pouches that other men carried with them as a sign of their personal vision. Because his medicine had to do with the successful carrying out of raiding expeditions, he wore the signs of the supernatural powers given to him by the Moon Deity only on these occasions. He was also a specialist in summoning rain and snow, and as a sign of this ability, he did not wear women's clothing, but instead vomited up four hailstones (Schaeffer 1965:222). Thus, his nursing or feeding of younger warriors was not an expression of feminine role behavior, but rather an expression of the symbolic manner, appropriate to his kind of medicine, or power, received from the Moon Deity, in which he passed these powers on to others. Four Bears thus actually borrowed a type of feminine power (feeding) in order to enhance a specifically masculine type of power (fighting).

In the case of the Osage warrior as well as of Four Bears, the cross-dressing is lasting, but is *determined by the situation.* In both cases, a change of gender role was not carried out. The Osage carried out a partial external change of gender in the domain of everyday life. In Four Bears' case, the cross-dressing took place in situations connected with his role as a specialist in empowering young warriors. The Osage put on women's clothes in order not to jeopardize his power as a warrior, whereas Four Bears donned women's clothes to demonstrate his specific power. Neither of the two men aspired to a consistent execution of the feminine gender role.

With one possible exception (a Kwakiutl mentioned by Ford 1941:131, who exhibited feminine behavior patterns, but who nevertheless was regarded as "the wisest man in the Quatsinos" and as a prestigious teller of myths), these cases exhaust the examples of a combination of cross-dressing with the masculine gender role. In these instances, feminine aspects were integrated into a predominantly masculine gender role. In other cases, commands received in a specific vision usually led either to ambivalence (i.e., to a combination of the masculine and feminine roles) or to unambiguously feminine gender role behavior. Fletcher and La Flesche's (1911:132) claim, however, that some men may have experienced a "berdache" vision but perceived themselves as so masculine that they preferred suicide to a change of gender role is questionable. The examples of the Osage warrior and Four Bears demonstrate that cross-dressing did not necessarily result in a feminine gender role or an ambivalent gender status, nor was such change even necessarily caused by the man's having a feminine gender identity.

The significant role played by the vision as an impetus to cross-dressing raises the question of the degree to which the vision functioned as a command, as well as the degree to which the visionary was disposed to follow through on the vision. Why is it that some males accepted the dictates of the vision without resistance (as, obviously, an Osage usually did with the *mixu'ga* vision), while others resisted?

Furthermore, the examples of the Osage and Four Bears contradict the view that a gender role change (however constituted) was a welcome "out" for men who shrank from the hard realities of a warrior's existence. Even if the women-men's crossing beyond the boundaries of the masculine role generally appears more strongly developed and salient in the war-oriented Plains groups than does the Osage warrior's mere everyday cross-dressing combined with a feminine manner of speaking, or Four Bears' donning of women's clothes as a sign of his power, the motivations for crossing beyond the boundaries of gender role are extremely complex. Consequently, these behaviors should not be interpreted, with any simplistic, blanket explanation, as flight from the high demands of the masculine role.

Alongside males who retained their masculine gender role in spite of cross-dressing, as well as those who gave up all the masculine role components in favor of feminine ones, one finds numerous transvesting women-men who combined elements of both gender roles. Aspects of the masculine role were sometimes retained to very differing degrees, but were usually integrated into the total role and not split off from it; such individuals engaged in *gender role mixing*. The status of the individuals concerned was usually ambivalent; that is, they were classified as women-men.

THE EARLIEST EXAMPLE: CABEZA DE VACA

Cabeza de Vaca described the "hombres amarionados impotentes" of the Coahuiltecan in the following words:

> . . . vi una diablura, y es: que vi un hombre casado con otro, y estos son unos hombres amarionados impotentes: y andan tapados como mujeres y hazen officio de mujeres, y tiran arco y llevan muy gran cargo . . . y son mas membrudos que los otros hombres y mas altos: Sufren muy grandes cargas. (Cabeza de Vaca 1555:36; my adaptation of orthography to modern Spanish)

> [I saw a piece of devilry, and thus: I saw a man married to another, and these are effeminate, impotent men: and they go about covered-up like women and they do the work of women, and they draw the bow and they carry very heavy load . . . and they are more brawny than the other men and are taller: they can withstand very great burdens.]

Here, the feminine role components are clothing and everyday occupations (especially carrying loads). At the same time, the *hombres amarionados* were active as archers, although it is unclear whether this was in connection with hunting, warfare, or both. In addition, Cabeza de Vaca's reference to the marriages of the *hombres amarionados* to men also points to the feminine aspects of their role and suggests that these were official marriages.

The emphasis on the unusual body size and physical strength of the *hombres amarionados* is curious. Indications appear repeatedly in the literature, however, suggesting that a feminine role—with or without the retention of masculine role components—was in no way chosen only or primarily by males who were especially feminine in their external appearance. In any case, it is extremely doubtful that Cabeza de Vaca's comments—especially his reference to the women-men as "amarionados impotentes"—could be used to justify Newcomb's (1961: 51) interpretation that some of the women-men were castrati. In Spanish, *amarionado*—or, as it more frequently appears, *amaricado* (Spier 1933:6)—describes an effeminate or homosexual man. "Impotente" designates in general the inability to procreate, without implying castration. Cabeza de Vaca obviously deduced—without closer examination—the infertility of the *amarionados* from their effeminacy, and probably also assumed that that infertility was the cause for their effeminacy, just as, for example, many of his contemporaries referred to women-men as hermaphrodites, although there are no indications that intersexuality was actually present (e.g., Hennepin 1699, Le Moyne 1603/1875; see also Simms 1903 and Kelly 1932; cf. a contrary view as early as 1727—Lafiteau, 1727/1974:52f.). Newcomb, then, obviously interpreted Cabeza de Vaca's term "amarionados impotentes" as meaning that castration had been performed on some of these males. In the event that Newcomb's interpretation regarding the Coahuiltecans were provable, we would be confronted with the only case in North America in which a gender role change had been mediated surgically. A further example of a supposed artificially induced genital atrophy (Hammond 1882, 1891) is likewise so doubtful that artificial effeminization among North American cultures can be discounted.

THE NAVAJO *NADLE:* A REINTERPRETATION

Very detailed information exists pertaining to the Navajo *nadle.* To the present time, these individuals have been discussed in the literature from the perspective that access to the occupational domains of both sexes helped them to gain considerable prosperity. This interpretation will be subjected to critical scrutiny in the following section.

The Navajo referred to both physical intersexes (usually referred to as "hermaphrodites" in the literature) and also to persons of the male and female sex who had carried out a gender role change as *nadle,* "being transformed" (Hill 1935:273). (Note that the term "hermaphrodites" is not really quite accurate, because hermaphroditism is only one of several possibilities for physically based sexual ambivalence; see Overzier 1961d). According to Hill (1935:273), the Navajo do in fact distinguish between "real *nadle*" (i.e. intersexes) and "those who pretend to be *nadle*" (i.e. "transvestites"). Not all so-called transvestites among the Navajo cross-dressed, however, so this term is unhappily chosen; further, it can lead to howlers such as "Transvestites wear the garb of either sex" (Hill 1935:275). When Hill was there, Klah wore both men's and women's clothing, switching off between them (Hill 1935:273), but when Reichard got to know him, he wore only men's clothes (Reichard 1950:141). His status as a *nadle* was not affected by this.

The distinction between "real" *nadle* and "those who pretend to be *nadle*" did not, according to Hill, have an effect on the cultural status of the two *nadle* groups; Hill claimed that the same status was held by "real" *nadle* and "those who pretend to be *nadle*" (Hill 1935:273). That the accuracy of this statement is limited will be explained below.

In spite of the concept of transformation inherent in the term *nadle,* the emphasis clearly does not lie on a *process* (of change), but rather on a *condition* or state of affairs (having a share in both sexes/genders at the same time). Not without reason are physical intersexes the "real" *nadle.* The person who moves from one gender to another by means of a gender role change is only the copy, so to speak, of the one who, from birth on, already combines both sexes. Like intersexes in the animal kingdom, the human "hermaphrodite" is regarded among the Navajo as bringing luck and prosperity (Hill 1935:274). The fact that both feminine and masculine spheres of activity are open to them is no doubt due to the culturally felt dual sexuality or bisexuality of the *nadle*: bisexual beings are associated with fertility. It is basically a matter of no importance whether this double-sexedness is physically conditioned (referring to persons with ambivalent sexual characteristics—"you can tell them when they are born," Hill 1935:273) or whether it arises from the psychic level and the person shows unambiguous sexual characteristics.

The important thing is that the *nadle* exhibits personality features that are ascribed to the other sex. An ambivalent sexual identity or extreme discrepancy between physique and behavior is just as able to lend the character of dual sexuality as physical ambivalence. The status of *nadle* is an ambivalent, nonmasculine and nonfeminine gender status which requires either physical or psychic-physical ambivalence. According to Reichard (1944:23), the respected chanter Klah received the status of a *nadle* merely because he "wove blankets and was not interested in women." In addition to this, however, as a child he had been emasculated during an attack by the Utes when his family came back from Fort Sumner (Reichard 1944:23). For one thing, this made him sexually ambivalent (in a certain sense, he was a "former" man); second, the physical infertility that resulted from this was relevant to the status of *nadle*.

Hill was certainly correct in his statement that unusual possibilities for acquiring material prosperity within the community were available to the *nadle*. In general, a *nadle* functioned as the head of a household. In addition, *nadle* had access to the occupational spheres of both sexes. Unfortunately, it is not always apparent from Hill's account whether he was talking about *nadle* in general, male-bodied or female-bodied *nadle*, or hermaphrodites. It seems like he was writing primarily about hermaphrodites and male-bodied *nadle*. Thus, the following discussion is meant to refer to these, unless otherwise specified. *Nadle* directed the planting and the fieldwork. The latter was primarily in the hands of the men (Hill 1938a:19, 53), although the women were also involved in many areas (Gifford 1940:17). Two characteristically masculine activities, hunting and warfare, were closed to *nadle* (Hill 1935:275). Most *nadle* were chanters; chanting was primarily a men's activity but one which was also practiced by women (Reichard 1950:xliv). In practicing this activity, *nadle* were, moreover, in no way depicted as superior to men and women (Hill 1935:275). Sheep-raising was open to both sexes, and not infrequently helped women in particular to acquire wealth (Underhill 1956:60). Specifically feminine activities that were performed by *nadle* include weaving, pottery, the tanning of hides, making moccasins, knitting, and midwifery (Hill 1935:275; midwives were usually women, although men could be present and sometimes assisted at childbirths; see Bailey 1950:54). Weaving was traditionally women's work (Stewart 1942:341), although in more recent times, both sexes have been reported to weave (Gifford 1940:48). In addition to this, *nadle* supervised the women at their work in the hogan and the preparation of meals during ceremonial meetings (Hill 1935:275).

The sources do not mention whether there were also feminine activities from which the *nadle* were barred. One form of specialization that was obviously not dependent on sex/gender, but for the practice of which *nadle* were preferred, was mediation between the sexes in matters of conflict and love (Hill 1935:275). The Cheyenne *heemaneh'* and the Oglala Lakota *winkte* were likewise popular and sought-after matchmakers, as were the Omaha *mixu'ga* (see Grinnell 1962, 2:38; Mead 1932:189, n.2; Williams 1986a:194). At dances, the male-bodied *nadle* assumed the feminine role and joked flirtatiously with men, just as women did (Hill 1935:275). If a *nadle* was murdered, the same amount of compensation had to be paid as in the case of a murdered woman, namely more than for a murdered man (Hill 1935:275). It was a special privilege of the *nadle* to have at her/his disposal the wealth of all of the members of the household (Hill 1935:275).

As Hill established (1935:275), access to the area of feminine tasks smoothed the *nadle*'s path to wealth, and above all the production and sale of ceramics, rugs, blankets, and basketware. Of course, the *nadle* also had access to non-gender-specific tasks—for example, sheep breeding—as well as to the total resources of the subordinate members of the household, which she/he could increase by means of shrewd business deals.

It is also the case, however, that because many of the profitable business areas, such as rug weaving, were extremely labor intensive, *nadle* could realistically take advantage of only a fraction of the economic opportunities available. Thus, although *nadle* were indeed associated "with all the wealth in the country" (consultant in Hill 1935:275), they did not necessarily accumulate great personal wealth. So, for example, the Navajo Kinipai (whom Hill dismissed as a failure in her culture on the grounds that in the interview situation she "refused to discuss or do certain things which would have been done or talked about by an ordinary Navajo without question" [1935:278]) was doubtless associated by the Navajo themselves with wealth as much as a certain *nadle* from the previous century who was regarded for a long time as the best weaver in his tribe (Matthews 1897:217, n. 30), or Klah, a renowned chanter (specialist in healing rituals) who at the same time wove rugs with patterns from sand paintings (Reichard 1950:141). The association of the *nadle* with wealth existed independently of the personal achievements of individual *nadle*. Presumably, many of them ultimately distinguished themselves in one of the occupations available to them, not least because as children they had already occupied a privileged position among their siblings, and while growing up had experienced a lot of support from their families (Hill 1935:274). If a *nadle* was consistently given the feeling by her/his family and community from childhood on that she/he was an extraordinary person, her/his motivation for achievement surely must have been considerable.

Just as *nadle* secured their prosperity primarily by means of feminine activities, so they were more strongly associated in the oral traditions with feminine than masculine areas of activity (see Chapter 20). Of interest in the present context is the role that the "hermaphrodites" play in the stories with regard to the relations between the sexes. In the Navajo origin story, it is definitely not the women themselves, but rather the hermaphrodites (*nadle*) who are given the credit for inventing the women's working implements (Matthews 1897:70). In one story, a conflict breaks out between the sexes, after which the men and the women live separately on opposite banks of a river and the *nadle* join the men (1897:72; O'Bryan 1956:7). The women—who believed that they could live without the men (Matthews 1897:71)—are not in a position to manage and cultivate the fields that have been entrusted to them, whereas the men live in abundance, because they succeed—by means of the *nadle* (referred to in the sources as "hermaphrodites")—in maintaining the sexual/gendered division of labor: "They had a good harvest. Nadle ground the corn and cooked the food" (O'Bryan 1956:7).

The story suggests that the Navajo themselves disapproved of the women's desire for autonomy. Further, in that the hermaphrodites take sides with the men and together with them maintain the arrangement of the relations between the sexes, it is they whom the Navajo ultimately have to thank for the return to harmony and cooperation between men and women. The fact that, in remote mythical times, the small number of *nadle* managed to perform all of the women's tasks for the men only makes their efficiency in the feminine role even more obvious. Correspondingly, in the oral traditions, and notwithstanding their double sexuality, the *nadle* are represented as being *better women than the women themselves.* They do that which should be the task of the women: first, they invent the utensils for women's work and then they remain with the men in order to uphold the complementarity of the gender roles. This striving to outstrip the women in fulfilling feminine role behavior also appears to have characterized the *nadle* in a nonmythical context; thus there are statements claiming that they carried out women's tasks better than the women themselves did (see Matthews 1897:217, n.30).

Contrary, therefore, to Hill's interpretation of the above-mentioned stories, it is not exactly the *nadle*'s ability to perform women's work in addition to men's work that gives the men the upper hand (Hill 1935:274). Rather, it is the *nadle*'s ability to fulfill the women's role better than the women themselves can (see O'Flaherty 1982:285f.). That the *nadle* also did men's work at the same time is thus not the issue.

In summary, it turns out that there are several levels on which the extraordinary qualities attributed to the *nadle* can be interpreted. For one thing, the Navajo themselves associated *nadle* with prosperity, for which they gave no further explanation. This association is shown in statements such as the following:

> If there were no nadle, the country would change. They are responsible for all the wealth in the country. If there were no more left, the horses, sheep, and Navaho would all go. They are leaders just as President Roosevelt. (Navajo consultant to Hill 1935:274)

> A nadle around the hogan will bring good luck and riches. (Navajo consultant to Hill 1935:274)

In this context, the fact that *nadle* were both capable of performing and also allowed to perform the activities of both sexes appears to have been a function of the fact that they were considered special: "They know everything. They can do both the work of a man and a woman. I think when all the nadle are gone, that it will be the end of the Navaho" (Navajo consultant to Hill 1935:274). They know everything—that is, they "know" the masculine and the feminine equally, on the basis of their dual sexuality, which alone enables them to fulfill both roles in the first place.

This leads to a second level from which the phenomenon can be perceived: dual sexuality is a condition which makes it possible to share in the roles of both genders and thereby to increase exponentially the potentials inherent in these roles, all of which then belong to a single person. Just as a hermaphroditic sheep promotes the fertility of the flock (Hill 1935:274)—even though it is itself sterile—an intersexual or hermaphrodite human promotes the economic "fertility" of his/her family. In terms of the economic success of the *nadle,* the combination of masculine and feminine productive activities seems at first glance to offer an obvious explanation, particularly when it can be shown that *nadle* were often in fact prosperous and successful. On closer inspection of the data, however, it turns out that this prosperity did not grow out of combining both gender roles, but instead resulted from the fact that the *nadle* worked more effectively and profitably in feminine activities than the biological women could.

This perspective on the *nadle*'s superiority invites a second level of interpretation. The dual sexuality of the *nadle* is said by the Navajo themselves to bring luck and wealth, but the actual material manifestation of this bringing of good fortune is due to the fact that *nadle* are "better" women than the biological women. Both in the oral traditions and in the everyday life of the tribe, *nadle* appear as guardians of the norms for gender-specific behavior, and indeed primarily *feminine* behavior. In the oral traditions, they are the ones who follow the men and preserve the "correct" sexual/gendered division of labor. Similarly, it is they who keep close watch on the women during the daily work in the hogan and while they are cooking for large gatherings on special occasions. Moreover, through their outstanding accomplishments in the area of women's handwork, *nadle* hurl a further challenge to the women.

So, *nadle* have an ambivalent gender status, but several rules are clearly in play. They have access to all feminine domains, but they are excluded from two characteristically masculine ones: hunting and warfare. Their gender status is thus ambivalent, and their gender role both masculine and feminine, but with a stronger emphasis on feminine role components, in the fulfillment of which they function as role models and guardians, and certainly exhibit great ambition.

In principle, the characteristics of the *nadle* have been equally attributed by the Navajo both to intersexes and to physically unambiguous women-men (and men-women). Nevertheless, there existed differences between the "real" *nadle* and the "those who pretend to be *nadle*," above all in regard to their relationships with partners. The type of relationship lived out by women-men with partners could, under certain circumstances, lead to at least the partial loss of the *nadle* status. The information given by Hill (1935:275f.) can be summarized as follows:

> HERMAPHRODITES: ("real" *nadle*) always dress as women, do not marry, and have sexual relationships exclusively with men.
>
> TRANSVESTITES: ("those who pretend to be *nadle*," male-bodied "berdaches") can choose between men's and women's clothing, marry persons of the same as well as of the opposite biological sex, and have sexual intercourse with men and with women. If they marry, they take on the clothing and activities of a man.

"If they marry men, it is just like two men working together," added one consultant (Hill 1935:276). This means that, at the moment they enter into a marriage, "those who pretend to be *nadle*" lose the privilege of carrying out both gender roles. Williams took the view that male-bodied *nadle* who were married to men continued to perform women's tasks: "Economically, the husband has both a wife and a husband, which partly explains the reputation these marriages have for economic success" (1986b:111). The remark from the consultant interviewed by Hill, however, speaks unambiguously against this, raising the question of how the sexual/gendered division of labor was handled in these marriages.

It is not clear from Hill's discussion whether the above rules also held for female-bodied *nadle*. If they did, then after the marriage of one of these to a woman, the picture that emerges is that of an ordinary wedded couple, with the usual sexual division of labor. The same is true when a biologically male *nadle* married a woman: apparently, at least partially, he gave up the status of *nadle*. (Among other things, the *nadle* status meant that even a biological male was addressed with female kinship terminology and was referred to as "she"; see Hill 1935:275.) A former *nadle* who married was not addressed with female kinship terms; even *nadle* were addressed as male or as female relatives according to the type of clothing they wore, so that after marriage, only male kin terms were used for them because they always wore only men's clothing (see Reichard 1928:150). A "real" nadle (i.e., a hermaphrodite or intersex), who as a rule remained unmarried, never underwent such a change of gender status.

Because the hermaphrodite is the "original" and the woman-man, with his/her unambiguous sexual characteristics, is the "copy," the transition to a masculine role occasioned by the marriage of "someone who pretends to be *nadle*" (i.e., who is sexually unambiguous) must be related to the fact that a lasting marriage relationship is apparently incompatible with the social role of the *nadle*. A pronounced, almost promiscuous sexual behavior is attributed both to hermaphrodites and to physically unambiguous women-men (Hill 1935:276). Kinipai—a hermaphrodite—estimated that in the course of her life she had had sexual relations with more than a hundred men (Hill 1935:278).

A further trait characterizes the sexuality of the "real," intersexual *nadle*: he/she is infertile and can neither engender nor conceive; that is, he/she cannot procreate. In the oral traditions, all of the children of First Man and First Woman with the exception of the firstborn hermaphrodite twins are capable of procreation (Reichard 1950:433). Intersexes are in fact infertile, even if they menstruate as a result of a developed ovary (Walter 1978:11; on infertility in intersexes see also Overzier 1961d). Because of intersexes' inability to conceive, the likelihood that a "real" *nadle* ever became pregnant is very slight. Apart from this, the preferred sexual practice between *nadle* and their male partners was anal intercourse ("sodomy," Hill 1938:276).

Thus the sexual life of "real" *nadle* was characterized by sexual relationships exclusively with men, frequent change of partners, and infertility. The moment "someone who pretends to be *nadle*" gave up one or more of these characteristics, he also lost some of the privileges associated with the status of *nadle*. As noted, however, in those cases where a male-bodied *nadle* married a man, it was precisely the *nadle* status that created the possibility of a marriage between two males in the first place. Homosexual intercourse between two biological males, neither of whom was *nadle*, drew harsh negative sanctions; moreover, according to the ideas of the Navajo, such behavior led to insanity (like other forms of forbidden sexual contact, for example, incest; Hill 1935:276).

A further aspect connected to the retention of *nadle* status is expression of the *nadle*'s ambivalence. The "real" *nadle* expressed this ambivalence directly through his physical dual sexuality. Someone who "pretends to be *nadle*"—apart from his manner of dressing—could express his ambivalence only through his actions. To maintain sexual relations with both sexes could—along with the discrepancy between biological sex and lived-out gender role and/or behavior pattern—express such an ambivalence, functioning as a substitute for the existence of male and female sexual characteristics. If a male-bodied *nadle* gave up the ambivalence in favor of an unambiguous partner relationship (especially with a woman), however, his culture apparently deprived him of his ambivalent gender status, even though he might have been able to return to it, for example, in the case of a divorce. "Those who pretend to be *nadle*" consequently partially lost their status in case of marriage, first, because as wedded persons they in principle became fertile, and second, because they gave up their sexual ambivalence through an unambiguous choice of partner.

AN INTERSEXUAL STONEY *WINKTAN'*

Lowie (1909:42) mentioned a Stoney *winktan'* who married a Cree man and who did both men's work and women's work. However, this combination of role components was unusual among the Assiniboine. In general, *winktan'* did only women's tasks, used the grammatical elements used by women, and in daily life associated freely with both sexes (1909: 42). In the case of the Stoney just mentioned, the fact that he was a genuine hermaphrodite with both male and female primary sexual characteristics (1909:42) was probably significant with regard to his combining the activities of both sexes.

WOMEN-MEN IN WAR

Notwithstanding their gender role change, women-men went to war regularly or occasionally among the Crow (Lowie 1912:226), Oglala Lakota (Williams 1986a:194), Illinois (Marquette 1959:129), Miami (Trowbridge 1938:68), Piegan (Schaeffer 1965:223), and Ojibwa (Henry 1897:164f.).

Except for the Illinois, among whom it was possibly the rule for women-men to participate in acts of warfare, such behavior appears to have been rare. The example of Piegan Woman, who although he acted out the feminine gender role in everyday life had regularly participated in raiding expeditions since his fifteenth year (Schaeffer 1965:223), suggests that the Piegan might have had a similar gender role combination. However, since only two cases of male gender role crossing are known from this tribe (Piegan Woman and Four Bears), it is difficult to generalize. Even Marquette's information concerning the Illinois has not gone unchallenged. All the other sources indicate that their women-men held a feminine gender role without engaging in any masculine activities (Hennepin 1699:163; Liette 1962:112f.; St. Cosme 1799; cited in Kellogg 1917:360).

All of the sources relating to the Crow also speak of a complete gender role change. Only Lowie (1912:226) mentioned a *bate* who, despite all attempts by the Indian agent to make him stop it, always wore women's clothes and had the reputation of being extraordinarily skillful in women's handwork. It is said that this *bate* once—and only once in his life—dressed in men's clothes and fought bravely in a skirmish against the Sioux (Williams 1986b:68). A similar situation holds for the heroic warrior's deed attributed to the Ojibwa *agokwa* Ozaw-wen-dib. With reference to this woman-man, Tanner noted only feminine role behavior, and stressed that Ozaw-wen-dib was said to be "very expert in the various employments of the women, to which all his time was given" (Tanner 1830:105). Henry, meanwhile, related of him that he was said to have once accompanied a group of Saulteurs (Saulteaux, a branch of the Ojibwa) on a peace mission to the Sioux. On the return trip, the Saulteurs were attacked by the Sioux. While the remaining Saulteurs made it to safety, Ozaw-wen-dib, who had managed to obtain from his companions the only available bow (a gift of the Sioux; the Saulteurs had evidently come unarmed to the negotiations, which were under White protection), collected the spent Sioux arrows and then shot them back at his adversaries. It was said that in so doing, he saved the lives of those in his group (Henry 1897:164f.). Apart from this, Ozaw-wen-dib is said to have been regarded as the fastest runner in the tribe (1897:164f.). It is possible that this was fully compatible with a feminine role. Female warriors occurred among the Ojibwa (Landes 1937:110f., 121), and nontransvesting women who went to war were no rarity on the Prairies and Plains (see Chapter 17).

With respect to the Oglala Lakota, the sources are in fundamental agreement. As a rule, *winkte* took over feminine role components, and some sources have explicitly denied that they went to war (Hassrick 1982:135; Lame Deer 1979:169). Williams' consultants confirmed this information, although one of them recalled that his grandfather had told him about a *winkte* who very definitely had gone to war (Williams 1986a:194). However, it turned out that he had not fought, but instead had taken care of the camp and the provisions and cared for the wounded (Williams 1986a:194).

It also holds true for the Miami that a complete assumption of the feminine gender role was the rule for women-men, although Trowbridge reported the case of a *waupeengwoatar,* or woman-man, who definitely went to war. In this case, however, the women's clothes were exchanged for men's clothes for the duration of the war expedition (Trowbridge 1938:68). The information is not sufficient to determine whether there is a parallel here to the Osage warrior mentioned above who did not undertake a complete gender role change, but instead merely wore women's clothing in everyday life, and regularly went on raids dressed in men's clothing. In any event, even among the Miami, warrior activities do not appear to have been components which could be integrated into the role of a *waupeengwoatar*; thus in the event of a war expedition, the masculine role had to be adopted once again, at least temporarily, together with all of its external attributes. It is also possible that these cases of women-men going to war are instances of gender role splitting in a tribe in which complete gender role change also occurred.

In contrast with this, Illinois women-men went to war completely within the framework of their assumed gender role, on account of which they were not permitted to use the characteristically "masculine" weapon, the bow. By contrast, the war club was regarded as an appropriate weapon for them (Marquette 1959:129). Clubs were very widespread as a weapon of warfare in all of North America, including the Prairies (Driver and Massey 1957:357ff. and Map 143). Among the Illinois, as elsewhere, women-men were probably not the only ones who used the club as a military weapon. Evidently persons who held a nonmasculine gender status were not permitted to carry weapons which were regarded as "proper to men" (Marquette 1959:129). The bow and arrow was evidently associated with masculinity to an extent that was not true for the war club, which, nonetheless, was also used by men. (Whether women of the Illinois also participated occasionally in war expeditions or raids, and whether they then were likewise permitted to arm themselves only with clubs, I don't know.)

WOMEN-MEN AS HUNTERS

Within the compass of the sexual division of labor in Native American cultures, another role which generally devolved on the man is that of hunter. This occupation was also retained by a few women-men after their gender role change, along with some preponderantly feminine activities. Mirsky (1937a:417) is the only author who mentioned that the Teton Lakota *winkte,* who in everyday life were the "most skillful of all" in performing women's tasks, also went on the hunt. Other authors have reported nothing about this with respect to the Teton Lakota, and have stressed the total dedication of the *winkte* to women's work, and their perfect mastery of it.

Some *tai'up* among the Mono used to exchange their women's clothes for a man's clothes from time to time in order to go hunting with the men (Gayton 1948:274). In everyday life, however, they dressed as women and accompanied them while collecting and grinding acorns. They also produced pottery (1948:274). However, there were also *tai'up* who merged completely with their feminine roles and who felt no need to undertake hunting expeditions with the men (1948:274).

These are the only two explicit indications that women-men hunted after as well as before their gender role change, so it is not clear how Linton (1936:480) arrived at his generalization that Plains "berdaches" hunted, as well as engaging in their feminine activities. Quite the contrary, a series of cases has been reported in North America expressly denying that women-men hunted in spite of a gender role change, with or without cross-dressing (for the St. Lawrence Eskimo, see Murphy 1964: 75; Eyak, Birket-Smith and de Laguna 1938:206; Flathead, Turney-High 1937:85; Hare, Broch 1977:100; Illinois, Hennepin 1699:163; Kutenai, Schaeffer 1965:218; Navajo, Hill 1935:275; Southern Paiute, Lowie 1924:282; Shasta, Holt 1946:317).

In a few cases, both warfare and hunting appear to have been retained by women-men as masculine role components, although in such cases, gender role splitting—especially in relation to the role of the warrior—was usually practiced, because these activities were obviously not easily reconcilable with the status of woman-man. In order to be able to pursue them, the woman-man had to define himself again temporarily as a man. Apart from this, hunting and fighting women-men appear to have existed alongside women-men in their respective tribes who did not pursue these activities. Whether or not they retained these masculine activities was evidently left up to them by their respective individual cultures.

WEWHA AND THE PRIVILEGES OF THE *LHAMANA:* ON GENDER ROLE COMBINING AMONG THE ZUNI

Among the Zuni *lhamana* as well, the emphasis lay primarily on the complete, perfect assumption of the activities and also the external appearance of a woman. In fact, Mathilda Coxe Stevenson (1904:310) reported that she was friends with Wewha, a *lhamana,* for years without realizing that Wewha was biologically male (see Figure 2). Moreover, Wewha was Stevenson's main consultant. (Stevenson is said to have been so hated in Zuni that hardly any other inhabitants of the pueblo made themselves available to her as consultants; Kalweit 1983:32.) *Lhamana* wove textiles (Gifford 1940:49; Parsons 1916:523; Stevenson 1904: 37), wove baskets (Gifford 1940:49), made pots (Parsons 1916:523; Stevenson 1904:37), and were expert plasterers (Parsons 1916:523); in

Wewha, Zuni, ca. 1884–1887. Reproduced by permission of the National Anthropological Archives, Smithsonian Institution (Photo No. 2235-B).

addition, Wewha, whom Stevenson had acquainted with the use of soap, did the laundry for the officers' families at Fort Wingate (Stevenson 1904:380). Within the household, *lhamana* carried out the most difficult of the women's tasks (Stevenson 1904:37).

Nevertheless, in common with all boys but in contrast to most girls, *lhamana* were initiated into the *ko'tikili,* or Kachina Society (Parsons 1916:527), and on the basis of this initiation took part in those dances in which the *kok'ko* (anthropomorphic deities) were personified. However, the *lhamana* were not admitted to the esoteric fraternities (Parsons 1916:528). Within the framework of the dances performed by the ko'tikili ("mythologic fraternity," Stevenson 1904:62) during the course of the year, which were essentially depictions of mythological events, there were also female deities to be found among the *kok'ko* portrayed by the masked dancers. These were portrayed by men (Stevenson 1904:104, 145, 181f.) with the exception of the Thla'hewe Ceremony held every four years to bring rain and promote the growth of corn. In this ceremony the Corn Maidens were portrayed by young girls. Even in these dances, however, other female figures were portrayed by male impersonators (Stevenson 1904:101f.). These could be *lhamana,* as on the occasion of the Shala'ko Ceremony, in which the *lhamana* U'k once took part in a Chaakwena Dance, playing the part of a female figure (Parsons 1916:527). But usually these impersonators were men. Stevenson mentioned that during the Thla'hewe Ceremony, one young male who later carried out a gender role change once took over the role of a certain virgin; this role fell to him, however, not because he was a potential *lhamana,* but rather because he was the grandson of a member of a certain priestly group, and only sons or grandsons of men from this group were allowed to personify the aforementioned virgin (Stevenson 1904:182).

There is one role, however, which within the framework of the ko'tikili performances was allegedly reserved for the *lhamana.* In a particular dance based on a mythical war between two groups of gods, one of the gods—Kor'kokshi—was, according to Stevenson, always portrayed by an *lhamana.* Kor'kokshi, who along with other gods had been taken prisoner by the opposing group of gods, the Kia'nakwe, had behaved in such an unruly manner that the Chaakwena (a warlike goddess, leader of the Kia'nakwe) dressed him in women's clothing in order to tame him (Stevenson 1904:37; see also below, Chapter 20). According to statements made by the Zuni, this was "the first instance of a god or a man appearing in woman's dress" (Stevenson 1904:37, n. a). The personifier of Kor'kokshi forced into women's clothes is called *ko'thlama,* "meaning a man who has permanently adopted female attire" (Stevenson 1904:37). Since Parsons rendered the designation for a woman-man as *lhamana,* however, it is to be assumed that "ko'thlama" refers specifically to Kor'kokshi, one of the *kok'ko,* in the role of a *lhamana.*

According to Stevenson (1904:37), Wewha always played the role of Kor'kokshi in the Kia'nakwe Dance. Even if this indicates that this role—which was an essentially masculine privilege, because the ko'tikili was composed of men—was in fact reserved for a *lhamana,* doubts are in order on several grounds in regard to possible special tasks of the *lhamana.*

Even if critical voices are raised regarding Stevenson's euphoric depiction of the outstanding position which her friend Wewha is supposed to have occupied in Zuni (see, e.g., Goldman 1937:344, n. 3), though, Wewha must really have been a distinctive and above all ambitious personality. Moreover, she obviously took sides in support of the traditional customs. In one case, for example, a man was accused of witchcraft; along with others, Wewha was energetically in favor of following custom and hanging him up by his thumbs until he confessed. A "general hubbub" broke out in Zuni until soldiers from the nearby fort put Wewha and the others who were involved in the incident temporarily behind bars (Stephen 1936:276). It is quite possible that Wewha temporarily attached functions to the status of *lhamana* which were otherwise not associated with it. It is illuminating in this connection that, according to

Kasinelu, Zuni, ca. 1938. (From Parsons 1939a:339.) Reproduced by permission of the American Anthropological Association from American Anthropologist *41, 1939.*

Stevenson (1904:374), the fetching of clay from a clay-bed up on the hallowed Corn Mountain, where men were not allowed, was supposed to have been the exclusive task of the *lhamana.* This report, however, was firmly contradicted some years later by Parsons' consultants (Parsons 1916:523). It was likewise contested that the *lhamana* fulfilled special functions in the religious domain (Parsons 1916:524). It is therefore conceivable that, by means of her domineering personality (see Stevenson 1904:20, 37, 311), Wewha temporarily integrated functions such as the portrayal of the Kor'kokshi as *ko'thlama* and clay fetching into the *lhamana* status—that is into her own personal status (possibly with the support of the priestly group then extant; Parsons 1916:524). Over a longer period of time, she would in any event have had "competition" from only one other *lhamana,* who—likewise an excellent weaver and potter (Stevenson 1904:37)—obviously restricted her ambitions to these feminine occupations.

The part of Kor'kokshi in ceremonies and dances was, to be sure, also taken over later by the *lhamana* Kasineli (also spelled Kasinelu; see Figure 3). However, in 1915—and possibly even earlier—it was a woman who appeared as Kor'kokshi, although three *lhamana* then lived in Zuni who from the standpoint of age (late twenties to early forties) surely were physically up to the demands of the dances. The woman was not a *lhamana,* but was somewhat masculine in her mannerisms, on account of which the Zuni in jest called her *katsotse,* "girl-boy" (Parsons 1916: 525). Consequently, the role of Kor'kokshi was not restricted in principle to a *lhamana.*

Moreover, regarding an initiation of the *lhamana* into the (male-dominated) ko'tikili, it should be noted that whether or not a boy took on the status of *lhamana* depended primarily on his inclination toward feminine activities. Although a preference for feminine over masculine activities could be manifested as early as childhood, women's clothing was not put on at this point in time (Stevenson 1904:37). Only on reaching puberty did the boy make the final decision to take on the status of a *lhamana* or not, and only then did he put on women's clothing, in case he ultimately did decide in favor of the feminine role (Stevenson 1904: 37). Until puberty, therefore, a boy's tendency toward the feminine gender role was reversible. However, the initiation into the ko'tikili took place before the onset of puberty—before, that is, the point in time at which the status of *lhamana* was assumed. (Stevenson 1904:104 spoke of "boys"; Lindig and Münzel 1976:134 gave ten to twelve years as the general age of initiation for the Pueblo Kachina Societies.) Thus, first of all, the boy was not initiated as a *lhamana,* but rather as a male person. Second, this initiation was deemed necessary in view of the possibility that, contrary to all indications during puberty, the boy might not undertake the last step, the assumption of the status of *lhamana,* but eventually decide to live as a man. Quite apart from the possible presence of feminine personality traits in them, if all boys were not initiated, a young male could lack important components of the masculine role in case he, against all expectation, did after all choose a masculine gender status. The only persons who were still being initiated into the ko'tikili as adults were rare cases of women who afterward, like men, could personify kachinas (Parsons 1939b:137). All boys were automatically accepted into the kiva of their ceremonial fathers (1939b:138). *Lhamana* were therefore not initiated as such, but did retain their membership in the ko'tikili if, during puberty, they decided in favor of a feminine gender role. As adults they would be eligible to portray the Kor'kokshi, but they also took over the parts of other female *kok'ko,* who were generally portrayed by men, but also in some cases by the few women who had been admitted into the ko'tikili (1939b:138).

It should be noted in passing that, strictly speaking, no biological male seems to have been less suited than the *lhamana* to personify the Kor'kokshi. In contrast to *lhamana,* whose decision in favor of the feminine role was voluntary, Kor'kokshi was forcibly coerced into women's clothing by the Chaakwena as a sign of subjection (Stevenson 1904:37).

Thus, membership of the *lhamana* in the ko'tikili can primarily be viewed as a masculine role component in combination with an otherwise feminine gender role. Meanwhile, the initiation took place independently of the *lhamana* status, although in case of a gender role change, membership was retained, but as an aspect of the masculine role associated with an otherwise feminine gender role. On closer examination, another interpretation also emerges: it becomes apparent that women were, under certain circumstances, definitely initiated into the ko'tikili as well, and that along with the parts of diverse feminine *kok'ko,* they also took on that of Kor'kokshi in the dances. As a consequence, the personification of Kor'kokshi and of female deities by *lhamana* can in principle also be interpreted as an aspect of the feminine gender role or surely at least not as an unambiguously masculine role component.

In the course of her life, the *lhamana* changed her gender status twice: once during puberty she crossed over from the masculine (boy) status into an ambivalent status (*lhamana*); and once after her death, when she returned—at least for the most part—to the masculine status that she had held before puberty. Dressed in a man's trousers and in a woman's dress, she was interred on the south side of the cemetery, which was reserved for men (Parsons 1916:528; Stevenson 1904:313).

A MASCULINE PRIVILEGE: THE USE OF THE SWEAT HOUSE

In the lists of the *Anthropological Records,* and pertaining to a number of California tribes and also some Great Basin groups, attention has also been given to a practice which likewise belonged to the masculine gender role: the admittance of women-men to the widely used "sweat house," which in many places was more a community or men's clubhouse, not to be confounded with the sweat *lodge* found in other regions of North America, which was exclusively used for ritual cleansing.

The question of whether or not women-men were allowed to spend time in this structure is a revealing one, particularly because women from a number of tribes were not admitted to it. In rare cases, the statement that male "berdaches" "sweat with males" (Driver 1937:90) is found (among some tribes, both sexes use the sweat house, but separately). In such cases, and also in those in which only men and women-men—but no women—are admitted, this custom is no doubt to be understood as a retention of a masculine role aspect, or at least as a masculine privilege when women-men are admitted to the sweat house. Table 1 lists the data from various groups.

First, it is striking that among most of the Shoshoni-speaking groups, women are totally banned from the sweat house, whereas both the Northwestern California groups and the intermediately situated Yokuts at least admitted them within limits. The information for the Kawaiisu

Table 1. Use of Sweat House by Women-Men

Tribe	To	Hu	Wi	C	Ma	Si	K	La	CY	Yu	Kl	Ch	Ki	Pa	Ka	OV	Mo	Yo	Tü	Ba
Women-men sweat with men																	▼	(▼)		▼
—not with men														▼	▼	▼		▼	▼	
Permitted in the sweat house	▼	▼				▼	▼	▼	▼	▼	▼	▼	▼							
—not permitted			▼	▼	▼															
Women not permitted										▼				(▼)	(▼)		▼	▼	▼	▼
Women permitted	▼	▼	▼	▼	▼	▼	▼	▼	▼	(▼)	▼			(▼)	(▼)	▼				
—only during ceremonies	▼	▼	▼	▼	▼															
—only old women							▼	▼			▼									

To = Tolowa; Hu = Hupa; Wi = Wiyot; C = Chilula; Ma = Mattole; Si = Sinkyone; K = Kato; La = Lassik; CY = Coast Yuki; Kl = Kalekau Pomo; Ch = Chumash; Ki = Kitanemuk; Pa = Panamint; Ka = Kawaiisu; OV = Owens Valley Paiute; Mo = Mono; Yo = Yokuts; Tü = Tübatulabal; Ba = Bankalachi.
(▼): Information differs for various subgroups of the tribe.
Kato: *Menstruating women are not permitted in the sweat house, and pregnant women have to pay a "fine" before entering (Essene 1942:57).* Yuki: *During ceremonies, women are permitted to enter the sweat house only to bring food to the men (Essene 1942:57).* Kawaiisu, Panamint-Koso, Owens Valley Paiute: *The sweat house is a meeting house for both sexes (Driver 1937:67).* Yokuts: *Among the Chukaimina, Nutunutu, and Paleuyami subgroups, women-men sweat with the men (Driver 1937:90).*

Sources: Driver 1937:67, 90; 1939:347, 321; Essene 1942:11, 31, 57; Harrington 1942:32.

is contradictory; Driver's (1937:115) consultants did not agree in regard to the admission of women. Differing information is also encountered for the three subgroups of the Panamint; only the Koso allowed women into the sweat house, which served as a meeting house for both sexes (1937:67).

The sources which explicitly reported that women-men sweated with the men are straightforward and clear. Among the Mono, Yokuts, and Bankalachi (a branch of the Tübatulabal), women were excluded from the sweat house. Thus, the use of the sweat house by both men and women-men in common can no doubt be seen as evidence for a significant masculine role component which is retained along with the feminine role. Driver's (1937:67) term for the sweat house, "clubhouse for males," is accurate to the extent that men spent a considerable part of the day there together. "Women pretenders" of the Ingalik obviously also regularly spent time in the Kashim, i.e., the men's house (Osgood 1958:262).

Where the sweat house was forbidden both to women and women-men, for example, among the Panamint, the Kawaiisu, and the Tübatulabal, it is probable that crossing over into a feminine gender role was complete, and that the gender status of the woman-man was so unambiguously nonmasculine that participation in the masculine social life of the sweat house was not considered.

Among the Wiyot, Chilula, and Mattole, women were allowed into the sweat house only during ceremonies, but women-men were excluded entirely. Without more precise information, this is difficult to interpret; it is likely, though, that women-men and women were excluded for similar reasons. In addition, it is likely that the exception allowing women during important ceremonies also held for women-men.

The rare examples in which the sweat house was open to both sexes without restrictions (i.e., the Sinkyone, the Coast Yuki, the Yuki [except during ceremonies], the Owens Valley Paiute, the Panamint-Koso, and possibly the Kawaiisu) do not permit an a posteriori conclusion with regard to masculine elements in the role and status of the women-men. Among the Tolowa and Hupa, it has been reported that "berdaches" had access to the sweat house at all times, whereas women did only during ceremonies. In cases in which women-men and old women were permitted to use the sweat house (the Kato, Lassik, and Kalekau-Pomo), it is probable that this is an instance of the granting of masculine privilege to postmenopausal women.

For the Kitanemuk and Chumash, it was not possible to determine whether both sexes used the sweat house. However, by taking into consideration the remaining eighteen tribes contained in the list, the general picture is clear: in the cases of eight tribes, the co-use of the sweat house can be seen as evidence for at least a partial retention of masculine role components; in six cases a sweat house ban for women and women-men probably indicates a complete feminine role and a clearly nonmasculine gender status; in the six additional cases, the sweat house was either completely open to both sexes or was open to women with minimal restrictions, so that the componential organization of the woman-man's gender status and role was not significant in terms of admission to the sweat house. A stronger emphasis on the feminine role is suggested among the Owens Valley Paiute, since it was claimed that "berdaches" did not sweat with the men. Even if women there did have access to the sweat lodge in connection with its function as a community house, only the men customarily sweated (Driver 1937:67; Essene 1942:11. According to Driver 1939:321, only old women sweated with the men).

"BERDACHE" SHAMANS AND A TRANSVESTING CHIEFTAIN: THE TOLOWA

Among the Tolowa, women-men not only had access to the sweat lodge, but also were able to retain wide-ranging masculine privileges. Gould (1978:131) reported a Tolowa "headman" who was at the same time a "transvestite shaman" (see Figure 4). Along with Dentalium beads which adorn his nose as a sign of prosperity, this chief wears women's clothing—a woven cap, a thick necklace made of common trade beads and coins, and a dance apron (1978:131).

The status of headman (also "rich-man," Drucker 1937b:244) was apparently restricted to men among the Tolowa. The prestige of the headman was based on his possessing and also displaying riches (Gould 1978:131). The degree of affluence required was considerable. A man needed

> a house big enough for a dance, valuables enough (own possessions and those he had the right to borrow from brothers-in-law, etc.) to equip a dance; a sweat house; hunting, fishing, whale, and sea-lion claims; canoes, nets, harpoons, and other gear for exploiting those rights; money enough to obtain allegiance of young men by buying them wives and paying weregild for wrongs committed by them. . . . His position thus was based on wealth; it was hereditary only in the sense that wealth was inherited. (Drucker 1937b:244f.)

Some rich-men, it has been reported, are supposed to have stopped working, letting their clientele perform all of their tasks for them (Drucker 1937b:245). This was not true of the headman just named. As noted, he was also active as a shaman. According to Gould (1978:134), shamans—or better, healers—among the Tolowa were usually women and "transvestite males." They all let themselves be paid richly for their services as healers. Drucker, however, asserted that there were both male and (preponderantly) female healers, but did not mention any "berdaches" in this profession. It is possible that some of the "powerful men shamans" (Drucker 1937b:258) cited by him were women-men, but his consultants expressly denied the existence of "berdaches" among the Tolowa, and Drucker himself disputed the claim that male shamans were not "normal" men (Drucker 1937b:260).

"Transvestite male shaman," Tolowa, ca. 1900. (From Gould 1978:131, Fig. 6.) Reproduced by permission of the Smithsonian Institution, © 1978.

The transvesting headman obviously turned to his own advantage the possibility opened to him among the Tolowa to fill components of both gender roles at once. It is unlikely that he obtained the position of a rich-man on the basis of the wealth that he acquired through his "shamanic" activity, however. Because a major part of all the available money (i.e., Dentalium) circulated among the few wealthy families, a poor man could not become headman in the first place, and second, the wealth and status of the rich-man was passed on to his descendants, whereby his brother or eldest son became the new headman (Drucker 1937b:242). Drucker mentioned that although "shamans" were indeed able to amass considerable fortunes, one should bear in mind that this only happened as the result of a very slow process (1937b:242). Consequently, inheritance remained the only possibility of becoming a rich-man. So it is to be assumed that the headman discussed here had inherited his position and then, in addition, had gone through his training as a "shaman" on the basis of a dream (1937b:258).

As has already been suggested, the sources pertaining to the Tolowa women-men are not unitary. Drucker's (1937b:260) and Barnett's (1937: 185) consultants disputed the existence of "berdaches" altogether. Driver (1939:347), on the other hand, not only affirmed the existence of women-men, but also stated that they wore women's clothes and performed women's tasks. A Wiyot consultant told Driver (1939:405) about a Tolowa woman-man who was supposed to be a "shaman" and married to a woman; both were said to have done women's work. At first glance, the previous assertions are not easily reconcilable with Gould's no doubt correct description of the (at least sometimes) transvesting "shaman"-headman.

In the case of the Tolowa, as among other tribes, there quite obviously existed parallel to each other several different degrees or grades of gender role change. As is evident in the cases of the Osage and Piegan, as well as—especially with regard to hunting and warfare—in the cases of the Illinois, Crow, Miami, Ojibwa, Lakota, and Mono, males could choose between a total and partial change to the feminine gender role. To summarize the information on transvestism and gender role change among the Tolowa: there, also, different degrees of adopting feminine role aspects were possible. The transvesting headman must have held a masculine gender status in order to be able to inherit the status of rich-man from one of his male relatives, or—what is less likely—in order to obtain that status by means of the fortune he acquired as a healer. If the women's clothing was first donned only after the man had already become headman, his masculine gender status must have been retained. Otherwise, he probably would have had to give up the headman status under pressure from his family or his clientele from the "town-lineage," on whose benevolence his position of power depended: " . . . if his kinsmen did his bidding it was out of respect for his wealth and his personality" (Drucker 1937b:244). Surely, the personality aspect should not be underestimated. As a shaman, the transvesting headman could heal, but he could also kill or injure (1937b:259), which certainly contributed to the fact that his habits of dressing, which were unusual for a chieftain, were overlooked. Whether wearing women's clothing was the expression of personal supernatural powers—as in the Piegan case of Four Bears—cannot be determined from the sources.

UNSPECIFIED ASSERTIONS REGARDING GENDER ROLE MIXING

In a number of sources, it is mentioned that male-bodied "berdaches" also carried out tasks of both sexes in Native American cultures other than those discussed above. In these additional cases, however, the individual activities were not specified in detail. Thus, Landes (1970:316) reported that the *mnetokwe* of the Prairie Potawatomi possessed the "work skills" of both sexes, but she produced examples only of a gender role change which aimed at the perfect imitation of exclusively feminine role components. Consequently, this tribe is discussed in the following chapter.

A Bannock *tuvasa* wore women's clothes and did women's work (Steward 1943 : 338), and "more vigorously than women" at that. Along with this, however, she/he also performed men's tasks (1943 : 385). It is also possible that a combining of the occupations of both sexes existed among the Nevada Shoshoni, of whom Steward (1941 : 252f.) wrote: "Transvestism . . . was unstandardized, varying with the individual. Some persons manifested slight, others great tendency to behave like the opposite sex."

SUMMARY

An obvious retention of masculine role aspects alongside cross-dressing and the taking up of feminine activities has been encountered to varying degrees in a number of Native American cultures, and even within the same culture. In some cases—for example, the Osage warrior in women's clothes, and Four Bears, who transvested only when he, as a medicine man, participated in preparations for raiding forays, or the transvesting Tolowa headman—we cannot speak of an actual gender role change. In other cases, a few components of the masculine role are retained; for example, sweating or spending time in the sweat house. With respect to the Navajo, it appears after closer inspection that it is not the *nadle*'s unique opportunity to combine two gender roles that fosters the *nadle*'s outstanding economic position, but rather the perfect mastery of feminine activities, combined with special privileges. Ideologically, the *nadle* were considered superior to both sexes, but practically, as noted, they were above all regarded as superior to women. Economically, they mainly competed with the women and not with the men. In Zuni, the initiation of the *lhamana* into the ko'tikili at first hints at the retention of a significant masculine role component. The initiation was carried out, however, while the prospective *lhamana* still occupied a masculine gender status. Remaining in the ko'tikili after entering into the ambivalent status of *lhamana* is, however, no clear evidence for holding onto elements of the masculine role, since under certain conditions even women gained membership in the ko'tikili and danced while playing the roles of female *kok'ko*. Even the role of Kor'kokshi in the Kia'nakwe Dance was not restricted to the *lhamana:* in 1915 the role was taken over by a woman, even though three *lhamana* were living in Zuni at that time. In Zuni, the emphasis likewise was placed on the perfect fulfillment of the feminine gender role.

Again, in other cases which are quite different in nature, a genuine double role (gender role splitting or bifurcation) can be observed, as for example among the Miami *waupeengwoatar,* who usually performed feminine tasks in women's clothes, but from time to time literally slipped back into the masculine role and, dressed in men's clothing, went on war expeditions. Cross-dressing in conjunction with masculine and feminine role components can, therefore, take the following forms:

1. only cross-dressing without the feminine gender role, either as (a) personal "medicine" (e.g., Four Bears) or (b) supernatural obligation (e.g., the Osage warrior)
2. cross-dressing with preponderantly masculine gender role (e.g., Tolowa)
3. cross-dressing in conjunction with masculine and feminine role components (often gender role splitting or bifurcation; e.g., Mono, Miami)
4. cross-dressing with preponderantly feminine gender role

Gender role change can take the form of a gender role split/bifurcation (separate living out of both gender roles), a gender role mixing (simultaneous living out of masculine and feminine role components), or merely gender role crossing (only minimal feminine activities in conjunction with cross-dressing).

It needs to be stressed once again that gender role change—not only in the case of the Shoshoni but also with other groups—obviously did not follow rigidly circumscribed rules; the individual had latitude, differentially determined culturally, in crossing beyond his gender role and also in the componential organization of an ambivalent woman-man status. The crucial factor in deciding whether a male received the status of woman-man was, first of all—and almost without exception—that he generally showed interest at all in feminine occupations. The few exceptions to this involve cases in which the parents destined a boy in early childhood to play the role of a girl. The extent to which he adopted other feminine role aspects—and also, by the way, the extent to which he decided to wear feminine clothing—was to a certain degree left up to him.

Chapter SIX

CROSS-DRESSING AND THE FEMININE GENDER ROLE

The carrying out of occupations which are culturally assigned to women within the framework of the sexual division of labor is an important aspect of the feminine gender role. As noted, the sources differ greatly with respect to the detail with which they describe which women's tasks were done by women-men. Where it is specified in what manner women-men filled the feminine role, it is remarkable that they frequently did not content themselves with equaling the women, but, if at all possible, they tried to surpass their role models.

CALIFORNIA

The characteristically feminine gathering activities have usually been cited as sex/gender-specific contributions to subsistence. In California, the seeds of various species of grass played an important role in the diet, along with acorns. Obtaining these seeds was the exclusive responsibility of the women, in contrast to gathering acorns, which was divided between both sexes: the men climbed the trees and struck the acorns to the ground, where they were collected by the women (Driver 1937:64, 1939:314; Essene 1942:7; Harrington 1942:8). Women-men accompanied the women in gathering grass seeds (Chumash, Harrington 1942:32; Gabrielino, Harrington 1942:32; Kato, Essene 1942:65; Kitanemuk, Harrington 1942:32; Lassik, Essene 1942:65; Nomlaki, Goldschmidt 1951:387; Pomo, Essene 1942:65; Salinan, Fages 1984:178f.; Yokuts, Gayton 1948:46, 236; Yuki, Essene 1942:65).

In the domestic sphere, women-men—like women—were responsible for processing what had been gathered. They cooked (Lassik, Pomo, Yuki, Kato, Essene 1942:65) and ground acorns (Maidu, Loeb 1933:183; Nomlaki, Goldschmidt 1951:387; Pomo, Gifford 1926:333; Tübatulabal, Voegelin 1938:47; Yokuts, Gayton 1948:106; Yurok, Kroeber 1925:46), which they probably also had helped to gather (Yokuts, Gayton 1948:106; Tübatulabal, Voegelin 1938:47). In addition to this they wove baskets (Lassik, Pomo, Yuki, Kato, Essene 1942:65; Pomo, Gifford 1926:333; Tübatulabal, Voegelin 1938:47; Wailaki, Loeb 1932:93; Yokuts, Gayton 1948:106; Yurok, Kroeber 1925:46). In connection with this, Essene (1942:65) mentioned in passing concerning the basket weaving of the Kalekau (Northern Pomo), Kato, Lassik, and Yuki, that the men there produced baskets, but men who made "fine baskets" were suspected of "homosexual tendencies." This remark quite obviously signifies that such men were seen as potential women-men. In the tribes just mentioned, women-men's baskets were thought to be at least as good as, or even better than, those produced by women (Essene 1942:65).

Sewing also belongs to the larger category of occupations that were practiced by women-men (Kato, Kalekau-Pomo, Lassik, Essene 1942:65; Yuki, Essene 1942:65, Foster 1944:186), as well as carrying wood (Maidu, Loeb 1933:183) and cooperating in the education of girls (Salinan, Fages 1984:178f., Hester 1978:502). Among the Achomawi, Atsugewi, and Klamath, women-men sweated with the women (Voegelin 1942:134); this also holds for two of the Wintu groups investigated by Voegelin as well as the Shasta (Voegelin 1942:134).

THE PLATEAU

Among the Plateau groups, women-men participated in gathering berries (Flathead, Turney-High 1937:85; Kutenai, Schaeffer 1965:218), in gathering roots (Kutenai, Schaeffer 1965:218), and also in making baskets and mats, in preparing lily seeds for consumption, and in cooking meals (Klamath, Spier 1930:52). The data on the Plateau tribes are extraordinarily meager, and for the Thompson and Sinkaietk, among whom women-men likewise existed, the data do not go beyond the information that there are supposed to have been persons who dressed and "behaved" like members of the opposite sex (Thompson, Teit 1900:321) and who preferred the clothing and occupations of women (Sinkaietk, M. Mandelbaum 1938:119).

THE NORTHWEST COAST

With reference to the Northwest Coast, little more is known about the Bella Coola and Bella Bella than that some males preferred feminine activities and wore women's clothing from childhood onward. Nonetheless, they customarily married and lent their wives a hand with all the women's work (McIlwraith 1948, 2:45). The same holds for the Haisla (McIlwraith 1948, 2:45; Olson 1940:200), and also of the Nootka, for whom Drucker reported merely a "preference [by some males] for work normally engaged in by the opposite sex" (1951:331). Among the Quinault, cooking and basket weaving belonged to the occupations of the "part women" (*keknatsa'nxwixw,* Olson 1936:99). It has been reported of the Tillamook women-men that they were valued as "shamans," but not which feminine tasks they performed on a day-to-day basis (Barnett 1937:189). Among the Kwakiutl, gender role change was found in differing componential manifestations, with and also without cross-dressing. Ford's consultant told in detail about his love affair with a Quatsino in women's clothes ("This man, her name was Frances," Ford 1941:129), but said little about what Frances did when she wasn't sleeping with the young Kwakiutl men. Ford merely stated that she sold baskets in the village (1941:130), but not whether she had also made them. Similarly, the information regarding the Eyak "transvestites" is generally restrained. It is said that they were men who lived like women and did women's work, but who did not hunt (Birket-Smith and De Laguna 1938: 206).

THE ARCTIC

Only a few statements pertaining to everyday feminine activities performed by women-men are available from the Arctic tribes for which gender role change has been reported. The Aleut and Kaniagmiut *shupans,* who were raised as girls, must have copied all aspects of the feminine role, including external appearance, with such deceptive authenticity that strangers to the tribe were not able to distinguish them from biological women (Dall 1897:402f.; see also Bancroft 1874:92). Murphy reported that some of the most powerful shamans among the St. Lawrence Eskimo were "transvestites" (1964:63, 74f.; Murphy and Leighton 1965:89), and also that a change of gender role was sometimes prescribed for the sick in order to make them unrecognizable to the spirits that were tormenting them (Murphy 1964:62f.). But apart from things like cross-dressing, short hair, and pipe smoking in the case of female patients, what particular form the gender role change actually took cannot be determined from this source. In addition, in regard to some nontransvesting *anasik* (males in a woman's role), it was not reported how their "acting like women" (Murphy and Leighton 1965:89) was expressed in detail, other than that one of them was constantly sewing and the other lay in wait for small boys.

THE SUBARCTIC

The Ingalik in Northern Alaska and the Ojibwa on the border of the Prairies and Plains are the only groups within this region for which gen-

"Ralph of Anvik, A berdache" (Ingalik). (From Osgood 1940, Plate 2.) Reproduced by permission of Yale University Publications in Anthropology, © 1940.

der role change with cross-dressing on the part of males has been reported. The Ingalik "women pretenders" preferred to spend their time with the women, by whom they were accepted and whom they equaled in feminine skills such as sewing and basket weaving (Osgood 1958: 261f.; see Figure 5). The Ojibwa are discussed in the following section, since the examples of women-men from this group are drawn primarily from the Northeast.

THE NORTHEAST

The sources are rich in detail for the Northeast. As noted, Marquette was the only writer who reported in regard to the Illinois women-men that they went to war. According to Hennepin (1699:163), they performed women's work—no further specifics are given—and stayed clear of hunting and warfare. Liette's (1962:112) remark that the women-men were said to have already shown their inclination toward women's tasks in childhood, when they spurned the bow and arrow and instead grasped "the spade, the spindle, the axe," suggests that as adults they engaged in raising corn, which in that region was women's work (see Driver 1961: Maps 4, 8). The spindle was used to produce yarn (from the wool of opossum and bison), out of which in the Prairie region blankets, headbands, neckbands, and anklebands as well as belts were woven (Driver 1961:150). In the Prairies, weaving was women's work (Driver and Massey 1957:340, Map 126). The ax served to procure firewood. Apart from these things, the Illinois women-men took part in games of lacrosse as female players (Liette 1962:124).

It should also be mentioned that along with the voluntary forms of gender role change already named, there existed among the Illinois a third, involuntary one. Bossu (1962:82) told of a warrior whom the Illinois forced into women's clothes as punishment for cowardice, which evidently was not an unusual procedure. This man regained his masculine status by going on the warpath against the Chickasaw alone and victoriously, whereupon he was rehabilitated (1962:82). All three sources—Marquette, Liette and Bossu—reported pertinent and accurate information. First, the changing of one's gender role while retaining the warrior's role has been documented for other tribes, for example the neighboring Miami. Second, the simultaneous occurrence of a voluntary gender role change, which is not regarded by members of the pertinent group as a humiliation, is not infrequently encountered along with the compulsory wearing of women's clothes by "failed" warriors, which is humiliating in character. For example, among the Winnebago, who were neighbors to the Illinois, those women-men whose vocations had been validated through visions were highly honored (Lurie 1953:710), whereas a cowardly or lying warrior in the last century was forced by decision of the tribal police to adopt the woman's role, in which he is said to have spent the rest of his life in shame (1953:711).

The *waupeengwoatar* of the Miami likewise carried out those women's tasks which related to the cultivation of maize—planting, hoeing, and harvesting—along with all of the housework (Trowbridge 1938:68).

Ojibwa *agokwa* took care of rearing children, the production and decoration of shoes (Kinietz 1947:156), and the manifold duties of the household (McKenney 1972:259). Tanner described an *agokwa* whom he personally knew as "very expert in the various employments of the women, to which all his time was given" (1830:105); as noted, Ozaw-wen-dib also performed heroic deeds in warfare against the Sioux (see Chapter 5). Overall, the sources suggest that the Ojibwa women-men generally strove to imitate feminine role behavior as exactly as possible—even extending to imitating the female voice and also the characteristic gait of women, with the toes pointed slightly inward (Kinietz 1947:156). Ozaw-wen-dib also imitated a woman's way of sitting and of walking, as well as female voice pitch (Henry 1897:163). At the same time, even Ozaw-wen-dib's brave exploits in war and his taking part in a drunken brawl do not necessarily speak against a highly developed feminine role; Henry (1897) and other traders repeatedly reported fights resulting from the consumption of alcohol (sometimes with fatal outcomes) in which the two sexes were evenly matched. (Ozaw-wen-dib "luckily" only lost an eye; he was said to have been "very quarrelsome" when drunk; Henry 1897:164.)

Landes (1970) provided a detailed report from the Prairie Potawatomi concerning the metamorphosis of a young male into a *m'netokwe,* which, however, took place at a time when the institution of gender role change was already disappearing. Thus, the young male—Yellow-Belly alias Louise—did not change into an Indian woman in traditional costume who did traditional Potawatomi women's work. Instead, as an employee in the home of a well-to-do Métis family, "she" assumed to perfection the clothing and household occupations of a woman according to the "White" model. In this case, cross-acting preceded cross-dressing (Landes 1970:198f.), and the cross-dressing took place gradually: aprons at first, then dresses, accompanied by increasingly feminine body language and feminine forms of speech (1970:199). In the house, Louise (as Yellow-Belly was soon called) did the dishes, swept the floor, dusted, and also worked as a cook. She made patchwork quilts and embroidered pillowcases (1970:198f.). Women's handiwork was also traditionally an area in which the *m'netokwe* excelled (beadwork; 1970:26). Together with the girls of the family, Louise gathered berries and nuts (1970:200), likewise a traditional area of women's work. She bought herself a sewing machine and made her own clothes, always with an eye on the newest women's fashions in the mail-order catalogues (1970:200). She rode horseback with a sidesaddle, took part in foot races, running with the girls, and at dance gatherings she danced with male partners (1970:199).

The statements concerning the Winnebago are more general. The women-men among them are supposed to have carried out feminine occupations—which are not specified any further—better than biological women; apart from that, they busied themselves as foster mothers for the children of relatives and sometimes were able to foresee future events, a form of specialist activity which was otherwise reserved for women (Lurie 1953:708ff.). Charlevoix reported concerning the Iroquois that the women-men—"hommes, qui n'avaient point de honte d'y prendre l'habillement de femmes" (men who were not ashamed to adopt the garb of women)—executed "toutes les occupations propre du sexe" (all the occupations appropriate to the sex) of women, but provided no details (1744:4).

THE PLAINS

Overview of Feminine Occupations

For the Plains, an entire series of sources again used general terms, stating merely that women-men wore women's clothes and performed both everyday household work and artistic handiwork, both of which were regarded as belonging to the feminine sphere. For the Cheyenne, Kroeber (1902:19) wrote, "ut femina cum feminis vixit" (she/he lived as a woman with [the] women), which suggests the practice of feminine activities. Kroeber (1902:19) also reported cross-dressing by the *heemaneh'*: "vestibus mulierum usa est" (They used the clothing of women). (Grinnell 1962 2:39, incidentally, denied cross-dressing by the *heemaneh'*.) Other sources are similarly general; for the Assiniboine, see Lowie (1909:42); Crow, Lowie (1912:226), Holder (1889:624), and Denig (1961:187f.); Oglala Lakota, W. K. Powers (1977:58); Santee Dakota, Landes (1968:112); Hidatsa, Dorsey (1894:517); Kansa, James (1823:129); Mandan, Maximilian (n.d., 2:78) and Bowers (1950:272); Omaha, Fletcher and La Flesche (1911:132f.); Oto, Fletcher and La Flesche (1911:132f.) and Irving (1838:112).

Sources that specified women's tasks in detail frequently emphasized handiwork such as beadwork and quillwork (Hidatsa, Bowers 1965:167; Ponca, J. H. Howard 1965:142; Crow, Lowie 1912:226; Teton Lakota, Hassrick 1982:135; Lame Deer 1979:169; Mirsky 1937a:417; Williams 1986a:194; Santee Dakota, Landes 1968:112). In one case, crocheting was also cited (Teton Lakota, Williams 1986a:195).

Gathering was the province of the women and the women-men. They dug for wild turnips (D. G. Mandelbaum 1940:256) and wild potatoes (Whitman 1937:50). Where corn was grown, women and women-men prepared the corn for storage (Oto, Irving 1838:112). They also butchered the game animals the men brought in (Hidatsa, Bowers 1965:167) and cooked the meals (Teton Lakota, Lame Deer 1979:169; Williams 1986a:195).

Frequently, it was reported that women-men mastered all of these women's tasks better than the women themselves (Bowers 1965:167; Hassrick 1982:137; Howard 1965:142; Lowie 1912:226; Mirsky 1937a:417; Whitman 1937:50; Williams 1986a:194). In the case of the Teton Lakota, the *winkte* are even supposed to have been visited by the women, because the latter hoped to obtain tips on embroidery or a recipe for an especially delicious meal from them (Mirsky 1937a:417). Holder (1889:624) reported that Crow *bate* were said to be so skilled in feminine occupations that they often found employment in "White" households.

One Teton Lakota who at the beginning of the 1980s defined himself as *winkte* (and practiced cross-dressing to the extent that he wore women's trousers; Williams 1986a:197) gradually adopted seven orphaned children and raised them, working as a nurse and cook in a home for the aged (Williams 1986a:198). Adoption of children by *miati* was also common among the Hidatsa; they took in orphans from their own tribe or children captured on raids and passed on property and ceremonial knowledge to them (Bowers 1965:167). The Teton Lakota *winkte* danced like women and are also said to have led the women's dances (Williams 19986a:194f.).

Androgynous Privileges in the Feminine Ceremonial Sphere

Hidatsa: "Captives" of the Holy Women

The Hidatsa *miati* even had access to the Holy Women Society, which was restricted to women (only the singer was male, but he was not a *miati,* or woman-man; Bowers 1965:324, 326). The participation of the *miati* within the Holy Women Society is discussed here, but some preliminary remarks are necessary pertaining to the sacred bundles concerned, since the bundle complex was widespread among many families and, as a result, the bundle-keepers should not be seen as religious specialists in a strict sense. The supernatural powers connected with individual bundles possibly represent a borderline case with respect to religious specialization. Sacred bundles played an important role among the Plains cultures. They contained various objects endowed with supernatural power and were unwrapped during certain ceremonies. Such bundles could be owned individually or by more than one person. Some sacred bundles were important to the welfare of the entire community, so owning them meant a great responsibility. Sacred bundles could be sold by one person to another according to certain culturally prescribed rules which differed among the various Plains tribes. Regarding the sacred bundles among the Mandan and Hidatsa, the bundles and certain rights associated with owning them were sold by family members to other family members (on sacred bundles, see Hartmann 1979).

The Holy Women Society was associated with two kinds of sacred bundles—the Woman Above Bundles and the Holy Women Bundles, respectively. In several families, these bundles were sold by the parents' generation to the children's, whereby rights to the bundles were acquired by both men and women. In the case of the Woman Above Bundles, it appears that male owners predominated (Bowers 1965:327, 332). Healing rituals performed with the aid of the Woman Above Bundles served to prevent miscarriages, premature births, insanity, paralysis, and other misfortunes which were attributed to the work of this malevolent deity (1965:330). Among the Mandan, who were very closely related culturally, the Woman Above Bundles also played a role in the war complex (1965:332).

What effectual consequences the possession of a Holy Woman Bundle had for a man is not quite clear. Bowers mentioned male owners of such bundles (1965:167), but later explained that rights to the Holy Women Society associated with these bundles were exclusively sold from mother to daughter (1965:324). Meanwhile, a comparison with the parallel ceremonies of the Mandan suggests that maybe the Hidatsa bundles were also acquired by married couples in common, whereby the man and the woman each obtained different ceremonial rights from the same bundle. This would explain the evidence for male owners of Holy Women Bundles and also the membership of the wives of Woman Above Bundle owners in the Holy Women Society (Bowers 1950:270f., 296ff.). The purchase of the rights by the daughter was occasioned by a dream in which she saw a benevolent deity such as Village Old Woman, the highest female deity (Bowers 1965:330).

Similarly, dreams were key in both the initiation of a male into *miati* status and *miati* membership in the Holy Women Society. The impetus to males' metamorphosis was a dream about one of the Holy Women, possibly Village Old Woman herself or the malevolent Woman Above (Bowers 1965:326, 330). The Hidatsa believed that such a male was "claimed by one of the Holy Women," and that he would become an imbecile if he did not comply with the meaning of his dream and put on women's clothes and carry out a gender role change (1965:326). Moreover, *miati* were said to be—without exception—the brothers or sons of men who possessed rights to the Holy Women or Woman Above Bundles (1965:167,330). According to the cultural ideology, only such males who stood in one of these kinship relationships to the corresponding bundle owners could undertake a gender role change at all (1965:167). Inasmuch as Bowers reported that *miati* bequeathed not only material property but also "ceremonial knowledge" to their adopted children, it is conceivable that rights derived from the Holy Woman Bundles were also passed on by them to their (adopted) children. However, this would hold only for those cases in which *miati* had to acquire these bundle rights themselves at all, in order to be able to become members of the Holy Women Society.

Since one of the Holy Women had laid claim to each *miati*, the *miati* as a group met with the Holy Women Society (Bowers 1965:326). Meanwhile, it remains unclear if the *miati* thereby acquired rights to a Holy Woman or Woman Above Bundle from one of her/his aforesaid relatives (or the wife of one of these men), as was the case among the Mandan. Bowers mentioned that Four Bears (or Mato-tope, a well-known Mandan who died in the late 1830s) died without having sold his People Above Bundle (the equivalent of the Woman Above Bundle of the Hidatsa) to his son, who was a "berdache" (Bowers 1950:296; a brother of Four Bears was also a woman-man; 1950:298). Perhaps, however, the purchase of a bundle by the *miati* was not actually required at all: "He was considered a 'prisoner' of the Woman Above and was *authorized* to participate in all ceremonies pertaining to the Holy Women *with whom he was classified*" (Bowers 1965:330, emphasis mine). At first glance, the *miati* appear to have been ordinary members of the Holy Women Society. On ceremonial occasions, they dressed and painted themselves the same as the female members did (1965:326). And together with the women, they carried out certain ritual acts during important ceremonies of the tribe—for example, at the Earth Naming Ceremony, a ritual associated with a special bundle that was supposed to summon the bisons (1965:433, 438); and also at the Sunset Wolf Ceremony, which was held in connection with the purchase of a certain bundle and which was associated with fasting, dances, and self-torture (1965:423). This last was similar to the Mandan Okipa Ceremony, which was supposed to secure the good fortune and prosperity of the tribe (Bowers 1965:410ff.; on *miati* as participants, see Bowers 1965:427).

However, in connection with the Sun Dance (Naxpike), it is clear that the role of the *miati* went beyond the ceremonial functions performed by the female members of the Holy Women Society. In particular, it is said to have been the responsibility of the *miati* to select the tree trunk for the center post from the driftwood in the river (Bowers 1965:167). Meanwhile, other *miati* helped the Holy Women (i.e., members of the Holy Women Society) dig the pit into which this post was to be placed (1965:315). The setting up of the side posts for the lodge associated with the Naxpike Ceremony was also supposed to devolve on the *miati* (1965:326; but see Bowers 1965:315, where it was stated that merely choosing the central post and tamping the earth around it was assigned to the *miati*). Bowers interpreted this to mean that *miati* executed tasks which were considered too difficult for the female members of the Holy Women Society (1965:326). This would mean that tasks were assigned to this society which its own *female* members could not perform. Without the *miati,* therefore, the Holy Women Society would not have been capable of fulfilling the entire range of their ritual functions.

Among the Hidatsa in general a strict division of labor prevailed, within the framework of which attention was paid, above all, to ensuring that boys and young men never performed feminine occupations (Bowers 1965:115): "This prohibition was fortified by ritual beliefs that those young men who performed women's customary duties were more likely to dream of the Woman Above and become berdaches. This resulted in a distinct sex dichotomy of labor" (1965:132). The only ones who were allowed to help the women to do weeding, to repair fences, or even to hoe the garden "if the work proved too much for the women" were old men (1965:132) who were too weak to go on hunts or on raids anymore. Feminine occupations, therefore, were in principle open to women, non-men, and no-longer-men.

Meanwhile, it simply appears unlikely that the core group of Holy Women—even if they were usually older women—would not have been physically able to set up posts (Naxpike), to heap up a mound on the edge of the village (Sunset Wolf), or to prepare the dance grounds (Bowers 1965:427, 438). According to Bowers' sketch (Figure 2 in Bowers 1965:313), nine posts apart from the central post had to be set in place. Eight Holy Women who were past menopause (1965:315) erected the side posts, while the *miati* stamped the ground firm around the central post, which had been erected by young men (1965:316). In 1879, when Good Bear sponsored the last Naxpike Ceremony (1965:309), no Hidatsa woman-man was available, so it was necessary to resort to a Sioux (1965:315). He chose the center post and stamped the earth firm around it, which indicates that he was familiar with this ceremony (only Williams 1986b:36f., in fact, mentioned that Oglala Lakota *winkte* fulfilled very nearly the same tasks at the Sun Dance as did *miati*). All of the other tasks were carried out by the Holy Women themselves, who in spite of their advanced age were obviously capable.

It seems unlikely, however, that selection of the center post for the Naxpike Ceremony should have been beyond the strength of even the most aged Holy Women, considering their other tasks, especially since young men from the village carried the tree trunk to the ceremonial site, not the *miati* (Bowers 1965:315). Much suggests that, in regard to the activities especially reserved to the *miati* inside the Holy Women Society, it is not a question of tasks primarily associated with the Holy Women, but rather of privileges which, at least among the Hidatsa, were related to the status of *miati*. Relevant here is an illuminating passage in Bowers' study, in which he explained that the *miati* "was authorized to participate in all ceremonies pertaining to the Holy Women with whom he was classified. *Since women were barred from actual participation in certain rites,* he was their representative when heavy work was required" (1965:330, emphasis mine). The *miati* stood in for the women, not because certain tasks were considered too difficult for the latter, but rather because certain rituals were closed to women which were open to the *miati* as non-women. Because he was a "prisoner" of the Holy Women, the *miati* was also held in esteem as holy (1965:330); this apparently was not true of the female members of the Holy Women Society.

Bowers noted that *miati* filled a great number of ceremonial roles and that they constituted "the most active ceremonial class in the village"

(1965:167), but did not go into detail. The ceremonial activities of the *miati,* however, must have been related to the fact that their initiation dream also contained individual "ritual instructions" (1965:167). Such dreams, thus, were visionary experiences that occurred not just as a one-time initiation, but repeatedly (1965:166).

The *miati*'s visions thus accomplished several functions. First, he was instructed to dress like a woman. Second, he was granted (independent of bundle purchase?) membership in the Holy Women Society. Finally, he received from the visions personal "power" or "medicine." Bowers aptly compared *miati* in their social position with *men* who possessed "unique and special mysterious supernatural powers" (1965:168). Their change of gender role provided them not only with the right to be received into the most significant women's ceremonial group, but with the kind of supernaturally bestowed personal power that was characteristic of the Plains region. On the Plains, the vision was mostly restricted to boys and men, in contrast to neighboring tribes (e.g., Woodland Algonquin, Hartmann 1979:152; Flathead, Turney-High 1937:33; for the Plains, see Weist 1980:259f.).

Miati did not become women through their visionary experiences, but instead—as Bowers aptly put it—became a "special class of 'females'" (1965:326), to whom were granted privileges denied to biological women. Power, which extended beyond the ceremonial functions of the Holy Women Society, was granted by the Holy Women only to those *males* who had dreamed of them: the latter had access to ceremonies which remained closed to the female members of the Holy Women Society. Probably related to their special spiritual power is that *miati* are supposed to have carried out everyday feminine occupations better than the women, and that their households were excellently organized (Bowers 1965:167). This echoes the case of the Navajo—the women-men were believed to have been better women than the women themselves, not least because of the nonfemale in them: "Being stronger and more active than the women, the berdache could do many things more efficiently and was never burdened down with childbearing" (Bowers 1965:167).

Mandan: Bundle Purchases

The references for the Mandan—who are closely related culturally to the Hidatsa—pertaining to the entrance of women-men into feminine ceremonial rights are less detailed. Among them as well, certain women held rights to the individual Holy Women Bundles and met at important tribal ceremonies (Bowers 1950:86). They bought the bundles with their husbands, to whom in turn particular tasks fell during the Okipa Ceremony because of the possession of such a bundle (Bowers 1950:124,

131, 271). Holy Women Bundles existed as separate bundles, but also as a part of the Small Hawk Bundles (the Small Hawk Ceremony promoted fortune in war and also in summoning the bison; Bowers 1950: 108) and evidently also as part of the People Above Bundles. Small Hawk Bundles contained masculine paraphernalia in one sub-bundle and Holy Women Bundles in a second sub-bundle, and were purchased by married couples who shared sex/gender-specific rights to an entire bundle (Bowers 1950:270f.).

A woman by the name of "Berdache," along with her sister and their common husband, was cited as one of the former possessors of the Small Hawk Bundle, which was passed on by purchase in the female line (Bowers 1950:270). In relation to this, however, it was not mentioned whether this woman actually was a woman-man or whether "Berdache"—that is, the Mandan word *mihdäckä* (Maximilian n.d., 2:289)—was her personal name. This possibility cannot be excluded altogether, because in another case among the Prairie Potawatomi, *m'netokwe* was both the general designation for women-men (Landes 1970:195) and the personal name of a quite obviously biological woman with twelve children (1970:376).

The daughters of Berdache's sister and her husband, themselves having meanwhile married, purchased the Small Hawk Bundle from Berdache after the deaths of their parents (Bowers 1950:270). It is consequently probable that Berdache was a *mihdäckä* because, in this polygynous marriage, evidently not she but rather her sister had given birth to the two girls (Bowers 1950:270). This suggests that Mandan women-men also came into possession of Holy Women Bundles, and by regular purchase within the framework of a marriage at that. This is also supported by the fact that an element of the female sub-bundle, a sacred bison robe, was associated with the deity Frog (or Toad) Earrings, who was regarded as equivalent to Woman Above, and like her, instructed males to put on women's clothes and to do women's work (1950:272). The sister of the Moon, Above Woman, with whom, inter alia, the People Above Bundle was associated, was also the effectual motivation for a gender role change, and beyond that, caused facial malformations, insanity, miscarriages, droughts, death, and other misfortunes (1950:296, 299). Inasmuch as gender role change among the Mandan was also the result of a "dream" or "higher inspiration" (Maximilian n.d., 2:78), it is probable that the vision experience was similar to that of the Hidatsa *miati*.

The facts that one of Four Bears' (the "Mato-tope" of Maximilian's n.d. and Catlin's 1844, 1926 reports) sons "dreamed of the Old Woman Above and dressed as a woman thereafter" (Bowers 1950:296) and that a brother of Four Bears was also said to have been a woman-man suggest that gender role change occurred at least as a tendency among brothers and sons of People Above Bundle possessors, and possibly also among relatives of Small Hawk Bundle possessors.

The bundles, meanwhile, could be sold to sons and daughters alike (Bowers 1950:296). Women who bought them together with their husbands received Woman Above rights and were permitted to wear the paraphernalia of this deity on ceremonial occasions. In any case, Four Bears' "berdache" son would obviously have been preferentially entitled to purchase the bundle on the grounds of his gender status. Other men, however, who bought People Above Bundles were not women-men (1950:296). Moreover, among the Mandan—as opposed to the Hidatsa—a vision was not a requirement for being entitled to purchase a bundle already in the possession of one's family (1950:343). Some men and women among the Mandan fasted, and by doing so, came into possession of *personal* bundles (1950:343f.). The decisive factor was that the seller regarded one of his children as suitable to continue the bundle line of descent (1950:343).

Thus, Mandan women-men, because they were pressured into a change of gender role by a vision of one of the Holy Women, obtained from that the right to acquire a bundle in an atypical fashion. This was in contrast to the situation among the Hidatsa, where a *miati* at least shared the Holy Woman vision with the women, who like him came from families which possessed Woman Above or Holy Women bundles. As among the Hidatsa, the Mandan woman-man was summoned or "claimed" by a Holy Woman, and as a buyer of a Small Hawk or a People Above Bundle, he received Holy Women rights just as biological women did.

The element of the "sacred" which was bestowed upon women-men by Holy Women among the Hidatsa and which extended beyond membership in the Holy Women Society seems to have been lacking among the Mandan. Possibly a *mihdäckä* acquired the bundle concerned simply as a "daughter" of the previous possessor, and became a suitable buyer because he quite obviously enjoyed the special attention of one of the Holy Women. The previously mentioned example of "Berdache," who purchased the Small Hawk Bundle together with her sister and her sister's husband, hints at this. A similar procedure, by the way, also may have prevailed among the Hidatsa, where the *miati* are likewise supposed to have been drawn primarily from families which had access to Holy Women or to Woman Above Bundles.

Thus, the association among the Mandan and Hidatsa of the women-men with certain feminine ceremonial groups or feminine privileges is related to the acquisition and sale of sacred bundles, which were themselves associated with female deities, the Holy Women. Rights to membership in the feminine ceremonial groups were a part of these bundles, but the rights also involved rights and paraphernalia for men. Women-men were usually consanguineal relatives of bundle owners. By sending visions, the Holy Women claimed these males for themselves, which resulted in a change of gender role. As "quasi-women," then, women-men could acquire rights to feminine bundle elements, and especially membership in the female ceremonial group.

For the Hidatsa, who emphasized the vision more strongly, the dream of the Holy Women also possessed features characteristic of a masculine vision experience, which invested the woman-man with considerable supernatural power, apart from feminine rights and duties. He was in addition more favored by the Holy Women than the female members of the group, and thus as a member of the Holy Women Society, he gained privileges which were withheld from biological women. The additionally bestowed supernatural power also led to a large number of ceremonial roles: "Their roles in ceremonies were many and exceeded those of the most distinguished ceremonial leaders" (Bowers 1965:167). Thus, unlike the Mandan *mihdäckä,* who as "quasi-women" inconspicuously bought into feminine bundle rights, the Hidatsa *miati,* as a "special kind of woman" who was inspired by the Holy Women and enriched by additional ceremonial knowledge, achieved a position of prime religious importance. Moreover, his/her position far surpassed that of the most esteemed women and was comparable to the role of the male "medicine men."

THE SOUTHWEST

The literature on the Southwest with regard to feminine everyday activities which were carried out after a change of gender role is scant. General "women's work" was reported from the Hopi (Beaglehole and Beaglehole 1935:65; Fewkes 1892:11), Santa Ana (Gifford 1940:163), the Yuma (Alarcón 1565:368) and Acoma (L. A. White 1943:325). The Isleta *lhunide* Palure was active as a plasterer and made the best cakes in the village, which "she" distributed to children (Parsons 1932:246). A woman-man from San Felipe was pleasantly remembered by Parsons' consultant because he washed the dishes when he came to visit her (1932:47). This woman-man, dressed as a man, worked in a store in Albuquerque, but he put on women's clothes—and evidently performed women's tasks—as soon as he came back to his home pueblo. In Laguna, the grinding of corn (maize) belonged to the feminine occupations of the *mujerados* (Hammond 1883:343), and among the Cocopa it was included in the tasks of the *elha,* the "male transvestite" (Gifford 1933:294). The *alyha* of the Mohave, who as boys played with *metates* (grinding slabs made of stone), as adults certainly ground corn on them (Devereux 1937:502). Since they were regarded as very industrious wives, they probably engaged in all the everyday feminine activities (1937: 513). A "well kept house" (1937:513) was no doubt among the incentives for a man to take an *alyha* as his wife. The Yuma *elxa* likewise ground corn and fetched water, which Forde (1931:157) evidently considered a significant example of women's work. Maricopa *yesa'an* occupied themselves at the metate, gathered mesquite, and carried out other unspecified feminine occupations (Spier 1933:242). It was reported of a Hopi *ho'va* that he came from his village, which was situated on First Mesa, to Mishongnovi in order to trade with the women there (Beaglehole and Beaglehole 1935:65). Another Hopi *ho'va* was well-versed in the fabrication of figure-decorated clay tiles (Fewkes 1892:11). The uncle of Don Talayesva clearly stood within the Hopi tradition of complete gender role change. He did not transvest, but he probably did women's work on account of his physical handicap—husking corn and looking after the children of his relatives and neighbors (Talayesva 1950:38).

Hammond (1882:348) maintained that the *mujerados* in Acoma did not have to work at all if they did not want to, but this is most unlikely. For one thing, Hammond himself cited women's occupations for the *mujerados* in nearby Laguna, which obviously were done on a regular basis (Hammond 1882:343). Second, Parsons (1918:181) reported that the Laguna *kokwimu* distinguished themselves specifically on account of a preference for feminine over masculine tasks, which motivated the gender role change in the first place. In any case, most of Hammond's ethnographic assertions (see below, chapter 8) are doubtful, and it is likely that *kokwimu* (*mujerados*) did pursue everyday feminine activities.

THE SOUTHEAST

The information on the Southeast is meager. Various older sources mentioned that "sodomy" was said to have been widespread in some tribes (e.g., Chickasaw, Romans 1962:70; Creek, Romans 1962:97), but this does not necessarily mean that gender role change was present. In regard to the Caddo, it is only known that women-men existed; details pertaining to their role and their status are lacking (Newcomb 1961:301). More precise information is available for the Natchez. Dumont (1753: 249) reported on the "chef des femmes," who "comme elles . . . travaille á la culture des terres & á tous les autres ouvrages qui leur sont propres" (the chief/boss of the women, who like them works at tilling the fields and at all the other tasks that are appropriate to them). In addition, if the women were prevented from accompanying a hunting or war expedition, then there came instead "cet homme habillé en femme qui sert á garder leur cabanage, á faire leur sagamité, & á pourvoir enfin a tous les besoins du ménage" (this man dressed as a woman, who helps to take care of their camp, to prepare/cook their sagamité, and in a word, to provide for all the needs of the household) (1753:250). Among the Karankawa as well, the women-men accompanied warriors on raids, particularly to look after the stolen horses, but also—proposed Fray Morfi (Newcomb 1961:74)—to be at the warriors' disposal for sexual intercourse. In this, they likewise would have taken the place of biological women. In the Southeast, it was no rarity for women to go on war parties, and occasionally to fight as well (Choctaw, Bossu 1962:164; Romans 1962:75; Houma, Gravier 1959:147ff.; Cherokee, Niethammer 1985:239; Creek and Seminole, McCloud 1977:27). The participation of Timucua "hermaphrodites" on war expeditions as described by Le Moyne (1875:7f.) also belongs to the feminine role area: in war, the Timucua women-men were said to have carried the supplies and also, on account of their physical strength, have otherwise served as "beasts of burden." They carried people who had died of disease and dead warriors to their place of burial, and took persons with infectious diseases to special places where the women-men took over their care (LeMoyne 1875:7f.). The first-named tasks otherwise devolved on women (Swanton 1946:713).

THE GREAT BASIN

Among most of the Great Basin groups, gender role change occurred both with and without cross-dressing. The criteria for classification as a woman-man did not emphasize assimilation to the female sex in external aspects, but rather an inclination for the activities of that sex. Several examples of combining women's clothing with feminine tasks have been reported.

The general assertion that women-men performed women's work is found with reference to the following: the Paiute in general (Steward 1941:312); the Northern Paiute (Stewart 1941:405); the Southern Paiute (Stewart 1942:298); the Nevada Shoshoni (Steward 1941:312); and also the Ute (Stewart 1942:298). Various reports from the Northern Paiute exist in regard to males in women's clothes who were especially engaged as laundry women (Lowie 1924:283; Steward 1933:238, "washing for white people"; Stewart 1941:440; perhaps all of these statements refer to the same person). Basket weaving is cited for the Northern Paiute (Lowie 1924:283) and Southern Ute (Gifford 1940:163); among the latter, as well as among the Western Mono (Gayton 1948:274), "male berdaches" also fabricated pots (Gifford 1940:163). Another woman-man in the same tribe cooked for a troop of boys who were always hanging around his house (Lowie 1924:282f.). He was also said to have possessed many horses, although it was not mentioned how he acquired these (1924:282). Another Shoshoni in women's clothes gathered seeds (Steward 1941:353). Among the Northern Paiute, beadwork also belonged to the *tübas'* sphere of activity (Stewart 1941:440). Finally, the women-men of the Wind River Shoshoni performed women's work of all kinds—"except to go to the menstrual hut," as a female consultant of Shimkin's (1947:298) put it.

SUMMARY

In regard to everyday women's activities, thus, the sources provide details to very differing degrees. As noted, women-men participated in female ceremonial groups. Specialist occupations such as that of medicine woman or of female buriers of the dead will be discussed separately. The occupations primarily named are those belonging to the subsistence domain—the gathering or raising and preparation of vegetable food products, as well as isolated references to processing the wild game brought in by the men from hunting. Further, only especially "typical" feminine subsistence activities were mentioned—seed-gathering in California, raising maize (corn) in the Northeast, digging for wild tuberous plants on the Plains, and gathering mesquite in the Southwest. Occasionally, it was also reported that women-men prepared meals. In addition to this, women-men were often active in areas of handiwork and artistic crafts which were specific to women. Depending on the tribe in question, they did ceramics (women's work everywhere in North America; Driver and Massey 1957:342, Map 129), made baskets (likewise women's work, with few exceptions; Driver and Massey 1957:335, Map 123), did beadwork or quillwork, or sewed clothing (women's work, Driver and Massey 1957:330, Map 119).

With respect to nonmaterial culture, the information is even more meager. In some tribes, the women-men made use of the sweat house together with the women; it was reported in a few cases that they collaborated in raising girls (Salinan) or even adopted children and brought them up (Teton Lakota, Hidatsa, Ojibwa). Only among the Mandan and the Hidatsa did they obtain access to ceremonial groups reserved to women. It is true that women-men among the Hill Maidu did, in isolated cases, join in puberty ceremonies for a girl (Loeb 1933:151), but they themselves did not undergo any ceremony of this kind, and probably participated in the festivities within the framework of their feminine role. Moreover, this participation was not tied to far-reaching ceremonial rights or duties. The status of the Hidatsa *miati* differed markedly from that of the female members of the ceremonial group. In this context, the women-men's supposed superiority in feminine activities is striking. In particular, this superiority was claimed for women-men in those groups in which legitimacy was granted to them through a vision or a dream, or in which the institution of gender role change was supported by supernatural prototypes and legitimations, although it was not restricted to these. The Hidatsa *miati* seem to have been less "quasi-women" than a special class of medicine *men* whose change of gender role expressed their personal medicine.

Women-men were often distinguished by their considerable ambition to fulfill the feminine role to perfection. In addition to everyday activities, this role consisted of another series of role components. These included specialist activities which devolved on women, feminine body-decoration (tattooing), feminine language (grammatical elements, expressions, vocal pitch and/or a woman's manner of speaking), and role aspects grounded in female physiology (i.e., forms of cultural expression related to menstruation and pregnancy). Before investigating these aspects, however, I will turn to change of gender role without cross-dressing.

Chapter SEVEN

Feminine Activities Without Cross-Dressing

The examples of feminine activities and occupations without cross-dressing fall into two groups. In a number of tribes, there have always been males who partly or exclusively formed the category of women-men who did not combine a special liking for women's work with putting on and dressing in women's clothing. In other cases, and under the influence of missionaries and Indian agents, a form of gender role change without cross-dressing gradually replaced the traditional gender role change which had included the wearing of women's clothing. Even in those cases, however, the status of "berdache"/woman-man nevertheless was retained and preserved, but in a form that was invisible to the representatives of the Indian administration and missions (and surely also to ethnographers). This indicates that even transvestism itself is a dispensable element of gender role change. In some groups, the institution even disappeared altogether, because younger and more strongly acculturated members did not share the responsibility for carrying it on. Even in these cases, however, some males who would have become women-men in earlier times found the ways and the means, despite pressure from both inside and outside the tribe, to pursue a way of life oriented toward feminine role models.

TRADITIONAL VIEWS: "FEMININE MALES"

The extent to which traditionally nontransvesting women-men appeared alone or simultaneously with transvesting ones cannot be definitely established in all cases. As noted, many ethnographers have not explicitly stated whether the persons described under the rubric "berdache," in addition to performing women's tasks, also transvested. It thus remains unclear whether the consultants were asked about males wearing women's clothing, or about males filling the feminine social role; or, on the other hand, whether consultants actually described the latter and the ethnographers then simply inferred the wearing of women's clothes according to the concept of gender role change—bound up with the designation "berdache"—which they themselves held. In order to undertake a preliminary differentiation of the phenomena which up to now have been indiscriminately lumped under the term "berdache," I will, in what follows, designate males who traditionally practiced only cross-acting, but not cross-dressing, as "*feminine males.*" This term will be used synonymously with "nontransvesting women-men." In the present context, by "feminine" I do not refer to an external femininity (of dress, gestures, etc.), but rather to the personality traits of a woman and an interest in a woman's activities. Because, apart from the absence of cross-dressing, feminine males usually exhibited all aspects of the woman-man status (including the characteristic classification into a special gender status), they are to be understood as a subgroup of women-men. (This, by the way, is in contrast to "masculine" women with interests in men's activities, who were usually not categorized as men-women; see Part 3).

In Shasta society, among whom both transvesting and nontransvesting women-men existed simultaneously (Voegelin 1942:134; her male consultant, with what she paradoxically referred to as "transvestite traits," wore men's clothing, but transvesting did occur in other cases), feminine males performed women's work and remained living with their parents like unmarried daughters. They did not hunt, but they occasionally accompanied men on the hunt in order to help bring back the game taken (Holt 1946:317). One male among the Kalekau Pomo was classified as a woman-man *(das)*; he wore men's clothes, but no hat (obviously in contrast to a "typical" Pomo man). Nothing is known of his activities (Essene 1942:65). Similarly, a Panamint male—the brother of the father of one of Driver's consultants, who likewise apparently did not transvest, was otherwise "just like a woman"—he made baskets and gathered grass seeds (Driver 1937:129).

Among the Paiute and Shoshoni, feminine males were grouped together with transvesting women-men and persons with ambiguous or atrophied genitals under the term *tübasa* or *tuvasa,* meaning "infertile" or sterile (Kelly 1932:157; Steward 1941:353; 1943:385; Stewart 1941:405, 440; 1942:352; see also above, Chapter 4). Feminine males performed women's work (Lowie 1924:282; Steward 1941:312, 353; Stewart 1941:405). It was specifically mentioned that among the Southern Paiute, such a male equipped with the collecting basket led the women in searching for grass seeds and that, like the women, he also roasted grass seeds (Lowie 1924:282). Another *tuvasa* worked as a housekeeper for whites (Steward 1941:353), and a third did women's work, but—in contrast to most women-men—preferred the company of men (Shoshoni, Steward 1941:353). Along with the term *tübasa/ tuvasa,* there existed others which referred specifically to persons who had carried out a change of gender role. Unfortunately, translations are not available for all of these. The Northern Paiute appear to have distinguished transvesting women-men from other *tübasa* by the word *tüdayapi,* "dress like other sex" (Steward 1933:238). The Lemhi Shoshoni had, besides *tübasa,* the term *tenanduakia* for "berdaches or transvestites of both sexes" (*tenap* = "man"; Steward 1943:385). Some Shoshoni groups designated "transvestites" in particular as *taŋgowaip* ("man-woman"; Steward 1941:353) or as *waip: siŋwa* ("half-woman"; Steward 1941:353). According to Hall (1993), the term *taŋgowaip* is properly spelled *tainna wa'ippe* (see also Miller 1972:164, 172: "man" in Shoshoni is *tainkwa*, "woman" *wa'ippe).* The translation given by Hall (1992, 1993) is the same as in Steward.

The Tewa *kwidos* are also included among the feminine males. Nothing specific has been reported concerning their day-to-day life, but both their gender role and their gender status must have been so distinctively androgynous that they probably did not transvest (Jacobs 1983:460). The extent to which gender role change in other pueblos was not necessarily connected with cross-dressing is not clear.

Talayesva's uncle among the Hopi obviously did not transvest any more than did Axa Hose Ihunide, "Old Father José Man-Woman," in Isleta, who wore "buckskin trousers" and moccasins, but who probably did women's work (Parsons 1932:246). This combination and also the way he was addressed—"Old *Father*"—similarly point to an androgynous, and not a quasi-feminine, status for some Pueblo women-men, in the context of which cross-dressing was left up to the individual.

Among the Pima, feminine males, together with (other male?) individuals who are "frightened by small things," come under the designation *wik'ovat*—"like a girl" (Hill 1938b:339). Hill stated that *wik'ovat* did not even perform the activities of the other sex, not to mention transvesting: "Their abnormal behavior manifested itself only in acting, talking, and expressing themselves like members of the opposite sex, showing an interest in duties and work of the other sex, and a marked preference for their companionship" (Hill 1938b:339). Meanwhile, all of these are characteristic forms of behavior which in other tribes almost invariably led to a person's carrying out a gender role change. Because there existed among the Pima a special test for determining whether a boy was a *wik'ovat* (Hill 1938b:340), it is likely that feminine males once definitely held a status which made it possible for them to live out their feminine interests. Virtually identical tests existed among the neighboring tribes (Northern Paiute, Stewart 1941:440; Papago, Underhill

1936:39; 1939:186; Shoshoni, Steward 1941:353; Ute, Stewart 1942: 298), and these always functioned as the entree into a recognized and institutionalized woman-man status.

Apart from the Great Basin, the Pima, and some Pueblos in the Southwest, cross-acting without cross-dressing seems to have been usual only in the Northwest, in the Subarctic, and possibly also (in one case) in the Arctic area. Further, cross-dressing by women-men was explicitly mentioned for only three out of a total of twelve Northwest Coast tribes which had gender role change (Bella Coola, Haisla, and Kwakiutl). Among the Kwakiutl women-men, feminine behavior without cross-dressing was apparently the rule (Ford 1941:130f.). A feminine male well known to Ford's consultant imitated feminine body language and did women's work (sewing, washing, patching garments, and picking berries) with the women, whose company he preferred. He cooked for the consultant himself and provided for him: "He acts towards me just as if he were my girl-cousin, and cooks for me and everything a girl would do" (1941:131). Another feminine male "behaved" like a woman and loved women's jewelry, but was married and was regarded as an expert in oral lore and in composing songs (1941:131).

The *aranu'tiq* of the Chugach Eskimo probably did not wear women's clothes, but rather men's clothes—or at least mixed costume. Birket-Smith's (1953) consultant mentioned such persons, who were said to be male on one side of their bodies and female on the other side. One *aranu'tiq* known to this consultant did the work of both sexes with great skill and carried the descriptive personal name "What Kind of People Are These Two?" (*Tyakutyik,* Birket-Smith 1953:94; this name, however, was also given to a chieftain's daughter in the village of Chenega, who was not an *aranu'tiq;* 1953:94). The Chugach Eskimo believed that *aranu'tiq* were two persons united in one, that they were more gifted than ordinary people, and that they were very lucky, like twins (1953: 94). The *aranu'tiq* were seen as twins within a single person (for similar ideas among the Teton Lakota, see Lame Deer 1979:169; among the Hopi, see Talayesva 1950:27). Such a description fits genuine hermaphrodites, but Birket-Smith did not specify hermaphroditism versus a form of partial gender role change with partial cross-dressing. Also conceivable is a subsuming of both phenomena under a generic term, as is sometimes found in the North American core area. In respect to the Eyak, neighbors of the Chugach Eskimo, the existence or nonexistence of cross-dressing cannot be ascertained clearly. Feminine males among the Eyak did not hunt, but preferred the life of a woman and women's activities (Birket-Smith and De Laguna 1938:206).

A modern example of situationally conditioned cross-acting was reported among the Hare. In a camp which had been pitched in connection with fighting forest fires, Broch (1977:97) came across a feminine young man who exhibited feminine behavior and functioned for the other men as a cook, nurse, and the object of jocular flirting. The men called him "mother," "auntie," and "mom," and joked erotically with him. In everyday life, however—in which he likewise worked as a cook—he was having an affair with a girl and was never treated by the men as a "berdache" (1977:100). Admittedly, he also did not go hunting and he set no traps, as other Hare men do (1977:100). Broch concluded that "berdache is a possible status within current Hare Indian culture," which, however, obviously can be lived out only in certain situations (1977:99). He established that the men's dealings with the feminine young man took place within a definite and secure connecting thread of "culturally defined codes" (1977:99). Inasmuch as the cultural patterns for dealing with males in a feminine role have been so clearly remembered down to such recent times, it is probable that this example is a remnant of a gender role change which was once possible on a permanent basis, but now, because of altered cultural conditions, can be practiced only in particular situations, for example, in a fire fighting camp, in which Hare men are among themselves. The young man reacted very aggressively when Broch also addressed him as "auntie," and Broch was probably correct in noting that "berdache is only a relevant status in exclusively Indian arenas" (1977:98f.). It is common in some groups to lavish (to some extent coarse) jokes on a woman-man or a feminine male without, however, his needing to feel mocked or disrespected. In this situation, it was clear to all involved that the woman-man was thoroughly respected—or at least accepted (Teton Lakota, Williams 1986a:194; Kutenai, Schaeffer 1965:218; Papago, Underhill 1936:43).

An additional aspect was involved in the case of the feminine Hare: the joking remarks of the men confirmed his temporary quasi-feminine status. They affirmed his sexual attractiveness and flattered him, saying that he looked after them better than their mothers and sisters could (Broch 1977:99). Within the framework of the cultural models operating *within* his own culture, the feminine male could sort out and interpret these remarks accurately. From a White man, to whom he naturally imputed the attitude of Anglo-American culture toward feminine males, the similar-sounding remarks took on a different meaning (although Broch did not intend this) and called forth a correspondingly different reaction. The feminine Hare must have assumed that the White man saw him not within one of the Indian cultural patterns, but instead as an effeminate homosexual "queen" in the sense of the Anglo-American interpretation of the situation, in which a feminine man did women's work and was constantly the butt of homoerotic teasing. According to Broch, the men did not have sexual contact with this male (1977:99). The unambiguous joking, however, suggests that at the time when an intact, permanent woman-man role was in existence, sexual relationships with men were also engaged in. Furthermore, Williams (1986b: 104f.) has pointed out that Broch's description in no way means that the feminine male had no sexual contact with other men in the camp.

Voegelin (1942: 134) cited cross-dressing for the Wintu, but Du Bois (1935: 50), by contrast, did not. Two feminine males who were still living when Du Bois' investigation was carried out did women's work and remained unmarried. It was said of a "shaman" from earlier times that he menstruated, had sexual relations with both sexes, and finally gave birth to two snakes (Du Bois 1935: 50). In this case, it may be that the imitation of female physiology was supposed to emphasize a gender role change; it may also be that it was the expression of a personal "power" possessed by the shaman, and for the most part had nothing to do with a gender role change. Moreover, in the cases of some hermaphrodites, the internal female reproductive organs were reported to be so well developed that menstruation did take place (Walter 1978: 11). Consequently, it is possible that this male was an intersexual, and probably one with primary development of male external genitalia (since he was obviously classified as a man). Furthermore, so-called genuine hermaphrodites have a vagina, so that—because of the possibility of heterosexual coitus in combination with menstruation—to ascribe to such a person the ability to give birth might also suggest itself, even though this was not possible on physiological grounds.

EXTERNAL INFLUENCES: CHANGE AND CONTINUITY

There are numerous cases in which women-men traditionally wore women's clothes, and later gave up this practice. With respect to this, three causes for this can be ascertained, all of which can be traced to the process of acculturation:

1. acculturation within the tribe, whereby the younger generation for the most part begins to encounter the institution of gender role change with rejection;
2. pressure on the part of the Indian agents, missionaries, or the non-Indian population generally, with whom a situation of continuing culture contact exists; and
3. forced conversion of women-men into "real men" by local Indian agents.

These causes cannot be separated from each other and in many cases work together, with the result that the women-men gave up women's clothing in favor of men's clothes. In many places, of course, the activities which belong to the area of women's work continued to be practiced, and special roles, primarily ritual in nature, survived which had traditionally been filled by women-men. For the representatives of the White culture, the women-men became invisible, while their status frequently was preserved (Jacobs 1968:30f; Williams 1986b:183ff.). Probable examples of this are the nontransvesting women-men in San Felipe, Isleta, and Laguna, on whom Parsons reported during the 1930s (Parsons 1932:246), and possibly also Don Talayesva's uncle among the Hopi (Talayesva 1950:38), as well as modern feminine males in the Hopi villages (Williams 1986b:52, 90, 101, 187). Consequently, the extent to which the males described in the literature as the "last berdaches" of a tribe in fact actually were the last of their special status cannot be determined with certainty.

Examples of coercive attempts on the part of White government officials to induce women-men to give up their clothing date primarily from before the turn of the century, but some cases are from the first third of this century. Representatives of the Anglo-American culture obviously believed that the woman-man would put aside his feminine ways of behavior along with his feminine clothing. However, cross-dressing is the most dispensable component of gender role change.

FORCED REVERSE METAMORPHOSIS: THE KWAKIUTL

In the case of Frances, the long-haired Kwakiutl in women's clothes referred to above, the forced reverse metamorphosis was successful. At the urging of the local Indian agent, he was transported to Victoria, where a policeman forcibly undressed him, determined him to be a man, cut off his hair, and dressed him in men's clothing (Ford 1941:130). In the eyes of the government officials, the rigorous measures bore fruit, for Frances remained a man and hired on to a schooner hunting seals (1941:130). Meanwhile, it is not possible to say whether or not he would have metamorphosed back, or at least have taken up a life as a feminine male without cross-dressing, according to the Kwakiutl model, since he died on that voyage.

INDIAN AGENTS AND ACCULTURATION: THE HIDATSA

As noted, on the occasion of the last Naxpike Ceremony, held in 1879, the Hidatsa had to ask a Sioux woman-man for assistance: the only Hidatsa *miati* still alive had fled to Crow Agency after "the Government agent forcibly stripped him of his female attire, dressed him in men's clothing, and cut off his braids" (Bowers 1965:315). It is unknown whether he ever returned to the Hidatsa. At that time, however, the woman-man status was still of sufficient importance to regard such a male as indispensable for carrying out the ceremony correctly. Admittedly, Hidatsa *miati* did not disappear on account of violent interventions from outside. The *miati* who took flight was already the only one left, a fact which surely cannot be traced to the devastating consequences of the smallpox epidemic of 1837 alone. Since the status of *miati* was closely tied to the traditional ceremonial system in its componential organization and legitimization, the women-men probably disappeared with the collapse of that system (Bowers 1965:168). Thus, a general process of culture change in the course of the years removed the foundations of the institution.

"AMUSING OR EVIL"? THE LAST WINNEBAGO *SHIÁŋGE*

In the case of the last Winnebago woman-man, or *shiáŋge,* his own brother took over the role, for the carrying out of which—among the Hidatsa—an Indian agent was required. At one time, the *shiáŋge* were legitimized in their gender role change on account of their visions and were highly esteemed (like some women who were endowed with prophetic gifts); they were also considered "better" at women's tasks than women themselves (Lurie 1953:708, 709f.). However, they experienced a decline because of external influences: ". . . the Winnebago had become ashamed of the custom because the white people thought it amusing or evil" (Lurie 1953:708). Thus it was that the brother of the last woman-man threatened to kill him, whereupon the *shiáŋge* donned a combination of men's and women's clothes (1953:708); however, he continued to perform women's tasks and helped his sister and half-sister in raising their children (1953:710).

SURVIVAL DESPITE EXTERNAL PRESSURE

The attempt of an Indian agent on the Crow Reservation around the turn of the century to induce Osh-Tisch, one of the three surviving *bate,* to put on men's clothing was unsuccessful (Williams 1986b:179). The other Crows protested, "saying it was against his nature" (Lowie 1912:226; see also Simms 1903:581). Apparently, the Crows were successful, because both Lowie and Simms encountered that *bate* in women's clothing. Yet with the collapse of the traditional culture, the custom eventually must have become invisible. Maximilian (n.d., 1:237) mentioned "viele Berdaches oder Mannweiber" (many berdaches or women-men) among the Crows in the late 1830s; around 1855 or 1856, Denig (1961:187) still knew two or three *bate* and stated that earlier there had been five or six. In Holder's time, five *bate* were alive (Holder 1889:623); Simms (1903:580) met three, and Lowie (1912:226) apparently met only one. After the death of Osh-Tisch, the last *bate,* the influence of Baptist missionaries brought the institution to a standstill for a time (Williams

1986b:183). Recently, however, males are said to have again taken on *bate* status, wearing a combination of men's and women's clothing (Williams 1986b:194).

The institution of the Lakota *winkte* underwent a similar change. In the 1920s and 1930s, pressure from missionaries and government officials grew: "I heard sad stories of winktes committing suicide, hanging themselves rather than change . . . after that those who remained would put on man's clothing" (Lakota man, age 25 years, quoted in Williams 1986a:194). In many Native American cultures, hanging is the characteristically feminine form of suicide (Landes 1938:235; Niethammer 1985:114). Nevertheless, *winkte* status has remained in existence even to the present time. One of Williams' (1986a:196) consultants identified himself as *winkte,* and although he wore men's clothes, he wore his hair very long. Another male, likewise a self-identified *winkte,* wore women's trousers and worked as a cook and as a nurse (1986a:197f.). In more recent times, other *winkte* have combined men's and women's clothing (1986a:193; T. H. Lewis 1973:312f.), as well as a young Omaha *mixu'ga* (men's outerclothing, women's underwear; Mead 1961:1452) and a Kutenai *kupatke'tek* (Schaeffer 1965:218).

Within the tribe, the attitude toward *winkte* worsened after World War II, with numerous young Lakotas attending "White" schools and losing respect for their own traditions (Williams 1986a:193, 194; 1986b:187ff.). Older Lakotas still showed the *winkte* acceptance and respect, and along with the traditionalists, other tribal members began to respect *winkte* again within the framework of the newly awakening consciousness of tradition during the 1970s (1986a:196). The modern *winkte* whose voices are heard or who are mentioned in Williams' essay are all very committed to, and involved in, traditional activities and thus preserve that aspect of the *wakan* which was attributed in such large measure to the traditional *winkte.* They also appear, as always, to be giving sacred names (1986a:197f), an activity which was counted among the tasks of the *winkte* in earlier times. Williams' consultants said little about day-to-day activities, mainly emphasizing "spiritual power," feminine personality traits, and sexual relations with men. These characteristics, however, because of the spiritual responsibility of the *winkte,* are distinguished from homosexual relations between two men (1986a: 193, 195, 196).

Among the Navajo, according to Williams, the *nadle* status held on firmly, and within the framework of the new strengthening of Native American consciousness, their number is even said to be increasing. Williams cited an eyewitness who claimed to have observed a meeting of 250 *nadle* in 1978 (Williams 1986b:199). I was not, however, able to confirm this optimistic estimate in my own fieldwork in 1992 and 1993;

neither was Wesley Thomas, himself Navajo, able to confirm this account. While a number of younger Navajo gays identify themselves as *nadle*, the traditional status of the *nadle* as a "third gender" seems to have almost disappeared (see Lang, 1997a).

Similarly, the Cheyenne *heemaneh'* seem to have disappeared. Grinnell (1962, 2:39) reported that the *heemaneh'* there "usually dressed as old men"—that is, they did not wear women's clothes (cf. Hoebel 1961: 77 and Kroeber 1902:19). Grinnell did not mention whether they wore women's clothes in earlier times, or whether, for example, the *heemaneh'* put on women's clothing during the Scalp Dance, in which they played an important role (1962, 2:40ff.). It is clear, however, that the institution must have disappeared by Grinnell's time. The five *heemaneh'* mentioned by him had all died "a long time ago" (1962, 2:39), and the last Cheyenne women-men, Pipe alias Pipe Woman and Good Road alias Good Road Woman, died in 1868 and 1879, respectively (1962, 2:39f.).

In more recent times, transvesting *heemaneh'* again have been said to live among the Cheyenne (Williams 1986b:194, 223). The old-time *heemaneh'* took on the "ways of women" (Grinnell 1962, 2:39) and were responsible for a number of special tasks (matchmaker, companion on war parties, and the Scalp Dance; 1962, 2:39f.). The contradictoriness of the sources regarding cross-dressing among the Cheyenne is most likely the result of the fact that putting on women's clothing is traditionally related to gender role change—as in other Plains tribes which had the "berdache" institution. It disappeared in proportion to the degree to which the pressure of the "White" culture became stronger and stronger, until finally—with the end of the traditional way of life—the foundations of the institution as such had also crumbled. (Most of the Prairie and Plains tribes had been driven onto reservations by 1878 at the latest; see Lindig and Münzel 1976:110; on the Cheyenne, see Brown 1974: 323ff.; Sitting Bull and his Lakotas surrendered July 19, 1881.) With the recent reawakening of the conscious awareness of tradition in the context of the American Indian Movement, institutionalized gender role change apparently has also been revived in some places, although it is likely that it survived in a less formal gestalt. While the American Indian Movement has been instrumental in reestablishing Native Americans' ethnic consciousness and pride, it has the reputation of not being gay-friendly itself, according to what Native American gays and lesbians told me during my 1992–1993 fieldwork.

NEW SELF-DEFINITION AS "HOMOSEXUAL": MOHAVE

In contrast to such continuation of the woman-man tradition, a certain Mohave of the 1960s defined himself as "gay" rather than *alyha* (Waltrip

1985:327ff.). In 1964 he lived on the Colorado River Reservation with his 83-year-old aunt. He was known generally as "homosexual" and was regarded by the local Whites as a kind of village idiot (1985:328). His fellow tribesmen treated him much like the Hare treated the feminine male described above. They made erotic jokes both with him and about him, and some also entered into short-term sexual relations with him (1985:328). He made his livelihood by making belts embroidered with beadwork, a feminine activity which he had learned from his aunt (1985:328). Aside from this, he appeared as a Bird Dancer; in this dance, performed by a man and several women (1985:328), the "homosexual" Mohave apparently danced in the man's role (see photo, 1985:331). In addition to this, he made necklaces, bolo ties, traditional cradle boards for infants, ceramics, and dolls (imitations of the ceremonial dolls used in the traditional cult of the dead; 1985:329) for the local arts-and-crafts market. This had also been taught to him by his aunt, who had a strong personality and was knowledgeable regarding the traditions (1985:329). As in the case of the Lakota *winkte,* a pronounced awareness of tradition as the outstanding personality trait of the woman-man is markedly noticeable: "It seems like I'm the only one that's keeping these traditions alive" (1985:329). However, a simultaneous identification with traditionally common patterns of gender role change is missing. In this connection, it may be significant that, in contrast to the *winkte*, the *alyha* had already succumbed to culture contact by Devereux's time (see Devereux 1937:498).

The last "real," old-time *alyha* and *hwame* must have died shortly after the turn of the century (Devereux 1937:521, 523); by Devereux's time, *alyha* and *hwame* had already ceased to transvest (1937:509). For the modern Mohave "homosexual" born around 1927, no incorporation into continuously passed-on models of role and status was possible. All that remained was a cultural acceptance of feminine behavior in males. Devereux mentioned that, although the Mohave institution of *alyha* had disappeared by the 1930s (the last singers who could hold the initiation had died at an advanced age; Devereux 1937:501), there were no prejudicial restrictions with regard to "homosexuality," although no "avowed homosexual" lived on the reservation (1937:498). This attitude was maintained into the 1960s, despite the disappearance of institutionalized gender role change: "The Indian boys tease each other about sleeping with him, yet their teasing is somehow not ridicule of him. Among the Indians he is accepted with equanimity, and their laughter is as much at themselves as at him" (Waltrip 1985:328). Thus, acceptance by his fellow tribe members made it possible for him to remain integrated within traditional cultural elements which had been preserved (Bird Dance), and also gave him the opportunity to pursue women's artistic handiwork while remaining incorporated in a circle of Native American friends (Waltrip 1985:331). That the White population regarded him as a nonthreatening "village idiot" is also likely to have given him considerable latitude for the practice of his role as a feminine male.

ACCESS TO NONTRADITIONAL AREAS OF WORK

After the collapse of the institution of gender role change, other feminine males sought opportunities for themselves outside of the traditional tribal structure which would accommodate their feminine interests. Kasinelu, the last "real" *lhamana,* was still alive in Zuni in 1938 (Parsons 1939a: 338; see Figure 3). After the death of Wewha, the two other surviving *lhamana* died in 1918 and 1937, respectively; during the preceding twenty years, only a single boy had shown tendencies toward becoming *lhamana.*

Stevenson (1904) reported that the *lhamana* were still esteemed, but even in her time there were signs of a change which possibly only Wewha's energetic personality could delay for any length of time. Earlier, it had been customary not to hinder boys in their decision to become *lhamana* (Parsons 1916:526; see also Gifford 1940:163). Stevenson stated, however, that Kasinelu's grandfather Naiuchi, who was a prominent figure in the Zuni priestly class, attempted with all available means to stop him from assuming the status of *lhamana,* even though his mother and grandmother would have liked to see a *lhamana* in their household (Stevenson 1904:38). This was in 1896, and probably after the death of Naiuchi in 1904 (1904:313), Kasinelu finally—as an adult—did ultimately put on women's clothes and assume the status of *lhamana* (1904:38). Shortly before the turn of the century, two additional males, who probably encountered less opposition from their families, did the same (1904:38). These must have been U'k, who died in 1937 at about the age of sixty, and Tsalatitsa, who died "in middle age" in 1918 (Parsons 1939a:339). These three males, who in 1916 were between their late thirties and early forties (Parsons 1916:521), were the last ones at Zuni who undertook a gender role change. This decline is without any doubt to be attributed to external influences and increasing acculturation (Parsons 1939a:338). Thus, there was no institutionalized form of gender role change available to Laspeke, the last boy who showed unambiguously feminine inclinations. Around 1916, the six-year-old was wearing boys' clothes, but with a long shirt over his trousers, a necklace, and a boy's haircut. He always played with girls and used feminine expressions and exclamations (Parsons 1916:521f.). In 1918 he was carrying his little sister in a cloth slung over his shoulder, as women and girls did (Parsons 1939a:338). He later attended an Indian boarding school, and finally chose a vocation which accommodated his feminine interests—as a "cook to an American roadmaking labor gang—another way of doing women's work!" (Parsons 1939a:338).

What is striking here is the fact that the *lhamana* obviously were dispensable in the ritual system of Zuni, in contrast to the Hidatsa example cited above. In 1915, the role of the *ko'thlama* was danced by a woman, even though three *lhamana* of the appropriate age were available (Parsons 1916:525). In contrast to the *miati,* other ceremonial tasks did not devolve on the *lhamana* (1916:524). The *lhamana* lacked the supernatural legitimization, the categorization as a "Holy Person," which the *miati* received. The only justification for the existence of the institution of the woman-man in Zuni was to enable males to practice feminine occupations within the framework of a special status. In contrast to institutionalized gender role change, the ritual system in Zuni persisted for many years, and the *lhamana* were not needed to obtain the clay for the visibly flourishing production of pottery. This suggests the possibility that males who earlier would have become *lhamana* could well have broken into the traditionally feminine domain of pottery in recent decades. In the meantime, men in other pueblos have made names for themselves as potters, although these neither were, nor are, women-men. Whether feminine males in Zuni today are active as potters alongside women is not known; some traditional *lhamana* were excellent potters (Parsons 1916:523; Stevenson 1904:37).

During the 1930s, two males of the Prairie Potawatomi, like Laspeke above, were seeking alternative opportunities for living out their feminine personality traits. These males had been introduced to Landes by members of the village community as potential *m'netokwe,* but they were deterred by culture change (Landes 1970:197f.). Both had grown up in strongly traditional family circumstances, one with his mother, who was a respected medicine woman in a family which supported his feminine interests. Landes did not mention how he earned his living. He spent his leisure time, however, having a female relative instruct him in beadwork (1970:197). Beadwork was traditionally a specialist occupation at which *m'netokwe* were especially expert (1970:26, 316). The second young man preferred to spend his time with another old medicine woman and worked as a grade school teacher. "He loved to care for the school children, to advise their parents, and to scrub the schoolhouse till it shone" (1970:197). His final aspiration, however, was to study medicine (1970:197). Both males distinguished themselves by their feminine interests and by imitating feminine ways of moving and of speaking, especially the teacher: "He walks like a [Potawatomi] woman, he talks like one, he likes housekeeping" (Landes' female consultant, 1970:197). Although he was supported by his aged protectress, his feminine mannerisms did not elicit enthusiastic support from all members of the tribe. However, the feminine inclinations of the two males provoked no more hostility than had those of Yellow Belly a generation before, when the institution of *m'netokwe* had already disappeared but was still remembered within the community (1970:196). Yellow Belly's employers, who were acculturated to White customs, approved of his metamorphosis only to a limited extent, but they did accept it, and the acceptance was greater by far among the tradition-oriented Potawatomis:

> "He is m'netokwe, something unusual. If (this female man) lived with us Indians, instead of you who are like Whites, and if (he-she) had learned the Indian ways, then we would have heard something extraordinary from the (creature)." (Old Potawatomi woman to Landes' consultant, who had been one of the daughters in the household mentioned above; Landes 1970: 186. Parentheses in the original.)

As Landes correctly explained, "berdache"/*m'netokwe* was definitely still functioning as a concept at that time (1970:197). Whether the two young males—who in the 1930s were looked up to as potential *m'netokwe*—did not put on women's clothes only because their social milieu was not as favorable as Yellow Belly's had been in his acculturated but tradition-oriented family and because their interests in feminine artistic handiwork were not as fully developed, is questionable (1970: 202). It seems more probable that, although the concept "m'netokwe" was still available, the institution itself—as Landes speculated elsewhere—in actual fact "could not survive fundamentalists' outrage in the general American world" (1970:316). Again, the conceptual equation of effeminate males with male homosexuals in the sociocultural milieu of Anglo-American everyday life, as well as the strongly negative attitude of both the White population and White legislation toward homosexuality (see Katz 1985), probably outweighed the at least tolerant attitude of their own group, in which effeminacy and interest in feminine tasks were not punished.

TRANSITIONAL PHASE BEFORE THE DISAPPEARANCE OF INSTITUTIONALIZED GENDER ROLE CHANGE

Both the Kutenai and the Klamath feminine males who, contrary to traditional custom, no longer wore women's clothes, should be seen as part of a transitional phase preceding the final disappearance of institutionalized gender role change. "Justine" (Kutenai), who was already very old in 1890, wore a combination of men's and women's clothing—a woman's dress with a man's leggings under it (Schaeffer 1965:218). She imitated the feminine way of speaking and sitting, but wore her hair cut short. She spent her time with the women, picked berries, and dug for roots. The Kutenai accepted her, and warm relationships bound her to a female relative and to the latter's husband, with whom she lived (1965:218).

Cross-dressing was likewise traditionally common among the Klamath. Spier (1930:51) was told by one consultant of five "berdaches" *(tw!inna'ek),* although it is not clear whether any of them were still alive at the time of his investigation. Another consultant of Spier's—the only *tw!inna'ek* whom he personally met—was a male in his sixties, who out of fear of an old female shaman had undertaken a gender role change with cross-dressing when he was sixteen; his cross-dressing, however, was retained only for a short time (1930:52). But he remained feminine and also persisted in doing feminine tasks (cooking and making baskets for sale), as well as engaging in feminine characteristics of speech and movement (1930:52). Apart from the traditional feminine task of basket weaving, he showed himself to be a traditionalist in that he was the only person who still wore a basket hat (1930:52).

CONCLUSIONS

In the vast majority of cases, cross-acting without cross-dressing represents a transitional form of gender role change: the institution of woman-man is disappearing, but is not yet forgotten. Increasing influences from the dominant "White" culture make the continued open existence of this institution impossible, and simultaneously lead to the increasing acculturation of younger tribal members, who, for example, in the context of their schooling to varying degrees adopt Anglo-American values and moral ideas. This process has partly been reversed in the course of the rise of the American Indian Movement since 1968 (Lindig and Münzel 1976:114ff.). Thus, for example, among the Lakota, with the strengthening of ethnic self-awareness, the *winkte* had regained respect in at least some communities when Williams conducted his interviews in 1982. This revival of the institution of *winkte* was only possible, however, because it had had a continuing existence throughout the years, however altered in its standing and its performance. A similar situation can be assumed for the Hare, among whom, to be sure, not a continuous but at least a situationally bound gender role change has been possible for feminine males in more recent times. In other cases, the woman-man institution had disappeared by the 1930s at the latest, after the institution had become invisible (cross-acting but no cross-dressing). Feminine males occasionally chose occupational areas within "female" areas of work, but usually outside of their tribal community. Coercive attempts on the part of White government officials to force feminine males into men's clothes and into a masculine role played a lesser part in this change than the gradual process of acculturation and the disappearance of those cultural elements in which women-men had filled fixed social roles.

By contrast, among the Paiute and Shoshoni groups of the Great Basin, gender role change existed in both forms (with and without cross-dressing) at the same time, at least in the 1930s, when the pertinent investigations were conducted for the *Anthropological Records*. The less fully developed kind of institutionalization in this region, in which gender role change of every degree and infertility of both sexes were subsumed under one higher category—that of the "infertile" or sterile individual—suggests the conclusion that gender role change both with and without cross-dressing was traditional there.

This variability notwithstanding, there are clues that the higher category *tübasa* was formed from subcategories which definitely contain differentiation and include traditional cross-dressing for women-men. The Southern Paiute called a male who was taking on a female role component *maipots* (Shivwits, Lowie 1924:282). Stewart (1942:352) reported the same designation from the same tribe for a woman-man in women's clothes. Another Southern Paiute group designated infertile persons as *tuvasawö,* but transvesting women-men as *onobakö* (Stewart 1942: 352). The Northern Paiute called transvesting males who crossed out of the masculine gender role *tüdayapi,* "dress like other sex" (Steward 1933:238); the Northern Shoshoni, it is true, designated both women-men and infertile persons identically as *tübasa,* but in addition to this they had available separate designations for both women-men and men-women (Steward 1943:385). Finally, the Nevada Shoshoni called women-men "half man, half woman" (Steward 1941:353), or *waip: siŋwa,* "half woman" (Steward 1941:353). Thus, the terms varied from group to group, but in every case the woman-man existed as a (sub)category distinct from "sterile," which frequently—but not always—indicated cross-dressing. The higher category designates infertility, while the lower category more closely characterizing the woman-man describes a mixture of male and female characteristics which are expressed in the pertinent individuals, and do not—as in other tribes—constitute an approximation to the other sex (e.g., *winkte,* "would-be woman," W. K. Powers 1977:58; *miati,* "to be compelled against his will to act the woman," Dorsey 1894:517; "woman pretender," Osgood 1958:261; *kupatke'tek,* "imitate a woman," Schaeffer 1965:218). Such a mixture could be expressed in a mere fondness for feminine activities without cross-dressing, as in a complete gender role change.

We should not, however, exclude the possibility that in this case, too, the sources were describing a transitional phase in which cross-acting began to replace complete gender role change. It is striking that the examples of cross-dressing in combination with cross-acting which were recalled by consultants in the 1930s already belonged to the past (Steward 1933:228; Lowie 1924:283, the example refers to 1894; Stewart 1941:440, "once saw a Kuyui man," "knew of a . . . man who wore dresses"; Steward 1941:353, "saw a Lida Shoshoni man . . . who dressed like a woman"; Steward 1943:385, "only one case in which a man . . . dressed like a woman."). Thus, the very different, but all general, "yes" and "no" answers given by the consultants of different groups in response to the question concerning cross-dressing may reflect at times *normative,* at times *factual,* componential organizations and manifestations of gender role change. If the consultants denied cross-dressing, then they were taking the actual situation at the time of the ethnographic interview as the basis; if they affirmed it, then they were orienting themselves on the traditional norms relevant to the woman-man status, even though these norms were often not adhered to by the 1920s and 1930s.

The literature on the Arctic and Subarctic groups taken up—although with reservations—in this chapter gives no particulars concerning a possible historical change in the institution of gender role change.

Among the Kwakiutl of the Northwest Coast, the feminine male was the "norm," whereas the one who at the same time transvested appears to have been the exception. Nowhere else does gender role change appear to have been so little tied to formal rules; thus, one can speak less of an institution per se than of distinctive possibilities for individual personality development. The spectrum extends from "Frances" through feminine males in a feminine role to the highly respected song maker and story teller who loved feminine jewelry and masculine men, but was married (Ford 1941:131). The basic underlying category which led to the Kwakiutl lumping these males together becomes evident from the text: Ford's consultant begins with "Frances," proceeds to nontransvesting males in feminine roles, then on to the story teller, and finally to men who have never touched their wives or who were "afraid" of women (1941:129ff). Common to all of these is that they avoided sexual contact with women and most of them showed some degree of effeminization. In addition, homosexual contacts during boyhood were quite usual (1941:68), and Frances was desired by the young men as a sexual partner (even though they were aware of "her" biological maleness), suggesting that the traditional acceptance by the Kwakiutl ranged widely, without any standardized form of legitimization for any of these phenomena. The difference between a heterosexual man who also sought male sex partners and a male who defined himself in terms of a completely feminine gender role and had exclusively male partners was seen by the Kwakiutl quantitatively and not qualitatively. This stands in contrast to the Lakota, who distinguished *winkte* and "gays" qualitatively from each other: *winkte,* endowed with spiritual potential, held an institutionalized status and enjoyed the respect of the community, whereas "gays," who had not taken a woman's role and who had not been granted the special power of a *winkte,* possessed no special status (Williams 1986a: 193, 195f.). The Kwakiutl, meanwhile, did not institutionalize homosexual behavior or "homosexuality," but instead institutionalized the possibility of avoiding masculine role norms, whether in the area of partner choice or occupations.

Whether the absence of cross-dressing has to do with a transitional phase or with a traditional juxtaposition of gender role change both with and without cross-dressing, all of these examples show that cross-dressing is not an indispensable element of gender role change. Quite obviously, the status of woman-man is assigned to a male primarily because he is feminine in his public persona and because he is interested in feminine occupations and activities and in feminine artistic handiwork. Women's clothing provides additional external proof of this, but is dispensable, especially when, under the pressure of White culture and law, it became necessary to make the women-men invisible to outsiders. The componential organization of a woman-man's social role was independent of whether or not he wore women's clothes. Further, in the traditionally small Native American tribal communities, people would have known whether a male had taken on the woman-man status regardless of cross-dressing, which also suggests that cross-dressing was a dispensable aspect of the woman-man status. Finally, other opportunities for signaling their femininity or nonmasculinity were open to women-men. These are the subject of the next chapter.

Chapter EIGHT

THE IMITATION OF "FEMININITY" AND INTERSEXUALITY

THE IMITATION OF "FEMININITY"

MIMICRY, GESTURE, AND LANGUAGE

In addition to the adoption of women's activities and the donning of women's clothing, it has also been frequently reported that women-men generally "behaved like women." The sources go into varying degrees of detail in regard to this. The most general statements maintain that within the framework of a gender role change, males "act like women" or had women's "manners," or that they "behave like members of the opposite sex" (Aleuts, Dall 1897:402; Crow, Simms 1903:580; Oglala Lakota, Lame Deer 1979:169; Dakota in general, Dorsey 1894:467; Holder 1889:623; Flathead, Teit 1930:384; Hidatsa, Holder 1889:623; Lillooet, Teit 1906:267; Maricopa, Spier 1933:242; Miami, Trowbridge 1938:68; Modoc, Ray 1963:43; Navajo, Reichard 1928:150; Nomlaki, Goldschmidt 1951:387; Ojibwa, Henry 1897, 1:163; Skinner 1911:151; Kinietz 1947:155; Omaha, Dorsey 1894:378; Skidi Pawnee, Dorsey and Murie 1940:108; Shivwits Paiute, Lowie 1924:282; Wind River Shoshoni, Shimkin 1947:298; Nevada Shoshoni, Steward 1941:353; Thompson, Teit 1900:321; Winnebago, Lurie 1953:710).

When this feminine behavior was specified further, the authors frequently mentioned that the female pitch of the voice was imitated—in the pueblo of the Acoma (Hammond 1882:346), among the Cheyenne (Grinnell 1962, 2:39, voice between male and female), Crow (Holder 1889:623), Flathead (Turney-High 1937:85), Hare (Broch 1977:97, "high-pitched laughter"), Klamath (Spier 1930:52), Laguna (Hammond 1882:346), Navajo (Hill 1935:273; Reichard 1928:150), Ojibwa (Kinietz 1947:156; McKenney 1972:259), Piegan (Schaeffer 1965:223), Prairie Potawatomi (Landes 1970:199), Quinault (Olson 1936:

99), and Yuki (Foster 1944:186; Kroeber 1925:180). The characterization of the voice pitch of the *heemaneh'* in Cheyenne society as between male and female suggests that it was less a matter of copying the female voice perfectly than of having one's own voice sound nonmasculine, which corresponds to the ambivalent status.

Where the language contained specifically feminine expressions, or where the kinship terminology differed according to the sex of the speaker, women-men frequently also adopted these "female" forms of speech. Thus, Lakota *winkte* spoke in "women's dialect" (Williams 1986a:195) and used feminine "terms of address" (Mirsky 1937a:417). Among the Santee Dakota, women-men likewise made use of feminine "forms of speech" (Landes 1968:112). The same thing was reported from the Osage (Fletcher and La Flesche 1911:132). Piegan Woman used specifically feminine exclamations (e.g., *Kyaiyo* [Oh me!] and *Kiye* [Oh gracious]; Schaeffer 1965:223). Among the Pima, feminine males customarily "expressed themselves" like members of the opposite sex (Hill 1938b:339). When s/he spoke Potawatomi, Yellow Belly (Louise) used the women's form of the language (Landes 1970:199). In Zuni, mastery of feminine speech forms was such an important part of the *lhamana*'s role that people laughed at an apparently somewhat feebleminded *lhamana* behind her back because she always "goes on talking like a man, she says ikina (younger sister, man speaking) instead of hani (younger sister, woman speaking)" (Parsons 1923:166, n. 5). The six-year-old Laspeke, on the other hand, had such a command of the feminine expressions, exclamations, and turns of speech that people admitted of him, "He talks like a girl" (Parsons 1916:522). Among the Assiniboine, the *winktan* likewise used the affirmative and imperative particles specific to women's language (Lowie 1909:42). A modern Hopi woman-man "consistently uses 'feminine talk' forms. . . . This is especially obvious in the frequent tongue smack. . . . Also, his inflection pattern is definitely female speech" (Williams 1986b:52).

A number of sources merely stated that women-men "talked like women," not specifying whether speech mannerisms, speech forms, and/or voice pitch are meant (Acoma, L. A. White 1943:325; Cocopa, Gifford 1933:294; Illinois, Liette 1962:112, "imitate their accent, which is different from that of men"; Klamath, Spier 1930:51; Kutenai, Schaeffer 1965:218, "woman's way of speaking"; Laguna, Parsons 1932:246; Mohave, Kroeber 1925:749; Nisenan, Beals 1933:376; Osage and Omaha, Fletcher and La Flesche 1911:132, "speak as a woman"; Omaha, Dorsey 1894:378, "speaking just as Indian women used to do"; San Felipe, Parsons 1932:247). One consultant reported to Spier (1930:51) of a Klamath *tw!inna'ek* that he had "tried to laugh like a woman," and Kroeber mentioned that Mohave *alyha* laughed and smiled "like women" (1925:749). The "high-pitched laughter" of the feminine Hare young man (Broch 1977:97) similarly indicates imitation of feminine laughing habits, just like the behavior of a Yuma male who, after a dream concerning women's work, awoke and "put his hand to his mouth and laughed four times. He laughed with a woman's voice and his mind was changed from male into female. Other young people noticed this and began to feel towards him as to a woman" (Forde 1931:157). Among the modes of feminine behavior taken on by women-men is also included gesticulations which a culture assigns as specifically feminine, and which has been reported from the Hare (Broch 1977:97), the Klamath (Spier 1930:52), and from Laguna (Hammond 1882:346). Among the Potawatomi, *m'netokwe* assumed a manner of walking which was typical of women (Landes 1970:199, "short steps"); similar phenomena were reported for Flathead (Turney-High 1937:85, "swaying hips"), Klamath (Spier 1930:52), Kwakiutl (Ford 1941:131), Luiseño (Boscana 1846:383), Ojibwa (Kinietz 1947:259, "turn in the toes"; McKenney 1972:259); and the proper women's way of sitting was found among the Kutenai (Schaeffer 1965:218), Mohave (Kroeber 1925:749), Navajo (Hill 1935:275; Reichard 1928:150), Pima (Hill 1938b:339), and Quinault (Olson 1936:99).

In addition to these forms of bodily expression, another set of behavior patterns defined by the relevant Native American cultures as specifically feminine was adopted by women-men. Among the Santee Dakota, *winkta* exhibited "the fears of water and of bodily exposure" regarded as typically feminine (Landes 1968:112), as well as feminine "coquetteries"—not specified in any more detail (Landes 1968:112). The young Hare feminine male threw sticks at muskrats (in order to drive them out of the camp) with movements "like a girl" (Broch 1977:98). Ingalik "women pretenders" adopted the "sweetness and reticence attributed to some women" (Osgood 1958:262). A woman-man from San Felipe behaved "shy like a girl" when he—dressed in women's clothes—visited women friends (Parsons 1932:247). A Kwakiutl feminine male showed a "feminine" way of throwing when playing ball, and split wood "like a woman" (Ford 1941:131). The Potawatomi Yellow Belly (or Louise) mastered the "White" feminine gender role to perfection; she never went out alone with a man, she danced like a woman (with male partners), flirted with young men like a "boy-struck girl," rode horses sidesaddle, didn't swear, didn't drink, didn't smoke, and didn't chew tobacco (Landes 1970:198ff.). Piegan Woman loved (women's) jewelry (Schaeffer 1965:223), as did the feminine Kwakiutl story teller, who otherwise did not transvest, even though "the way his body acts is like a woman" (consultant in Ford 1941:131): "He has earrings on his ears—women's earrings—and all kinds of women's brooches on both sides of his breast, and wore women's rings" (consultant in Ford 1941:131).

External Appearance: Hairstyle and Body Decoration

In most parts of North America, the sexes were distinguished not only by clothing, but also by hairstyle. In the East and on the Central Plains, the men shaved their heads, leaving only some parts to form a pattern, or a line of hair standing from front to back through the middle, to which the roached headdress (made from porcupine and deer hair) was attached (see Driver and Massey 1957:325, Map 113). It has been reported for a number of groups that women-men wore their hair long—the Choctaw (Bossu 1962:169), Illinois (Liette 1962:112), Kansa (James 1823:129), Osage (Fletcher and La Flesche 1911:132), Klamath (Spier 1930:52), and Kwakiutl (Ford 1941:129). In the latter two groups, the men did not shave their heads but did wear their hair shorter than the women did. In other cases, both sexes wore their hair long, but had different hairdos or decorated the hair differently (see, e.g., Catlin 1926, re the hairstyles on the Plains, the Crow men's pride concerning their hair, and the hairstyle of the women of the Crow and other tribes). Holder (1889:623) mentioned that the Crow *bate* whom he examined had his hair parted in the middle, like the women, and braided. Flathead *ma'kali* also wore their hair after the manner of women (Teit 1930:384). One photo (Scherer 1975:163; see Figure 2 of the present book) shows that Wewha also imitated the hairstyle of the Zuni women—as all *lhamana* surely did (see also Stevenson 1904, Plate 94). Piegan Woman wore her hair "women's style" (Schaeffer 1965:223), and so did Louise, who in addition had a fondness for decorative combs (Landes 1970:199). Yuki *iwap-naip* also parted their hair in the middle, after the pattern of the women (Foster 1944:186).

A liking for women's jewelry has already been reported from the Prairie Potawatomi (Landes 1970:199), Piegan (Schaeffer 1965:223), Kwakiutl (Ford 1941:131), and Winnebago (Lurie 1953:710), but was certainly not restricted to women-men of these tribes.

Tattooing was widespread, in some cases restricted to women (e.g., Yurok, Yuki) and in other cases existing in different patterns for both sexes (e.g., Ojibwa, Mohave). Unfortunately, only in very few cases have the sources specified whether women-men were tattooed in the manner of women. The Aleut *shupans* were, like the women, tattooed on the chin (Bancroft 1874:92, n. 129). Furthermore, after puberty they plucked out the hairs of the beard, which—in contrast to other North American groups—was not customary among the Eskimo, Aleut, and tribes of the Northwest Coast (see, e.g., the photographs in Scherer 1975 and in Curtis Graybill and Boesen 1979). The women-men among the Illinois were adorned with tattoos on the cheeks, just as the women were, but also had tattoos on the chest and the arms (Liette 1962:112). The Mohave *alyha* also received the tattoos which otherwise were reserved to women (Devereux 1937:501). The Pomo *das* (Essene 1942:31) and the Yuki *iwap-naip* (Kroeber 1925:180; S. Powers 1877:132) were embellished with women's tattoos. However, tattoos were denied to the *elha* of the Cocopa, who also did not have the nasal septum pierced through, as did the men (Gifford 1933:294); this was also true in the case of the Kato and Lassik women-men (Essene 1942:31).

At least in the Cocopa example, this carried with it far-reaching consequences for the individual, because one's fate after death was related to the tattooing or piercing of the nasal septum (Gifford 1933:291); this was also true for the Mohave (Kroeber 1925:279). In other cases, the consequences of not being tattooed were less serious. A Yurok explained the custom in these terms: "an untattooed woman looks like a man when she grows old" (Kroeber 1925:78); the style of tattooing on the female chin practiced among them was widespread in northwest California (Kroeber 1925:77), where gender role change was also found almost universally.

Tattooing—for women only, or differently formed depending on sex—occurred among the following California tribes where male gender role change was also found, as well as among most groups in California to varying degrees (Kroeber 1925:808): Yurok (Kroeber 1925:77; the following page citations from Kroeber refer to tattooing), Sinkyone (Kroeber 1925:146), Yuki (Kroeber 1925:173), Shasta (Kroeber 1925:293), Achomawi (Kroeber 1925:311), Wintun (Kroeber 1925:357), Maidu (Kroeber 1925:406), Costanoan (Kroeber 1925:467), Yokuts (Kroeber 1925:519f.), Juaneño (Kroeber 1925:641, 675), Diegueño (Kroeber 1925:721), and Mohave (Kroeber 1925:729).

One possible explanation for the absence of tattooing on the part of women-men is that, in some regions, this form of body decoration was applied within the context of a girl's puberty ceremony. On the central North Pacific coast, the girl, after her time of seclusion, was tattooed on her wrists and her legs (Driver 1941:26). In Northern California, by contrast, tattooing was not performed within the framework of the elaborate puberty ceremony (1941:35), and in Southern California it was only occasionally performed during this ceremony (1941:35) because separate group ceremonies existed there which were specifically related to the tattooing of children (1941:36). On these occasions, both the ears and the nasal septum were pierced, too. In other regions in which puberty ceremonies for girls were held (see Driver 1941:32ff.), tattooing was either not usual, or was independent of the ceremonies. Consequently, wherever either the tattooing of women was performed in connection with female puberty rites or it was supposed that a girl had already undergone these, it is unlikely that women-men were adorned with tattoos. Instead, because of the absence of menarche, this ceremony was not even considered for them.

Wherever a woman or a girl could have herself tattooed at any point in her life if she wanted to, tattooing was probably also open to women-men. The fact that female tattooing of women-men was denied for three groups and was not mentioned in other cases, however, may also be because the status of woman-man was so different from that of women that the acquisition of women's tattoos by women-men did not even arise as a possibility, and it may not even have been considered by the women-men themselves. Meanwhile, where men and women wore different tattoos, and where men pierced the septum, but women received tattoos instead (e.g., Achomawi, Kroeber 1925:311; Maidu, Kroeber 1925:406), the lack of any kind of body decoration may very well have designated the gender status of the woman-man as neither masculine nor feminine. The Mohave and the Pomo, on the other hand, pierced the nasal septum of the men (Kroeber 1925, Plate 65; Kroeber 1925:240) and also tattooed women-men with feminine patterns; the men also wore tattoos (1925:729ff.). In connection with this, however, the scanty nature of the sources does not exclude the possibility that women-men elsewhere had themselves tattooed as an expression of their feminine gender role, too, and that this practice is not reflected in the sources.

Tattooed women-men seem to have made an extraordinarily strong adaptation to the feminine gender role. Mohave *alyha,* for example, copied femaleness even to the extent of imitating physiological aspects (Devereux 1937:511f.); the Pomo *das* sometimes cried like babies in order to make people believe that they had given birth to a child (Essene 1942:65), and Aleut *shupans,* who were raised as girls from infancy, imitated women so perfectly that outsiders were not able to tell the difference (Dall 1897:402f.). The women-men among the Illinois also strived for such perfection ("omit nothing that can make them like women," Liette 1962:113). These examples suggest that a specifically cultural element such as women's tattooing was seized upon in the context of a more or less complete gender role change.

The Imitation of Female Physiology

Elements of female physiology which were either imitated or claimed for themselves by women-men include menstruation, pregnancy, childbirth, and nursing, as well as external sexual characteristics such as the presence of female genitalia and breasts. Examples of actual intersexuality do not belong in this context, and therefore are discussed in a separate section (see below, "Intersexuality").

Examples of the imitation of female physiology and bodily functions by women-men are rare. Under the heading "Berdaches," the *Anthropological Records* reported a "belief that [male "berdaches"] may become pregnant" for a local group of the Southern Paiute and also for two local Ute groups (Stewart 1942:298), without giving more information. In all three cases, cross-dressing together with performance of feminine activities by women-men was specified, and in one of the Ute groups, also marriage with a man (1942:298). Because the statement "male berdache has female organs" is generally denied (1942: 332), it is improbable that intersexes were involved. At the same time, it is not altogether clear just how—in the pertinent groups—a pregnancy on the part of a woman-man who lacked "female organs" occurred. Furthermore, the term *tuvasawuts/tuvasawits* (Lowie 1924:382; Stewart 1942:352) among the Ute and *tuvasawuts* among the Southern Paiute (Stewart 1942:352) contains the morpheme *tuvasa/tübasa* (sterile, infertile), noted earlier in relation to the "sterility" criterion for women-men. Lowie's (1924:282f.) Southern Ute consultant mentioned no possibility of pregnancy on the part of women-men. Thus, a possible misunderstanding with respect to the information given by Stewart cannot be discounted. This could have occurred because Paiutes and Utes not infrequently classified women-men and infertile persons of both sexes under the term *tuvasa,* even though an infertile woman—unlike a woman-man—can certainly become pregnant under some circumstances. Thus, information pertaining to infertile women would have been entered under the rubric "Berdache." Meanwhile, just in case the information from the consultant actually did in fact refer to women-men, it could also have referred to a phenomenon encountered among the Mohave and Pomo, namely the simulation of pregnancy and/or childbirth. This was culturally integrated into the role of woman-man, a kind of behavior which is quite possible in other groups as well.

Whereas the *das* among the Pomo restricted themselves to imitating a baby's crying in order to make their fellow humans believe that they had given birth (Essene 1942:65), Mohave *alyha* imitated the entire physiological pattern of a woman (Devereux 1937:510). They insisted on the equivalent female designations for their genitals; their penis *(modar)* had to be called "clitoris" *(havalik),* and their testicles *(hama)* had to be called "labia maiora" *(havakwit)* (1937:510). As Devereux (1937:510) remarked, it is noteworthy that the penis and clitoris as well as scrotum and labia are actually developmental-biological equivalents, and are undifferentiated in the fetus until the sixteenth week of gestation, when they begin to develop into either the female or the male external genitals (see also Walter 1978:9). The *alyha* had their anus *(hivey)* called "vagina" *(hithpan)* (1937:510). Joking which disregarded this terminology could have painful consequences for the joker (1937:510).

In spite of female designations for their genitals, the sexual reactions of the *alyha* naturally remained those of males, and erections caused them great embarrassment:

> You may play with the penis of your [*alyha*] wife when it is flaccid. I often did, saying, 'Your cunnus is so nice and big and your pubic hair is nice and soft to touch'. Then my alyha wife would loll about, giggling happily . . . she liked to be told about her cunnus. When alyha get an erection, it embarrasses them, because the penis sticks out between the loose fibers of the bark-skirt. They used to have erections when we had intercourse. Then I would put my arm around them and play with the erect penis, even though they hated it. (Consultant in Devereux 1937:511)

If an *alyha* found a husband, she simulated menstruation by scratching her thighs until they bled. She then submitted to all of the puberty regulations prescribed for girls, and afterward followed the rules obtaining for the days of menstruation each month (Devereux 1937:511). The husband correspondingly had to observe the Mohave customs pertaining to the first menstruation, and similarly had to abide by all of the regulations which the culture applied to him (1937:512).

The simulation of pregnancy by *alyha* likewise followed the culturally prescribed patterns. The feigned menstruations were no longer produced, and the *alyha* and her husband complied with the usual taboos surrounding pregnancy, with the *alyha* being more strict than biological women, even taking into account otherwise obsolete taboos (1937:512). In contrast to most Mohave women, *alyha* boasted about their "pregnancy," but continued to have both oral and anal intercourse with their partners, which in the case of biological women was regarded as harmful to the fetus (1937:512). They stuffed pieces of cloth and bark under their dresses, and then concocted a strong purgative. After one or two days of severe abdominal cramps—which the *alyha* referred to as labor pains—they went into the woods, took the squatting position of women in childbirth, and emptied their intestines over a hole. After burying this "stillbirth" (1937:512), they went home and began to mourn the stillborn child (1937:512f.). In the meantime, the husband was primarily the one who had to bear the brunt of the derisive commentary, and the Mohave were keen on mockery and ridicule:

> People used to tease me about my wives' imaginary children . . . they would kick a pile of animal dung and say, 'These are your

> children.' And yet I had real children once and they died. Were they not dead they would now take care of me in my old age. (Kuwal, one of Devereux' consultants, who had been married to *alyha* and also to biological women; Devereux 1937:513)

Nowhere else did women-men probably come as close to the totality of a feminine gender role without gaining the feminine gender status. The initiation ceremony, in the course of which a woman's dress was put on a boy, did not make him into a "woman," but endowed him with the status of an *alyha* (Kroeber 1925:748). Devereux (1937:508) reported that "after the fourth song he is declared a homosexual." This is formulated incorrectly, though, because he was not declared a homosexual, but rather a woman-man/*alyha;* Devereux, however, uses "homosexual" and "*alyha*" synonymously. As the coarse jokes which Devereux repeatedly cited indicate, it is not a matter of a "shift from one sex to the other" (1937:509). The "shift" (to the other sex) was the complete fulfillment of the feminine role by the boy, who would then be established in his *alyha* status, but this did not constitute a shift from one sex to the other in Mohave categories of thought. From their standpoint, he was obviously a biological male in the clothing and social role of a woman. One did not court an *alyha* like one did a young girl whom one contemplated marrying (1937:513), and particularly during coitus, a man did not forget that his "wife" had male genitals. In spite of this, an *alyha* was rarely teased—"He was an alyha, he could not help it" (Devereux 1954:513). Her husband, though, could be teased, and frequently was.

Some general remarks are in order at this point regarding Devereux' estimation of the institution of women-men among the Mohave. Devereux was probably in error when he spoke of a "humoristically viewed homosexual cluster" in the context of institutionalized gender role change (Devereux 1937:507). The Mohave joked about sexual behavior of *every* kind, as Greenberg (1986:185) noted in comments about Devereux' (1951) investigations of Mohave humor. Devereux reasoned that *alyha* and *hwame* (men-women) were "humoristically viewed," and thus not taken seriously, on the basis that even though *alyha* were given appropriate feminine personal names, they were refused a feminine clan name (1937:507) and that, in the event of a marriage between a *hwame* and a biological woman, no change was made in the gentile affiliation of the child (1937:514). Devereux accounted for both these situations by stating that "gentile continuity is past joking" (1937:514). Most probably, however, these phenomena had less to do with "joking" than with practical matters regarding gender status and descent.

The Mohave took the *alyha* and the *hwame* much more seriously than Devereux' comments imply. The initiation ceremony for *alyha* as described by Devereux was in fact anything but humoristic. Rather, it was a serious effort to enable boys and males who had an obviously feminine or ambivalent gender identity to live out this identity in the framework of an elaborated copy of the feminine gender role and within a special gender status.

The Mohave's descent group system "comprises patrilinear, exogamous, nameless groups of totemic reference" (Kroeber 1925:741). All the women of a particular descent group carry a "clan" name in addition to a personal name (1925:741). With the possible exception of the rule of exogamy, this system played hardly any role at all in women's everyday life (1925:741)—or in the life of an *alyha.* The situation of a *hwame,* who could, to be sure, lay claim to the paternity of a child, but who could not pass on "his" descent group membership to that child, was more difficult.

The refusal of clan names and/or the heredity of descent group membership to *alyha* does not, however, seem to indicate so much that the descent group system was a cultural element which, to the Mohave, was "past joking." Instead, it seems much more to point to a very realistic way of viewing the limits of gender role change. A patrilineal transmission of descent group membership is based irreversibly on the biological reproduction of the members of this group. Neither *alyha* nor *hwame* shared in this means of reproducing the descent groups. They neither procreated nor gave birth. Their status was neither masculine nor feminine, but rather just *alyha* or *hwame.* In view of such a status, an alteration of the rights associated with the descent groups was out of the question. The imitation of female bodily functions by the *alyha* took place in the framework of precisely fixed cultural rules of the game. Neither the village community as a whole nor the *alyha* themselves assumed, therefore, that menstruation or pregnancy, for example, were actually being experienced by the *alyha.* What was in fact happening, from the naming of male genitals with female terminology to anal birth, so to speak, was a transference of female bodily functions onto a male physique, combined with a feminine gender role which was being played out to perfection.

Such a discrepancy between gender role and gender status—(which arises because status is at least co-dependent on biological factors which cannot be copied)—is also apparent in other Native American cultures and, in one case, was explicitly formulated. A female consultant of Gayton's among the Western Mono mentioned that women-men "dressed as women" and had "male consorts," but, she added, "they never had any babies" (Gayton 1948:274). It should be noted here that the Western Mono applied a common term, *tai'up,* both to males who had undergone a partial or total gender role change and to bachelors who had had no sexual intercourse with women (Gayton 1948:274). Thus, the

Mono provide another example of the higher category of infertility found among the Shoshoni-speaking groups. The remark by Gayton's consultant, however, clearly indicates that transvesting *tai'up,* despite a gender role change—*and in contrast to women*—could not become pregnant. The Navajo interviewed by Stewart (1942:298), when asked by him whether (male-bodied) *nadle* were able to become pregnant, also denied that this was possible.

Hammond reported a peculiar piece of information pertaining to the Laguna *mujerados.* A *mujerado* whom Hammond examined medically told him that he had nursed several children (Hammond 1882:344). According to Hammond's description, this was not a simple case of gender role change, but rather an obviously pathological bodily change which had led to atrophy of the genitals, a strong development of mammary glands, and to a change of the voice register (1882:344). (In view of the rarity of this kind of hormonal disturbance, it does seem odd that Hammond found two males in both of the neighboring pueblos of Acoma and Laguna who had undergone such a physical metamorphosis. His medical descriptions, however, are treated here as fundamentally accurate). At the time of the examination, the *mujerado* was forty-five years old, and had already been changed in the manner described for seven years. Before the change, his body and genitals were said to have been those of a normal male (1882:345). All of this suggests that a grave disturbance of the hormonal balance appeared in this male at the age of thirty-eight years. Hammond hypothesized that this genital atrophy (with general physical effeminization as the consequence) was artificially induced through excessive masturbation and excessive riding, but this explanation can be dismissed at once on medical grounds. According to more modern medical knowledge, effeminization might have been caused, for example, by a tumor (Pfäfflin 1987, written communication). Further, more recent information from Parsons (1918:181f.) suggests a completely different explanation of the genesis of the *mujerado* (see also Bandelier 1966:326, who visited the Pueblos in 1880–1882).

Hammond was strongly fixed on impotence as the topic of his investigation, and was imprisoned in nineteenth-century etiological models of this phenomenon. He claimed to have obtained his information concerning artificial effeminization through masturbation and riding "from authentic sources, including the subjects themselves" (1882:347). More recent cultural-anthropological knowledge, however, indicates that he may have been intentionally misinformed. Although the present work is a cultural-anthropological investigation, some medical aspects are of interest here, especially since there is some evidence that a distinction was also made in Laguna and in Acoma between physically effeminized *mujerados* and *kokwimu*—those who underwent a voluntary change of gender role. The results of research in the medical literature show that the cause of the effeminization—in particular that exhibited by the *mujerado* from Laguna whom Hammond examined—is to be sought in a grave hormonal disturbance, possibly evoked by a testicular or adrenal tumor. In regard to testicular tumors, for example, Overzier and Hoffmann (1961:411) described atrophied genitals, shriveled testes, hypospermia or aspermia (insufficient or absent sperm), reduction of libido and potency, and possibly a rise in the voice register, as well as gynecomasty, that is, a female development of the breasts—exactly the symptoms which the *mujerado* exhibited. Such hormonal disturbances can even lead to the formation of colostrum, or milk secretion, in males (1961:420). A similar picture is encountered in cases of adrenal or suprarenal tumors (1961:441f.). In the case of a benign tumor, this transformation can last for many years without any lethal consequences for the sufferer. Thus, the *mujerado*'s claim to have nursed several children cannot be supported by medical evidence. However, the possibility that he secreted milk cannot be dismissed. The alleged nursing, which the *mujerado* him/herself reported (Hammond 1882:344) may, on the other hand, have merely been an affirmation of his by all means very feminine overall appearance and bearing, and also of his feminine role; it is also possible that the *mujerado* had taken children to his well-developed breasts, which possibly did secrete small amounts of milk. In contrast to the simulations of menstruation and pregnancy enacted by the Mohave *alyha,* in this case an imitation of female physiology (nursing) was apparently grounded in an actual physical anomaly.

The simulation of female breasts on a biological male underlines the feminine in one's appearance. Such simulation can only occur, of course, if the women's clothes cover the upper part of the body so that it can be "stuffed out." Landes (1970:199) reported that Yellow Belly/Louise always wore "bulging corsets" with his/her women's clothes of European cut, although nature had made him flat-chested. A photo in Scherer (1975:163; and Figure 2 of the present work) shows Wewha, who quite obviously stuffed out her Zuni woman's robe at chest level, or at least draped the blanket in such a way as to create the impression of an imposing female bosom.

An imitation of the female physique can also result if, instead of imitating female physiology (menstruation) or bodily features (breasts), a male conceals characteristics of his male physique (above all the external genitals). This has been reported in only one case, for the simple reason that scarcely any researcher has ever caught sight of an unclothed woman-man. Holder (1889:624) noted that the Crow *bate* he examined hid his genitals between his upper thighs, a practice which he had carried out ever since childhood, especially when swimming together with the women. As a result of this artifice, he created the impression that he actually did have female genitals (or just *not* male ones), although it is likely that the other tribe members knew perfectly well that he was a *bate* and not a woman or a hermaphrodite.

Plucking out the hairs of the beard by the Aleut and Kaniagmiut *shupans* has already been pointed out in another context. That this practice was particularly emphasized indicates that the men in these tribes usually did nothing to prevent their beards from growing, in contrast to other cultures in North America. (Ingalik boys, for example, rubbed their faces with a muskrat tail—which, as everyone knows, is hairless—in order to avoid beard growth; Osgood 1958:261).

The last example leads into the topic of the next chapter, because it evidently has to do with a genuine hermaphrodite. Once when Frances entered the house of the brother of Ford's consultant in order to sell baskets, the consultant wanted sexual intercourse with her, which she declined with the words, "Not this time, I've got my monthlies" (Ford 1941:130). Thus Frances was borrowing the woman's argument, related to female physiology, that sexual intercourse at certain times is impossible. Although she was not actually menstruating, she imitated the culturally appropriate behavior of a menstruating woman. The seclusion of women during menstruation was meant to keep men away from menstrual blood, and was widely practiced on the Northwest Coast (Drucker 1963:174f.). Frances' behavior was thus atypical to the extent that she went around during her "menses" and sold baskets. Admittedly, the Kwakiutl racked their brains over the question of Frances' true sex, although they categorized her as more likely to be male on physical grounds ("This man, her name was Frances," Ford 1941:129). After her death on a seal hunting schooner, during which she was playing the masculine role, the men examined her and found a vaginal opening behind the normal male genitals (1941:130). Consequently, it is altogether possible that Frances actually menstruated: two thirds of the genuine hermaphrodites menstruate (Overzier 1961b:210). It must be noted, however, that hermaphrodites and other intersexes are extremely rare, and that the exact nature of Frances' intersexuality cannot be determined on the basis of these external characteristics. In any case, at least some degree of intersexuality, a masculine overall appearance, and the status of woman-man seem to have coincided in Frances. Whether or not she in fact menstruated is secondary in the context of the culture, since the Kwakiutl did not know about her intersexuality during her lifetime. Her reference to her menstruation was understood by those involved as the imitation of feminine role behavior coming from a woman-man, and was respected as such.

In conclusion, an imitation of female physiology and physique occurred individually in greatly varying forms, but—taking the entire subcontinent as a whole—was only very rarely reported. For the most part, imitation was restricted either to claiming or to simulating menstruation and birth. Since a complete simulation of female bodily functions was reported only for the Mohave, the question of whether women-men in other cultures may have observed regulations pertaining to menstruation cannot be answered. If there were more data, it would be possible to determine whether simulations of menstruation were rare. If they were, this would mean that women-men were able to fill all of the feminine role aspects without having periodically to be restricted by menstrual or pregnancy taboos. Numerous activities were not prohibited to them every month or in connection with pregnancy and birth, and they were, unlike women, always available as sexual partners. This would be particularly enlightening in light of the fact that women-men are frequently portrayed in the literature as promiscuous. That the village woman-man was sought out by a substantial number of men may indicate that he was available as a quasi-female sexual partner for men for whom intercourse with their wives was prohibited because of menstruation, pregnancy, or childbirth.

PHYSICAL ANOMALIES AND PECULIARITIES

Intersexuality

Intersexuality—an ambivalence of the external and/or internal sexual characteristics—has rarely been reported with reference to women-men. The few believable examples derive partly from reports of medical examinations and partly from reports by consultants. The fact that so few intersexual persons could have shaped the institution of gender role change in its essentials has already been discussed in relation to the example of the Navajo *nadle*. Among the Navajo, aspects of physical intersexuality became the fixed points in relation to which non-intersexuals—"those who pretend to be *nadle*"—had to orient themselves. The concept of the *nadle* was thus shaped by physical ambivalence. Hill's (1935:273) consultant Kinipai, according to her own testimony and that of other Navajos, was a "hermaphrodite." However, the acquisition of *nadle* status was not tied to the presence of intersexuality. Biologically unambivalent persons assumed this status, just as did Klah, who was said to have been emasculated as a child (Reichard 1944:23). The lack of a genuine intersex in one generation would not have brought down the institution; the foundation of the status of *nadle* quite obviously was the concept not only of a physical but also of a psychic ambivalence in regard to gender membership. Within such a conceptualization of dual sexuality (*Zwiegeschlechtlichkeit*), intersexuality, nonmasculinity because of emasculation, and the inclination of a physically unambivalent male toward feminine role behavior obviously are "the same" (on the Navajo classification of certain phenomena or concepts as "the same" in other contexts, see Reichard 1950:7f.). Although this concept appears most clearly in Navajo society, it has probably existed in similar form in other tribes. In the latter cases, however, it was not the intersexual who was the "genuine" or "actual" woman-man, but instead the male with an unambivalently masculine physique who carried out a gender role change. This may be related to the fact that, in the Navajo conception of the world, the outstanding role of intersexes/hermaphrodites represented a unique phenomenon as far as its markedly developed form is concerned, and, as noted, actual intersexuality appeared only very rarely.

In a number of sources which described gender role change at first without the presence of intersexuality, intersexes were referred to by the consultants as belonging to the "berdache" category of their tribe along with males who were physically unambiguous. Thus, Lame Deer (1979: 169) reported intersexual *winkte* with both male and female genitals; Ford's (1941:130) consultant said the same about Frances; and Holder (1889:623) spoke of a Klamath woman-man with a "rudimentary" penis. In another case, M. Mandelbaum's (1938:119) consultant portrayed a Nez Percé woman-man who was allegedly "sexless" and who was not able to have intercourse either with men or women. It is unclear whether or not this in fact was a case of so-called Genuine Agonadism (Overzier 1961a:348ff.), which is characterized by the lack of gonads and gonadal ducts (*Geschlechtsgänge*). The affected persons have a small, penis-like external genital, but not a vagina, so they cannot penetrate and cannot be penetrated vaginally; oral intercourse with both sexes is possible, of course, as is anal intercourse with male partners.

In contrast to all other sources on the Ojibwa, Skinner (1911:152) reported that at least among the Northern Saulteux their women-men "invariably [were] supposed to be hermaphrodites." The term used, "split testicles" (Skinner 1911:151; no Native term given), suggests a genital deformation which can occur in association with intersexuality (see the illustrations in Overzier 1961c:242f., "pseudohermaphroditism," and also Illust. 116d, p. 357, adrenogenital syndrome). Other sources, however, cited another term for women-men among the Ojibwa—"man-woman" (McKenney 1972:258) or *a-go-kwa* (Tanner 1830:105); Tanner did not explicitly translate *a-go-kwa* as "man-woman," but it must have this meaning. The suffix *-kwa* or *-kwae* means "woman" or "female" in the Algonquian languages (e.g., Potawatomi, *m'netokwae,* Landes 1970:195). A *separate* designation ("split testicles"), therefore, seems to have existed for intersexes, although these persons actually were integrated into the status of woman-man. Why Skinner apparently obtained the word for "intersexual" in response to his question about "berdaches" cannot be ascertained. No other source equates the Ojibwa women-men with intersexes.

Kelly (1932:158) mentioned "hermaphrodites" for the Northern Paiute. Since she maintained at the same time that these donned "the clothing of the opposite sex" (1932:158)—which makes no sense in view of intersexes' or hermaphrodites' sexual ambivalence—it can be assumed that the author meant physically unambiguous women-men. Since the Northern Paiute assigned both infertile persons and "berdaches" alike to the category *düba's* (sterile; 1932:157), intersexes—who are always sterile—should also have fallen under this category, not as "transvestites," but on the basis of their sterility. As noted, Stewart (1942:298) stated that male "berdaches" could become pregnant, but also that all groups denied the presence of female genitals on the part of women-men (1942:332). Two additional Northern Paiute groups are supposed to have maintained that "male berdaches" had "female organs" (Stewart 1941:405). Here also, however, *tüvasa* designates "any sterile person as well as the sexually abnormal usually considered transvestites" (Stewart 1941:440). Instead of presupposing intersexuality, it probably makes more sense to assume a mistake in communication in which sterile *women* (who had "female organs") ended up under the rubric of male "berdaches" in the *Anthropological Records*. Similarly, females in a man's role—who likewise fell under the category *tüvasa*—were described in the same source as having "male organs" (Stewart 1941:405). If, in answer to Stewart's question, the consultant had *sterile* but not *transvesting* persons in mind, then the statements regarding the supposed presence of genitals of the opposite sex are no longer astonishing. What is meant are neither "berdaches" nor intersexes, but rather infertile men or women. Despite this, intersexes would also fall under the category of *tüvasa*—not because of their dual sexuality, but because they were infertile.

With respect to the Northern Shoshoni, Steward's (1943:338) consultants mentioned—with reservations—three groups in which "female organs" were mentioned in connection with male-bodied "berdaches." What has just been said about the possible misunderstandings surrounding the categoy *tüvasa* holds here as well. In the *Anthropological Records* list, "female organs" in connection with male "berdaches" were mentioned for three groups of the Nevada Shoshoni (Steward 1941:312). The first example was a Lida Shoshoni male "who had neither beard nor breasts," who cross-dressed and did women's work, and did not marry (1941:353). In two of these groups, however, it was also reported that the "berdaches" did not wear women's clothing or do women's work (1941:312). How, though, could a "berdache" status have been established at all for these two groups? The footnotes pertaining to the individual groups provide clarification: in one of them, the Shoshoni of Elko, one "berdache" was a feminine male—in a manner which was not specified—who had a wife and children; another "berdache" from Elko, however, had "breasts and male genitals," but dressed as a man, did men's work, and did not marry (1941:353). This latter example probably led Steward's consultants to say that female organs, too, might be present in women-men. The "berdache" from the second group, the Snake River Shoshoni, had no breasts, but reportedly did have "male and female genitals," and was active as a doctor (1941: 353). The non-transvesting "berdaches" in a masculine role who were said to have had female organs turn out, therefore, to be intersexes. Other examples of both transvesting and non-transvesting women-men from the same region include a male "housekeeper" in men's clothing, and a transvesting Lida Shoshoni male who performed women's tasks (1941:353). Another nontransvesting woman-man is supposed to have had an "abnormally small penis" (Steward 1941:353). He did women's work and was active as a doctor. The relatively indeterminate Shoshoni concept of woman-man obviously comprised every male who was not unambiguously masculine, and thereby also included cases of physical intersexuality: "Transvestism . . . was unstandardized, varying with the individual" (1941:353). Shimkin also reported a case of obviously underdeveloped genitals ("minute genitalia") in a transvesting woman-man of the Wind River Shoshoni who did women's work (1947:298). Shimkin noted that there existed "no recognized social role whatsoever" for "berdaches" among the Shoshoni. Thus, in some Shoshoni-speaking groups, infertility, nonmasculinity, and/or intersexuality obviously would have allowed a person to come under the category of *tüvasa;* but whether or not that person undertook a gender role change at the same time remained up to the individual.

Rumors also circulated in regard to Yellow Belly/Louise, alleging that she was a hermaphrodite (Landes 1970:198). But the available information instead suggests that deliberate myth formation was involved. At birth, the boy was said to be "formed like a boy," but he later supposedly underwent a metamorphosis into female sexual characteristics. Since he had already begun to wash himself at an early age, however, no one was able to witness this transformation (1970:198). Whether Louise actually was in fact intersexual can neither be confirmed nor disconfirmed. Of greater interest in the present context, in any case, are the reasons which could have moved her, her mother, or other persons to start rumors concerning a bodily transformation.

The status of *m'netokwe* in Potawatomi society was not traditionally associated with intersexuality, and the two modern potential women-men interviewed by Landes (1970:196f.) were biologically unambiguous, effeminate males. Only Landes' heavily acculturated female consultant (for whose parents Louise had worked) reported—on the basis of hearsay—on Louise's transformation or possible intersexuality. Even she described Louise's general appearance as "like a male, tall, with coarse features" (1970:198). It would seem that Louise lived at a time (end of the nineteenth century) when the institution of gender role change was losing its former respect. The family of the female consultant apparently treated Louise with good-humored acceptance; traditional Potawatomis, by contrast, saw her as a *m'netokwe*—someone endowed with supernatural power—and regretted that she lived in the acculturated family and not in a traditional milieu (1970:196). Notably, the acculturated family accepted and perhaps elaborated on the rumors about Louise's physical metamorphosis, whereas the traditional Potawatomis did not consider physique at all in their evaluation of Louise as *m'netokwe.* On the contrary, her effeminacy and her inclination toward women's tasks were much more important. The acculturated family obviously needed a "modern" explanation for Louise's gender role change, which was taking place before their very eyes. In view of her striving for the role of an *acculturated* or "White" woman, Louise certainly could have provided additional encouragement to interpretations such as these (see Landes 1970:199 on Louise's fondness for stylish jewelry and non-Indian women's clothing). Louise was not attempting to achieve the role of a Potawatomi *m'netokwe,* but rather of a "modern" woman. In the immediate environment of the acculturated mixed-blood family, intersexuality was probably a more plausible explanation for the gender role change than a vocational call based on a visionary experience.

The two *mujerados* with atrophied genitals whom Hammond (1882) examined were probably actual intersexes, although, as noted, the cause was most likely a severe hormonal disturbance appearing during adulthood, and in all likelihood traceable to a tumor. *Mujerado,* the term reported to Hammond for these males, is different from the one later told to Parsons—*kokwima* or *kokwimu* (Parsons 1918:181f. and also 181, n. 6; 1923:166). Parsons herself used the term "man-woman" in English, which is obviously a translation of *kokwimu.* The Spanish word *mujerado,* by contrast, grammatically implies a forced change from the male to the female sex, and is best translated as "effeminized male." Bandelier (1966:326) used the term *amujerado,* adding that the Pueblos called such persons *qo-qoy-o* (i.e., *kokwimu*). *Mujerado* is obviously the Spanish translation of *kokwimu* (see also the corrupted form *mojaro;* Roscoe 1988b:58), but it contains an element of forced change that is lacking in the Keres word. Independently of this, the possibility also exists that a distinction was made in Acoma and Laguna between literally (i.e., physically/phenotypically) "effeminized" males and "berdaches." First, there existed the status of *kokwimu,* which was chosen by a male "merely because he prefers woman's work to man's" (Parsons 1918:181; see also Bandelier 1966:326), without any symptom of intersexuality. Such persons were designated as "she" and addressed with female kinship terms (Parsons 1923:166). The males examined by Hammond, however, had undergone another kind of transformation—not a change of gender role, but rather a *change of sex:* "by some means or other the sex of this person had become changed *from male to female,*" whereupon the male "assumed the garb of a woman, lived with women, and followed their occupations" (Hammond 1882:343, emphasis mine). That the Laguna *mujerado* told Hammond "with evident pride" of his once large penis and "his testicles . . . 'grandes como huevos'" (big as eggs)(Hammond 1882:345) likewise does not fit very well with a voluntary gender role change. There is no case known in the literature in which a woman-man recalls his former masculinity with wistful nostalgia. The "chief" who accompanied Hammond, incidentally, spoke of the *mujerado* in the masculine form (1882:344; see also Bandelier 1966:326). This case may represent the integration of a *mujerado*—a man become a woman—into a status which resembles but is not identical with that of the *kokwimu.* In the one case, the desires of the individual were accommodated; the other case had more to do with the necessity of finding an appropriate status in society for a man who was suddenly becoming a physical woman. Further, gender role change by physically unambiguous males appears to have been the actual institution which made possible the integration of physically ambivalent persons. People at Laguna obviously did not make a fundamental conceptual distinction between physical and physical-psychic ambiguity of sex membership.

The remark by Spier and Sapier (1930:221) that the "transvestites" among the Wishram were probably "real hermaphrodites" was not verified by these authors on the basis of evidence. Referring to the Yuki *iwap-naip,* Foster likewise mentioned that at least one of them was "definitely" intersexual, but offered no details (1944:186).

One Stoney *winktan* exhibited both male and female genitalia ("mentula parva, infra illam cunnus" [a small penis, and beneath it a vulva]), but his general appearance suggested that he was male, since the Cree—among whom he turned up as the wife of a man—took him for a man until the husband enlightened them to the fact that he was a "berdache" (Lowie 1909:42). In contrast to other Assiniboine *winktan,* this one performed both women's *and* men's tasks, instead of exclusively women's (Lowie 1909:42). Although he did not undertake a complete gender role change and was intersexual, his Cree husband classified him as a woman-man.

Consequently, and as is clearly evident from the preceding discussion, intersexes could be integrated into the status of woman-man. Unfortunately, with the exception of the examples from Laguna and Acoma, hardly anything is known about the biographies of such persons. In contrast to biologically unambiguous male women-men, who in most cases—even in Laguna and Acoma—assumed that status during puberty at the latest, both of these males undertook the change of gender role as adults, because they underwent their physical transformations at this point in time. Innate intersexuality, however, is frequently already visible at birth or in the first years of life. It is known that, as a child, Kinipai already enjoyed the preferential treatment to which the *nadle* was entitled (Hill 1935:278). Among the Navajo, this also held true for non-intersexual children who were classified as *nadle* because of their behavior. With regard to intersexual children, however, the classification as *nadle* obviously took place soon after birth: for the Navajo, one characteristic of the "real nadle" was that "you can tell them when they are born" (consultant in Hill 1935:273). In other Native American cultures as well, therefore, intersexual women-men with ambivalent external sexual characteristics who held the status of woman-man as adults must, in principle, already have been classified as such from birth onward, and not on the grounds of a special preference for women's work, a vision, or other omens which ultimately led physically unambiguous boys or males to take on the status of woman-man. Their entrance into the woman-man status is atypical, both in terms of the point in time and also in terms of the manner of their recruitment. Only among the Navajo did the intersexual *nadle,* or hermaphrodite, appear as the genuine woman-man. Nevertheless, in general there were two possibilities of acquiring the status of woman-man: through the divergence of role behavior and sexual characteristics, and through an ambiguity of the sexual characteristics themselves. Which of these two kinds of women-men is the actual model in a given culture at given time seems to be less significant than the concept of a principled equivalence—or at least great similarity—of both kinds of sexual ambiguity (see Williams 1986b:21f.).

Masculinity and Femininity in Outward Appearance

In the literature, one finds rare indications of a third means of entering into the status of woman-man, namely through the custom of raising boys from soon after birth as girls, without either their behavior or their physique necessarily playing any role in the matter. (Presumably, especially "feminine" male infants were from time to time selected for the feminine role). It is probably because of their female socialization from the very beginning that the début of such women-men into their women's role was so perfect that outsiders were not able to distinguish them from women.

Thus, on the occasion of a wedding on Kodiak, the priest was made aware only at the last minute that he was about to unite in wedlock a couple consisting of a man and a woman-man (Dall 1897:402f). The persona which the Aleut *shupans* projected was likewise feminine (1897:402). Similarly, Luiseño *cuit* were brought up as girls from infancy, which had the effect that as adults they "in almost every particular . . . resembled females" (Boscana 1846:282). In other cases, femininity was not instilled in a boy in the course of his socialization, but rather was already present before he assumed the woman-man status. One of Williams' (1986a:196) consultants portrayed budding *winkte* as especially pretty babies whose voices already sounded "effeminate." The two *mujerados* described by Hammond had been so severely effeminized by pathological hormonal changes that the one from Acoma, according to Hammond (1882:346), looked more like a woman than like a man, even when unclothed. From Hammond's perspective, the *mujerado* in Laguna could not be distinguished from the women whom he joined to grind maize (1882:344). Likewise, Parsons' (1932:246) female consultant described Palure from Isleta as "very pretty"; and men from the pueblo took great delight in passing "her" off onto unsuspecting Whites or Mexicans as a bed partner.

Meanwhile, Osgood's (1958:262) claim that the contemporaries of the Ingalik "men pretenders" and "women pretenders" (Osgood did not give the Native terms) did not in general recognize their real sex should be treated with caution. It is likely that the biological sex of an individual was perfectly well known to the inhabitants of the village in which that person grew up. "Men pretenders" and "women pretenders" assumed the role of the opposite sex during childhood; if that role was performed to perfection and the overall appearance of a "woman pretender" approached that of a woman, such a "deception" of persons at least from other villages could, admittedly, have been possible. More probable than a genuine failure to recognize biological sex membership, though, is that the villagers simply no longer mentioned the biological sex of the women-men and men-women, a respectful rule which, as noted, was also usual among the Navajo (Hill 1935:279).

A story told by Osgood (1958:262) also supports this interpretation: a father warned his "woman pretender" son against going into a *kashim* (men's house) in which another, powerful, "woman pretender" spent time, so that this male could not harm him. The Ingalik believed that "woman pretenders" were extraordinarily envious of each other (1958:262), which likewise indicates that it was generally known who held this status—and therefore who was biologically male. The report of a Mohave woman should also be seen in the same light: one of her acquaintances had taken an *alyha* for a "real" woman, until one day the *alyha* "lifted something . . . and as the fibers of the bark-skirt parted his penis became visible" (Devereux 1937:506f.). Devereux commented that "the 'astonishment' was a mere flower of speech, in view of the fact that sex and transvestites were regularly discussed" (1937:507). Habituation must also have played a role, if the sex of a woman-man at birth was no longer mentioned. This is indicated, for example, by a remark of Maria Chona (Papago) in Underhill (1936:43), referring to her relative Shining Evening: "Yes, just like a woman. We have forgotten he is a man."

Nevertheless, only in a very few cases were the women-men really so "female" from the standpoint of their overall appearance that not a trace of ambiguity clung to them with respect to their sex/gender membership. As noted, reports maintaining that their biological sex was not at least generally known to their co-villagers should be interpreted as meaning that this knowledge was not *expressed.* The outward appearance of a woman-man frequently contradicted even his feminine role and women's clothing. Schaeffer (1965:223) described Piegan Woman as a large, good-looking male with large hands. Osh-Tisch, the Crow *bate* described by Lowie (1912:226) and by Simms (1903:580), was large and bulky, "almost gigantic in stature" (see also the photo in Williams 1986b, Plate 12). Holder (1889:623f.) also portrayed the external aspects of the *bate* whom he examined as thoroughly male, including his voice register. According to Holder (1889:623), a male voice and "features" also characterized a Klamath woman-man he knew. Justine (Kutenai) was described as large, heavy-set, and as having a deep voice (Schaeffer 1965:218). The intersexual Stoney *winktan* looked so masculine that the inhabitants of the village to which his Cree husband took him at first thought he was a man (Lowie 1909:42). The Cree *ayahkwew* Fine-day looked like a man and had a man's voice (D. G. Mandelbaum 1940:256). Reichard (1950:141) described Klah as masculine in appearance, voice, and "manner": "Had there been no rumors or whispers, no white person would have picked him out of a Navaho crowd as abnormal." Kinipai (the intersexual) also had masculine-looking hands and shoulders, as well as a masculine-appearing face (Hill 1935:273; see also Figure 1 of the present work). Ozaw-wen-dib (Ojibwa) was masculine "both as to manners and courage" (Henry 1897:163), and the Oto *mixo'ge* portrayed by Irving (1938:112) was large, with masculine facial features. Yellow Belly/Louise, too, was not particularly feminine in her appearance (Landes 1970:198), and one of the other feminine males was "strong and squarely built," with a deep masculine voice (1970:197).

Along with the Crow *bate* just mentioned, the Coahuiltecan women-men were described not only as masculine in appearance, but also as especially big and powerful: "mas membrudos que los otros hombres y mas altos" (more brawny/corpulent than the other men and taller; Cabeza de Vaca 1555:36). Bodily strength was also a characteristic of the Timucua women-men (LeMoyne 1875:7). Finally, Stevenson (1904: 310) described Wewha as the strongest and tallest person in all Zuni; this was confirmed by a photograph (Williams 1986b, Plate 10). Furthermore, other photographs show Wewha as a quite masculine-looking *lhamana* (Scherer 1975:163; Stevenson 1904, Plate 94; Figure 2 of the present work). It is hardly credible that Stevenson (1904:310) was convinced for many years of the female sex of her friend, but this was apparently the case: "Gossip goes that Mrs. Stevenson took Wewha to Washington without knowing 'she' was a man" (Parsons 1939b:65, n.). Of course, in Zuni Wewha was always referred to as "she" and her biological sex was "carefully . . . concealed" (Stevenson 1904:310). Meanwhile, it is also probable that Stevenson was the only person in Zuni who did not know that Wewha was a *lhamana* and not a woman.

All of these examples indicate that although external femininity was a possible attribute of the woman-man status, it was not a necessary component of it. Similarly, a markedly unfeminine outward appearance is no barrier to a gender role change. Yet even in the case of an exact imitation of feminine role behavior and of a distinctively feminine appearance, no transition into the status of "woman" was possible, but merely into the status of "woman-man." This status was open to a male completely independently of physical femininity. Just as little, incidentally, would a male with a more feminine body build probably have been forced to undergo a gender role change, and at most then only if he, like the two *mujerados,* had undergone a genuine bodily metamorphosis. The most important criterion for undertaking a gender role change on the part of physically unambiguous male individuals was the subjective desire to do so, expressed by interest in feminine tasks, by a vision experience, or by a combination of both of these. In the latter case, an interest in women's work and in other aspects of feminine role behavior usually preceded the vision. It is precisely the phenotypically very unfeminine women-men who, like intersexes, illustrate with particular clarity the sexual ambiguity accompanying the woman-man status, the simultaneous presence of maleness/masculinity and femaleness/femininity in the psyche and in the physique, or even in the physique alone. Even in a single individual, the psyche and the physique can express a dual ambiguity. This is the case when a biological male puts on the clothing and the role of a woman (ambivalence in biological sex versus social role) and at the same time retains aspects of the masculine role (ambivalence in the social role).

Chapter NINE

Women-Men as "Shamans," Medicine Persons, and Healers

Women-men have been reported to have carried out the most varied activities as specialists (see Map 3). They were active as healers ("shamans"), medicine men, gravediggers, conveyers of oral traditions and songs, and nurses during war expeditions; they foretold the future, conferred lucky names on children or adults, wove, made pottery, arranged marriages, and made feather costumes for dances; they had special skills in games of chance; they led scalp-dances; they fulfilled special functions in connection with the setting up of the central post for the Sun Dance; and some ethnographers have even imputed to them the specialist role of tribal prostitute. In the following, specialist activities are understood to be those which go beyond the realm of everyday occupations such as subsistence acquisition, food preparation, the making of objects for one's own use, the raising of children, and so on, and which require special skills on the part of the person performing them. Thus, in many places, all of the women of a group wove or made pottery for their own use, but they could become specialists if they began to produce in larger quantities and for a wider circle of consumers. In the same way, numerous medicaments certainly were generally known, but the "medicine man" or his female equivalent was destined in a special way for the healing profession through supernaturally granted skills. Specialist activities were also frequently subordinate to the sexual division of labor; according to the sources, some are supposed to have been reserved especially for women-men. In what follows, the specializations of the women-men are investigated against the background of the masculine and feminine role spheres.

Map 3. Specialist Occupations of Women-Men (Male "Berdaches")

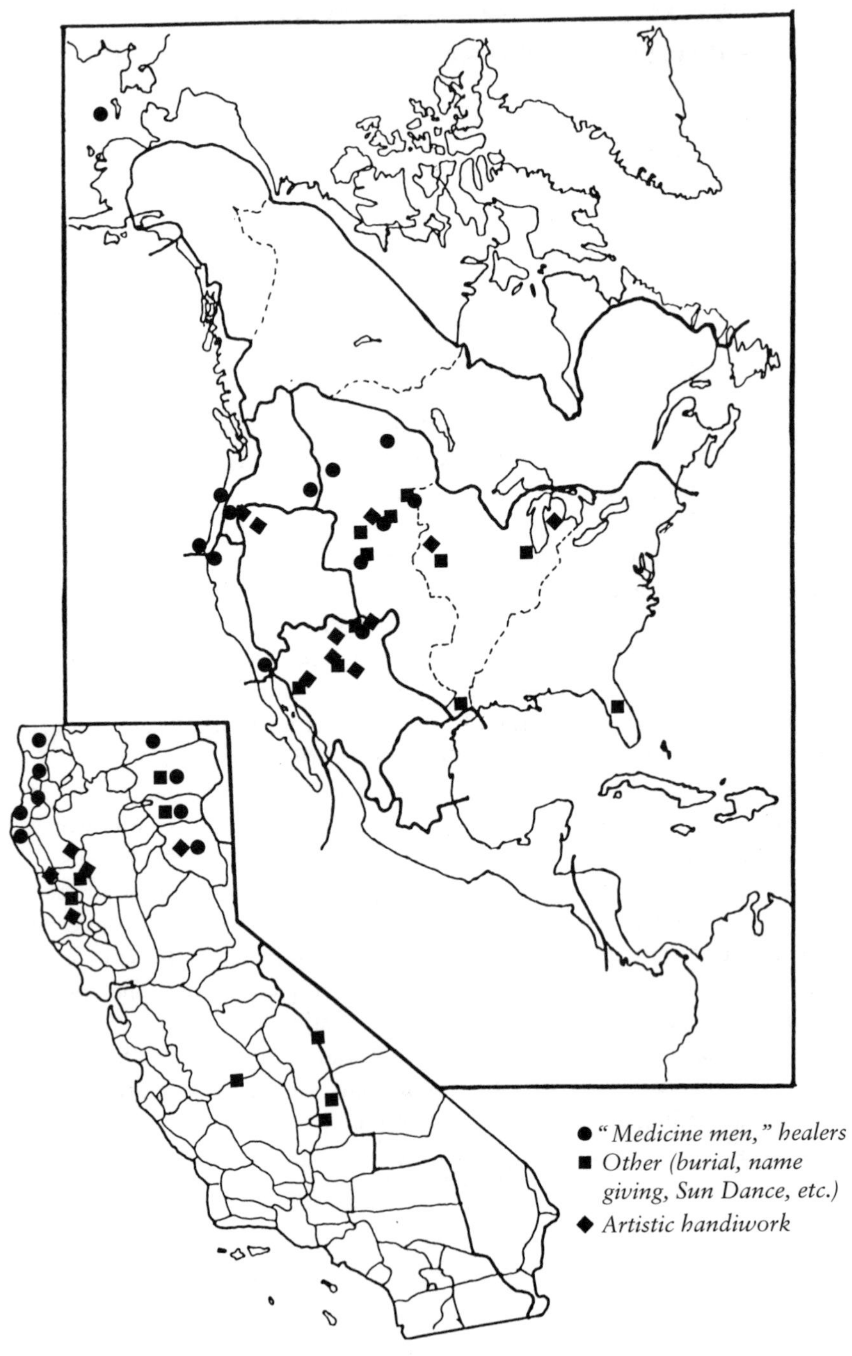

INTRODUCTION

Because of the close connection between Siberian shamanism and gender role change, ethnographers generally asked very specific questions about a possible connection between these phenomena; consequently, the sources are quite detailed on this question. The *Anthropological Records,* in particular, often refer to whether "berdaches" were skilled in medicine and healing ("shamans") or not. Here, the terms "medicine man" or "medicine person" (a person endowed with supernatural powers, usually also including healing skills) and also the term "healer" (endowed with special healing powers) are used rather than the term "shaman," which is frequently employed in the literature in an undifferentiated manner (see, e.g., Eliade 1957, Findeisen 1957, Ohlmarks 1939). Reports concerning women-men as medicine people fall into three groups: (1) women-men were not medicine people; (2) some women-men were medicine people; and (3) all women-men were medicine people (see Table 2).

The reasons for excluding women-men from the status of medicine person seldom appear in the literature. Essene reported that his consultants from the Kato, Lassik, Pomo, and Yuki reacted strongly against the idea that a *murfidai* (hermaphrodite or "berdache") could be a "shaman" (Essene 1942:65). In other cases, this occupation was restricted to men (see Table 3).

Regardless of whether women-men were able to become "shamans," medicine people, or chanters, most supernaturally legitimized healers were men. When women-men could be medicine people, they were often considered "holy people" if their gender role change involved a supernatural experience (e.g., *wakan, manitu,* etc.). Meanwhile, it is striking that wherever women-men could become medicine people, the percentage of female-dominated healing activity was higher. There are no reported cases in which the medicine person role was restricted to women-men. Further, a gender role change did not necessarily involve occupation of the healer role, except among the St. Lawrence Eskimo (Murphy 1964:62f., 74f.). Kroeber (1925:46) stated that all of the Yurok *wergern* were "shamans," but Driver (1937:347) maintained that only some had taken this path. The Yurok themselves explained that *wergern* underwent a gender role change because they were "impelled by the desire to become shamans" (Kroeber 1925:46). Healers, however, could be men, so it is unlikely that men would have changed gender to become "shamans"; this was also true for other groups. Nowhere, in fact, was the institution closed to men, and in eight cases among the cultures concerned here, it was restricted to men exclusively.

Table 2. Women-Men as Medicine Persons/Healers

Tribe	Women-Men Are Medicine People/Healers	Medicine People/Healers Are Usually:
Bankalachi	No (Driver 1937:109)	Men (Willoughby 1963: 59f.)
Chumash	No (Harrington 1942:32)	Men (Willoughby 1963:59f.)
Chugach-Eskimo	No (Birket-Smith 1953:94)	Men and Women (Birket-Smith 1953: 88, 126)
Diegueño	No (Drucker 1937a:46)	Men (Willoughby 1963:59f.)
Gabrielino	No (Harrington 1942:32)	Men (Willoughby 1963:59f.)
Kato	No (Essene 1942:31, 65)	Men (Willoughby 1963:59f.)
Kawaiisu	No (Driver 1937:109)	Men (Willoughby 1963:59f.)
Kitanemuk	No (Harrington 1942:32)	Men (Willoughby 1963:59f.)
Lassik	No (Essene 1942:31, 65)	Men and Women (Willoughby 1963:59f.)
Maricopa	No (Spier 1933:242)	Men (Spier 1933:238)
Mono	No (Driver 1937:109)	Men (Willoughby 1963:59f.)
Northern Paiute	No (Kelly 1932:158; Steward 1933:238; Stewart 1941:405)	Men and Women (Willoughby 1963:59f.)
Southern Paiute	No (Steward 1941:312; Driver 1937:109; Stewart 1942: 332)	Men (Willoughby 1963: 59f.); Kelly 1939:151
Panamint	No (Driver 1937:109)	Men (Willoughby 1963:59f.)
Pomo	No (Essene 1942:31, 65)	Men and Women (Willoughby 1963:59f.)
Salinan	No (Harrington 1942:32)	Men (Willoughby 1963:59f.)
Coast Salish	No (Barnett 1955:149)	Men (Barnett 1955:149)
Shasta	No (Holt 1946:317; Voegelin 1942:134)	Women (Willoughby 1963:59f.)
Nevada-Shoshoni	No (Steward 1941:312)	Men (Steward 1941:258)
Tübatulabal	No (Driver 1937:109)	Men (Willoughby 1963:59f.)
Ute	No (Stewart 1942:332)	Men and Women (Stewart 1942: 315)
Wintu	No (Voegelin 1942:134)	Men and Women (Willoughby 1963:59f.)
Wishram	No (Spier and Sapir 1930:221)	Men and Women (Spier and Sapir 1930:238, 241)
Yana	No (Sapir and Spier 1943:275)	Men (Willoughby 1963:59f.)

Table 2. Continued

Tribe	Women-Men Are Medicine People/Healers	Medicine People/Healers Are Usually:
Yokuts	No (Driver 1937:109)	Men (Willoughby 1963:59f.)
Yuki	No (Essene 1942:31, 65)	Men and Women (Driver 1939: 360) Men (Essene 1942:41; Kroeber 1925:196)
Yuma	No (Drucker 1937a:46)	Men and Women (Willoughby 1963:59f.)
Achomawi	Yes (Voegelin 1942:134)	Men and Women (Olmstedt and Stewart 1978:232) Men (Voegelin 1942:152, 157ff.; Willoughby 1963:59f.)
Atsugewi	Yes (Voegelin 1942:134)	Men (Willoughby 1963:59f.)
Chetco River	Yes (Barnett 1937:189)	Women (Barnett 1937:189; Drucker 1937b:258)
Cheyenne	Yes (Grinnell 1962, 2:40)	Men (Grinnell 1962, 2:127ff.)
Chilula	Yes (Driver 1939:347)	Women (Kroeber 1925:137)
Cree (Plains)	Yes (D. G. Mandelbaum 1940: 256)	Men and Women (D. G. Mandelbaum 1940:254, 245)
Lakota (Teton)	Yes (Hassrick 1982:136; Lame Deer 1979:170; Williams 1986a:194, 195, 197)	Men (W. K. Powers 1977:63)
St. Lawrence Eskimo	Yes (Murphy 1964:74f.; Murphy and Leighton 1965:72)	Men and Women (Murphy 1964:75)
Flathead	Yes (Teit 1930:384) No (Turney-High 1937:85)	Men and Women (Fahey 1974: 14) Men (Turney-High 1937:27ff.)
Hidatsa	Yes (Bowers 1965:167)	Men (Bowers 1965:167, 168, 256)
Klamath	Yes (Spier 1930:51f.; Voegelin 1942:134)	Men (Willoughby 1963:59f.)
Maidu	Yes (Voegelin 1942:134)	Men (Willoughby 1963:59f.)
Mattole	Yes (Driver 1939:347)	Women (Willoughby 1963:59f.)
Modoc	Yes (Ray 1963:43) No (Voegelin 1942:134)	Men and Women (Willoughby 1963:59f.)
Mohave	Yes (Devereux 1937:516; Kroeber 1925:749)	Men and Women (Drucker 1941:158; Williams 1986b:35)
Navajo	Yes (Gifford 1940:163; Hill 1935:273, 275; Reichard 1950: 141)	Men (Reichard 1950: xliv)

TABLE 2. CONTINUED

TRIBE	WOMEN-MEN ARE MEDICINE PEOPLE/HEALERS	MEDICINE PEOPLE/HEALERS ARE USUALLY:
Piegan	Yes (Schaeffer 1965:221f.)	Men (Gerhards 1980:94)
Tillamook	Yes (Barnett 1937:189)	Women (Barnett 1937:189)
Tolowa	Yes (Gould 1978:131, 134; Driver 1939:347)	Women (Gould 1978:134; Willoughby 1963:59f.)
Wiyot	Yes (Driver 1939:347)	Women (Willoughby 1963:59f.)
Yurok	Yes (Driver 1939:347; Kroeber 1925:46)	Women (Willoughby 1963:59f.)

Note. Yes/No *refers to sources on a given tribe: different information is given for subgroups within the tribe. Among the* Wind River Shoshoni, *women could become healers only after menopause (Shimkin 1947:312); healers among the* Northern Shoshoni *were of both sexes.* Flathead: *Male "shamans" exclusively were discussed by Turney-High (1937:27 ff.).* Hidatsa: *See text. Medicine persons whose powers were comparable to those of* miati *were male (see Bowers 1965:167; medicine persons generally seem to have been male, see, e.g., Bowers 1965:168, 256). Regarding the sacred bundles, a cooperation between men and women was emphasized, with both sexes equally acquiring the powers of the respective bundles.* Chilula: *According to Kroeber (1925:137), healers were predominantly female in northern California. This apparently also held true for the Chilula.* Piegan: *Four Bears was not a woman-man but has been included in the discussion here for the sake of completeness.* Cheyenne: *Grinnell (1962, 2:127ff.) mentioned that both men and women were "doctors." His discussion of Cheyenne medicine persons, however, suggests that these were predominantly male. Those "doctors" who accompanied raiding parties were in any case exclusively men (1962, 2:141) or women-men, not women. Female "doctors" among the Cheyenne seem to have specialized predominantly in applying herbal cures (see Niethammer 1985:206).*

TABLE 3. SEX OF MEDICINE PERSONS (TRIBES LISTED IN TABLE 2)

MEDICINE PERSONS/HEALERS ARE:	WOMEN-MEN ARE MEDICINE PEOPLE/HEALERS (N = 21)	WOMEN-MEN ARE NOT MEDICINE PEOPLE/ HEALERS (N = 27)
Exclusively or predominantly men	10 (47%)	18 (67%)
Exclusively or predominantly women	6 (29%)	1 (4%)
Both men and women	5 (24%)	8 (29%)

THE PLAINS: STATUS AMBIVALENCE AND SUPERNATURAL POTENTIAL

The statements of two consultants from Williams' (1986a) essay underscore the association of the status of woman-man with special latent supernatural spiritual power:

> Winktes know medicine, but they are not medicine men. They have good powers, especially for love medicine, for curing, and for childbirth. They can tell the future. (194)

> Winkte are wakan, which means that they have power as special people. Medicine men go to winkte for spiritual advice. Winktes can also be medicine men, but they're usually not because they already have the power. An example of this power is the sacred naming ceremony. (197; consultant self-identified as *winkte*)

The supernatural instruction and legitimization of the *winkte* related, therefore, to gender role change as well as to capabilities which had to be acquired separately by other medicine men. Although *winkte*—as recipients of latent supernatural power—were very definitely "medicine men," they formed a special subgroup within this status. Both the acquisition of supernatural knowledge and the classification of the *winkte* as a *wakan* (sacred, unusual, or strange) person correspond to masculine patterns. Like the Hidatsa *miati,* the *winkte* were equivalent to the medicine *men* who dominated the spiritual life of the tribe.

Within this masculine pattern, feminine elements seem to have conferred personal medicine upon the males who exhibited them. Part of Four Bears' (Piegan) personal medicine, for instance, seemed to be a function of his cross-dressing for particular ceremonies. Likewise, for the Oglala Lakota, transvesting was much more the expression of a very personal medicine than it was either the expression of a feminine gender identity or of a quasi-feminine status. Just as other males carried the various symbols of their supernatural helpers with them in medicine bags, the *winkte* "carried" (wore) pieces of women's clothing. This applies to the *miati* as well, on whom—along with functions in the Holy Women Society—a series of special ritual activities devolved. Thus, just as the Hidatsa medicine man surrounded himself with a number of "individual rules of conduct" (Bowers 1965:168), the *miati* and the *winkte* "surrounded" themselves with feminine role behaviors. Similarly, the Cheyenne *heemaneh'* were described as "doctors or medicine men," although other additional ritual tasks also fell to them (Grinnell 1962, 2:40). Among the Lakota, the Hidatsa, and the Cheyenne, thus, women-men seem to have been a special class of medicine people comparable to the medicine *men* of their cultures; in their sexual ambivalence, they were male androgynes in O'Flaherty's sense (1982:285f., 333f.). On the one hand, their gender role change was the expression of an ambivalent gender identity. On the other hand, their borrowing and exhibiting of feminine role aspects expressed a kind of power that was reserved for men in their respective cultures.

Among the Plains Cree, the role of the medicine person seems to have been mixed. There were numerous "women doctors," and some of the most respected healers were women (D. G. Mandelbaum 1940:245, 254). The most important rituals of the tribe, however, were performed by men (1940:245). Although the sources do not explicitly mention legitimization of the woman-man's status through visions, these were usual for both sexes (1940:252). Girls did not undergo vision quests, but they were definitely considered to be susceptible to visions during their menstrual seclusion. Women-men (*aayahkwew*) among the Plains Cree usually became "noted shamans" (1940:256).

The example of the *aayahkwew* Clawed Woman shows, however, that his specific powers as a healer were masculine rather than feminine, and that his gender status as a woman-man, while ambivalent, was still nonfeminine enough to make contact with menstrual blood dangerous to him (just as it was dangerous to any male in his culture, but not to the women). Clawed Woman was an extraordinarily successful healer until he died, according to the Cree, because he borrowed a dress from a woman which she had worn during her menstrual period, which rendered it dangerous to men. (He had lost his own dress while gambling; D. G. Mandelbaum 1940: 257.) Had he held any degree of feminine gender status, no one would have thought that contact with this garment would have led to his death (Williams 1986b:83f.). But his gender status was mixed, as indicated by what the Cree said about him: "He wanted to be called piecuwiskwew, because Thunder is a name for a man and iskwew is a woman's name; half and half just like he was" (D. G. Mandelbaum 1940:256). Several other facts, too, suggest that his healer role was not a function of his *aayahkwew* role. For one thing, Clawed Woman removed his dress during healing rituals, and practiced in a breech-cloth, indicating that he assumed a masculine role during his healing. Further, he was once seen suddenly holding bear-claws at a curing session (D. G. Mandelbaum 1940:257). This implies that it was not his woman-man status, but instead probably a spirit helper in the form of a bear, that conferred his healing power on him. Moreover, the status of healer among the Plains Cree was independent of sex/gender. Consequently, it is unlikely that *aayahkwew* assumed the role of healer as a further aspect of their feminine gender roles. It is possible that the vision experience that may have legitimized the gender role change also destined *aayahkwew* to learn the curing profession, but in contrast to the *winkte*'s vision, it did not bestow corresponding powers.

The Arapaho *haxu'xan* "could do supernatural things" (Kroeber 1902:19), but whether they were active as healers or as ritual specialists in general was not reported. Their power, however, was obviously not tied to the women's role, but instead was based on a special vision experience, a "supernatural gift from animals or birds" (1902:19). A *haxu'xan* is said to have invented the custom of collecting rainwater during storms: this water was "powerful" and made people foolish, and therefore was regarded as a kind of narcotic drug (1902:19, 21).

In the Plains, thus, gender role change was combined with healing activity within the framework of the masculine spiritual domain. In this region, women-men did not become healers as "women," but instead as males with an ambivalent gender identity and a special visionary experience. They sought this vision experience as boys or as men, and not within the framework of a feminine gender role. Since the vision quest did not occupy such an outstanding position in other Native American cultures—and also did not fall so markedly within the masculine role domain—it is impossible to generalize beyond this area. In fact, outside the Prairies and Plains region, vision experiences did not always legitimize alternative social personae such as women-men (Mirsky 1937a: 415f.). When Ququnok patke, the "female berdache" of the Kutenai, told her fellow tribe members that her sex had been transformed from female to male and that she had thereby acquired great spiritual power, some Kutenai believed that she had gone out of her mind (Schaeffer 1965:197). It is likely that they would have thought the same of a man: even though vision-inspired gender role change was possible for Kutenai males (not females) (1965:217), the idea that the change would confer supernatural capabilities was foreign to the Kutenai.

CALIFORNIA: HEALING ACTIVITY AS THE EXPRESSION OF GENDER ROLE AND PERSONAL CAPABILITIES

Several kinds of "shamans" existed in California, with men and women often specializing in different areas (see Driver 1939:360; Essene 1942: 41ff.; Harrington 1942:39; Kroeber 1925; Voegelin 1942:152ff.). ("Shaman" is the term usually encountered in the literature on California and has therefore been retained in this section.) Among the Yurok, almost all "shamans," or healers, were female; the few male "shamans" did not heal so much as entertain by means of rattlesnake sleights of hand and other tricks (Kroeber 1925:63ff.). Serious *wergern* (women-men) "shamans" thus would have modeled themselves after the female "shamans" (1925:46). Among the Wiyot, too, women dominated healing activities, and it is likely that women-men participated in this sphere (1925:117).

In other cases, classes of "shamans" can be distinguished on the basis of the kind of supernatural power involved. Usually men appeared as "bear doctors" or as "rattlesnake doctors"—a role which diverges from general healing activities (see, e.g., Kroeber 1925: Pomo, 259; Yuki, 196; Maidu, 427; Yokuts, 512). Moreover, the bear doctor was not a healer, but rather a werewolf-like creature (1925:259, 854). Kroeber's information regarding women-men "shamans" is not detailed, so it is impossible to determine whether they practiced in feminine specialist areas where these existed. Even in places where the curing profession was almost exclusively restricted to women, however, a male did not have to undergo a gender role change in order to practice.

Generally, it seems that in California the healing activity of women-men was independent of their woman-man status, especially where both sexes could become "shamans." Contrary to the situation on the Plains, California males do not seem to have been destined, on the basis of visions or dreams, to undergo a gender role change and become "shamans" imbued with supernatural powers. Rather, consultants usually reported that "berdaches" were simply born as women-men (Achomawi, Voegelin 1942:228, but see also Voegelin 1942:134, where a dream is mentioned; Atsugewi, Voegelin 1942:228; Modoc, Voegelin 1942:228; Nisenan, Beals 1933:376; Shasta, Voegelin 1942:228; Wintu, Voegelin 1942:228; Yokuts, Kroeber 1925:497, "call of their natures"). Like any other person, however, women-men could be the recipients of dreams which conferred specialist capabilities.

Where women dominated healing activities, the women-men's adoption of the healer's role was most likely related to their gender role; the "shaman" role was part of their quasi-feminine status. This also explains why women-men typically did not assume the healing role in groups in which male "shamans" predominated. It was not that women-men were not allowed to be "shamans," but rather that this occupation was simply uninteresting to them: it was an aspect of the masculine, and not of the feminine, gender role.

Some evidence suggests that California women-men were considered less spiritually endowed than other people in a few cases. Among the Maidu, "berdaches and other incapable men" (Loeb 1933:175), that is, both women-men and men who had failed to meet the stringent training requirements for the secret society, were alike classified as *suku* ("dog" in Wintun; Loeb 1933:175, 185; see also Chapter 16 below). Similarly, R. C. White (1963:145f.) reported that the Luiseño *cuut* lacked *ayelkwi* (supernatural potential in the broadest sense), and since this lack could be recognized at birth, such boys were assigned to the *cuut* status from the time they were small (see also Boscana 1846:283). Thus Voegelin's statement that Maidu "berdaches" were "shamans" (1942:134) seems doubtful.

With regard to those remaining California tribes among whom women-men functioned as "shamans" despite male dominance, at least the Atsugewi *yaawaa* turned to the occupation of rattlesnake shaman, which was mostly restricted to women (Voegelin 1942:159). On the other hand, the neighboring Achomawi assigned the rattlesnake specialty to the masculine role domain, whereas the occupation of "singing doctor" or "soul-loss doctor" was open to women (1942:157). In these healing activities, however, stronger spiritual powers were in general attributed to men (Kroeber 1925:314); they acquired these powers in the framework of a vision quest undertaken at the time of puberty (1925:314). If, as Voegelin (1942:134) asserted, gender role change by Achomawi *yaawaa* occurred after puberty, it is probable that these women-men acquired their healing capabilities in the "masculine" way and later continued to practice as women-men.

THE PLATEAU

Among the Klamath, there seems to have been no fundamental relationship between gender role change and healing activities. The majority of the curers were male, and greater spiritual powers were attributed to male "shamans" than to female ones (Spier 1930:107). According to Spier, White Syndey [*sic*], a "berdache shaman," made a considerable fuss over his abilities but was not particularly esteemed by the Klamath (1930:52). Williams, on the other hand, claimed that White Syndey (White Cindy) was thoroughly respected and well liked, although the Klamath feared the curses uttered in his outbursts of rage; as a powerful "shaman," he even "outrivaled the chief in power" (1986b:41). Other Klamath *tw!inna'ek* evidently did not practice curing; nor did a latent supernatural power inhere in women-men on the basis of their sexual/gender ambiguity.

Only one woman-man was reported to have practiced as a "shaman" among the Modoc, and his/her status as healer does not seem to have been related to gender ambivalence (Ray 1963:43). Both males and females could become "shamans," but women could do so only after menopause. Thus healing was not a specifically feminine activity.

The sources are contradictory in regard to the Flathead. Teit (1930:384) reported that Flathead women-men, whose gender role change occurred at the injunction of guardian spirits, as a rule became "shamans" and devoted themselves to healing activities. According to Turney-High's (1937:85) Flathead consultants, however, "berdaches" did not have supernatural capabilities, nor was their gender role change legitimized by a vision. The vision quest was customary for both sexes (Turney-High 1937:33), as was the healer's role, although men seem to have predominated (women more often became herbal physicians; see Fahey 1974:14). Turney-High's (1937:27f.) report suggests that it is unlikely that the gender role change was connected to the vision leading to the profession of "shaman."

THE NORTHWEST COAST

In the case of the Tillamook, women-men's activity as healers seems to have been part of the expression of their feminine gender role: most "shamans" were female (Barnett 1937:189). Furthermore, stronger powers were attributed to women serving in this capacity, and unmarried healers of both sexes were the most highly valued (1937:189). It is not known whether the higher esteem in which female "shamans" were held also extended to women-men healers. Similarly, the healing activities of the women-men at Chetco River were related to their feminine role, since this specialty fell within the feminine role domain there as well (1937:189).

Among the Tolowa, "shamans" were usually women and women-men (Gould 1978:134), but not all women-men practiced curing activities (Driver 1939:347). Both male and female healers could demand high fees (Gould 1978:134) and attain high prestige in the Tolowa social structure, which was based on wealth (1978:131). The headman discussed in Chapter 5 who wore women's clothes and practiced as a healer (see Figure 4) exhibited so many elements of a masculine gender status that the adoption of healing activity in the framework of a feminine role cannot be assumed. Another Tolowa was likewise a woman-man and a "shaman" and worked together with his wife in feminine occupational areas (Driver 1939:405). This suggests that women-men could have taken on the role of healer in the framework of either a feminine or masculine gender role.

THE NAVAJO *NADLE:* LATENT SUPERNATURAL POWER WITHOUT SUPERNATURAL HEALING CAPABILITY

In Navajo society, the occupation of "chanter" is primarily restricted to men, but is in principle open to women, and when they enter it, they acquire considerable prestige and can pass the chants (healing rituals) on to other women (Reichard 1950: xliv). Reichard (1928:150) said about the *nadle* that "some are medicine men but it does not follow that an individual knows medicine because he is a berdache." The only really renowned *nadle* chanter of his time seems to have been Klah, who was classified as a *nadle* not because of his feminine tendencies, but because of a violent emasculation (Reichard 1950:141). He transvested only some years after this event, and later wore men's clothes (Reichard 1950:141). It was expressly said of another *nadle* that he "didn't know any medicine" (Reichard 1928:150); that is, he did not possess ritual knowledge. Stewart's consultants (1942:332) denied that *nadle* were "shamans"; Gifford (1940:163) mentioned a "shaman" of the Eastern Navajo who donned women's clothing in 1935 and began to weave.

Hill stated that most *nadle* learned and mastered one or more chants with proficiency. One *nadle* in White Cone was one of the last Hail Way Chanters. Kinipai specialized in healing rituals to cure mental illness caused by incest, and in addition was a well-known midwife. *Nadle* were not, however, said to be better qualified as chanters than other persons (1935:275). This at first seems surprising in view of the latent potency attributed to them as hermaphroditic bearers of good fortune and wealth. It is likely, though, that even the hermaphrodites of the origin story were gifted more on the material than on the spiritual plane (e.g., the invention of household objects). Furthermore, the status of *nadle* does not require supernatural legitimation. A child becomes *nadle* because he/she is physically intersexual or behaves like the opposite sex. Such backgrounds, meanwhile, are most definitely found in the Plains region as well. On the Plains, however, the vision experience—the individual's direct, personal contact with the supernatural—bestows supernatural power on the divergence of physical sex and role behavior. Such a concept is missing in Navajo society. Supernatural powers are not bestowed from such a source, but instead are based on quite definite and thoroughly worldly capabilities of the individual, for example, the ability to conduct a complicated chant with word-for-word accuracy (see, e.g., Reichard 1944:23), which is key to the efficacy of the ritual. His luck-bringing dual sexuality is of no help to the *nadle* if he is not capable of performing a healing ritual in all of its complex recitations and orders of events. The occupation of chanter is primarily one of technique, not a supernatural gift. Whoever learns and masters this technique as *nadle*—like Klah and Kinipai—gains the same good reputation and high esteem as ordinary men and women who can perform curative rituals (and who achieve corresponding successes). The *nadle*'s success as a chanter is due to his/her personal abilities, and not to his/her ambivalent gender status. The *nadle*'s luck-bringing characteristics lie in the material, not in the spiritual, domain.

Within this area, however, they are definitely "medicine persons" with special potential. The analogy with intersexual animals is significant here: Hill (1935:274, n. 1) reported that intersexual sheep mean that "you will have many sheep and grow rich." It is possible that sexual intercourse with *nadle* filled a similar function in increasing at least men's luck and prosperity, which would help explain the tremendously high number of sexual partners which Kinipai is said to have had in the course of her life (according to her own statements, over one hundred men), especially since Kinipai was a "real," that is, intersexual, *nadle*.

THE MOHAVE *ALYHA:* DESTINED TO DREAM

According to Kroeber (1925:749), the Mohave *alyha* specialized in healing a certain venereal disease which likewise bore the name "*alyha*." Devereux did not mention this, but he did report that it was convenient for "shamans" who specialized in healing syphilis to take an *alyha* as a wife (1937:516). *Alyha* and *hwame* (especially the latter) could become "exceptionally powerful shamans"; it was also said that they were successful in gambling games (1937:516). Dreams—to which all Mohave attached great significance—legitimized both gender role change and "shamanistic" occupation (1937:502; Kroeber 1925:748, 754f.). Mohave "shamans" were of both sexes, without a preponderance of men or women (Drucker 1941:158; Williams 1986b:35), although stronger powers were ascribed to female "shamans" (1986b:35). Williams (1986b:35) stated that "berdaches" were considered superior to both sexes with respect to their powers, but this is not confirmed in Devereux's report or other sources. In Mohave oral traditions, the god Mastamho destines the existence of "shamans" as well as *alyha* and *hwame* (Devereux 1937:501).

That *alyha* frequently became "shamans" explains an additional characteristic which the Mohave ascribed to them: *alyha,* it is said, died young (Kroeber 1925:749). They had this in common with other "shamans" as well as with warriors: "Doctors and brave men are alike. The latter say, 'I do not wish to live long.' A doctor says: 'I shall not live a long time. I wish to die. That is why I kill people. Why do you not kill me?'" (Consultant in Kroeber 1925:778). "Shamans" who, on account of a failed harvest, or because of cases of death, aroused the Mohaves' suspicions were frequently killed (1925:778f.). Thus, *alyha* (and some *hwame,* too) died young not because they were "berdaches," but because they were "shamans." If they were suspected of witchcraft, they were killed just like any other shaman was.

The relationship of the *alyha* to the supernatural in Mohave society is at first difficult to recognize because dreams did not transform their recipients into sacred or holy persons, like the vision quest on the Plains. The Mohave did not have the concept of a guardian spirit (Kroeber 1925:775); dreams bestowed supernatural potential on "shamans," but no supernatural status (Kroeber 1925:778f.). Their abilities could be questioned, and they could be killed (1925:779). Neither did they have the power to put curses on people (Devereux 1937:510f.). *Alyha* nonetheless did possess spiritual power. This is shown in the fact that they themselves frequently became "shamans" and also in the fact that they were the preferred partners of male "shamans." It is possible that their special link to the supernatural was established by the dream that caused their gender role change. They did not necessarily receive "shaman" dreams, although they could. Typically, *alyhas'* first dream was followed by others which brought success at gambling. It is unlikely that the latent spiritual power of the *alyha* derived from their sexual ambiguity. Even so, as with the women-men of the Plains region, the *alyhas'* cross-dressing and cross-acting were manifestations of direct contact with the supernatural.

BETWEEN TWO CONTINENTS: THE ST. LAWRENCE ESKIMO

The St. Lawrence Eskimo occupied a cultural position between those of the North American Arctic and Siberia. Among the St. Lawrence Eskimo, both sexes filled the role of "shaman," and males who had carried out a gender role change were regarded as especially powerful (Murphy and Leighton 1965:72), as were "normal" men (Murphy 1964:75). Murphy's (1964:75) conjecture that for the *anasik* (women-men), gender role change and the shamanic call occurred simultaneously through a spirit-helper may well be true, particularly since the St. Lawrence Eskimo were in a transitional zone between the traditional Eskimo cultures and the Siberian groups (Murphy and Leighton 1965:71). The transvesting Eskimo shaman's call was probably a variant of the Siberian form (see Bogoraz 1907:449ff.). As among the St. Lawrence Eskimo, Chukchee shamanism included cross-dressing for curative purposes (1907:450). The Chukchee, though, had both complete gender role change and a partial gender role change which was lacking among the St. Lawrence Eskimo, along with transvesting as a disguise to protect against malevolent spirits (1907:450). Unfortunately, Murphy and Leighton did not give further information on the cultural background of the *anasik* status; they interpreted the role of the transvesting shaman as the only opportunity in the culture of this Eskimo group to follow one's homosexual inclinations, since the people disapproved of homosexual behavior (Murphy 1964:63f., 74f.; Murphy and Leighton 1965:89). It cannot be determined whether the *anasik* practiced as shamans in the framework of a feminine or a masculine gender role. It is evident, however, that their reputation and high standing corresponded to that of their male colleagues. Since details pertaining to gender role change were not reported, it is not clear whether *anasik* cross-dressed but otherwise retained a masculine role, as was at least partly the case with the partially transformed "soft men" of the Chukchee. In any case, all *anasik* were shamans (but not vice versa); gender role change and shamanism were associated to a greater extent than among cultures of the North American subcontinent.

CONCLUSIONS

Women-men's participation in the role of "shaman," medicine man, or other healer must be seen in connection with the sexual division of labor and ideas concerning supernatural powers. Where the curative activity lay preponderantly within the feminine role domain, women-men seem to have expressed the feminine gender role via the role of healer. Women-men did not become "shamans" in only two cases in which the healers of the tribe were preponderantly female. Where medicine people or healers were predominantly male, it is likely that this role would not have been attractive to women-men because it belonged to the masculine area of activity. This interpretation seems more plausible than Essene's (1942:65) idea that women-men were not eligible to take over the function of healer in some tribes on account of their gender status, although this was also true in some cases. Among the Lassik and the Pomo, for example, both sexes could become healers, but not women-men (Essene 1942:65). Exclusion of women-men from the healer profession was also found among the Chugach Eskimo, Northern Paiute, Wintu, Yuma, Northern Shoshoni, and Ute, although in these groups the women-men's status was not explicitly cited as the reason. Although DuBois' (1935:50) Wintu consultants and also two of the Wintu groups interviewed by Voegelin (1942:134) denied that "berdaches" could become "shamans," one Wintu local group affirmed the existence of this practice. Generally, thus, it seems to have been somewhat unusual, but not impossible, for women-men to take up this occupation in these cultures.

In other instances, it is inexplicable why women-men did not become healers. The *elxa* of the Yuma, for example, possessed more supernatural power than ordinary males (Forde 1931:157). Although most Nevada Shoshoni consultants denied that "berdaches" could become healers, Steward (1941:353) reported on two groups in which males who held the Shoshoni equivalent of the woman-man status became "doctors." Thus, *tüvasa* were not generally excluded from the healer role. Why the Chugach Eskimo women-men were not able to become shamans is not clear, particularly since they were highly esteemed and were regarded as more skillful than ordinary humans, as well as luck bearing (Birket-Smith 1953:94). Here, too, the information is both contradictory and full of gaps.

In any case, whenever consultants denied that women-men could be healers, it may be that this activity was not considered appropriate to the feminine gender role or that women-men were regarded as unfit for this occupation.

Reports have affirmed that women-men practiced the occupation of "shaman" in twenty-one Native American cultures. Women were the main practitioners in one-third of these cases, and the occupation was obviously chosen by the women-men as an aspect of their feminine gender role. Where men were the primary healers or medicine men, the women-men moved partly within the domain of the masculine gender role, both with respect to their status as medicine "men" and also with regard to acquisition of the necessary supernatural powers. Women's clothes and components of the feminine gender role appeared there as the expression of the personal "medicine" of a woman-man. In such cases, women-men were not healers in the framework of the feminine gender role, but—despite their ambivalent gender status—they were males with a special kind of supernatural power. Even among the Hidatsa, where the *miati* had access to the Holy Women Society, their kind of latent supernatural power distinguished them both qualitatively and quantitatively from the women. Within the ritual group, they held a special status which could not be filled by a woman. Consequently, the women-men's activity as healers in groups in which visions legitimated gender role change was at bottom only one aspect of their status as holy or sacred persons (*wakan, manitu,* etc.). This means that especially in the Plains region itself, still other ceremonial roles were classified as belonging to the woman-man, which at first glance seem to have belonged neither to the masculine nor to the feminine gender role.

It is a characteristic of the vision-stressing cultures on the Prairies and Plains that women-men were regarded as holy persons. By contrast, this quality of the holy or sacred was almost entirely lacking in the women-men of California. The literature even suggests that some women-men there were actually characterized by spiritual deficits. Insofar as information is available, it is remarkable that in the majority of California tribes, women-men were not active as "shamans," whether because they were regarded as not having the necessary spiritual gifts or because the "shamanic" function was predominantly carried out by men and therefore held no attraction for women-men. Women-men in the role of healers were also the exception on the Plateau and in the Great Basin, even if one considers the inconsistency of the data for the latter region. Both the transvesting Tolowa chieftain and White Syndey, who was competing with a local chief for power and prestige, show highly developed elements of masculine role behavior. Considered in general terms, a weighting of the healer's role in favor of one sex is not very pronounced in either of these two culture areas, so women-men probably did not take up this occupation in order to consolidate and emphasize their feminine gender role. Nor were they in principle excluded from it on account of their quasi-feminine or ambivalent status. Thus, the most likely explanation is that women-men (like other persons) became healers on account of personal abilities.

The same holds true for the Navajo *nadle,* particularly since chanters were esteemed on the basis of skill. Among the Modoc and the Klamath, as well, curative activity was not strongly associated with gender role change, and the latter was not associated with supernatural power. In the case of the Mohave *alyha,* a latent spiritual power underlay their "shaman's" function; this latent power, however, seems to have had little to do with gender role change itself, but instead with the special ability of the *alyha* to receive dreams. *Alyha* were no more holy than the Mohave "shamans." Finally, the *anasik* of the St. Lawrence Eskimo were instructed to undertake a gender role change from the same spirit-helpers which bestowed shamanistic capabilities on them.

Women-men, therefore, exercised the function of a healer under the following conditions:

1. Within the framework of their feminine gender role.
2. On the basis of visions that became manifested in the external, visible symbol form of gender role change, making the woman-man a holy/sacred person and destining him to become a healer or medicine man.
3. On the basis of visions or dreams which conferred on the woman-man supernatural healing capabilities, independently of a certain gender status or of his gender role change.
4. On the basis of visions which called a woman-man especially to become a "shaman" and at the same time required a gender role change.

The distinction between 2 and 4 (the latter represented by the St. Lawrence Eskimo alone) consists in the fact that in the first case, the woman-man became qualified as a healer, but also—and independently of it—had access to latent spiritual power, part of which was reserved for him on account of his gender status. The orders of his spirit-helper primarily consisted of the requirement that he had to undertake a gender role change in order to avoid suffering harm. In the case of 4, the assumption of shamanistic activity is emphasized. In one case (4), gender role change is the secondary phenomenon; in the other (2), the qualification as medicine man or healer (see Bogoraz 1907:450 with reference to the Siberian variant, and Lurie 1953:508 with reference to the Prairie and Plains variant).

Chapter TEN

OTHER SPECIALIZED OCCUPATIONS OF WOMEN-MEN

SKILLED HANDCRAFT SPECIALIZATIONS

In Native American cultures, women's specialist occupations and activities involved producing objects which every woman usually knew how to fabricate, for example, pottery among the Pueblos, baskets in California, or rugs among the Navajo. Women-men were also active in these areas, especially in the Southwest, where weaving and the production of pottery underwent a renaissance after the turn of the century, in part because of increased tourism. In Bunzel's (1929) time, most of the potters there were female, and there were virtually no women-men left among the Pueblos. The few men who became renowned as potters (primarily designers of the decorative patterns), such as Julian Martinez, Popovi Da, Tony Da, or Joseph Lonewolf, were not women-men (Arizona Highways 1974). Men evidently penetrated this branch of handcrafted folk art only when it began to produce prestige objects and profits: in this case, a feminine role area had become a prestige occupation appropriate for both sexes.

Women-men do not seem to have been active in the area of men's specialist occupations, although a Hopi woman-man who died in 1891 produced painted clay tiles which were used on altars in the kivas, which belonged to the masculine sphere (Fewkes 1892:11; Parsons 1939b:354).

Women-men were often specialists in women's handcraft areas that offered them the opportunity of making a name for themselves, particularly within their feminine role, such as through the production of high-quality pottery and textiles. Stevenson (1904:37) described the *lhamana* as the best weavers and potters in Zuni. Stevenson (1904:38) also portrayed a *lhamana* as one of the richest "men" [*sic*] in Zuni; this wealth was no doubt the result of hard work and competence in the area of women's handcrafted artwork. Other *lhamana* worked as washerwomen for officers' families stationed at Fort Wingate (1904:380). Roscoe (1988b:58) wrote of a *mojaro* from Acoma, who—like other women-men—was counted among the best potters there. One of the last women-men in Laguna was a renowned potter who introduced typical Zuni ceramic designs into Laguna after a visit to Zuni (Bunzel 1929:57). Valentino (Dyamu) from Laguna was known as an excellent potter (Parsons 1932:246). A *tüvasa* of the Paviotso at Pyramid Lake specialized as a washerwoman for Whites (Lowie 1924:283). Kasinelu and Tsalatitse from Zuni were first-class plasterers, as was also Palure from Isleta (Parsons 1932:246). Kasinelu was, in addition, an outstanding potter (Parsons 1916:523). House plastering was women's work in Zuni (Gifford 1940:22). Of the other six *lhamana* on whom Parsons obtained information, two were skilled weavers (Parsons 1916:523). Navajo *nadle* were often active in the feminine occupation of weaving (Gifford 1940: 49; Hill 1935:275; Reichard 1950:141; Stewart 1942:341), as well as pottery and basket weaving (Hill 1935:275). The proceeds from such work contributed significantly to the *nadle*'s prosperity (1935:275).

Oglala Lakota *winkte* fashioned beadwork and quillwork in "top quality" (Williams 1986a:194), just as they are said to have performed all women's tasks better than women themselves (1986a:195). Mirsky (1937a:417) also attested to the "exceptional skill" of the *winkte* in beadwork, saying that they were "most skilful of all in womanly arts and crafts." Hassrick (1982:137) mentioned that handcrafts produced by *winkte* were greatly sought after and sold very well.

Where the traditional culture was tottering, women-men readily chose women's professions according to the Anglo-American model. Louise became a housekeeper to a prosperous family (Landes 1970:196); one of Williams' (1986a:198) *winkte* consultants became a nurse and a cook in a home for the aged; and Laspeke from Zuni became a cook with a road-building company (Parsons 1939a:338)—women's work according to traditional ideas.

Spier's (1930:52) Klamath woman-man consultant wove baskets for sale, as women otherwise did. Papago women-men were gifted producers of pottery and baskets (Underhill 1939:186); Ponca *mixu'ga* produced the best quillwork and beadwork in the tribe (J. H. Howard 1965:142f.). With regard to the Kato, Lassik, Pomo, and Yuki, women-men wove "as good or better baskets than women" (Essene 1942:65); and the Maidu women-men specialized in the production of the feather costumes used in dances (Loeb 1933:175; on the costumes, see Dixon 1905:284ff.). The latter case is clearly a matter of a feminine specialization, because *suku* were regarded as unfit to do men's work (Loeb 1933:175).

ROLES RELATED TO DEATH AND WAR

The burial of the dead and the war complex are two main areas of activity which have been reported as relegated specifically to women-men, particularly in California (death) and the Plains (war). That women-men had special functions in connection with burial festivities has been reported from the Achomawi and Atsugewi (Voegelin 1942:134), Bankalachi (Driver 1937:90), Mono (Gifford 1933:44, n. 39a; Driver 1937: 90), Tübatulabal (Driver 1937:90), and Yokuts (Driver 1937:90; Gayton 1948:46; Kroeber 1925:497; Wallace 1978b:455), although detailed information is available only for the latter two groups. More detailed information concerning the functions of women-men at burials is likewise available from the Oglala Lakota (Williams 1986a:195) and from the Timucua (Le Moyne 1875:8).

Women-men have also been reported as accompanying warriors on raiding expeditions to care for the wounded (Cheyenne, Grinnell 1962, 2:40, Hoebel 1960:77; Achomawi, Voegelin 1942:134; Oglala Lakota, Williams 1986a:194; Huchnom, Foster 1944:228; Karankawa, Newcomb 1961:74; Timucua, LeMoyne 1875:7f.). Women-men also had special ceremonial roles associated with the Scalp Dance (Cheyenne, Grinnell 1962, 2: 40f.).

Women-men performed special functions in connection with the Sun Dance in three cases (Crow, Lowie 1935:48, 312f.; Hidatsa, Bowers 1965:167; Oglala Lakota, Williams 1986b:36f.). A further special task of women-men in some tribes was to bestow auspicious names on various individuals (Oglala Lakota, Hassrick 1982:137, Lame Deer 1979: 169f., W. K. Powers 1977:38, 58, Williams 1986a:194, 195; Papago, Underhill 1939:186). Moreover, among the Winnebago (Lurie 1953: 708) and the Oglala Lakota (Lame Deer 1979:169; Williams 1986a: 194), they possessed the gift of soothsaying, but this was not restricted to them exclusively. An additional role frequently assumed by the women-men was that of mediator between lovers or married persons.

Burial and Mourning Ceremony

Women-men primarily functioned in some tribes as gravediggers, and had no particular responsibilities during mourning ceremonies (Bankalachi, Driver 1937:90; Mono, Driver 1937:90; but see Gifford 1933: 44, n. 39a). In other tribes, however, they distinguished themselves in the framework of mourning ceremonies or performed functions in connection with both mourning and burial, as, for example, among the Tübatulabal (Driver 1937:90). Whereas Voegelin's (1938:47) Tübatulabal consultant denied any activity on the part of *huiy* (women-men) as gravediggers or as "professional mourners," Driver's consultant mentioned a function at the mourning ceremony (Driver 1937:90). Driver characterized women-men as the exclusive gravediggers among both the Tübatulabal and Bankalachi (a branch of the Tübatulabal). This was a paid occupation (Driver 1937:99). According to Kroeber (1925:497), the Yokuts *tongochim* (*tonochim* in some subgroups) were both grave-diggers and leaders of the mourning ceremony held immediately after the death and then annually. They alone are supposed to have prepared the dead for burial or cremation (Kroeber 1925:497). They also functioned as professional mourners before the body (Kroeber 1925:500), and among the Tachi Yokuts they led the Tonochim Dance *(tonochmin hatim)* on the occasion of the first public gathering after a death had taken place. In the course of this dance, they could enrich themselves materially, either by randomly helping themselves to property which had to be liquidated by the real owners after the dance, or by "capturing" persons who had overstepped a line drawn by one of the *tonochim* on the dance floor: the "prisoner" then had to be ransomed (Kroeber 1925:500). At the annual mourning ceremony as well, the *tonochim* led the singing and, even though they had already been paid for their services, once again received valuables as presents, provided of course that these did not have to be burned along with the images portraying the deceased (Kroeber 1925:500f.).

Other information, meanwhile, indicates either that these tasks, which formerly were the privilege of women-men, were eventually extended to common persons, or that they possibly were never restricted to women-men. One possible source of confusion is that, in many Yokuts groups, *tongochim* means "gravedigger," but in others it means "berdache"; in still others, it means both (see Driver 1937:99; Gayton 1948:46, 106, 149). It is also conceivable that the mourning ceremony and the burial were restricted to women-men only in some Yokuts subgroups, but that in other local groups, these were also—or even exclusively—performed by ordinary men and women, as indicated by Driver's tables (1937:90, 99). There and also in Gayton (1948:46, 149), the term *tongochim* was the professional designation for the gravedigger, but no reference was made to women-men. This profession was inheritable from father to son among the Choinimni Yokuts, and Gayton's (1948:149) consultants disagreed that *tono'cim* were "berdaches," stating that "they were just plain men and women." It was the same among the Tachi Yokuts—the grandmother of a female consultant of Gayton's (1948:168) had been a gravedigger. Among the Paleuyami Yokuts, women-men and men shared this task in such a way that there were always two men and two women-men who buried the dead, and who together were called *tonocim.* They also performed a dance, the *to'onoci'ma,* at the annual mourning ceremony (1948:46). Gayton's (1948:46, n. 12) conjecture that these pairs were in each case bound by a "homosexual" relationship cannot be proven. But the facts that Yokuts women-men did not generally enter into relationships with men (Driver 1937:90) and that the marriage (mentioned to Gayton 1948:106) of a woman-man to a man was cited as the cause of the woman-man's death both speak against Gayton's hypothesis. The corpse handlers of the Wukchimni Yokuts were obviously women, although women-men also took over this task occasionally (1948:107). It is possible in this case that women without daughters raised their sons as daughters in order to pass on the gravediggers' profession. However, this was not required to safeguard the profession's existence, since female gravediggers could when necessary be named by the village chieftain (1948:107). The Michahai Yokuts and the Waksachi Yokuts had women-men who were gravediggers, although the women-men took up this profession only if they had received instructions to do so in a dream (1948:226).

Among the Mono, too, gravedigging and mourning functions were not restricted to women-men. In two of the groups consulted by Driver (1937: 90, 99), a "normal individual" was also able to carry out this task; and in all cases, any functions of women-men in connection with the mourning ceremony were denied. Where non-"berdaches" were gravediggers, the office was inheritable from father to son; this is also true in one case in which women-men were named as gravediggers (1937:99). Gifford (1933:44, n.39a) thought that the leader of a wake at which he was present (occasioned by the death of a woman) was a "berdache." Finally, Gayton's (1948:274) consultants denied any activity on the part of Mono women-men in connection with the bewailing and burial of the dead. The professional singers at the Mono lamentation were both men and women, and either these people or a strong woman carried the corpse to the grave or to the pyre (Gayton 1948:274). According to Driver's (1937:138) Entimbich Mono consultants, gravediggers were married and had children; Driver assumed that gravediggers were usually women. Further, Driver's (1937:138) suggestion that the married gravediggers could not have been "real berdaches" is doubtful, since gender role change was not necessarily accompanied by same-sex relationships.

Timucua women-men were entrusted with the task of burying the dead both in everyday life and during war expeditions (see Figure 6). Le Moyne (1875:7f.) explained that women-men possessed especially great physical strength. Thus, they also carried the provisions on war expeditions, and they loaded persons with infectious diseases onto their shoulders and carried them to a special place in order to nurse them back to health (1875: 7f.). A passage from Swanton (1946) suggests that these activities belonged to the feminine role domain and were therefore not restricted to the women-men: "The male concubines or berdaches *relieved women of*

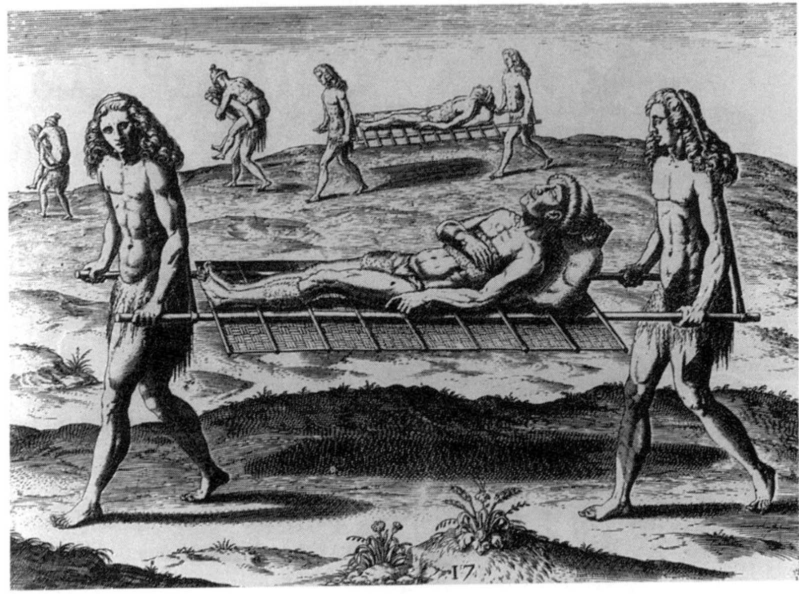

Timucua "Hermaphrodites" carrying the sick. (From Le Moyne 1970 [1603], p. XVII.) Reproduced by permission of Reprint-Verlag Konrad Kölbl KG, © 1970.

much of their labor. They carried provisions for a war party, undertook the burial of the dead, and removed those who had contagious diseases to special places where they could be taken care of" (Swanton 1946:713; emphasis mine). Only Williams said anything concerning the *winkte* playing a role at Oglala Lakota funerals. A female consultant, whose grandfather had been *winkte,* told Williams (1986a:195): "When someone died, it was the winkte who was the first one people came to, to help out at the funeral and the ceremonies." The *winkte* who were interviewed by Williams did not, however, mention these functions themselves.

In regard to the California tribes, it is remarkable that in four of the six tribes in which women-men were active as buriers of the dead and/or as leaders of the mourning ceremonies, they did not also become "shamans" (Bankalachi, Mono, Tübatulabal, Yokuts; see Table 2.) At a certain time, or in certain subgroups of the Bankalachi, Yokuts, and Tübatulabal, however, they had at least a formal monopoly on the burial of the dead; they likewise seem to have constituted the major part of this specialist group among the Mono. The attitude toward women-men in California was generally benevolent, but they were not regarded as being endowed with special supernatural powers. In places where non-

"berdaches" also carried out this activity, it should not be classified as feminine, except in one subgroup of the Yokuts. The same holds true for the Tachi Yokuts, where women were gravediggers as well (Gayton 1948:31). The Yokuts' explanations of why a person became a gravedigger are prosaic: someone "grew up that way," "with a desire 'to get rid of the dead'. They had no special totemic or dream helper" (Gayton 1948:168). The Yokuts also referred to dreams sent by the dead which moved someone to take up this occupation (1948:226).

The sources for all of the tribes indicate generally that the job of corpse handler and undertaker was not restricted on the basis of gender. However, since women usually (and exclusively among the Tachi Yokuts) became gravediggers, it is probable that women-men were welcomed eagerly as co-workers when it was a matter of laboriously excavating a grave with digging sticks, or of carrying a corpse, which occasionally had to be managed by a single person. This is true of the Achomawi (Voegelin 1942:135) and of the Yokuts (Gayton 1948:236), although among the Michahai Yokuts and the Waksachi Yokuts, a man had to carry a male corpse, and a woman a female one (Gayton 1948:336). The women-man's feminine gender role, combined with his male physical strength, made him well suited to such a task.

Thus, particularly in California, it is likely that the woman-man's activity as gravedigger (and other death-related activities) should be seen as an expression of his feminine gender role rather than as a function of an association between women-men and the supernatural. Because activities such as carrying the corpse required physical strength and at the same time often devolved upon women (one of Gayton's 1948:236 consultants described Yokuts corpse handlers as "big women"), they would have been viable tasks for women-men. In contrast to "shamanistic" activity, which in the groups concerned was clearly dominated by men (see Table 2), the occupation of gravedigger offered the women-men a profitable and certainly prestigious feminine role component.

The *winkte* may have been involved in the organization of mourning ceremonies and of burials, although such participation is mentioned only once in the literature. In Oglala Lakota society, the public lamentation for the dead was the task of the women (Hassrick 1982:325), and carrying the corpse to the burial scaffold devolved specifically on old women (1982:326). According to Hassrick (1982:325f.), organization of mourning was the responsibility of a male *wicasa wakan,* or holy man (Walker 1980:79). Since Williams' consultant said that *winkte* were called upon to help out at funerals and mourning ceremonies, they seem to have participated both in the practical aspects of the funeral (otherwise taken care of by women) and in the ceremonial aspects (that otherwise devolved on the *wicasa wakan*). Thus, the particular ambivalence of the *winkte* status found expression through participation in both masculine and feminine role components.

Roles in the War Complex

In a few of the tribes in which women-men went to war, they did not go to fight themselves, but rather to fulfill other tasks. The *heemaneh'* of the Cheyenne were frequently requested to accompany warriors, primarily in large war expeditions, in order to take charge of the wounded (Grinnell 1962, 2:40). Apparently the *heemaneh'* were valued in war expeditions; Hoebel suggested that because of their "self-abstinence and denial of their natural-born sex," they possessed a "high 'psychological' potential of stored-up virility," "which is just what the Cheyenne feel is necessary for successful fighting" (1960:77). The Cheyenne themselves offered a simpler explanation: the *heemaneh'* were "good company and fine talkers," and beyond that were very skillful healers (Grinnell 1962, 2:40). It is also conceivable that, as in the case of the Natchez "chefs des femmes" (Dumont 1753:249), they cooked for the warriors and kept the camp in order, particularly on the bigger raids; among the Plains tribes, this was the job of small boys or, occasionally, of some women (Hartmann 1979:166).

In the Plains region, however, the medicine persons who accompanied war parties were male (see Hartmann 1979:106), which also holds true of the Cheyenne (Grinnell 1962, 2:141). Thus, although the *heemaneh'* may have brought to bear certain aspects of their feminine role (cooking), as medicine *men* they accompanied the warriors in a function which clearly belonged to the masculine role, namely as specialists who, during fighting in enemy territory, were able to attend to wounds promptly and knowledgeably. The same holds true for the individual *winkte,* who in their women's role looked after the warriors' camp, but who otherwise fulfilled the masculine role of the battlefield surgeon (Williams 1986a:194; see Hartmann 1979:106 on male medicine men in Oglala Lakota war parties).

One of the two Achomawi groups affirmed "nursing in war" by women-men (Voegelin 1942:134), but they denied any activity on their part as healers/"shamans" (1942:134). Their male "shamans" always went into battle along with the warriors, but evidently less as healers than as a guarantee of supernatural assistance (1942:109). For the Achomawi, "war" actually took on quite a different form than it did on the Plains. For them, as in California generally, it was more a matter of acts of revenge and family feuds of narrowly limited scope (Kroeber 1925:843), although the Achomawi in addition had to fear surprise attacks from their northern neighbors, on account of the trade in slaves customary there (Kroeber 1925:308). The women-men's function as caregivers is the same as what women did when someone was injured during a raid or feud. Women-men did not function as supernaturally legitimated healers, either because they were excluded from or were not interested in this masculine activity.

The task of the Huchnom *iwap k'uti* of carrying wounded and dead warriors home clearly belonged to the feminine role domain (Foster 1944: 228). Men feared this task, because it was inauspicious to be smeared with blood; most women, however, "were not strong enough" (Foster 1944:228). Thus, the *iwap k'uti* combined the female immunity against pollution through contact with blood with male physical strength, so that, in the context of the feminine gender role, they were especially well suited for the evacuation of the dead and wounded.

As noted, the evacuation or rescuing of the dead or wounded among the Timucua fell within the feminine role domain (Swanton 1946:693). In the case of the Karankawa, the participation of women-men was probably also a component of the feminine role, especially since it was stressed that they "conduct themselves in every way like women" (Newcomb 1961:74); during raids, the women-men watched over the horses which their warriors had stolen, so that they did not run away (1961:74).

The Cheyenne *heemaneh'* also led the Scalp Dance, which was held after the return of a war party. The best scalps were given to them, and they carried the scalps into the village on long poles (Grinnell 1962, 2: 40). On the Plains, the Scalp Dance was generally a women's dance (Niethammer 1985:241). Among the Cheyenne, the dance was choreographed to a certain extent by the *heemaneh'*, but biological women also danced with scalps (Grinnell 1962, 2:41). Moreover, the *heemaneh'* filled the clown's function at the Scalp Dance (Grinnell 1962, 2:41). Within the framework of the celebrations after a successful war expedition, the other dances at the closing of the ceremony possessed an erotic element, and were likewise led by the *heemaneh'* (Grinnell 1962, 2:41f.).

It is likely that women-men took part in the Scalp Dance in other tribes as well—not necessarily in a privileged position, but rather in the framework of the usual feminine gender role. Among the Papago, for example, a woman-man sometimes danced around a captured Apache scalp, threatened it with a bow, and shouted insults at it: "See what you are reduced to! The men will not look at you, but I, even I, can shoot you" (Underhill 1939:186). At the welcoming celebration for returning warriors, Mohave *alyha* tied wooden phalli around their hips like the old women did and "copulated" with the men who had stayed behind, whom they insulted by calling "*alyha*"—which means not only woman-man, but also "coward" (Devereux 1937:517).

Thus, the Cheyenne *heemaneh'* participated in war expeditions in a masculine role—that of medicine men—but afterward, in their feminine role, they received scalps (like the women who stayed behind) and, still in the same role, led the Scalp Dance. The fact that they were given the best scalps is surely because they were being recognized for their services in the war party. Their function as leaders at the victory celebrations should be seen as a function of their masculine supernatural "medicine," which was stronger than the women's. The *heemaneh*'s masculine power thus conferred on him/her the privilege not only of participating in the Scalp Dance, but also of leading it. Generally, the women-men did not have privileges of this kind in Mohave or Papago society, where the specific vision-dependent legitimization, which makes the recipient a holy person with a very specific kind of latent supernatural power, was lacking. (Grinnell did not explicitly mention that the *heemaneh'* status was legitimized through visions, but the overall Plains pattern and also the Cheyenne componential organization and formulation suggests it.)

The Cheyenne *heemaneh'* are an especially apt example of the Plains tendency for women-men to be able to retain aspects of both gender roles, or to alternate back and forth between the roles. An additional expression of the ambivalent status of the *heemaneh'* is, moreover, that they possessed both masculine and feminine forms of their names, and that their voice register is said to have lain somewhere between that of males and females (Grinnell 1962, 2:39f.).

Roles in the Sun Dance

Participation of men-women in the Sun Dance has been reported from only three tribes. In the case of the Hidatsa, it was the responsibility of the *miati* to select a suitable tree trunk for the center post of the dance bower from driftwood in the Missouri river (Bowers 1965:167), and later to stamp down the earth around the center post, which in the meantime had been erected by young men. Together with the female members of the Holy Women Society, the *miati* also set up the side posts (Bowers 1965:315, 326). According to Lowie (1919:424f.), however, one or two expert young Hidatsa *men* tracked down the driftwood log like an enemy (the typical Sun Dance pattern; see Spier 1921b:465), and other men then set it upright on its base. Among the Crow, the first post (the Crow Sun Dance bower did not have a center post) was felled ceremonially by a chaste and respectable woman, by a war captive, usually female, and also by a *bate* (Lowie 1935:312). The woman struck the trunk of the tree four times with a tine from the antler rack of a wapiti (North American elk, *Cervus canadensis*), the female captive painted a black ring around it, and then the *bate* touched the tree with an ax and subsequently felled it (Lowie 1935:313). According to Lowie, the tree represented an enemy who would be "felled" later on by means of the ceremonies of the Sun Dance (1935:313). The felling of the other trees necessary for the structure of the dance bower was handled without ceremony by young women (1935:313). Before the felling of the first tree, the *bate* used to hide themselves, but the village police tracked one of them down: "Amidst general merriment he would cover his face with bashfulness" (1935:312). After the villagers had shot at the fallen tree and young men had touched it with their coup-sticks, the role of the *bate* ended—"he slunk away" (1935:313), "hid in the crowd, being ashamed" (Lowie 1915:32). The general amusement at the recruitment of the *bate* may be related to the symbolism of felling the tree, since, in general, the *bate* was a nonwarrior.

In the early 1980s, Williams (1986b:36f.) recorded the *winkte*'s role in the Lakota Sun Dance. The *winkte* felled the tree for the center post, and after the tree had been carried to the dance grounds, the *winkte* recited a prayer. After that, the post was erected, and finally the *winkte* stamped down the earth around the center post (1986b:36f.). Williams noted that the blessing of a *winkte* was apparently necessary for the success of important rituals: "It was no accident that Terry [the *winkte*] had been asked to bless the Sun Dance pole; this was the proper way of assuring a successful ritual" (1986b:37).

At least among the Hidatsa, the *miati* participated in the erection of the Sun Dance bower as members of the Holy Women Society. The women set up the side posts; the *miati* could take part in this, but did not have to (Bowers 1965:316, 326). Just as in the case of the *winkte* and the *bate,* they were associated either with the center post or with the first, ceremonially most significant, post. As noted, the felling of the tree symbolizes the "felling" of an enemy—an activity which clearly belonged to the masculine role. Among the Crow, a woman hinted at the felling symbolically before the bate carried it out, and both the *bate* and the woman captive at the same time went through "sham motions" which represented the killing of an enemy (Lowie 1935:313). Within the symbolic framework of these actions, the killing of an enemy was temporarily shifted into the feminine role sphere.

Among the other Plains tribes, felling the center post was not the job of the women-men, but usually the job of the men (Spier 1921b:466, 467; see also Goddard 1919:301, 307; Skinner 1919b:288ff., 1919c: 313; Wallis 1919:326; Wissler 1918:254). Felling the center post devolved upon women among a few tribes (Oglala Lakota, Spier 1921b: 467; Walker 1917:106; Kiowa, Spier 1921a:440; Crow, Lowie 1915: 33; Arapaho and Arikara, Spier 1921b:467). Among the Oglala Lakota and the Crow, at least, the felling of the center post evidently devolved regularly on women, either symbolically (indicated by their touching the post with the antler tine, as in the Crow case) or actually, as in the Oglala Lakota situation (Lowie 1915:33; Walker 1917:106). At the same time, however, these three Siouan language-speaking groups are exactly those groups of the Plains region which conceded women-men the most distinctive spiritual position, a status which otherwise was held only by important medicine men. Traditionally, it has been reported for both the Lakota and the Hidatsa that women-men performed a large number of ritual functions which were supernaturally legitimized. In the case of the Crow *bate*, this latent spiritual power appears in less highly developed form. Today they play a leading role in connection with the singing of love songs at certain tribal festivals (Williams 1986b:53). Traditionally, however, their power was expressed through their execution of all feminine tasks to perfection; they possessed the biggest and most beautiful tipis and were "highly regarded for their many charitable acts" (Simms 1903:580). Their activities as healers or as ritual specialists certainly must have counted as "charitable acts" as well.

As males in a feminine gender role, the *winkte* and *bate* took up an occupation that in their own tribes had been transferred from the masculine to the feminine gender role (Spier 1921b:467). At the same time, having a nonwarrior such as a woman or a woman-man fell the center post or the first post certainly reinforced the warriors' own perception of their masculinity and male prowess.

OTHER SPECIALIZED OCCUPATIONS

Among the special tasks of the *winkte* was that of giving children names that were regarded as especially auspicious (Hassrick 1982:137; Lame Deer 1979:169f.; W. K. Powers 1977:38; Williams 1986a:194, 195, 1986b:37f.). In Oglala Lakota society, and within a ceremonial context, each child was ultimately given a name which replaced the name that the child had received at birth. Relatives were generally asked to perform the name giving, but sometimes *winkte* also participated (W. K. Powers 1977:38). Usually only boys received *winkte* names (Hassrick 1982:137; Lame Deer 1979:169). A *winkte* name ensured spiritual protection as well as long life and health (Williams 1986b:37). In contrast to Mohave *alyha*, longevity was attributed to *winkte* themselves (1986b:38), and thus, through the ceremony of name giving, they handed on some of their own latent spiritual power and longevity to others. Hassrick's (1989:313) remark that *winkte* names were often said to be "unmentionable" suggests that these names were erotic in nature, like the names which Papago women-men bestowed on adults. Although these names were sexy and funny (Lame Deer 1979:170), the fact that they were "unmentionable" probably had less to do with their being erotically colored (or "pornographic," as Hassrick 1989:313 chose to put it), than with their being *secret* names (Lame Deer 1979:169); if they had been uttered, they would have lost their efficacy.

The naming ceremony proceeded as follows. First, a boy's father sought out a *winkte* and "flirts with him sexually" (Williams 1986b:37). Then the *winkte* underwent an exhaustive ritual preparation, sought visions, and also gave the boy spiritual instruction. These preparations culminated in a ceremony with the boy and his family during which the *winkte* presented the boy with a medicine bag (1986b:37f.). The preparations were so extensive that a *winkte* was not able to hold more than four such naming ceremonies in a year (1986b:37). It is also claimed that persons with *winkte* names assumed some *winkte* characteristics (Williams 1986a:195). Just as the *winkte*'s femininity was an expression of his/her special latent supernatural power, so the same power found expression in persons who received a portion of that power from a *winkte*.

Also restricted to males were the "obscene nicknames" which were given by Papago women-men. Although a supernatural aspect did not manifest itself, the men were proud of these names, "since they were often bolder than those bestowed by women" (Underhill 1939:186). The names were bestowed when a man had "visited" the woman-man (1939:186), that is, when the two had had sexual intercourse. The Papago "berdache" name was an expression of intimacy. Similar names were bestowed on men by women whom they had married or with whom they had had a sexual relationship; women also liked to give them to their divorced ex-husbands (1939:177). The men regarded such names as a proof of prowess and were also regularly called by their "sexual name" (1939:177). The privilege which the Papago women-men here appropriated for themselves was, therefore, originally a feminine one. They adopted it and surpassed the women by making sure that the names they gave were even more shockingly crude than those given by the women. This parallels the excellence generally attributed to women-men in components of the feminine gender role domain.

Lame Deer (1979:170) told Erdoes that a *winkte* name was worth as much as an expensive horse, and named Sitting Bull, Black Elk, and Crazy Horse as examples of the kind of success which these names could bring. The fact that these cases involved male war leaders and medicine men, and that only boys received *winkte* names, indicates that the power passed on by the *winkte* was masculine in nature. Williams (1986b:37) suggested that *winkte* were brought into a large number of ceremonial occasions, just as, in regard to the Hidatsa *miati,* Bowers (1965:167) spoke of a number of additional ceremonial roles which they held in addition to their already-mentioned functions. Since those additional functions were not specified, these brief statements must suffice to hint at an important religious position for the women-men in these tribes, which was possibly extended to other Plains groups as well. Such an aura of the sacred or holy surrounding women-men cannot be established for other regions. In the present context, this much can be gleaned from the preceding discussion: while it is true that the bestowing of sexual names fell both to *winkte* and to Papago women-men alike, this took place against completely different cultural backgrounds. *Winkte,* who were regarded as medicine persons, gave the names on the basis of their androgynous latent supernatural power, whereas Papago women-men did so as an expression of the feminine gender role which they had chosen.

Matchmaking is another specialized occupation sometimes held by women-men. The Cheyenne *heemaneh',* for example, were popular as matchmakers: they helped young men persuade girls to elope with them, brought gifts to the girls on behalf of the boys, and were sent to a girl's parents in order to arrange a marriage (Grinnell 1962, 2:39). Navajo *nadle* fulfilled similar functions and served as a court of appeals in case of marital disputes (Hill 1935:275). These functions were not the exclusive privilege of the women-men, however. Among the Cheyenne, the messengers of infatuated men could just as well be relatives, and preferably older women (Grinnell 1962, 2:137). *Heemaneh',* though, appeared to be considered especially well suited to the task, and it is striking that it was the *men* who asked them for help. *Heemaneh'* were generally regarded as especially eloquent (Grinnell 1962, 2: 39f.), and *nadle* as especially good at bringing good fortune. The Omaha *mixu'ga* were also active as matchmakers (Mead 1932:189, n. 2), and *winkte* were considered to be specialists in the preparation of "love medicine" (Williams 1986a:194). The women-men's particular qualification for mediating between the sexes was doubtless their ambivalent gender status, which combined both the masculine and the feminine, and which was so highly developed in precisely these groups. Where their status was less characterized by gender role mixing and more by quasi-femininity, such special tasks did not devolve on them.

Essene (1942:31, 65) reported that Pomo and Kato women-men acted as "tribal prostitutes" who were for sale in both tribes during the 1930s at the price of 25 cents, and earlier for payment in the form of a short bead necklace. Williams' (1986b:170) conjecture that Whites were the customers in these cases, because Indians usually did not pay cash, seems doubtful, since Essene explicitly said that beads were the usual payment in earlier times. (The traditional currency of the Pomo, as everywhere in California, consisted of beads which were produced from mussel shells, Kroeber 1925:248f., 824f.) In any case, it is not clear whether women-men were classified as prostitutes (in the European sense) by the members of their own group. Frequent changing of partners has been reported for women-men of many tribes. Papago men sought out the women-men, but along with this, there were "playful women" who, suggestively clothed and painted, went to drinking parties or to puberty ceremonies, and there entered into short-term liaisons, even with married men (Underhill 1939:183). Gifford (1926:333) wrote the following about a Pomo *das:* "Many men associated with him for short periods, some sleeping with him. None married him permanently." It is likely that Essene's classification of the women-men as "tribal prostitutes" was based on these kinds of short-lived, serial partner relationships, although it is possible that the *das* actually did receive beads (or later, money) as gifts from his lovers. Regardless, the term "prostitution" as a characterization of the promiscuous sexual life of the woman-man is just as unhappy and misleading as that coined by Fages in 1769—that the *joyas* of the Salinan were "sodomitas de profesión," that is, "professional homosexuals" (Fages 1984:163). Palure, a woman-man from Isleta, though, is said to have been "rented" to Whites or Mexicans regularly by the men of his village—sometimes three or four times a night. In these situations, he was evidently passed off as a woman, and according to Parsons' (1932:246) description, it was more a matter of a practical joke carried out with Palure's consent, than of professional prostitution.

A final type of specialization has been reported in regard to the Yuki *i-wa-musp:* some of these were said to have locked themselves in the "assembly hall" of the village from time to time, and there recited aloud "legends" and "moral tales" and likewise the tribal history "in a sing-song monotone to all who chose to listen" (S. Powers 1877:132), all of which contributed primarily to the education of the children. Such a task was independent of the activities of the (mostly male) "shamans," who were oriented to curing (see Kroeber 1925:196f.), not to passing on oral tradition. This instruction in the traditions seems to have taken place at least for the boys who were undergoing initiation into the Taikomol-woknam (men's secret society) (Kroeber 1925:184f.). The assembly hall mentioned by Powers is the dance house (see Kroeber 1925:175), which was apparently accessible to women except during ceremonies of the men's society, although *i-wa-musp* likewise had access (Essene 1942:57). Whether the recitation of the oral traditions was tied to a particular gender role cannot be ascertained. The *i-wa-musp*, however, were regarded as a "kind of order of priests or teachers" (S. Powers 1877:132), which suggests a masculine role domain. In any case—and in contrast to other California groups—they were regarded as suitable keepers and transmitters of supernatural knowledge.

CONCLUSIONS

It can be determined that, with respect to certain activities that women-men customarily took up in some groups, the feminine gender role was usually involved. In other cases, their activities had to do with aspects that were not tied to any particular gender role. The sources are sometimes contradictory and inconsistent, especially pertaining to the functions of women-men in the framework of the burial of the dead. Among the three neighboring, Siouan-speaking groups—the Crow, Hidatsa, and Oglala Lakota—women-men participated in outstanding ritual roles. In these groups, women-men held a position resembling that of males with extraordinary spiritual powers, and at the same time they occupied a highly ambivalent gender status. This also holds true for the Cheyenne, but to a more limited degree. Even here, these ritual functions were not fundamentally bound to the status of woman-man, but in the total context of the Plains cultures, mostly contained feminine role components which in a very few groups became the privilege of women-men. Where such an association of the women-men with androgyny and spirituality was lacking, and where they usually performed special tasks alongside *both* men and women, their specialization is best explained by means of the combination of feminine gender role and masculine physical strength. Where women-men assumed responsibilities in the framework of the war complex, these tasks usually lay in the feminine role domain as well, except when the women-men accompanied the warriors in a masculine function as healers.

Chapter ELEVEN

Partner Relationships and Sexuality

▼

Women-men usually had sexual relationships and partnerships with persons of only one sex, but sometimes with members of both sexes. This could vary within a tribe, but also within the life span of an individual: some women-men carried on relationships with men, while others allied themselves with women. Some women-men among the Paiute, Shoshoni, and Ute formed bonds with men, others with women, and again others remained unmarried. Whether a woman-man took a male or a female partner must to a great extent have been left up to his own wishes, and must also have been partly dependent on the degree to which he acted out the feminine gender role. Many women-men did not enter into any lasting relationships whatsoever, others co-habited with men, and one even co-habited with two men (Kelly 1932: 158; Lowie 1924:282; Stewart 1941:405, 1942:298, 332). In any case, the available data do not support a general classification of women-men as "homosexual." With the possible exception of the Tewa *kwidos* (Jacobs 1983), women-men *never* entered into relationships with one another. The reason for this is not entirely clear. Among some tribes, women-men regarded and addressed each other as "sisters"; such relationships might have precluded sexual relations as incestuous.

The association of "berdache" with "homosexuality" that permeates the literature has a significant impact on the reliability of the sources. Same-sex relationships in the framework of the woman-man institution, and sometimes also between two persons of the same gender status and the same social role, were not prohibited in most Native American cultures, but they most definitely were prohibited in the ethnographer's culture, which the consultants very well knew. Thus, consultants often responded negatively when they were asked about the "berdaches'" relationships with men. A Paiute consultant gave Stewart (1941:440) the characteristic answer to the question regarding "berdaches": they did not exist, "because our Indians were good and taught their children right." Other consultants from neighboring Paiute local groups, less cautious toward the White ethnographer, answered the question regarding the existence of "berdaches" affirmatively (1941: 405, 440). Thus, it cannot be ascertained how many consultants gave negative answers regarding women-men's same-sex relationships because they knew what the ethnographer wanted to hear. As for relationships or marriages of male "berdaches" with women, many ethnographers simply did not ask (see, e.g., Driver 1937:90; Essene 1942; Harrington 1942; Voegelin 1942:134).

PARTNER RELATIONSHIPS WITH WOMEN

In some tribes, women-men had short-term or long-lasting relationships with women. Bella Bella and Bella Coola males who had already changed gender roles as children and had cross-dressed married women and together they performed women's tasks. Some Haisla women-men also married women (McIlwraith 1948, 1:45; Olson 1940:200). A Crow *bate* likewise was married, and the couple showed the "anomaly of husband and wife in the same dress attending to the same domestic duties" (Denig 1961:188). The Hare feminine male described by Broch (1977:99f.) had a steady girlfriend, although in relation to her he adopted a masculine role; his feminine role was restricted to specific situations. At least one Klamath *tw!inna'ek* was apparently married to a woman (Spier 1930:51), and the same was true of some Kwakiutl feminine males who were classified by their people as women-men (Ford 1941:131). Marriage with women was forbidden to most *winkte* by their guardian spirits, but some nonetheless married and had children without giving up their *winkte* status (Williams 1986a:193); the grandfather of one of Williams' female consultants was a *winkte* (1986a:195). By contrast, among the St. Lawrence Eskimo, marriage to a woman and the *anasik* status were mutually exclusive. A man from this group who was viewed as a potential *anasik* ultimately married a woman, which put off the consultant: "He isn't always a real anasik because later he got a wife" (Murphy and Leighton 1965:89). "Real" *nadle* (hermaphrodites/intersexes) also did not marry or have sexual relations with women, but "those who pretend to be *nadle*" did (Hill 1935:276). As noted, if a *nadle* married, he/she apparently had to forfeit *nadle* status at least for the duration of the marriage (Hill 1935:276). Sometimes the woman-man status was so markedly defined as nonmasculine that sexual bonds to women were not even considered.

As noted, one Osage warrior married while he was a *mixu'ga* and produced several children (Fletcher and La Flesche 1911:133), but he had taken on a feminine gender role only partially. The same held true for the medicine man Four Bears. He was married and the father of several children, but despite situationally specific cross-dressing, he was not a woman-man (Schaeffer 1965:221). One Quinault woman-man had sexual relations exclusively with old women, which—it was said—led to his early death, because sexual intercourse with old women "poisoned" young men (Olson 1936:99). The fact that the woman-man could be "poisoned" in this way indicates that, notwithstanding his feminine gender role (1936:99), he also must have held a very highly developed nonfeminine gender status (on this, see also the Cree example of Clawed Woman; D. G. Mandelbaum 1940:257).

One Shoshoni *tüvasa* married, although it is not known whether he retained his special status afterward; he probably lost it, since he was no longer "*tüvasa*" (infertile): he was, in fact, the great-grandfather of one of Steward's consultants (Steward 1941:353). Another Shoshoni, who was described as "feminine in unspecified characteristics," likewise married and had several children (1941:353). Finally, a Tolowa woman-man was married to a woman, and the two performed women's work together (Driver 1939:405).

Apart from enduring relationships, intercourse with women has sometimes been represented as being possible for women-men. This holds true for the "women pretenders" of the Ingalik (Osgood 1958:261) and for the Crow *bate*. The *bate* examined by Holder claimed to have had sexual intercourse with women. Since he had already carried out his gender role change by the age of five years, this intercourse had to have occurred within the context of his status as a *bate* (Holder 1889:623f.). Trowbridge (1938:68) reported that the *waupeengwoatar* of the Miami occasionally used their constant association with women for the purpose of engaging in "carnal connection" with them. Also, the men of the Papago village where Shining Evening lived joked with their wives that they couldn't be certain that their children were actually theirs, seeing as how Shining Evening was constantly with the women. The men would call out to the children, pointing to Shining Evening: "Run along! Over there is your daddy!" (Underhill 1936:43). This implies that Papago women-men at least theoretically could have sex with women, even though the sources, including Underhill, have almost unanimously stated that they had sexual relationships only with men. Maybe this accounts for the joking on the part of the men. In Zuni, Wewha was said to have been the father of several children, although Stevenson reported that *lhamana* never married women and rarely had "any relations" with them (Stevenson 1904:38).

A considerable number of sources have stated that consultants denied that "berdaches" had any sexual contacts with men. As noted, however, consultants had reason to dissemble. In addition, even if such denials were true, it is doubtful that the women-men in those groups had intercourse with women instead. Further, even if "berdaches" did not marry or co-habit with men, as many consultants reported, they still could have had either fleeting or multiple, repeated sexual contacts with men. It is also possible that women-men were asexual in some tribes, as Gifford (1933:294) reported for the Cocopa *elxa* (according to Drucker 1941:163, however, Cocopa *elxa* did marry men). Some women-men may also have been asexual among the Cree (D. G. Mandelbaum 1940:256) and the Ingalik (Osgood 1958:261). The sources are contradictory; the existence of relationships or intercourse with men is sometimes affirmed and sometimes denied within the same tribe.

The data on partnerships and sexuality of women-men are summarized in Tables 4 and 5. It is apparent that women-men's sexual relationships with women, whether fleeting or lasting, were common in only a few groups. Such relationships were relatively more common in Subarctic groups and on the Northwest Coast, although even in these areas, relations with women were certainly not the only option. Where relations with women did occur, they tended to parallel women-men's relationships with the men of the respective group (see Maps 4 and 5).

In some cases, married transvesting or feminine males continued to fulfill an essentially masculine gender role, and therefore were not "berdaches" in the narrower sense of the definition. This is true, for example, of Piegan Four Bears (Schaeffer 1965:221), of the Osage warrior described in Fletcher and La Flesche (1911:133), and of the Kwakiutl "feminine" story teller (Ford 1941:131f.). It is probably also true of the feminine Shoshoni male from Elko (Steward 1941:353), as well as the feminine Hare (not married, but having an affair with a woman) who held a status similar to that of the woman-man, but only in certain situations (Broch 1977:100), in which he/she possibly had sexual relations with men (Williams 1986b:104f.). Navajo *nadle* had to change to a masculine role if they married a woman (or even a man; Hill 1935:276).

In other cases, both partners carried out women's work. Because husband and wife usually formed an economic unit, particularly in regard to the management of subsistence acquisition, having a couple consisting of "two wives" might have led to problems, especially where a large part of the food supply was secured by the man's hunting activity. However, married couples consisting of "berdache-and-wife" did not live in isolation, but rather within the framework of a larger unit of associated families, so the couple was probably able to cover the meat requirements with the help of male hunters in the family, and could themselves contribute

Table 4. Partner Relationships of Women-Men (Male "Berdaches")

Tribe	With Men	Not with Men	With Women	Not with Women
Achomawi	Voegelin 1942: 134			
Aleut	Bancroft 1874, 1: 92; Dall 1897: 402			
Arapaho	Kroeber 1902:19			
Assiniboine	Lowie 1909:42			Lowie 1909:42
Atsugewi	Voegelin 1942: 134			
Cheyenne	Hoebel 1960:77			
Chumash	Harrington 1942: 32			
Cocopa	Drucker 1941: 163			
Costanoan	Harrington 1942: 32			
Crow	Holder 1889:624		Denig 1961:188	
Dakota-Teton	Williams 1986a: 194		Williams 1986a: 193	
Dakota-Santee	Landes 1968:153			
Diegueño	Drucker 1937a: 27	Drucker 1941: 163		
Gabrielino	Harrington 1942: 32			
Huchnom	Foster 1944:227			
Juaneño	Kroeber 1925: 647			
Kaniagmiut	Bancroft 1874: 92; Dall 1897: 402			
Kato	Essene 1942:31	Driver 1939:372		
Kitanemuk	Harrington 1942: 32			
Klamath	Spier 1930:52; Voegelin 1942: 134		Spier 1930:51	Spier 1930:52
Luiseño	Boscana 1846: 283			
Maidu	Voegelin 1942: 134			

Table 4. Continued

Tribe	With Men	Not with Men	With Women	Not with Women
Maricopa	Drucker 1941: 163; Spier 1933: 242			
Mohave	Devereux 1937: 501			
Mono	Gayton 1948: 274	Driver 1937:90		
Navajo	Hill 1935:276	Stewart 1942:298	Hill 1935:276	
Nisenan	Beals 1933:376			
Ojibwa	McKenney 1972: 259; Skinner 1911:152; Tanner 1830:105f.			
Omaha	Dorsey 1894:378			
Paiute (Northern)	Stewart 1941: 405	Stewart 1941:405		Kelly 1932:148; Steward 1933:238
Paiute (Southern)	Lowie 1924:282; Steward 1941: 312	Stewart 1942:298		Steward 1941:253; Stewart 1942:298
Papago	Drucker 1941: 163; Underhill 1939:186	Gifford 1940:163		
Piegan	Schaeffer 1965: 223		Schaeffer 1965: 221	
Pomo	Essene 1942:31; Gifford 1926:333			
Ponca	J. H. Howard 1965:142			
Salinan	Harrington 1942: 32			
Shasta	Voegelin 1942: 134			Holt 1946:217
Shoshoni	Steward 1941: 312, 1943:338	Shimkin 1947: 298; Steward 1941:312, 1943: 338	Steward 1941: 353	
Ute	Stewart 1942: 298	Gifford 1940: 163; Stewart 1942:298		Stewart 1942:332
Winnebago	Lurie 1953:708			
Wintu	Voegelin 1942: 134			Du Bois 1935:50

TABLE 4. CONTINUED

TRIBE	WITH MEN	NOT WITH MEN	WITH WOMEN	NOT WITH WOMEN
Yuki	Essene 1942:31; Foster 1944:186; Kroeber 1925:180	Driver 1939:372		
Yuma	Drucker 1937a:27; Forde 1931:157			
Zuni	Parsons 1916:526; Stevenson 1904:38			
Bankalachi		Driver 1937:90		
Chilula		Driver 1939:372		
Eyak		Birket-Smith and De Laguna 1938:206		
Hupa		Driver 1939:372		
Kawaiisu		Driver 1937:90		
Lassik		Essene 1942:31		
Mattole		Driver 1939:372		
Panamint		Driver 1937:90		
Pima		Hill 1938b:339		
Sinkyone		Driver 1939:372		
Tolowa		Driver 1939:372	Driver 1939:405	
Tübatulabal		Driver 1937:90		
Wiyot		Driver 1939:372		
Yokuts	Gayton 1948:106	Driver 1937:90		
Yurok		Driver 1937:90		
Bella Coola			McIlwraith 1948, 1:45	McIlwraith 1948, 1:45
Bella Bella			McIlwraith 1948, 1:45	McIlwraith 1948, 1:45
St. Lawrence Eskimo	Murphy and Leighton 1965:89		Murphy and Leighton 1965:89	
Haisla			McIlwraith 1948, 1:45; Olson 1940:200	
Hare			Broch 1977:100	

Table 4. Continued

Tribe	With Men	Not with Men	With Women	Not with Women
Kwakiutl			Ford 1941:131f.	Ford 1941:132
Osage			Fletcher and La-Flesche 1911:133	
Quinault			Olson 1936:99	
Ingalik	Osgood 1958: 261	Osgood 1958: 261	Osgood 1958: 261	Osgood 1958:261
Cree		D. G. Mandel-baum 1940:256		D. G. Mandelbaum 1940:256
Chugach-Eskimo				Birket-Smith 1953: 94
Flathead				Teit 1930:384
Illinois				Marquette 1959: 129
Iroquois				Charlevoix 1744: 4f.
Kutenai				Schaeffer 1965:218
Lillooet				Teit 1900:267
Panamint		Driver 1937:90		
Potawatomi				Landes 1970:352

Note. Information for one and the same tribe may be contradictory because (1) different authors (and their respective consultants) may have disagreed about whether women-men of a given tribe had relationships with men or with women; or (2) in some tribes, it was possible for women-men to enter into relationships with both women and men and/or to live as "singles," entering into no formal relationships or marriages with either sex. Shoshoni: *The information is given with reservations in the sources.* Navajo: *Information does not apply to intersexes, but only to physically unambiguous women-men.* Papago: *It is not clear from Underhill's account whether relationships occurred with men or women. She reported that male transvestites "might marry," but did not indicate whether the woman-man's spouse would have been male or female.* Ute: *Information given with reservations in the source.* Yurok: *The relationship between a woman-man and a man mentioned by Gayton was apparently atypical and was said to have "killed him" (i.e., the woman-man concerned; Gayton 1948:106).* St. Lawrence Eskimo: *The woman-man mentioned in the source, however, who lived with a woman, was not regarded as a "real"* anasik, *which suggests that it was customary for* anasik *to enter into relationships with men.*

TABLE 5. SEXUALITY OF WOMEN-MEN (MALE "BERDACHES")

TRIBE	WITH MEN	NOT WITH MEN	WITH WOMEN	NOT WITH WOMEN
Acoma	Bandelier 1966: 326; Hammond 1882:347			Bandelier 1966: 326
Apache (Tonto)	Gifford 1940:163			
Crow	Holder 1889: 624; Kroeber 1902:19f.; Maximilian n.d., 1: 237		Holder 1889:624	
Dakota-Teton	Dorsey 1894: 467; Hassrick 1982: 137; Williams 1986a: 193f.			
Dakota-Santee	Landes 1968:113			
Eskimo (St. Lawrence)	Murphy and Leighton 1965: 89			
Flathead	Teit 1930:384			
Hidatsa	Henry 1897:348; Holder 1889:623			
Hopi	Williams 1986b: 107			
Illinois	Hennepin 1699: 163; Liette 1962: 112; St. Cosme 1799 (cited in Kellogg 1917: 360)			
Ingalik	Osgood 1958: 261	Osgood 1958: 261	Osgood 1958: 261	Osgood 1958:261
Iroquois	Charlevoix 1744: 4f.			
Isleta	Parsons 1932: 246			
Karankawa	Newcomb 1961: 74			
Klamath	Holder 1889:623		Holder 1889:623	
Kwakiutl	Ford 1941:129ff.			
Laguna	Hammond 1882: 347			
Mandan	Maximilian n.d., 2:78			

Table 5. Continued

Tribe	With Men	Not with Men	With Women	Not with Women
Natchez	Dumont 1753: 249			
Navajo	Hill 1935:276, 278		Hill 1935: 276	
Nez Percé	M. Mandelbaum 1938:119			
Paiute-Southern	Stewart 1942: 298	Stewart 1942:298		
Papago	Drucker 1941: 163; Underhill 1939:186	Gifford 1940:163	Underhill 1936: 43	
Piegan	Schaeffer 1965: 221			
Pomo	Essene 1942:30, 31; Gifford 1926: 333			
Quinault	Olson 1936:99		Olson 1936:99	
Salinan	Fages 1984:163			
Sauk	Catlin 1926, 2: 244			
Ute	Stewart 1942: 298	Stewart 1942:298		
Yuma	Alarcón 1565: 368			
Zuni	Stevenson 1904: 38		Stevenson 1904: 38	
Chilula		Driver 1939:372		
Hupa		Driver 1939:372		
Kato	Essene 1942:30, 31	Driver 1939:372		
Mattole		Driver 1939:372		
Pima		Hill 1938b:339		
Potawatomi		Landes 1970:351		
Shoshoni (Wind River)		Shimkin 1947: 298		
Sinkyone		Driver 1939:372		
Tolowa		Driver 1939:372		
Wiyot		Driver 1939:372		

Table 5. Continued

Tribe	With Men	Not with Men	With Women	Not with Women
Yuki		Driver 1939:372		
Yurok		Driver 1937:405		
Miami			Trowbridge 1938: 68	
Cree		D. G. Mandelbaum 1940:256		D. G. Mandelbaum 1940:256
Cocopa		Gifford 1933:294		Gifford 1933:294

Note. In contrast to Table 4, in which the partner relationships/marriages entered into by women-men are listed, this table lists all cases where the sources explicitly *stated with whom women-men had sex. Information may be contradictory for one and the same tribe because (1) different authors (and their respective consultants) may have disagreed about whether women-men of a given tribe had sex with men or with women; or (2) in some tribes, it was possible for women-men to have sex with both women and men.* Navajo: *Information does not apply to intersexes, but only to physically unambiguous women-men (the Navajo category of "those who pretend to be nadle").* Papago: *Underhill's description suggests that it was only jokingly alleged that women-men had heterosexual intercourse.*

significantly to the band's food supply by their own doubled gathering activities. (On communal hunting and gathering by extended families on the Plains, see, e.g., Hartmann 1979:78.)

Where the woman-man was also active as a curer or religious specialist—as, for example, among the Tolowa (Driver 1939:405) and the Oglala Lakota—the married couple would have been economically secure. Tolowa "shamans" of both sexes were often rich (Drucker 1937b: 242; Gould 1978:134), and Williams (1986b:218) reported that a modern Oglala Lakota *winkte* kept a large stack of gifts which he had received as thanks for his services stored in a corner of his house. Further, women-men may in some cases have participated in masculine subsistence activities (contrary to the statements in the sources). They also may have been paid for artistic handcrafts. In many places, women-men were prosperous, so marriage to a woman would not have posed economic difficulty. Benedict commented that the husbands of women-men were often teased by the community because the woman-men had made a lazy and worry-free life possible for them. Especially on the Plains, women-men were among the wealthiest persons of their respective tribes (Benedict 1949:244). It may be that the woman-man's ambition to perform feminine specialist activities to perfection was motivated by the desire

Map 4. Relationships and Sexuality of Women-Men (Male "Berdaches") with Men

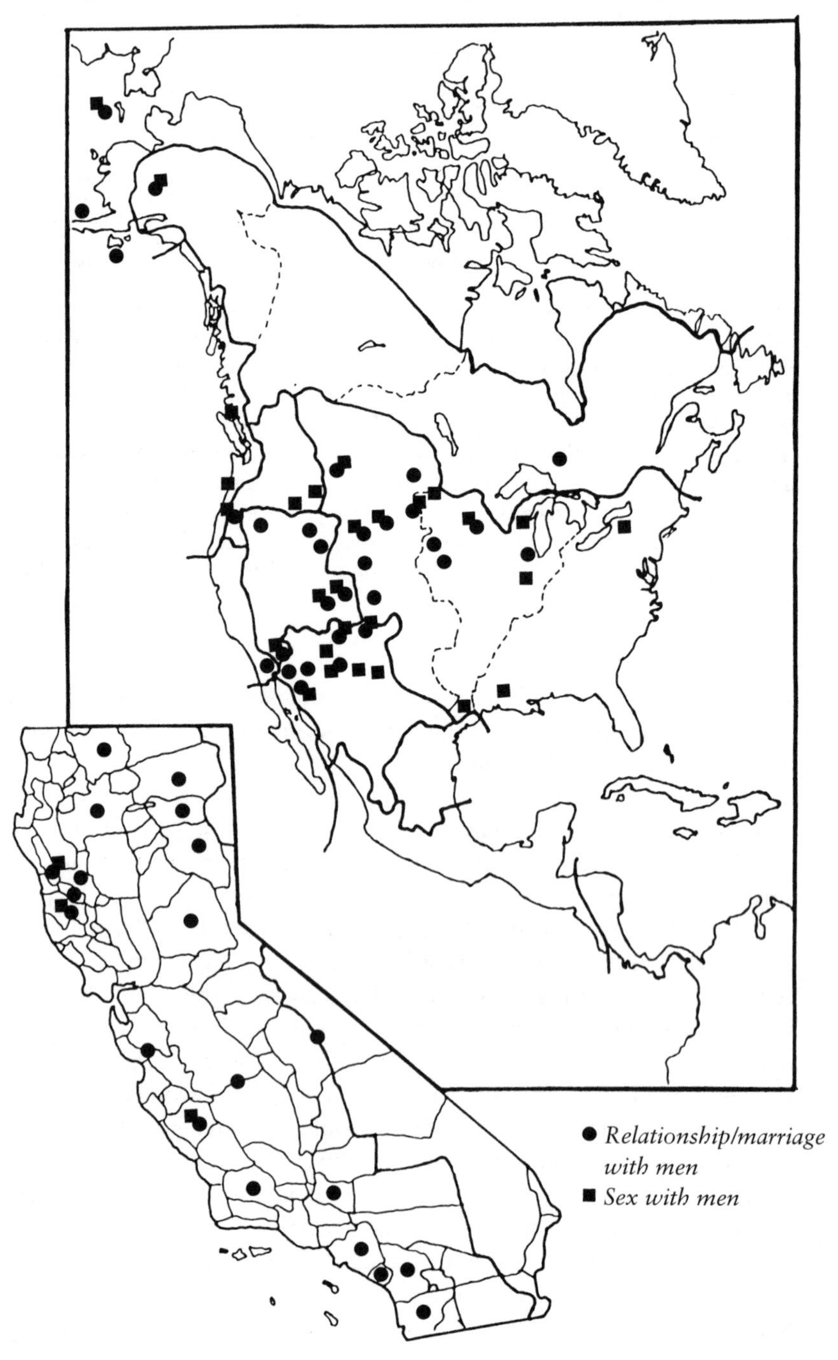

Map 5. Sexuality and Relationships of Women-Men (Male "Berdaches") with Women

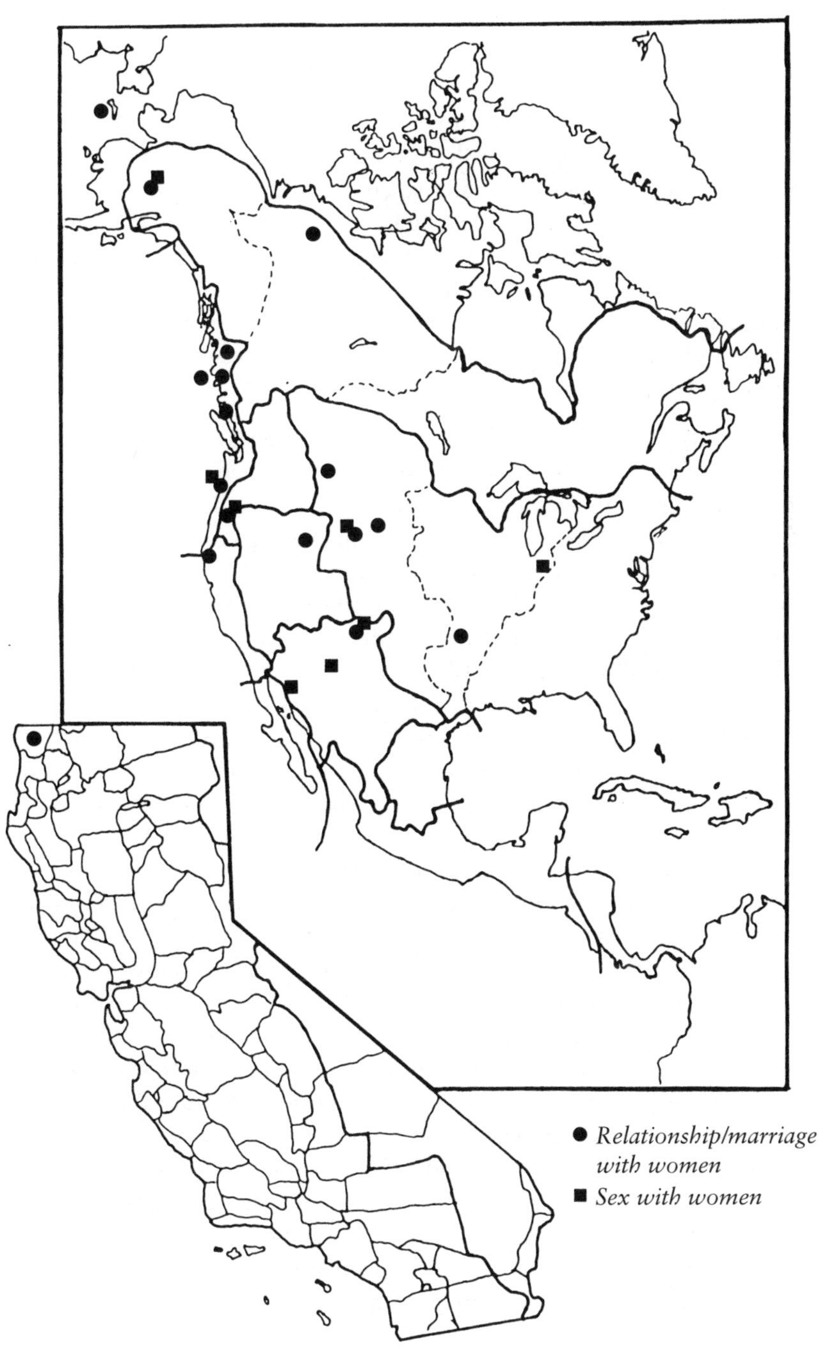

for material security, above all where these activities were profitable and where women-men remained unmarried (and thus had to provide for themselves).

PARTNER RELATIONSHIPS WITH MEN

Most women-men entered into partner relationships with men; these comprised everything from fleeting, short-term partnerships to long-term relationships and formally solemnized marriages. In other cases, however, they did not form lasting bonds of any kind, but instead lived alone or with members of their respective birth families and received men for occasional sexual encounters. Just as women-men in some tribes could have relationships with men as well as with women, so there often existed within the same tribe several parallel forms of partner relationships with men.

MARRIAGES AND LONG-TERM RELATIONSHIPS WITH MEN

In Aleut and Kaniagmiut society, marriages between men and *shupans* were so commonplace that one couple wanted to enter into this bond in the presence of a European priest (Dall 1897:402f.). In this case, the bridegroom was a chieftain, which suggests that marriages with *shupans* had prestige value: "The husband regarded his boy-wife as a major social accomplishment, and the boy's family profited from association with their new wealthy in-law" (Williams 1986b:45). Since wealthy Aleut men usually maintained polygynous marriages (Dall 1897:388, 402), it is likely that the *shupans* were not exclusive wives, but rather part of a polygynous marital relationship. This also holds true for women-men in a number of other tribes. Cheyenne *heemaneh'* often lived as second wives in the household of an already-married man (Hoebel 1960:77). Hidatsa *miati* were sometimes co-wives in extended households, but also established their own households with older, childless men (Bowers 1965:167). From time to time Oglala Lakota men likewise took *winkte* as second or third wives (Williams 1986a:194), apparently within the framework of a marriage ceremony (1986a:197). As in the Aleut case, respected Oglala Lakota men also seem to have liked to take women-men as wives: "Chief Crazy Horse had one or two winkte wives, as well as his female wives, but this has been kept quiet because Indians don't want whites to criticize" (Williams 1986a:196, consultant self-identified as *winkte)*. Unlike women, *winkte* could practice polyandry; some "higher class winktes" are said to have had up to twelve husbands (1986a:196). Since these husbands must also have had female wives, the *winkte* probably lived by themselves, since it is hardly likely that they continually moved from one marital tipi into the next. A certain woman-man of the Shivwits-Paiute was also married to two men, "sleeping with them on alternate nights" (Lowie 1924:282). Finally, an Ojibwa *agokwe* who earlier had made unsuccessful advances to John Tanner also married into a polygynous household: "This introduction of a new inmate into the family . . . occasioned some laughter . . . but was attended with less uneasiness and quarreling than would have been the bringing in of a new wife of the female sex" (Tanner 1830:106). This last remark suggests that *agokwa* did not threaten the wives' position within the marital relationship. Tanner (1830:105) also noted that Ozaw-wen-dib had already had several husbands. Thus, it is true that Ojibwa *agokwe* were taken in marriage by men, but the ties were not lasting. Of course, the same holds true for opposite-sex marriages as well (see Landes 1938). Separations from *agokwe* were possibly simpler than separations from women, since *agokwe* did not have the same backing and support from their families of birth. Owaw-wen-dib's father, for example, most strongly disapproved of his gender role change, and could hardly have been of help to him in the event of marital problems (see Henry 1897: 163). For this reason alone, the two wives of Ozaw-wen-dib's newest spouse would not have feared being forced out of their position, because the *agokwe* would probably not have remained in the family long enough to affect the existing privileges of the women. In addition, there seems to have been no doubt that the status of the woman-man wife was subordinate to that of the other wives. Apart from these considerations, Ozaw-wen-dib was more than fifty years old at the time, and probably represented no sexual threat, but he certainly constituted a valuable acquisition in the area of feminine occupations.

Because polygyny was common in most of the Plains tribes, particularly for respected men (Hartmann 1979:77), and since it likewise occurred in the Prairie region and in parts of the Northwest and the Subarctic, as well as in other regions of North America (see Driver and Massey 1957: Map 153, p. 398 and 399f.), it is likely that women-men were frequently members of polygynous marriages in these areas, a circumstance which is not explicitly mentioned in the literature. Two aspects of such arrangements should be emphasized. First, the work capacity of women-men was seen as outstanding, so a woman-man must have been welcomed into the household as a valuable asset. However, entering into a lifetime monogamous marriage with a woman-man might also have been to a man's disadvantage, because marriage partners typically wanted to have children who could support them in their old age. The Mohave Kuwal, for example, suffered from childlessness as an old man; the children of his female wives had all died, and his *alyha* wives had not, of course, had any children (Devereux 1937:513). It must not be forgotten, though, that the possibility of adoption existed in principle (see Bowers 1965:167; Williams 1986a:198, 1986b:55ff.), and further, that relatives could take over providing for one's old age in place of children.

Aside from the groups already mentioned, the marriage of men to women-men without indication of polygyny has been reported from the Arapaho (Kroeber 1902:19); Assiniboine (Lowie 1909:42); Coahuiltecan (Cabeza de Vaca 1555:36); Cocopa (Drucker 1941:163); Santee Dakota (Landes 1968:153); Juaneño (Kroeber 1925:647); Klamath (Spier 1930:52); Luiseño (Boscana 1846:283); Maricopa (Spier 1933:242); Navajo (Hill 1935:276, only "those who pretend to be *nadle*"); Nisenan (Beals 1933:376); Omaha (Dorsey 1894:378); Southern Paiute (Steward 1941:312); Ponca (J. H. Howard 1965:142); Shoshoni (Steward 1943:338, only in one local group); Winnebago (Lurie 1953:708); Yuki (Kroeber 1925:180); and Zuni (Stevenson 1904:38). Moreover, the co-habitation of men and *alyha* can also be regarded as marriage; the Mohave did not have a marriage ceremony (Kroeber 1925:747) and among them, living together with *alyha* or *hwame* followed the same patterns as did the establishment and dissolution of opposite-sex partnerships (e.g., the man's wish to separate because of his *alyha* wife's "infertility"; Devereux 1937:514). On the other hand, *alyha* were not courted as ordinary girls were, but rather like widows, divorcees, and women known to be promiscuous (1937:513). Consequently, they occupied the status of women who did not go into a marriage "untouched"—only "ordinary girls" who had never been married could in principle be courted in their respective parents' homes. Since, however, a separation of the partners was simple and apparently not rare, the open, publicly displayed type of bride wooing more likely represented the cultural norm than the exception. *Alyha* wives were regarded as robust workers (1937:513), which was also true of the Luiseño *cuit.* Because the latter were supposed to be stronger than women, reported Boscana (1846:283), they were better suited than women for carrying out the arduous tasks required of female spouses, and chiefs in particular liked to marry them. On the occasion of the wedding, however, merely a large festive banquet was given, instead of the formalities and ceremonies which otherwise were customary. The *kwit* of the neighboring Juaneño were also eagerly married in public because they were robust workers (Kroeber 1925:647), although it is not known whether these marriages differed from those between partners of the opposite sex.

Like Kuwal's *alyha* wives, other women-men were probably also frequently only one element in a series of marriages which men entered into during the course of their lives. White Syndey (Klamath) was married twice to men, although the second husband later took a woman and founded a family (Spier 1930:52). By contrast, Yuma *elxa* and men are said to have forged lasting marriages (Forde 1931:157).

In the preceding discussion, only those cases have been considered in which it was expressly a matter of formally solemnized marriages (identical with or similar to marriages between partners of the opposite sex), or with the particular form of co-habitation which, in the absence of formal solemnization of marriage, took the place of the latter in certain groups. With few exceptions, however, the sources are not clear, and marriage and co-habitation are not distinguished (but see Stewart 1942: 298, who entered both "Lives with man" and "Marries man" in his tabulation).

As marriage partners of men, therefore, women-men entered into polygynous, monogamous, and serial marriages. Repeatedly cited is the woman-man's ability to perform women's work—including the production of prestige objects such as beadwork—more efficiently and with greater endurance and stamina than biological women. This holds for all tribes in which women-men entered into marriages with men, and also for an entire series of groups in which they co-habited with men.

These abilities were especially advantageous for prominent men, who were typically obliged to undertake acts of public benefit to the village community, and for this required the assistance of their wives. For example, Omaha wives whose husbands occupied outstanding positions in the tribe often had to prepare meals for many persons and, in addition, had to produce handcrafts which the husband could give away in order to consolidate his status (Niethammer 1985:137). Southern California chiefs had similar obligations (1985:137), for the fulfillment of which a single wife was just not enough. In other parts of California as well, generosity was what characterized the proper chief, who "through the possession of several wives, or through contributions, was in a position to conduct himself with liberality, especially toward strangers and in time of need" (Kroeber 1925:834).

Such a combination of affluence, generosity, and social position existed on the Northwest Coast to an especially pronounced extent. When it came to outshining and thereby ousting a rival by means of an especially opulent potlatch, heavy demands were placed on the entire association of related extended families (see Benedict 1949:160ff.; Drucker 1963:132). It might seem odd at first that it was precisely in this area that women-men did not become wives, but instead married women or engaged in short-term sexual relationships with men. This is probably because the Northwest Coast had a complicated system, unique to North America, of inheritance of privileges, names, and "coats-of-arms" that was bound up with opposite-sex marriage. Polygyny as such was also common on the Northwest Coast (Driver and Massey 1957:400), and the bride price connected with it was very high. The privileges obtainable through marriage or inheritance were usually connected to biological sex, so marriage of a man from the upper stratum of society to a woman-man would have created a terrible mess in the complex system of passing on privileges. A passage in the literature even hints, at least for the Bella Coola, that women-men—who like "hermaphrodites" were called *sx'ints*—were rendered unfit by their gender role change to continue to hold the privileges of males. If it turned out that a man was not able to "strengthen" a certain privilege adequately (the right to occupy a very special seat in the house, McIlwraith 1948, 1:167) by bestowing gifts, it was said of this privilege, "It has become hermaphroditized" (McIlwraith 1948, 1:171)—that is, it has become weakened or worthless. The woman-man could not bring feminine privileges with him/her into the marriage, either. Thus, at least for a man of the upper social stratum, marriage to a woman-man would not have been worthwhile under the best of circumstances, and in the worst case, would have brought with it serious disadvantages. Whether, by contrast, men from the lower social class took women-men as wives is an open question. Even women-men who were married to women apparently relinquished participation in the masculine competition for prestige—if they belonged to a social class for which this even came into consideration—since they and their wives did women's tasks together (McIlwraith 1948, 1:45).

Where such a complex system of rights and privileges was lacking, however, it was precisely respected men who took women-men as wives in polygynous marriages, as, for example, among the Luiseño, Oglala Lakota, Aleut, and Kaniagmiut. In view of the large number of California tribes from which the co-habitation of men and women-men has been reported, it is likely that they were also regarded there as welcome human labor, especially in the households of prominent men, and likewise among the Omaha, Cheyenne, Arapaho, and other Plains tribes. In the Plains, too, women-men certainly must have increased the prestige of the men with whom they formed ties on account of their status as medicine persons (*wakan,* etc.). In any case, marriage between women-men and men suggests that both parties viewed the woman-man as occupying a feminine gender role. In the cultures under discussion, moreover, it was appropriate for any person who occupied a feminine gender role to enter into a marriage with a man.

In some cases, bonds between "berdaches" and men have been explicitly denied in the literature. The example of the Eyak may be illustrative because individuals of indeterminate gender were not seen as desirable marriage partners. The Eyak, in fact, did not have an institutionalized "berdache" status, but rather a category of men who merely failed in the masculine sphere, who, according to Birket-Smith and De Laguna

(1938:206), were called "no good." These men were regarded as too lazy to hunt, did not transvest, and did women's work, less because they wished to (and probably not very efficiently, either) than because they were incompetent in masculine subsistence activities.

In regard to the Pima and the Cree, it is possible that relationships between women-men and men occurred in earlier times, although D. G. Mandelbaum reported that the Cree *aayahkwew* Clawed Woman remained single all her life. First, the Plains Cree are closely related culturally to tribes which allowed such marriages (e.g., the neighboring Ojibwa and Assiniboine). Second, Lowie (1909:42) indicated that a Cree once married a Stoney "berdache" and took him along to his village. In regard to the Pima, it is doubtful that Hill accurately portrayed the traditional status of the *wik'ovat.* Even if it is true that during the 1930s there was "no cultural niche and such abnormal behavior was definitely stigmatized" (1938b:338), there actually once was a test to determine whether a boy was a *wik'ovat* (1938b:340). Further, it is clear that *wik'ovat* once was a culturally recognized woman-man status. In neighboring tribes in this area as well, women-men occupied a legitimized status (Papago, Maricopa, Cocopa). Thus, it is probable that Pima *wik'ovat,* too, were able at one time to enter into marriages with men in the context of institutionalized gender role change.

In regard to a number of Northern California tribes, the sources are contradictory. Driver (1937, 1939) consistently reported that "berdaches" never married or had sex with men (see Tables 4 and 5). Other ethnographers obtained different information, even from the same tribes: Essene's Kato consultants affirmed that "berdaches" co-habited with men, and so did the Mono interviewed by Gayton (Essene 1942:31; Gayton 1948:274). Driver's Yuki consultants denied that relationships with men had taken place, but such relationships were affirmed to other researchers (Essene 1942:31; Foster 1944:186; Kroeber 1925:180). In regard to the Yokuts, Gayton (1948:46, n. 12) reported that one female consultant told her about a relationship between her uncle, who was a woman-man, and a man; the consultant said that this relationship, however, had negative consequences: "Finally he took a man and that killed him. He said that he hated women" (1948:106). Of course, it is also possible that the ethnographers influenced the answers in each case (see Williams 1986b:185ff.).

Sexual Contacts Outside Long-Term Relationships

Some women-men participated in short-term sexual contacts rather than marriages or other long-term relationships. Table 5 summarizes the data for all tribes for which the sources explicitly reported that women-men actually had sex with men (and women), regardless of whether these contacts took place within long- or short-term relationships. Some earlier authors portrayed male "berdaches" as extremely promiscuous or hinted at orgiastic activities that supposedly occurred curing certain ceremonies, with the women-men as prominent actors. Such accounts have to be read with caution and may not be very reliable because they reflect the authors' own bias rather than historical facts. Moreover, certain sexual acts may have had a completely different meaning in the Native American cultures where they were practiced than in the culture of the ethnographer or early chronicler. This holds true especially for cases of seemingly "promiscuous" extramarital sexual activities in certain ritual contexts.

Not all *winkte* married men. If they stayed single, they lived in their own tipis (Hassrick 1982:135; Mirsky 1937a:417; Williams 1986a:194), where they were visited by the men (Williams 1986a:194), preferably when the men's wives were menstruating or pregnant (1986a:194), and therefore when sexual intercourse was forbidden to them. A similar situation probably held for the Santee Dakota; Landes traced the popularity of the *winkta* among the men to their "complete hospitality" (1968:112). Teit's (1930:384) statement that young men visited the Flathead women-men now and then in order to "joke" with them can be interpreted in much the same way. According to Henry, Hidatsa *miati* also maintained sexual contacts with men apart from lasting relationships; the Hidatsa were "much given to unnatural lusts and often prefer a young man to a woman. There are many berdashes among them, who make it their business to satisfy such beastly passions" (1897:348).

This kind of portrayal also occurs in other—primarily earlier—sources. Even if these authors might have distorted or exaggerated the actual facts of the matter in their efforts to depict the Indians of certain tribes as especially "depraved," their statements nonetheless indicate that, for the men of many groups, intercourse with women-men outside of marriage-like relationships was common. This also holds true for the Illinois (Hennepin 1699:163; Liette 1962:112). Sexual relations of men with women-men have likewise been reported from the Iroquois (Charlevoix 1744:4f.); Karankawa (Morfi in Newcomb 1961:74); Klamath (Holder 1889:623, also on White men as sexual partners); Kwakiutl (Ford 1941:129ff.); Mandan (Maximilian n.d., 2:78); Navajo (Hill 1935:276, 278); Nez Percé (M. Mandelbaum 1938:119—a woman-man who turned up among the Sinkaietk and "attempted to ply the trade of prostitute at a communal gathering"); Papago (Underhill 1939:186, women-men's "sex life" with men was a "community institution"); Pomo (Essene 1942:31, "tribal prostitute"; Gifford 1926:333); Salinan (Fages 1984:163, "dado que todos estos gentiles son harto propensos a este abominable vicio" [given that all these heathens are very

The "Dance to the Berdash (i-coo-coo-a)" of the Sauk. (From Catlin 1973, Vol. 2, Plate 296.) Reproduced by permission of Dover Publications, Inc., © 1973.

prone to this abominable vice]); Sauk (Catlin 1926, 2:243f.); Yuma (Alarcón 1565:368); and Kato (Essene 1942:31, "tribal prostitute"). Young men visited the *lhunide* Palure from Isleta, staying late at night, and they were scolded for it by their parents. Since the men from the locality made a joke out of "renting" Palure to Whites and Mexicans, sexual contacts also between the *lhunide* and the local men can probably be assumed, even though Parsons (1932:246) contested this.

Against the background of other information available about the kachina ceremonies of the Pueblos, Hammond's (1882:347) references to *mujerados'* participation in the springtime "saturnalia and orgies" in Acoma and Laguna—in the course of which "pederastic ceremonies . . . form so important a part in the performances"—are incomprehensible. Hammond reported that his consultants were uncommunicative regarding these "pederastic purposes" of the *mujerados*—who Hammond (1882:348) claimed had been artificially effeminized especially for this purpose. The consultants, however, were probably uncommunicative because there *were* no pederastic purposes.

The Sauk—among whom the *i-coo-coo-a* were regarded as "medicine and sacred"—honored their women-men at least once a year by means of a "Dance to the Berdash," in which apparently only those men who had had sexual intercourse with an *i-coo-coo-a* were allowed to participate (Catlin 1926, 2:244; see Figure 7).

The popularity of women-men as occasional sexual partners for many men can probably be accounted for by a number of circumstances. First, along with unmarried young men, the women-men's partners in these short-term sexual relationships were probably married men. In spite of widespread polygyny in many places, men who were not high-status public figures or extraordinarily successful hunters generally did not have more than one wife. Sexual intercourse with one's wife, however, was frequently not possible (when she was menstruating, was pregnant, or had given birth and there was a post-partum sex taboo), and sex was also often prohibited just before hunting trips or military expeditions (Niethammer 1985:283f.; Williams 1986b:101). One of Williams' (1986a:194) male consultants hinted that Oglala Lakota men sought out *winkte* when they could not have intercourse with their menstruating or pregnant wives. Moreover, it was probably preferable to visit a *winkte* than to initiate an affair with a woman, because the latter could have grave consequences for both parties involved in those cultures where premarital or extramarital sexual relationships were prohibited for women. For the men's part, sexual variety was probably also a factor, although the division of roles during intercourse with women-men corresponded to the male-female pattern, that is, with the man as the "active" and the woman-man as the "passive" partner (Williams 1986b:96f.). According to Williams, among the contemporary Pueblos, the woman-man still functions as a substitute for the wife when she is indisposed or if the couple is quarreling (Williams 1986b:101).

Such a function of the woman-man as the sexual partner of the men during times in which intercourse with their wives was forbidden to them can, with some certainty, also be assumed for the other tribes from which active and "promiscuous" sexual activity has been reported. The interpretation of the promiscuous women-men as "tribal prostitutes" (Essene 1942:31) can also be understood in the light of this. In most of the tribes, married women and unmarried girls had only limited opportunity for extramarital sexual activity (see Niethammer 1985:308, 292ff.), although there was occasionally a class of women who had more freedom (e.g., Creek, Swanton 1946:703; Papago, Underhill 1939:183f.; Salish, Niethammer 1985:309). There also existed a group of women among the Oglala Lakota who had had a vision of the Double Woman (Anukite), and who on the basis of the vision were permitted to live out their sexual freedom (Mirsky 1937a:416; W. K. Powers 1977:59). Anukite was also the guardian spirit of the *winkte* (see M. N. Powers 1986:16f.; W. K. Powers 1977:59). The term "prostitution," though, does not seem to be appropriate for all of these forms of promiscuity, first because the aspect of material gain was not important in these groups, and second, because the cultural stigma associated with prostitutes in the West did not attach to the promiscuous women and women-men: the "wild" women of the Oglala Lakota were *wakan* (sacred, extraordinary) and so were the *winkte* (M. N. Powers 1986:39; W. K. Powers 1977:58). Among the Papago, neither promiscuous women-men nor "light women" were stigmatized. As one of Underhill's (1939:184) female consultants put it, "The light woman can't help it. . . . Her heart bubbles over."

Thus, the sexual contacts between women-men and men resembled the masculine and feminine role patterns, but the woman-man occupied a special position because of the sexual freedom granted to him, which generally differed from the culturally approved woman's role.

Roscoe (1987:166 and n. 11) brought up another aspect of sexual intercourse between women-men and men: the conveying of spiritual potency or power. Kehoe described how, in an entire series of Plains tribes, a man transmitted spiritual power to another: the more powerful man had intercourse with a woman, and then the recipient had sexual intercourse with the same woman (usually the wife of the recipient). In this kind of ceremonial sexual intercourse, the woman functions as the transmitter of the supernatural powers from one man to the other (Kehoe 1981:99ff.). Sexual intercourse between a man and a woman-man may have served a similar purpose under certain circumstances, with the woman-man serving as both the giver and the transmitter of power. Erikson (1949:183) mentioned that men used to seek out "berdaches" before going on war expeditions "in order magically to increase their own ferocity."

As noted, women-men with latent spiritual power corresponded to men with comparable powers, especially among the Plains tribes. Among the Navajo, *nadle* were endowed with a similar potential and were associated with fertility and prosperity, but not, as on the Plains, on the basis of vision experiences, but rather because of their dual sexuality. Furthermore, the Navajo believed that during sexual intercourse (between whatever partners) all secrets, including secrets that refer to special powers, are betrayed from one partner to the other. In the oral traditions, for example, Self Teacher learns the key to setting free the wild animals while having intercourse with Deer Owner's Daughter, and Coyote exchanges his powers and capabilities for those of Changing Bear Maiden (Reichard 1950:139). Thus the latent spiritual power of the *nadle* could probably be transmitted to both men and women during sexual intercourse, since non-intersexual *nadle* had sexual relations with members of both sexes. This aspect of sexual intercourse with women-men is rarely mentioned in the sources, but it may have been important, especially on the Plains and among the Navajo, and perhaps even among the Mohave, where *alyha* were desired by "shamans" as wives.

ON "HOMOSEXUALITY" AND "HETEROSEXUALITY"

I have so far intentionally avoided the terms "homosexual" and "heterosexual" to refer to the relationships entered into by women-men. Sexual relationships between women-men and men are, it is true, "same-sex," if one considers the given anatomical and genetic circumstances of the persons involved. But they differ from homosexual relationships in several important ways. Homosexuality is a Western construct in terms of its cultural organization and manifestation, as well as the subjective feelings involved (see Williams 1986b:215ff.). In the West, a male homosexual relationship comprises two males who both occupy a masculine gender status and have a masculine gender identity (see Dannecker and Reiche 1974:351ff.; see also Stoller 1968:179; on the gender identity of homosexuals of both sexes, see also Luria 1979:179). Homosexuality in the Western sense, however, was neither formally institutionalized nor culturally approved by the majority of Native American cultures in North America. Overall, the data support Williams' (1986b:215) finding that "men who are not berdaches are expected to marry women.... There was not a recognized way for two masculine men to become formally married." This holds true not only for marriages, but also for homosexual relationships in general. Marriages with women-men were, by contrast, possible, but apparently for the most part were not explicitly encouraged (Williams 1986b:215).

The gender identity of women-men is not the same as that of gay men, either. Women-men were interviewed on this question only rarely, but the interviews conducted by Williams suggest that women-men do not have a masculine *or* a feminine identity: "A winkte has two spirits, man and woman, combined into one spirit. . . . As a winkte, I accept my feminine nature as part of my being. I dress as a man, but I feel feminine and enjoy doing women's things. I would be terribly scared to be considered as a man" (1986a:196). The women-men I interviewed in 1992–1993 likewise did not see themselves as either men or women, but as a gender of their own that combines the masculine and the feminine. Because their gender identity is thus decidedly nonmasculine (yet at the same time nonfeminine), they also strongly resented a classification of their same-sex relationships as "gay" because their partners are of a gender different from their own, and they do not identify themselves as men (see Lang 1995, 1997a). Williams (1986b:2, 51) also reported that "berdaches" generally create the impression of androgyny rather than of pronounced effeminacy. Money and Erhardt's (1972) definition suggests that the gender identity of women-men is ambivalent because it contains both masculine and feminine components. Consequently, women-men are not comparable to Western society's transsexuals, either (see Stoller

1968:179, 187ff.; Williams 1986b:79f.); they do not feel themselves to be "held captive in the wrong body." The ambivalence of their gender status is retained, even if one of the two partial identities predominates. Thus, modern women-men do not, in general, identify themselves as homosexual in the sense of the "gay" of Western culture (1986b:218ff.), although some males who traditionally would have been women-men attempt to integrate themselves into the White-dominated homosexual subculture (1986b:219ff.). And in modern times, numerous members of American Indian cultures also straightforwardly define themselves as "homosexual." They do sometimes see themselves in the tradition of the "berdaches" (Gay American Indians and Roscoe 1988; see Jacobs, Thomas, and Lang 1997a), but this is more an expression of the acceptance of alternative sexual behavior than an embrace of the old-time woman-man status in the narrower sense. For traditional Native Americans, "gay" (homosexual) and *winkte* (or *heemaneh',* or *alyha,* or other statuses and roles of those usually referred to as "berdaches" in the literature) are not synonymous:

> Some younger people today are called winkte, but I don't think they are real winkte because they don't have spirituality. They are just 'gay'; there's a difference . . . winkte means 'different'. It is neither man nor woman, but a third group different from men and women. That is why winktes are regarded as sacred. (Consultant in Williams 1986a:193)

According to Callender and Kochems (1986), women-men do not constitute a "third sex," but rather a combination of masculinity and femininity. Because of this ambivalence, the right devolves on them to live out sexual relationships with men. Research during the past twenty years has also shown that while women-men did not constitute a third *sex* within their cultures, they constituted a third *gender* on the basis of their combining of masculine and feminine features (see Jacobs, Thomas, and Lang 1997a; Kessler and McKenna 1977; Martin and Voorhies 1975). If the feminine component surrounding and within them were to lapse and disappear, they would no longer be classified as women-men, but as "gays" instead. Seen from the woman-man's standpoint, intercourse with a man is not "homosexual": first, he is living out his sexuality within the framework of an entirely or predominantly feminine gender role; and second, his gender identity is no more masculine than is his status—as Williams' examples all show.

Likewise, the woman-man's partner seeks him out not as a man, but rather as a woman-man within the feminine gender role which he is living out. During the sexual act, according to Williams, women-men nearly always take over the receptive role, and anal intercourse is practiced, whereby the man takes on the penetrating role traditionally termed "active," and the woman-man takes on the so-called passive role as the recipient partner. For most contemporary women-men, a reversal of these roles is unimaginable (1986b:98f.). Such a strict division of roles is not characteristic of the role patterns of homosexual relations between two men who both identify as such, each of whom generally alternates between both roles during anal intercourse (see Dannecker and Reiche 1974:208ff.).

Furthermore, sexual contacts with women-men appear less as a fundamental alternative to sexual intercourse with women, as in the West, than as an equivalent to it. The division of roles stays the same: intercourse is merely anal instead of vaginal, although in a number of tribes anal intercourse was also practiced with women (Mohave, Devereux 1937:514; Pomo, Niethammer 1985:291). The special status of the women-men also explains, for example, why, according to Navajo ideas, homosexual (anal) intercourse between men resulted in madness, but intercourse between a man and a male-bodied male *nadle* did not (Hill 1935:276).

Yet, because the women-men were of a gender different from "man" and "woman," sexual relations with women-men cannot be described as heterosexual, either. Furthermore, these acts were probably also not subjectively experienced as heterosexual, either by the women-men themselves or by their male partners. The possible aspect of the transmission of specific supernatural latent power through intercourse with a woman-man is likewise not a part of either Western heterosexuality or homosexuality. In such a case, the woman-man, by being both the donor of power and the medium through which that power is transmitted to a man during intercourse, combines a man's and a woman's role, as noted above. The transmission of power through sex, of course, holds true above all for the Plains (and possibly also the Northeast), where women-men were regarded as holy persons.

Consequently, just as the woman-man was neither man nor woman, but rather combined aspects of both sexes, so sexual intercourse with him was neither heterosexual nor homosexual in the strict sense, but was instead a combination of both. The imposition of the Western polarization between homosexual and heterosexual does not do justice to the complexity or variety of cultural expressions of woman-man sexuality. The best way to characterize women-men's (and men-women's) sexual relationships with either men or women is "hetero-gender," which helps to clarify how sexual relationships were viewed and classified in Native American tribal cultures. Regardless of whether, for example, a woman-man formed a relationship with a man or a woman, his partner's gender was always different from his own. It is probable that hetero-gender relationships were usually condoned in those Native American cultures that had institutionalized gender role change. A hetero-gender relationship might comprise a man and a woman, a woman-man and a man, or a man-woman and a woman. Unlike hetero-gender relationships, homo-gender relationships were usually not culturally sanctioned. A homo-gender relationship would comprise a man and another man, a woman and another woman, a woman-man and another woman-man, or a man-woman and another man-woman. There are hardly any examples of two women-men or two men-women entering into a relationship. Homosexual (and, at the same time, homo-gender) relationships between two men or two women have been reported from a number of Native American cultures, but these apparently were not formally recognized in the respective cultures, unlike same-sex relationships entered into by women-men and/or men-women. In Native American classifications of sexual relationships, greater importance was attributed to gender status than to physical sex. Thus, certain same-sex relationships were viewed as quasi-heterosexual while others were not, and only those relationships culturally constructed as quasi-heterosexual received formal cultural recognition. Thus, sexual relationships between women-men and men and between men-women and women were culturally constructed in such a way that they did not fundamentally call into question the normativity of heterosexual marriage. In any case, homo-gender relationships in Native American societies seem to constitute the closest cultural equivalent to Western culture's concept of "homosexuality" (see Lang 1997b; Tietz 1996).

Contemporary Native Americans who are familiar with their culture's traditions of gender role change, when asked whether there is any difference between a gay man and a woman-man, will usually say that gays and women-men are not the same. In defining the status of women-men, contemporary Native Americans will usually stress occupational aspects; if they come from cultures where visionary experiences are stressed, they will also emphasize the spiritual element inherent in the woman-man's role and status. Gays (and lesbians), on the other hand, are viewed as acting on the basis of sexual preference (see Lang 1997a, 1997b).

Thus partners of women-men did not experience themselves as "homosexual," and moreover drew a sharp conceptual line between themselves and women-men. Devereux (1937:518) reported that it was an insult to call someone *alyha* who did not hold this status. Among the Yuma, "casual secret homosexuality" was widespread between persons who did not hold the status of women-men or men-women, but the participants involved did not want to be designated as *elxa* or *kwe'rhame* (Forde 1931:157). The Tewa *kwidos* were clearly distinguished from both homosexual and heterosexual men and women (Jacobs 1983:460).

This demarcation between women-men and other people who engage in homosexual behavior, however, does not necessarily suggest a negative attitude toward women-men, but rather a classification which distinguishes clearly between intercourse with biologically and genetically same-sex "berdaches" and same-sex non-"berdaches." Even where sexual relationships between masculine men are culturally accepted, they are seen as different from relationships between men and "berdaches." The status of woman-man is in actual fact neither masculine nor feminine, but "androgynous"—a mixture of the masculine and the feminine (see Williams 1986b:81ff.; on the question of homosexuality see also Williams 1986b:110ff., 215ff.). Moreover, it is important to recognize that a person is not classified as a woman-man on the basis of a sexual preference for the biologically same sex, but rather on the basis of a *preference for activities and occupations of the other sex*. This is a direct contrast to Western homosexuality, which is based exclusively on the choice of sexual partners (see Callender and Kochems 1986:176). In this respect, from a cultural anthropological standpoint, the institution of woman-man (and man-woman) cannot be seen as institutionalized homosexuality, even though same-sex relationships were often an integral part of women-men's roles and lives. What is institutionalized, rather, is a gender role change founded on opposite-sex occupational interests. This has frequently been neglected in anthropological approaches that have overemphasized sexuality, following the Western practice of classifying people on the basis of their sexual behavior as "homosexuals" or "heterosexuals," and not taking into account the complexity of how women-men's roles and statuses were seen in non-European cultures. Same-sex relationships were often part of the woman-man's role, but they were a consequence of gender role change rather than the underlying cause for a male's taking up the culturally defined role of a woman. For someone who occupied a feminine role from childhood, taking a male partner was just a logical consequence in many Native American cultures once a woman-man had reached marriageable age and had acquired the knowledge and skill to do a woman's share of work within the sexual/gendered division of labor.

GENERAL LIVING SITUATION: LIFE WITH THE PARTNER AND FAMILY

Separate Households and Households with Partners

Even as adults, women-men often continued to live in their families of birth (see Williams 1986b:54), which certainly relates to the fact that they often did not marry. In other cases, they lived alone or founded separate households with a male or female life partner.

If unmarried, Oglala Lakota *winkte* traditionally lived in their own tipis (Hassrick 1982:136; Mirsky 1937a:417; Williams 1986a:193, 194); some lived together with their life partners and sometimes also with their children (Williams 1986a:194). According to Hassrick (1982:136), a *winkte*'s parents pitched a tipi for him as soon as he began to have sexual relationships with men. This corresponds to the custom of putting up tipis for newly married couples (see Hassrick 1982:111). Hassrick (1982:135) also asserted that *winkte,* along with widows and orphans, were banished to the outer margin of the camp circle, but this is doubtful. Far from being avoided, *winkte* received not only men in their tipis but also women, who obtained advice from them concerning beadwork and who appreciated their culinary skills (Mirsky 1937a:417). There also existed a loose connection among the individual *winkte,* but although they called one another "sister" (Hassrick 1982:136; Lame Deer 1979:170; Williams 1986a:194), they did not form a closed group, as did other Oglala Lakota who were bound by vision experiences of the same type (the *heyoka,* e.g., and women who had had a Double Woman Vision; DeMallie 1983:241f.; W. K. Powers 1977:58f.).

In other cases, women-men were constantly being visited by relatives or took in adoptive children (Williams 1986b:54f.). On the basis of their diligence and their many functions, Oglala Lakota *winkte* seem to have gained a high degree of economic independence, which made it possible for them to found their own households. T. H. Lewis (1973:312f.) reported that one *winkte* lived with his sister, but this living arrangement seems to have been the exception. That particular *winkte* was already over sixty years old, and had possibly moved in with his sister in order to avoid living alone in his old age. Further, Lewis' report dates from a time when the institution of *winkte* had reached a low ebb.

Flathead women-men also lived alone (Teit 1930:384; Turney-High 1937:85). In contrast to the *winkte,* they had no special ritual roles, nor did they do any men's tasks (in contrast to some *winkte,* who hunted; Mirsky 1937a:417), so they lacked the *winkte*'s opportunities to achieve prosperity and esteem (see Turney-High 1937:85). Niethammer (1985:138) indicated, however, that because of the abundant food resources in the Plateau region, women were able to live without the direct support of their families by exchanging some products of their gathering activity for meat and fish. This is doubtless true of the women-men as well.

The Klamath *tw!inna'ek* whom Spier (1930:52) interviewed was also economically independent and lived alone. Spier reported that he was proud of his culinary arts, and it is probable that he, too, was integrated into a larger extended family, which gave him access to all of the foodstuffs he needed in order to cook. He also made baskets to sell (Spier

1930:52). This is also true of Papago women-men, who often lived alone. The women-men's talents as potters and basket weavers also must have contributed to their economic self-reliance (Underhill 1939:186). As Shining Evening put it, "Here are my hands and here [is] the clay. I can have what I want. Give me a bottle of whiskey" (Underhill 1936:44). He lived at first in the house of his parents and his married brothers, and then alone, and was famous for his cooking. After the death of his father, he took in his mother, for whom he was "both a son and a daughter"—"only he was often away, drunk" (Underhill 1936:51).

Shimkin (1947:298) was told about a Wind River Shoshoni woman-man who also lived alone. The information pertaining to other Shoshoni groups is less certain (Steward 1941:353). An example mentioned by Lowie indicates that women-men among the Great Basin groups were economically independent, since a certain *tuwasawits* of the Southern Ute not only had access to a great number of horses, but could also afford to lodge and feed a whole crowd of boys at his place (Lowie 1924:282). Of course, in the Great Basin, vegetable foodstuffs gathered by the women constituted the major portion of subsistence (Driver and Massey 1957:424, 425, Map 162). Thus, women-men—and women—were not as dependent on male providers as they were in regions in which hunting predominated (Prairies and Plains, Arctic, Subarctic; see Driver and Massey 1957:424f., Map 162).

The available data on the Yuma *elxa* are mixed. Forde (1931:157) maintained that Yuma *elxa* entered into lasting relationships with men and lived with them; Alarcón (1565:368), by contrast, reported that sixteenth-century *elxa* were promiscuous; he also noted that they were permitted to help themselves to anything that they needed to live on from the houses in the village.

Wherever the sources maintain that "berdaches" entered into enduring relationships with men or women, it can be assumed that, according to the traditional customs of their respective tribal groups, they either founded separate households or integrated themselves into an already existing larger extended family. In some instances, other possibilities were open to them, as with the Hidatsa *miati,* who either moved into an existing polygynous household or founded their own households with elderly, childless men and then filled out the household with adoptive children (Bowers 1965:167). Occasionally, too, they seem—contrary to the customary rule of uxorilocal residence—to have moved into the maternal household of their husbands or remained in their family of birth, but probably only if they did not marry (1965:159). *Winkte,* too, could live alone, with their family of birth, in monogamous marriages, or in polygynous marriages.

Life in the Family of Birth

Women-men who had neither the wish nor the opportunity to found their own households, whether alone or with a partner of either sex, continued to live in their families of birth or with members of their extended families. Zuni *lhamana* usually stayed in their parents' home, where they were highly valued by the women for their capacity for work (Stevenson 1904:37). Wewha, who had become an orphan early on, stayed during her entire life with relatives who had adopted her (1904:37), and she apparently occupied a central position among them because of her distinctive personality (1904:311). The *lhamana* Kasinelu, the grandson of the priest Naiuchi, lived in the home of her/his parents and grandparents (1904:38, 317). A *kokwimu* from Laguna lived in a house together with her/his mother (Parsons 1923:237). Another *kokwimu* lived with a married couple; however, together with the wife and her lover, the *kokwimu* murdered the husband, and the three of them went to prison (1923:272). After she/he had returned from prison, the *kokwimu* seems to have lived alone. She/he was in no way ostracized socially, though, since she/he apparently often visited her/his mother's brother in Oraibi and related tearfully to the assembled family how she/he had dragged the corpse of the murdered man to the railroad tracks (Parsons 1932:246). One *kokwimu* from Laguna lived with his uncle, where he ground maize, baked unleavened bread, and fetched water. In the village, they called him Naiya Huye, or "Mother Huye" (1932:246).

A *das* of the Pomo about whom Gifford (1926:293) received information was supposed to have lived in a house with his sister's daughter and her husband. This was unusual, since in most cases, the husband's, not the wife's, relatives lived with the family (1926:299, 303). Members of a larger extended family divided into three "fireside groups" lived in this particular household. The *das* was not the only member of the family who had been taken in and provided for in an atypical fashion. The entire family exhibited a tendency to integrate relatives whose ties were with the women instead of with the men of the family (see Figure 8). The mother of one of the wives lived with the latter's family segment in the northern part of the house, and the mother of the other wife lived with the segment in the southern part (1926:293). This was an extremely unusual arrangement (1926:299) which may have occurred because both of the wives in the household had come from another locality. In the customary pattern, the *das*, as a mother's brother, should have had to find accommodation in the home of a sister's son, but he lived with a sister's *daughter*. It is likely that this woman, whose name was Baken, did not have any brothers. The *das* probably moved into Baken's household, and not into one of her sister's, because Baken's home was very prosper-

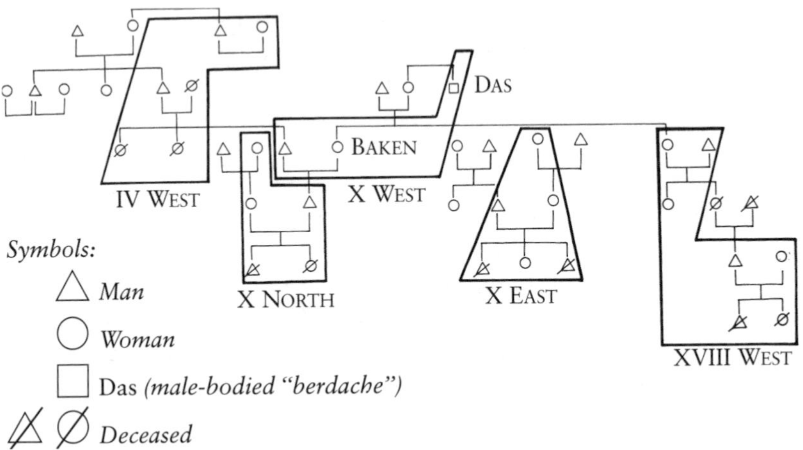

Inhabitants of House X of the village community investigated by Gifford [Pomo]. (After statements in Gifford 1926.)

ous and thus able to support and integrate the unmarried "mother's brother." One of the men in the family was a skilled fisherman, another was the only local producer of nets for hunting ducks, and a third, Baken's husband, was one of six arrow makers in the village (1926: 328f.). This particular *das* repeatedly had short-term lovers, but none of these formed lasting bonds with him (1926:333). Other *das,* however, did enter into permanent relationships with men (Essene 1942:31), in which case they probably moved into their partner's home.

In other groups as well, unmarried women-men apparently preferred to remain with members of their respective families of birth than to found their own homes. Shasta *gitukuwahi* lived "like unmarried girls . . . at home" (Holt 1946:317); one of the Michahai Yokuts *tono'cim* lived at his sister's place (Gayton 1948:236); a Panamint woman-man lived at his parents' home (Driver 1937:129); and the *i-wa-musp* interviewed by Powers (S. 1877:132) lived with "a family," although it is not clear whether this was his family of birth.

The Kutenai *kupatke'tek* Justine lived together with a female relative and her husband (Schaeffer 1965:218). The last Winnebago *shiáŋge* resided with his sisters, whom he helped to raise their children (Lurie 1953:710). After she had given up her position as housemaid with the acculturated family, the Potawatomi *m'netokwe* Louise moved into her sick father's home and kept house for him and her unmarried brother (Landes 1970:200).

Regardless of whether women-men lived monogamously or polygynously with husbands, stayed in their families of birth, or maintained their own households, they spent most of their time with women, and in many groups, a preference for the company of women was specifically named as the typical characteristic of the woman-man.

In those places where women-men were either primarily or exclusively entrusted with women's work, they performed feminine occupations—depending on the region—such as gathering, making pottery, weaving baskets, and grinding maize together with the women of the family or of the village. They never seem to have been forced into social isolation, even when they lived alone. The particular kind of living situation probably varied in any one tribe, both between individual women-men and for an individual woman-man during the course of his/her life. Wewha stayed single, but another Zuni *lhamana* married a man; some *winkte* married, while others lived alone. When, under White influence, the marriage of *shiáŋge* and men was prohibited among the Winnebago, there remained no other choice for the last woman-man than to reside in his family of birth. White Syndey married two men, and another Klamath *tw!inna'ek* lived alone. Again, for other women-men, times of solid and lasting partnerships probably alternated with times of living alone, or of a temporary return to their families of birth. In areas where gathering activity by women accounted for most of the food, women-men were also able to survive by themselves if they remained either temporarily or permanently without a male partner. In the rare cases in which they hunted *and* gathered, they likewise attained economic autonomy. Even in those regions where the hunting activity of the men provided the major portion of the food, women-men could survive without a partner, since they were included in the distribution of foodstuffs, either as part of a larger extended family or as part of the village community. Thus, even when the means of obtaining food were dominated by men, women-men were not forced into entering into an enduring partnership with a man in order to be assured of a livelihood.

Chapter TWELVE

ENTRANCE INTO THE STATUS OF WOMAN-MAN

Why some persons resisted the customary socialization into the role prescribed by their culture for persons of their sex of birth is a question which is not answerable on the basis of the available evidence. Psychological approaches to the question have been disappointing. Hassrick's (1982:136) conjecture that *winkte* were victims of excessive maternal care is unverifiable; the idea that the "berdache's" status provided the only possibility of escape from the dangerous life of the warrior—expressed by Hassrick, Hoebel (1958:589), Linton (1935:480), Opler (1965:111), and others—is untenable. As far as the homosexual niche theory is concerned (see Chapter 3), as Callender and Kochems (1983:444) have cogently argued, a preference for same-sex relationships was more likely a *consequence* of gender role change than a *motivation* for it.

The question of an ultimate "cause" of the wish for a gender role change seems to have brought forth only negligible interest on the part of the members of the pertinent Native American cultures themselves: one merely accepted the child's nonmasculinity (or nonfemininity) as a part of the latent personality or potential with which the child had been endowed by nature (Williams 1986b:53). Since a third gender status was institutionalized in most of the Native American cultures under discussion, a radical divergence and subsequent chasm between sex of birth (i.e., biological sex) and chosen gender role was not regarded as deviant, and so did not require an explanation. This stands in direct contrast to Western culture, which prescribes a sexual/gender dichotomy and defines any nonconformism as deviant and undesirable: "Western psychiatrists seem most interested in finding a 'cause' that will supposedly explain why a boy becomes effeminate. The motivating factor in much of this research seems to be to find a way to prevent such a behavior"

(Williams 1986b:53). Green's (1974, 1987) long-term studies are an example of the problems connected with explaining how and why boys grow up to be transsexual—that is, how and why they come to choose a feminine role and identity for themselves. Contrary to Green's (1987: 99ff.) expectation, the effeminate "sissy boys" whom Green and his team observed did not develop a transsexual identity. On the contrary, most of the "sissy boys" (two-thirds) became *homosexual* or *bisexual* young *men*.

Further, the socialization of a child into the cultural role assigned to its sex of birth is an extremely complex process. Many individual, family-related, and societal components influence the personality formation of the child, so that one might pose the question in reverse: Why don't more people cross out of the standard gender role planned for them? Since no detailed biographies of women-men and men-women exist, the question of the very individual circumstances and relationships in which they grow up cannot be answered.

For these reasons, the question of a psychologically based cause of gender role change is set aside here in favor of focusing on the actual practices and customs surrounding the initiation of a gender role change. Generally, the woman-man was seen as having been born with a dual nature, and was accepted as such. Group acceptance of the woman-man was usually contingent on some kind of proof that the individual was indeed a woman-man, such as the appropriate choice of a feminine object during the "berdache" test or a specific dream or vision. These tests or proofs varied across groups. Often, a boy was allowed to wait until puberty to decide finally for or against the feminine gender role he had chosen for himself. Fathers, in particular, sometimes attempted to force woman-man sons into a masculine role. Ultimately, however, the choice to assume the woman-man status was generally accepted as soon as the child or young person had given proof of his or her woman-man or man-woman nature in the culturally prescribed manner.

"FEMININE BOYS": EARLY INDICATIONS

Regardless of whether a dream or vision finally supported the change of gender role through a supernatural legitimation, an interest in activities and (often, but by no means always) clothing of the opposite sex often became noticeable during childhood.

If a boy among the Bella Coola and their neighboring tribes exhibited a marked skill in performing women's tasks, his parents concluded that he "would rather be a girl," and from then on clothed and treated him as such (McIlwraith 1948, 1:45). Cocopa *elxa* talked "like girls," sought out female company, and refused to learn masculine tasks (Gifford 1933:294).

Timucua "hermaphrodites" and women while gathering. In the foreground, a woman is loading a carrying basket onto a woman-man. (From Le Moyne 1970 [1603], p. XXIII.) Reproduced by permission of Reprint-Verlag Konrad Kölbl KG, © 1970.

Crow *bate* already showed a preference for feminine tasks as children (Denig 1961:187; Lowie 1912:226; Simms 1903:581); the same is true of the Santee Dakota (Landes 1968:112); Oglala Lakota (Mirsky 1937a: 417); Illinois (Liette 1962:112); Maricopa (Spier 1933:242); Mohave (Devereux 1937:502); Navajo (Stewart 1942:298); Nootka (Drucker 1951:331); Southern Paiute (Stewart 1942:298); Papago (Underhill 1936:39, 1939:186); Ute (Stewart 1942:298); Yurok (Kroeber 1925: 46); Hidatsa (Bowers 1965:105, 115, 132); Pomo (Gifford 1926:333); and Laguna (Parsons 1918:181). An early preference for female company (see Figure 9) has also been reported from the Cheyenne (Kroeber 1902: 19, "ut femina cum feminis vixit" [he lived as a woman with the women]); from Acoma (Hammond 1882:346); from the Chumash (Costansó 1984a:42, "vivian como las Mugeres, se acompañaban con ellas" [they used to live as the women, and kept company with them]); the Cree (D.G. Mandelbaum 1940:256); Crow (Denig 1961:187; Holder 1889:623; Lowie 1912:226); Flathead (Turney-High 1937:85); Gabrielino (Harrington 1942:32); Ingalik (Osgood 1958:261); Kitanemuk (Harrington 1942:32); Kutenai (Schaeffer 1965:218); Kwakiutl (Ford 1941:31); Laguna (Hammond 1882:343); Maricopa (Spier 1933:242); Miami

(Trowbridge 1938:68); Nisenan (Beals 1933:376); Nomlaki (Goldschmidt 1951:387); Natchez (Dumont 1753:249); Oto (Irving 1838:112); Northern Paiute (Steward 1933:238); Papago (Underhill 1936:43; 1939:186); Piegan (Schaeffer 1965:223); Pima (Hill 1938b:339); Potawatomi (Landes 1970:196f.); Salinan (Fages 1984:178f.); Wind River Shoshoni (Shimkin 1947:298); Tübatulabal (Voegelin 1938:47); Yokuts (Gayton 1948:46, 106); and Yuma (Forde 1931:96).

One could recognize the Omaha and Ponca *mixu'ga* in boyhood because they were constantly playing with girls (Dorsey 1894:379; J. H. Howard 1965:242); the same is true for the Mohave *alyha,* who played with dolls and *metates* (Devereux 1937:502), and also Papago women-men, who preferred girls as playmates (Underhill 1936:39). Such children also often eschewed activities that were appropriate for boys. Sometimes they were very active in asserting their wishes for a girl's role and successfully resisted their parents' will: Cocopa *elxa* refused to learn how to ride horseback and to shoot with a bow (Gifford 1933:294); Crow *bate* could not be induced to play or work together with other boys (Denig 1961:187); in contrast to "all other small boys," Illinois women-men spurned bows and arrows (Liette 1962:112), and Maricopa *yesa'an* threw the bow away and turned to the *metate* (Spier 1933:242).

Among the Hopi, by contrast, opposite-sex interests did not indicate that a child was a potential woman-man, but that the next child born to the family would be a girl, according to one consultant (Beaglehole and Beaglehole 1935:29). The Beagleholes did not say how the Hopi recognized women-men as children.

A self-identified *winkte* reported that Oglala Lakota *winkte* were recognizable as babies: "He is a beautiful baby and the sound of his voice is effeminate; it is inborn. The mother realizes this soon, and allows the boy to do feminine things" (Williams 1986a:196). In such cases, the young women-men were typically raised as *winkte;* thus one cannot in principle speak of a gender role *change.* Such raising of boys as girls has been reported from the Aleut and Kaniagmiut (Dall 1897:402), in one source from the Illinois (Hennepin 1699:163), and also from the Juaneño (Kroeber 1925:647), Luiseño (Boscana 1846:283; R. C. White 1963:146), the Yuma (Alarcón 1565:368), and from the Zuni; the parents' motivation was that there were no girls in the family (Gifford 1940:163).

Even in cases for which the sources did not explicitly mention early interest in feminine activities, such interest can be inferred. Among the Kato, Pomo, Yuki, and Lassik, according to Essene, a man "may make coarse baskets without reflecting on his masculinity but a male maker of fine baskets is suspected of homosexual tendencies" (1942:65). Since occupations such as basket weaving begin in childhood, the young males who engaged in it must have been recognizable as future women-men. Ford's consultant speculated that Kwakiutl women-men "get that way when they are growing up" (Ford 1941:132), suggesting that a feminine gender role emerged early in that group as well.

In other cases, however, it appears that the gender role change did not begin early and proceed gradually, but instead was carried out very suddenly during puberty or later—sometimes against the male's will—on the basis of an order received in a vision. Some Omaha *mixu'ga* are said to have been driven to such despair that they committed suicide rather than obey the order (Fletcher and La Flesche 1911:132). This, however, is very improbable. For one thing, the gender role change there definitely began before the vision quest (Dorsey 1894:379; Mead 1961:1452, 1970:260f.). For another, the position of the *mixu'ga* was not despised, as Fletcher and La Flesche reported. *Mixu'ga* were popular as matchmakers (Mead 1932:189), could be members of the men's warrior society (Mead 1970:261), married men, and were well respected (Dorsey 1894:378f.). Further, it is unlikely that males were visited by visions which ran against their own predilections, as Dorsey (1894) reported. The *mixu'ga* who allegedly committed suicide because he was not able to defy his vision, even though his father had given him arrows and a bow (Dorsey 1894:379; Fletcher and La Flesche also probably had this example in mind), can be interpreted alternatively: the young man may have killed himself not because of his vision, but because of the pressure from his father to give up the gender role which he had chosen and which was legitimated by a vision. This interpretation is also supported by a parallel from the Wind River Shoshoni, where women-men sometimes chose voluntary death as *wi'yagait,* which consisted of hurling themselves at an adversary during a war party, armed with only a flute or a rattle (Shimkin 1947:298). In this Shoshoni group—in contrast to the Omaha—the woman-man status was not institutionalized. Most often, the family reacted with sympathy, but the community was merciless (1947:298). Some form of legitimation through dream or vision was often required. Where such legitimation was not planned for within the religious system of a particular group, the woman-man sometimes met a tragic end, as among the Wind River Shoshoni. For the most part, however, his predilection for feminine activities sufficed to allow him to grow into his woman-man status gradually and with the acceptance of his culture.

FAMILY IMPETUS

In a very small number of tribes—Aleut, Kaniagmiut, Juaneño, Luiseño, and in some cases probably also among the Illinois, Yuma, and Zuni—

the family of birth had an influence on the gender role change to the extent that the family assigned the feminine gender role to a boy soon after birth. Even here, however, he did not acquire the status of "woman" (or even at first "girl"), but rather a status of his own: *shupan* among the Aleut and Kaniagmiut (Dall 1897:402); *kwit* among the Juaneño (Kroeber 1925:647); *cuut* or *cuit* among the Luiseño (Boscana 1846:283; R. C. White 1963:146); *lhamana* in Zuni (Parsons 1916:521; Stevenson 1904:37); and *elxa* among the Yuma (Forde 1931:157). Among the Yuma in the sixteenth century, there is supposed to have existed the established number of four women-men; on the death of a woman-man, the next boy to be born is said to have been chosen as the successor. Alarcón claimed that the women-men's function consisted in being available for purposes of sexual intercourse to all unmarried young men (Alarcón 1565:368). Hennepin (1699:163) attributed a similar function to the Illinois women-men.

In other groups, the family of birth affected gender role change to the extent that women-men preferably came from certain special families or descent groups, or relatives of theirs were already supposed to have been women-men. The last five Cheyenne *heemaneh'* all belonged to the same "family"—Ottokanih, or Bare Legs (Grinnell 1962, 2:39), by which term a larger extended family is to be understood (1962, 2:39; on family and camp groups, see Grinnell 1962, 1:96ff.). It cannot, however, be determined whether the status of *heemaneh'* was always tied to membership in this family; other men from the Bare Legs family became warriors (1962, 1:193f), and other sources on the Cheyenne have not mentioned the association of the *heemaneh'* with this family group. And, although the vision quest was customary among young Cheyenne (1962, 1:80ff.), Grinnell did not connect the status of *heemaneh'* with this custom. Among the Cheyenne, the vision quest, or fasting and self-sacrifice, seems to have served primarily as a means of mollifying supernatural beings, and although visions apparently could occur, they did not have to. As in the other Plains tribes, there existed among the Cheyenne some groups of persons, however, who had acquired special powers through visions. Curers obtained their abilities from supernatural beings, but could pass on their powers to other people (1962, 2:127ff.). Similarly, the gift of soothsaying was supernaturally bestowed (1962, 2:112f.). Because the *heemaneh'*, like healers and seers, were seen as persons with special latent supernatural power, it is likely that their status among the Cheyenne was also legitimated through visions, independently of any possible association with the Bare Legs family.

The status of the *miati* among the Hidatsa was legitimated by both family connections and visions. Nonetheless, the membership of the *miati* in certain families seems to have been more a tendency than a prerequisite. As noted, *miati* were usually supposed to have been brothers or sons of men who had possessed rights to Woman Above or Holy Women Bundles (1965:167). An early interest in women's tasks was seen as a sign that a boy might receive a vision from Woman Above, and as a result of this assume the status of *miati* (1965:132). A male did not have to carry out a change of gender role in order to acquire rights to the bundles related to female deities, but an example from the Mandan, whose culture was closely related, indicates that fathers typically sold such bundles to "berdache" sons (Bowers 1950:296). Among the Hidatsa, by contrast, the bundles were usually sold to a child and that child's spouse (Bowers 1965:296). Bowers (1965:323f.) did not mention whether, as the special favorite of the Holy Women, a *miati* was required to undertake a bundle purchase, as was necessary for the women of the Holy Women Society in the case of a Holy Woman dream. The connection between bundle-owning families and *miati* in Hidatsa (and possibly Mandan) thought is plausible, in any case, because the Holy Women initiated gender role change. Further, boys in these families grew up in close contact with the Holy Women Bundles and with the ideas connected with them. Because Hidatsa thinking related the Holy Women, their bundles, and the *miati* with certain families, it is possible that the development of some boys into women-men was preprogrammed culturally. Other information suggests, however, that young men from any family could receive visions from the Holy Women, assume the status of *miati*, and be accepted into the Holy Women Society without having purchased a bundle. At the same time, it is significant that the powers bestowed on the *miati* by the Holy Women exceeded those powers associated with the bundles (1965:167). Regardless, the Holy Women did not turn *miati* into "daughters" of bundle owners, but instead into a special class of medicine men whose rights went far beyond those connected with the bundles.

In the case of the Mandan, a loose association of the *mihdäckä* with certain families (and bundles) is likewise recognizable (Bowers 1950:296). Bowers' female consultant did not posit such a relationship (1950:298f.), but the family of Mato Tope (Four Bears)—which had a People Above Bundle—included several women-men.

Among the Mono, Gayton (1948:274) reported that numerous women-men appeared in particular families, but did not develop this further. Tlingit *gatxan* were likewise supposed to have occurred in a particular family line. A woman from this "sib" had married the Sun and brought a *gatxan* into the world as her eighth child. Because of this, *gatxan* were continually reincarnated in this line (De Laguna 1954:178). Such a conception of the change of sex/gender was not unusual in

Tlingit thought, and it also suggests a physical sex change during a birth—likewise in the framework of a reincarnation (1954:183; on a similar idea among the Bella Coola see McIlwraith 1948, 1:45; on the idea of the "change" of a woman into a man because of menopause, see De Laguna 1954:178). A grandfather of Klah is supposed to have been *nadle* (Hill 1935:273), although it should be considered that Klah apparently did not enter this status on the basis of feminine inclinations, but because of forced emasculation (Reichard 1950:141).

The Oto informed Whitman (1937:50) that the few women-men in their tribe were all from the same descent group (Elk), which is confirmed by some gens-origin legends, in which Elk either appears as a "transvestite" *(mixo'ge)* or is associated with one (Whitman 1937:50, 22, 29). The rivalry of the descent groups, meanwhile, comes out very clearly in their origin legends. In the origin legend of the Elk gens itself, Elk is definitely not a *mixo'ge;* on the contrary, his power over fire is emphasized (he is "superior to chiefs"; "Elk creates chiefs"; Whitman 1937:31). A non-transvesting Quinault woman-man who performed women's work (cooking, basket weaving) had a sister who likewise carried out a change of gender role (Olson 1936:99).

Foster (1944:186) reported that there was no tendency for women-men to come from certain families among the Yuki, but one of his consultants indicated that children of pairings between closely related persons were supposed to have become *iwap-naip* with particular frequency.

Thus, the family of birth affected gender role change through the parents' socializing of a boy as a "girl" and through the association of women-men with very specific families or descent groups, which was usually based on mythological-religious ideas. As shown by the Hidatsa example, such an association did not in every case release one from the requirement of a formal legitimation of the woman-man status by means of a vision. In other cases, by contrast, young males seem to have grown into this status gradually, above all in places where this status was assigned to them by their own parents.

IMPETUS FROM VISIONS AND DREAMS

Particularly in the Prairies and Plains, as well as in the hunting and gathering communities of the Southwest, visions and dreams played a significant role in legitimating entrance into the woman-man status. The vision quest played an important role in the lives of boys and men, but to a much lesser extent in the lives of girls and women (see Benedict 1922, 1923). They fulfilled this function to a considerably lesser extent in the Plateau area, and in only a few isolated cases in California.

The Holy Women

The typical vision of an emergent woman-man in the Prairies and the Plains areas often either contained or was sent by a female deity who was regarded as threatening or ambivalent rather than as benevolent. The Holy Women of the Hidatsa, who either appeared to a *miati* in frequent visions or made him dream of a sweetgrass loop (Bowers 1965:326), were not all benevolent, especially Woman Above, who not only coerced males to assume a woman's role but also caused miscarriages, premature births, insanity, and paralysis (1965:330). Village Old Woman and the other female deities created by her, in contrast, were benevolent (1965:330). Usually it seems to have been Woman Above who decisively influenced *miati* (1965:166, 330). However, males who dreamed of the sweetgrass loop were not necessarily forced to become *miati;* they seem to have had the choice. After such a dream, the feminine role components that had been taboo for boys were open to them, because *miati* "had been claimed by a Holy Woman and therefore nothing could be done about it" (1965:326). Similarly, Dorsey (1894:517) reported that the *miati* was seen as having been "impelled against his will to act the woman." At once pitied and regarded as holy or sacred on account of this supernatural compulsion, *miati* could change gender role, which was otherwise culturally prohibited, and even enjoyed great esteem (see Bowers 1965: 326).

The equivalent of Woman Above among the related Mandan was the deity Frog (or Toad) Earrings, who was connected with nearly the same diseases and likewise with some bundle rites (Bowers 1950:272, 296f.). She, too, let males know that they should carry out a change of gender role through dreams, as well as by letting them find women's work utensils: "If he picks it up, but few do, he dresses like a woman" (1950:298f.). As for the Hidatsa, such a vision legitimated gender role change (but did not force it), thus fostering acceptance by a community that otherwise probably would not have approved of males in a woman's role; the transformation was seen as having been ordained by a higher power.

The Moon Deity: A Dream Test

In Omaha society, too, gender role change was seen as ordained from above. In the characteristic visions of the prospective *mixu'ga,* the Moon Deity appears with arrows and a bow in one hand and a burden strap in the other, and she asks him to take hold of whichever piece of equipment he wants. He tries to grab the bow, but she swiftly crosses her arms, so he gets the burden strap. If he does not react fast enough to grasp the bow, or if he does not wake up from his dream in time, he must take on the status of *mixu'ga* and carry out a gender role change (Dorsey 1894:

378; Fletcher and La Flesche 1911:132f.). This is the form, here set in a dream, of a "'berdache' test" actually carried out in other tribes. In spite of the deception, however, the intention of the Moon Deity must be seen here as benevolent: supernatural beings in Omaha culture did not send visions out of malice, but out of a "feeling of pity" and "compassion" for the vision seeker (Fletcher and La Flesche 1911:131). Further, *mixu'ga* typically had already manifested feminine personality traits, so the "compassion" of the Moon Deity was in harmony with the vision seeker himself, even if the act of the goddess was formulated as coercive and deceptive (Dorsey 1894:378; Fletcher and La Flesche 1911:132f.).

In Winnebago society, the Moon Deity was likewise responsible for the assumption of the woman-man status, but she did not deceive the vision seeker; rather, she threatened him with death if he did not comply with her orders; at the same time, though, she also promised him prosperity if he obeyed her (Lurie 1953:708f.). She also rewarded him with the gift of prophecy and with the ability to perform women's tasks better than any woman (1953:708). Sauk women-men also characterized their gender role change as "an unfortunate destiny which they cannot avoid, being supposed to be impelled to this course by a vision from the female spirit that resides in the moon" (Keating 1825:227f.). Keating's interpretation of the destiny as unfortunate is doubtful, however; the Sauk *i-coo-coo-a* was treated as respectfully as women-men in other Prairie and Plains tribes (see Catlin 1926, 2:244). Jacobs also mentioned a case in which the Moon Deity influenced gender role change, but no vision was present: the Tewa accounted for the androgyny of the *kwidos* by saying that their genitals had been exposed to the full moon "at a critical time during early infancy" (1983:460).

Other Deities

In several cases, the details regarding visions and the deities involved are sketchy. The "female" who instructed the Miami males within the framework of a vision to undertake a gender role change (Trowbridge 1938:68) was most likely the same Moon Deity as in the neighboring Prairie tribes. However, the sources do not mention the sex of the supernatural beings who were responsible for the "extraordinary dreams" by which Ojibwa *agokwa* were prompted into their gender role change and from then on became "saints, or beings in some degree inspired by the Manitou" (Kinietz 1947:155). A vision experience also lay at the basis of the "superstition" which, according to Marquette (1959:129), inspired the gender role change of the Illinois women-men. Other sources suggest that this change had already started in childhood (Hennepin 1699:163; Liette 1962:113; St. Cosme 1799, cited in Kellogg 1917:360); thus the vision served to make the woman-man status official and granted the highly honored recipient latent supernatural power (see Marquette 1959:129). A "principe de Religion" (religious principle), not further specified, also lay at the basis of the Iroquois woman-man status (Charlevoix 1744:5); this was probably a vision experience, but nothing further can be ascertained, since Charlevoix is the only source on the Iroquois women-men.

A certain Kansa woman-man underwent a gender role change "in consequence of a vow he had made to his mystic medicine" (James 1823: 129); this suggests a vision experience which legitimated the gender role change and established a male as a woman-man. In a dream at the height of his career, a certain Oto warrior received a visit from the Great Spirit, who informed him that he had reached the pinnacle of his fame and that he should henceforth give up all claim to the warrior's rank and adopt the clothing and occupations of a woman (Irving 1835:195f., 1838: 113). The villagers disapproved of this metamorphosis; "neglected and scorned by those who had once looked up to him with love and veneration," the woman-man henceforth languished as "one of the lowest of the nation" (1835:200).

A vision experience of indeterminable origin also legitimated the status of the Potawatomi *m'netokwe* (Landes 1970:190, 196), although the gender role change had already been intimated in childhood (1970: 195). Together with the vision experience, however, there also came an innate potential of "power," comparable in the eyes of the Potawatomi to the inborn ability of some people to understand the language of infants (1970:196). It may be that the potential was there from childhood, or that the innate potential only began to blossom under the influence of the visions. Two modern feminine Potawatomi males were taken for visionaries, although they had never mentioned having visions (1970: 190f.). The same held true for Louise; an old woman simply named her "*m'netokwe*" because she had undertaken a gender role change (1970: 196); the vision experience, though, was apparently tacitly presupposed.

In Arapaho society, the vision which legitimated the status of a *haxu'xan* was a "supernatural gift from animals or birds," and was not specified further (Kroeber 1902:19). In relation to this, Kroeber did mention the mythically transforming Wapiti Women and Bison Women (1902:19) who were found among the Arapaho just as elsewhere in the Plains area, but he did not say whether one of these mythical beings appeared in visions of the *haxu'xan*. An early tendency toward gender role change is also intimated here, since *haxu'xan* are said to have had a "natural desire to become women" (1902:19) that surely manifested itself in boys.

Denig (1961:188, n. 38) reported that "dreams" legitimated the status of the Crow *bate;* and, again, a boy's interest in the feminine role had obviously begun long before puberty (1961:187). Further, the act of clothing the boy in a woman's dress occurred in early puberty (1961: 187), surely after a vision. The sources are unclear regarding the source of such visions. The "witch" Hicicawia, "Red Woman," is one possibility; in the oral traditions, she, together with Coyote's wife, is responsible for the origin of the women-men at the beginning of the world (Lowie 1918:28f.). In other stories, she possesses the traits of the female deities of the Mandan and Hidatsa (Lowie 1918: 52f., 70f., 1922:316; Maximilian n.d., 2:145). (The Crow are a splinter group of the Hidatsa, separating from them around 1700; see Kehoe 1992:298; Maximilian n.d., 2:138.) Red Woman often appears as the adopted grandmother of the Morning Star ("Old Woman's Grandchild"). One version of this story features the motif of choosing between a shinny stick (female) and a bow and arrow; this is not related to gender role change, but has to do with ascertaining the sex of the intruder in the female deity's garden (Lowie 1918:53). Thus, the sources do not explicitly identify Hicicawia as the sender of the *bate* visions, but some of the stories suggest that she may have been.

Among the Flathead up on the Plateau, "guardian spirits" legitimated gender role change, which had apparently already begun at the age of seven or eight—before the vision quest (Teit 1930:384). Two Klamath *tw!inna'ek* likewise formulated their gender status as the result of "esoteric situations," which surely refer to visions (Spier 1930:51). Another Klamath male carried out a gender role change, including cross-dressing, out of fear of a female "shaman" because the latter "took a fancy in him." He soon exchanged his women's clothing again for men's garb, but he continued to live in a feminine gender role all his life (1930:52).

A guardian spirit also instructed Kutenai visionaries to adopt the status of a *kupatke'tek* (Schaeffer 1965:217). It is not known whether this was the Moon Deity who conferred supernatural powers on their close Piegan neighbor Four Bears, whose endowed powers were tied to the obligation to don women's clothes when he practiced as a medicine man, but who was not classified as a woman-man (1965:221f.). Similarly, the details regarding the "dream revelations" that legitimated the status of Assiniboine *winktan* were not specified (Lowie 1909:42).

Anukite: Too Much of the Feminine

In several instances, feminine deities such as Anukite and Deer Woman were considered instrumental in gender role change; these complex deities personified femininity and conferred it on people in various ways. The Ponca seem to have assumed that *mixu'ga* were influenced by the Moon Deity, but they also told J. H. Howard (1965: 74f., 78, 142f.) that Deer Woman was the one responsible: a man who allowed himself to be seduced by her became a woman-man. According to other statements, however, sexual intercourse with her led to death, not a gender role change (1965:78). This interpretation of Deer Woman as lethal to men corresponds to the idea found among the neighboring Oglala Lakota (W. K. Powers 1977:59). There, however, the Deer Women were closely related to Double Woman (Anukite), and can be regarded as manifestations of her. Anukite appeared to Oglala Lakota *winkte* in a dream, making them choose between feminine and masculine utensils (1977: 59). As Anukite, Double Woman turned men into feminine *winkte;* as Deer Woman, she seduced men, and immediately then turned herself into a doe or a hind; this encounter led to the death of the man (see W. K. Powers 1977:58f., 197). It is tempting to see in Deer Woman the Ponca equivalent of Anukite, although even there Deer Woman would only have been an embodiment or personification; the person appearing to the *mixu'ga* would be a further manifestation of the same supernatural being. (In reference to animals, *minquga* means "hermaphrodite" in Omaha, Dorsey 1894:379; according to Fletcher and La Flesche 1911:132, *miqu'ga* means "instructed by the moon.") To the Oglala Lakota, Anukite was not identical to the Moon Deity, but instead was her female adversary (Walker 1917:82).

The deity Ite (Face), instigated by the Trickster Iktomi, is supposed to have tried to contend with the Moon Deity for the latter's place at the side of her husband, Wi (Sun; Walker 1917:164ff.), even though Ite herself was already married to the god Tate and was the mother of the four wind gods. Skan, who was highest among the gods in rank (1917:82), punished Ite for her infidelity by giving her, in addition to the beautiful face she already had, another face so horrible that whoever saw it died or went insane. Henceforth her name was not Ite (Face), but Anog Ite (Anukite)—"Double Woman" or "Two-Faced" (1917:166).

If Anukite appeared in a male's vision, he had to undertake a gender role change and acquired the status of a *winkte* (W. K. Powers 1977:58), but only if, when she offered him masculine and feminine objects, he chose the feminine ones (1977:59). If a man saw a *pte winkte* (an intersexual bison), a gender role change also ensued (Lurie 1953:709). Powers (1977:58) spoke of a hermaphroditic bison-cow—a contradiction unless it is understood symbolically as a female androgyne. Williams' (1986a:197f.) consultants mentioned visions of a white buffalo calf and also of a long-dead *winkte* who appeared to a certain young man. Again, the gender role change began earlier, and the vision put the official stamp on it:

> To become a winkte, you have a medicine man put you on the hill for a vision quest. You can see a vision of the White Buffalo

> Bull Calf if you truly are a winkte by nature, or you might see another vision if Wakan Tanka wants you to. (Consultant self-identified as *winkte* in Williams 1986a:196)

Double Woman could also appear before a woman; the woman then acquired extraordinary skill in quillwork and tanning, became diligent and generous, and became especially gifted in the seduction of men (W. K. Powers 1977:58); this, in turn, could lead to her becoming the "lewdest and worst woman of the band" (Mirsky 1937a:415). DeMallie (1983:247) interpreted these women as the equivalents of the male *winkte,* "distinctly masculine by not marrying, behaving aggressively, and soliciting promiscuous intercourse."

This interpretation is problematic, however. In her efficacious relationships with humans, Anukite was as ambivalent as she was in her mythic deeds. After her moral lapse in the world of the gods, she appeared to be quite benevolent, and, with Iktomi's help, led the first Lakota out of the underworld and up into the present one (Walker 1917:181f.). Anukite's gifts to *winkte* were the same as her gifts to women. Above all, she conferred excellence in women's artistic handiwork, paired with promiscuous sexual activity. Female Double Face vision seekers, meanwhile, clearly did not represent—as DeMallie thought—an "intermediate category between male and female" like the *winkte,* characterized by extraordinary skills in women's artistic handiwork and "active and disapproved forms of sexuality" (1983:247). Anukite's two faces signify more than merely fitting and unfitting sexual behavior (W. K. Powers 1977:197); she embodied *ambivalence* in the broader sense. According to one source, she could turn herself into a man—a "malevolent being who harms people" (Deloria 1978:19ff.) who was held up to children as a kind of bogeyman (1978:20, n. 1). Thus, she embodied not only the ambivalence of the feminine role—seductress of the Sun versus generous hostess for the first Lakota who climbed out of the underworld (see Walker 1917:182)—but also the ambivalence of gender role per se. At the same time, when it came to feminine skills, she constantly gave too much of a good thing. She made some women not just attractive but excessively sexual; she made others not just efficient but compulsively hard working (see Mirsky 1937a:415f.).

Thus, she clearly did not make the women who dreamed about her into nonwomen; rather, she made them *too* feminine. Further, this excess femininity was sufficient to transform even a male, if he had the general innate tendency. It makes sense that Anukite offered a potential *winkte* a woman's hand-working tool instead of trying to seduce him, as she would have done with a masculine male.

As Williams (1986b:29) emphasized, Double Woman and the Moon

Deity have in common the aspect of transformation, of change. This aspect of transformation is particularly apparent with Anukite, first in her metamorphosis from Ite to Anukite, and second in the various personae that she adopted later on when dealing with humans. Anukite shared this combination of ambivalence and latent power for transformation with the *winkte,* who never lost their ambivalence (androgyny) even after their transformation (gender role change).

The significance of the intersexual bison, or *pte winkte* (Lurie 1953: 709; W. K. Powers 1977:58), cannot be determined on the basis of Oglala Lakota oral traditions as recorded in the literature, although according to W. K. Powers (1977:58), the word for hermaphroditic animals was also *winkte* (see the Omaha term *te minquga,* "hermaphroditic bison," Dorsey 1894:379). Wohpe (Beautiful Woman), the female culture bringer of the Lakota, finally transformed herself into a white bison cow or calf (Hassrick 1982:251). In her essential character, Wohpe was the exact opposite of Anukite (see Hassrick 1982:248ff., 253). Apparently she was the only Lakota deity who changed herself or himself into a white bison, but it is unlikely that the bisexual bison seen by some *winkte* in their visions could have been a manifestation of Wohpe. She was not sexually ambivalent, and in contrast to Anukite, she embodied the feminine cultural ideal and was clearly benevolent when she appeared. Thus, *winkte*'s vision of the white hermaphroditic bison was probably a function of the sexual ambivalence of the animal, which embodied no particular deity but was nevertheless regarded as possessing supernatural power.

Other Dreams

According to the sources, dreams played a significant role within the context of gender role change only in two California tribes. Achomawi women-men "act upon a dream" (Voegelin 1942:134), but at the same time were said to have been "born that way" (1942:228). According to S. Powers (1877:133), the Achomawi also had a "berdache" test. In regard to the Yuki, Powers' consultants hinted at a combination of spiritual direction and the *i-wa-musp*'s own will as the impetus to a change of gender role (1877:132). Their function as "priests and teachers" indicates that latent spiritual power was attributed to them (1877:132).

Outside of California, dreams during childhood (and according to the Mohave, even dreams already experienced in the womb) were regarded as the cause of a boy's interest in the feminine gender role in a number of tribes, including the Cocopa (Drucker 1941:163); Maricopa (Drucker 1941:163; Spier 1933:242); and Mohave (Devereux 1937: 502; Drucker 1941:163; Kroeber 1925:748). According to Drucker (1941:163), dreams also played a significant role among the Papago, although Underhill (1936, 1939), who dealt with the topic of gender role change there more intensively, did not mention dreams. Drucker (1941: 218) pointed out that dreams were probably of decisive importance only in those rare cases in which people took on the status of "berdaches" as adults. Underhill stressed an early inclination toward women's work and female company.

Like visions, dreams occasionally also had a specific character. Maricopa *yesaa'n* dreamed of a mountain of the Sierra Estrella range named *"avialyxa',"* ("berdache" mountain), in whose interior a supernatural "berdache" lived. Sometimes the women-men dreamed of another particular "berdache" mountain; both mountains appeared in those dreams as young girls. The mountains decided who would dream of them by means of a game of chance. If one of the "berdache" mountains lost the game, the tribe connected with that mountain (Maricopa or Yuma) lost a man, who then became a woman-man (Spier 1933:242). These dreams are supposed to have begun early in childhood, but the status of woman-man was not assumed until puberty (1933:242).

Yuma *elxa'* had similar dreams: a hill shaped like a *metate* (a characteristic woman's tool) which lay at the foot of the mountain *avikwala'l* (Pilot Knob) appeared to them in a dream (Forde 1931:157). Dreams involving arrow weed also incited a person to change gender role, since this plant was "believed to be liable to change of sex itself" (1931:157). No additional information is available concerning the dreams of the Mohave *alyha*.

The Maricopa also told Spier that too much dreaming was dangerous because it caused a "change of sex" (1933:242; see also Williams 1986b:184). At the same time, the Maricopa characterized dreams as the path to success (1933:243f.); thus it is unlikely that the Maricopa saw many dreams as harmful. Given this attitude toward dreams, no one could dream of "any one thing" too much (1933:242) and be harmed by it, as Spier's consultant said about the women-men. A further statement by Spier's consultant indicates that frequent dreams of a *specific kind* caused gender role change: "The change was caused by some spirit" (1933:242)—namely by one of the supernatural "berdaches" residing in the nearby mountains. Spier (1933:242) further speculated that *yesaa'n* received excessive supernatural powers which would be taken away from them by resentful and malevolent spirits who would then transform them into women. These speculations, however, are not supported by the information given by his consultants.

Visions and Dreams as Sources of Legitimation

In Native American cultures in which visions during puberty played a significant role, they usually served to legitimate the recipient's future actions, including gender role change. A tendency toward opposite-sex interests and behavior was typically present at a young age. Consequently, gender role change cannot actually be interpreted as the *result* of a vision experience. Rather, the vision functioned to consolidate the recipient's woman-man status in the community, which opened up culturally patterned functions and types of interactions.

As noted, some sources have stressed the compulsion aspect of the vision experience. Williams (1986b:29), however, pointed out that reluctance on the part of the vision seeker was also a common pattern in other vision experiences, particularly when recipients were required to become holy persons, which involved a great burden of obligations toward the community. Further, resistance on the part of the recipient served to strengthen the idea that the vision was divinely inspired; the recipient was thus spared any further social pressure to conform to the masculine role (1986b:30; see also Erikson 1949:183f.: "Thus the dreamer's deviant urges present themselves to him as a prophecy from a spiritual source and as a public obligation."). Of course, such attempts at reeducation hint at conflicting attitudes toward boys who did not want to fulfill the usual masculine role. Further, social pressure to fulfill the masculine role held true even where women-men were consistently and definitely respected. Without divine support, the boy's behavior was often defined as undesirable and even deviant, and was subject to strong negative sanctions, particularly on the part of his family (Bowers 1965:132; DeMallie 1983:248; Hassrick 1982:136; Lame Deer 1979:169; Maximilian n.d., 2:79; see also Chapter 18 of this volume).

Wherever spontaneous dreams, as opposed to the *pursued* visions of the Prairies and Plains, had already begun in childhood, the process of gender role change took a different course. In such cases, the dream was seen as the cause of the boy's interest in women's occupations. If this interest persisted until puberty, the boy was initiated into the status of woman-man within the framework of a public ritual or celebration. In places where dreams were not related to a gender role change—or were not seen as sufficient for legitimation—a person occasionally went a third way, that of the "berdache" test, as it is usually referred to in the literature.

Finally, in a whole series of Native American cultures, a test or supernatural legitimation by means of either visions or dreams was explicitly denied—for example, Acoma (Bandelier 1966:326; L. A. White 1943:325); Bella Coola, Bella Bella, and Haisla (McIlwraith 1948, 1:45; "berdaches" are influenced "in some mysterious way" by the supernatural hermaphrodite *Sx'ints,* but apparently not by a vision or dream); Diegueño (Drucker 1941:163, "cause unknown"); Chugach Eskimo (Birket-Smith 1953:94); Hopi (Beaglehole and Beaglehole 1935:65;

Fewkes 1892:11; Williams 1986b); Kwakiutl (Ford 1941:132); Laguna (Parsons 1918:181); Lillooet (Teit 1900:267, although the "change" immediately after puberty suggests visionary influence); Mono (Gayton 1948:274); Navajo (Hill 1935:273); Nisenan (Beals 1933:376, "made that way"); Southern Paiute (Drucker 1941:163, "cause unknown"); Coast Salish (Barnett 1955:128); Shasta (Voegelin 1942:228, "born that way"); Sinkaietk (M. Mandelbaum 1938:119); Walapai (Drucker 1941:163); Wintu (Voegelin 1942:228, "born that way"); Yokuts (Gayton 1948:48); and Zuni (Stevenson 1904:37).

In places where a legitimation by means of visions, dreams, or tests was lacking, a boy's interest in feminine occupations seems to have sufficed to establish and consolidate his status as a woman-man. Among the Bella Coola, for example, if a boy showed skill in doing women's tasks, his parents dressed him accordingly, "realizing that he wants to be a girl," and henceforth raised him as a girl (McIlwraith 1948, 1:45). A Pomo *das* began, like girls, to put on a deerskin skirt at the age of five or six years, at which time he was taught all of a woman's tasks (Gifford 1926:333). It is probable that gender role change took a similar course in other tribes for which this phenomenon represented more a profane or secular matter than a spiritual affair. If the boy showed an inclination toward the feminine role, his parents and the community accepted this (possibly after initial resistance) and allowed him to grow into the feminine gender role gradually.

Sometimes the community demanded a final decision of a young male, without his having made use of a test or a ritual. In Zuni, this decision fell at puberty. If a young male wanted to continue to do women's work, then he had to don women's clothing (Stevenson 1904:37), which obviously confirmed his status as *lhamana*. As long as Navaho *nadle* were not intersexes, they had to decide as young adults, in which event the issue of clothing was unimportant, since they could wear either men's or women's clothing, as they liked: "A boy may act like a girl until he is eighteen or twenty-five, then he may turn into a man or he may not" (Navajo consultant in Hill 1935:273).

Finally, information concerning dreams, visions, or other forms of legitimation of gender role change is totally lacking for numerous Native American cultures; this is true, for example, for all of the tribes of the Southeast in which a woman-man status existed.

TESTS AND RITUALS

Tests and rituals, which served either to determine whether a boy was really ready for the gender role change or to initiate him publicly into the status of woman-man, apparently existed in only a few Native American cultures. Further, such practices have only seldom been described in detail. Consultants sometimes explicitly denied tests and rituals, as among the Bankalachi (Driver 1937:109); Chilula (Driver 1939:372); Diegueño (Drucker 1937a:27); Kato (Driver 1939:372); Galice Creek (Barnett 1937:194); Hupa (Driver 1939:372); Kawaiisu (Driver 1937:109); Maricopa (Drucker 1941:218); Mattole (Driver 1939:372); Mono (Driver 1937:109); Southern Paiute (Driver 1937:109; Stewart 1942:298); Panamint (Driver 1937:109); Sinkyone (Driver 1939:372) Siuslaw (Barnett 1937:194); Tillamook (Barnett 1937:194); Tolowa (Driver 1939:372; Barnett 1937:194); Tübatulabal (Driver 1937:109); Tututni (Barnett 1937:194); Wiyot (Driver 1939:372); Yokuts (Driver 1937:109); Yuki (Driver 1939:372; Kroeber 1925:180); and Yurok (Driver 1937:109).

Tests

Tests were encountered among the Achomawi (S. Powers 1877:133); Klamath (Spier 1930:52); Northern Paiute (Stewart 1941:405, 440); Papago (Drucker 1941:163; Underhill 1936:39; 1939:186); Pima (Drucker 1941:163, with reservations; Hill 1938:340); Nevada Shoshoni (Steward 1941:312, 353); and Ute (Stewart 1942:298). They are, thus, restricted to the Great Basin and some hunting and gathering communities of the Southwest, as well as to groups of the Uto-Aztecan language family. The existence of a test among the Achomawi (Hokan language family) of California is probably explicable in terms of influences from the neighboring Paiute groups.

The "berdache" test proceeded everywhere according to the same basic pattern. It enabled the boy either to reverse his decision or to take on the full status of a woman-man. That which on the Plains was frequently represented in a vision experience—a choice between a man's and a woman's work tool—was carried out in reality through the test.

The Northern Paiute had a potential *tüvasa* sit down on a paper sheet or on dry grass, placed arrows and a bow on one side of him and women's handiwork tools on the other, and then set fire to the sheet or grass on which he was seated. In one bound, the frightened boy grabbed one set of objects and escaped: "If he takes the bow and arrows, he is normal. If he takes the objects associated with women, he is tüvasa and will be funny and never make babies" (consultant in Steward 1941:440). The Ute, meanwhile, used a similar test after a boy had begun to exhibit a tendency toward being *tuvasawut* (Stewart 1942:298). The Nevada Shoshoni set a potential *taŋgowaip* in a "circle of sagebrush with a bow and a basket. The brush was set on fire and the young man was required to seize either the bow or the basket and run out" (Steward 1941:353).

The Papago built a small enclosure out of undergrowth and sat the boy who was interested in women's work inside, placing a bow and arrow on one side of him and and basket-weaving tools on the other. They then set fire to the enclosure and waited to see what the boy would choose (Underhill 1936:39, 1939:186). In one case, they even ran the test several times, and the boy—Shining Evening—always chose the feminine objects (1936:39). Thus they were giving him several chances to reverse his decision. A boy's decision made in such a way was, therefore, *reversible.*

This also holds true for some other cultures, independently of the kind of legitimation of the woman-man status. One *winkte* even went "in and out of a winkte role" (Williams 1986a:197), which represented the exception among the Oglala Lakota, however. Among the Klamath, a spontaneous test similar to that usual in the Great Basin in one case resulted in a certain young male's *giving up* his *tw!inna'ek* status. Lele'ks, who was later to become a renowned military leader, wore women's clothes and did women's work as an adolescent. One time, after he had lain down to sleep after gathering lily seeds, some men placed arrows, a bow, and also women's working equipment next to him, and then leaned over him and shouted out loud. Lele'ks jumped to his feet and seized the bow. Soon afterward, he proceeded to go on a vision quest and—on the basis of his visions—became one of the most capable chiefs of the Klamath and the husband of seven wives (Spier 1930:52f.). Admittedly, the sources do not say anything about whether this was the accepted way to consolidate or revise the choice of a young *tw!inna'ek*. Lele'ks' fellow tribesmen must have come on the idea of conducting the "test" from the example of their Northern Paiute neighbors, since tests were not customary in California and on the Plateau. The Achomawi, of whom S. Powers (1877:133) reported that they set women-men inside a "circle of fire" and had them choose between bow and arrow and a "woman-stick" (obviously a digging stick), were also neighbors of the Northern Paiute.

The procedure with the brush hut, bow and arrow, and a woman's utensil, in this case a basket, was also practiced by the Pima (Hill 1938b: 340), indicating that there once must have existed a clearly formulated woman-man status in Pima society, as among the neighboring Papago. Gender role change in institutionalized form no longer existed there during Hill's time, and if Hill's account of the general attitude expressed toward the *wik'ovat* is accurate, feminine males were held in very low esteem by the Pima during the 1930s (Hill 1938b:339f.). It should be noted that the true nature of the test most probably came as no surprise at all (see Bleibtreu-Ehrenberg 1984:99; Williams 1986b:24f.), but instead quite consciously left the choice to the boy. As soon as he was led to where the test was to take place, he must have known what was in store for him. From this point of view, the test was actually a ritual rather than a spontaneous "test."

Rituals

The sources pertaining to formal rituals that consolidated the status of woman-man are meager. Several Native American cultures had special "berdache"-making rituals at one time, but these were already obsolete at the time the investigations were made, and there is no further information about them. This is true of the Chumash (Harrington 1942:32, 45), Cocopa (Drucker 1941:163, 218), Gabrielino (Harrington 1942: 32, 45), Kitanemuk (Harrington 1942:32, 45), and Salinan (Harrington 1942:32, 45).

Among the Yuma *elxa'*, whose gender role change was attributed to dreams, the new status was "publicly recognized" in some cases. Friends were invited, and the *elxa'* prepared a banquet for them (Forde 1931: 157). This apparently represented his first official act in his new status immediately following the legitimizing dream experience. The festive meal organized by the *elxa'* was not absolutely necessary; it did not contribute to the legitimation of his gender role change, but rather to the recognition of his new status by his friends and family.

Kroeber (1925:748f.) and Devereux (1937:504ff.) described the *alyha* ritual of the Mohave in detail. Along with elements of a standardized ritual, it also contained elements of a test—the boy was "surprised" by the celebration (1937:508). At the same time, the ritual served to formally acknowledge the child's woman-man status (1937: 509). The occasion for holding this "initiation ceremony" (1937:508) was decided upon by the boy's relatives, after all attempts up to his tenth year of life to change his behavior had come to nothing. Any singers who had received songs for the *alyha* ritual in dreams (Kroeber 1925:748) were notified, as were the inhabitants of the surrounding settlements. On the appointed day, the boy was led by two of his female relatives to a circle drawn by the singer in the center of the crowd of people (1937: 508). This was the test component: if the boy did not want to adopt the status of an *alyha,* he would not enter the circle. If he did enter it, though, four songs were sung, to which the boy danced like a woman. "After the fourth song he is proclaimed a homosexual" (i.e., an *alyha,* 1937:508). The women then carried him to the Colorado River, bathed him, and dressed him in a woman's skirt which had been made especially for the occasion. Later he received a feminine name (1937:508f.). This ritual was, in fact, "both an initiation and an ultimate test of his true inclinations" (1937:508). At the same time (as among the Yuma), a dream experience lay at the root of the gender role change, which had been developing since an early age (Devereux 1937:502; Kroeber 1925:748).

The element of surprise is lacking in several reports (Devereux 1937; Kroeber 1925). In spite of differences in such rituals, they had in common the public nature of the ritual, the collaborative assistance of special singer(s), women who presented the *alyha* with the woman's skirt, and the *alyha*'s bath in the river (Kroeber 1925:748f.; Devereux 1937:506ff.). Some reports suggest that the ritual served to indicate grudging acceptance on the part of the boy's parents ("If our child wishes to go that way, the only thing we can do is to make it adopt the status of a transvestite," Devereux 1937:503). Public recognition of the boy's entrance into the new gender status seems to have been the central function of ritual practices related to gender role change.

CONCLUSIONS

Thus, several cultural patterns associated with the initiation of males into the status of a woman-man are recognizable. The first premonitory indications of a gender role change typically became apparent in childhood. After this time, five regionally distinct basic patterns are evident:

1. If neither dreams nor visions in childhood were regarded as essential for a gender role change, and if at the same time the mere inclination of a boy toward feminine activities was not seen as sufficient for classification as a woman-man, the boy was subjected to a test during puberty in order to determine whether he was really serious about his decision. If, during the test, he decided in favor of the symbols of the feminine role, the status of woman-man was conferred on him. The test, rather than a dream or vision, legitimated his status (Paiute, Ute, Shoshoni, Papago, possibly Pima). When dreams or visions did have an influence on gender role change but did not suffice as a means of legitimation, either a test or a ritual typically occurred which if successful conferred the woman-man status on the boy (Mohave, possibly Klamath, Achomawi).
2. When visions or dreams were considered central, a standardized vision or dream experience served to legitimate and consolidate the gender role change and to establish a young male in the socially accepted status of woman-man (visions: Prairies, Plains, Plateau; dreams: Maricopa, Cocopa).
3. When neither dreams nor visions played a significant role culturally, but the emphasis lay rather on the personal inclinations of the individual, and at the same time the woman-man status was culturally defined and was connected to special role aspects and privileges, the potential woman-man had to make a final, binding decision at some point in his life (Navajo, Zuni).

4. In some cases, the individual's desire to assume the role and usually also the clothing of the opposite sex was sufficient. Dreams, visions, tests, or rituals were not required. In such cases, the woman-man usually manifested his inclinations from childhood and was brought up as a quasi-girl. Even in these cases, however, he did not grow up to be classified as a woman in his culture, but as a woman-man holding a separate, "third," gender status that differed from both women's and men's (California, Northwest Coast).
5. When the feminine role was assigned to a boy shortly after birth, he received the status of woman-man immediately. This would not constitute an actual gender role *change*. Nonetheless, his gender status was that of woman-man, not "girl" or "woman" (Arctic, parts of California).

Chapter THIRTEEN

Women-Men in Native American Cultures: Ideology and Reality

WOMEN-MEN AS THE "BETTER WOMEN"

As noted in Chapter 6, women-men were widely reported to have equaled or excelled women at specifically feminine occupations on the basis of either greater physical strength (carrying, digging) or greater skill (beadwork, pottery). A variety of explanations for this purported superiority have been offered. Here, these explanations are examined critically, and an alternative is presented.

The notion that women-men were physically strong was widespread. For example, Coahuiltecan women-men were highly valued and esteemed as load carriers on account of their physical strength (Cabeza de Vaca 1555:36), and, as noted, physical strength was thought to qualify women-men for tasks that were traditionally assigned to women in other groups as well. The Juaneño *kwit* (Kroeber 1925:657) and the Luiseño *cuut* (Boscana 1846:283) were regarded as especially robust housewives. Underhill's (1936:39, 43f.) female consultant Maria Chona found her "sister-in-law" Shining Evening "very convenient": not only was she usually in a cheerful mood, but she also did the strenuous task of grinding corn (maize) for the women; she could also dig up and carry more roots than the women, and on longer trips, she carried the consultant's baby for her when she became tired. Zuni women also felt a *lhamana* to be a great relief and help in the household because she did double the amount of work and generally performed the tasks that were the most difficult physically (Stevenson 1904:37). On account of their physical stamina, *lhamana* were also highly esteemed and valued by the White families, especially as washerwomen (Stevenson 1904:380). A certain Oto *mixo'ge* was no doubt also regarded as especially efficient at digging for wild potatoes on account of his strength (Whitman

1937:50), just as were Plains Cree *aayahkwew* (D. G. Mandelbaum 1940:256).

In addition to being recognized for their physical strength, women-men were often portrayed as excellent housewives. Crow *bate* possessed the biggest and most beautiful tipis, were considered to be experts in handiwork and in the culinary arts, and were also "highly regarded for their many charitable acts" (Simms 1903:580). The *bate* examined by Holder was so well versed in all the tasks of women that White families often employed him (Holder 1889:624). Piegan Woman, who lived with a series of men, was regarded as an "excellent housekeeper"; she/he cooked, collected firewood, dried meat, tanned hides, sewed clothing, and also knew how to do beadwork (Schaeffer 1965:223). All of this did not, of course, prevent her/him from going on raiding expeditions with the men (1965:223). Louise and other Potawatomi *m'netokwe* likewise demonstrated great skill in feminine activities (Landes 1970: 195, 198ff.). Moreover, Louise and Shining Evening were always up to date in everything pertaining to fashion (Landes 1970:200; Underhill 1936:51). A Bannock *tüvasa waip* "did women's work more vigorously than women" (and did some men's work as well; Steward 1943:385). Following the traditional patterns of interaction in dealing with women-men, Hare men also flattered the feminine male Sony, saying that he took care of them better than their own mothers or sisters could (Broch 1977: 99). Hidatsa households that were organized around a *miati* were said to have been especially well ordered, because *miati* worked harder than women and surpassed them in many occupations (Bowers 1965:167). Oglala Lakota *winkte* supposedly could "do anything, everything better than women" (Williams 1986a:195), and Mohave *alyha* were regarded as especially diligent wives (Devereux 1937:513). The Ojibwa *agokwa* Yellow Head was "very expert in the various employments of women, to which all of her time was given" (Tanner 1830:105). The Chugach Eskimo *aranu'tiq* were held to be more adroit at the respective tasks of both sexes than either men or women themselves (Birket-Smith 1953:94). On account of their competence as cooks and/or organizers of the feminine work domain, Navajo *nadle* and Oglala Lakota *winkte* were brought in for major gatherings and burials (Hill 1935:275; Williams 1986b:36); the supervising of women at their work can also be deduced for the Natchez women-men on the basis of their designation as "chefs des femmes" (bosses/chiefs of the women; Dumont 1753:249). Winnebago *shiáŋge* are likewise supposed to have generally performed women's tasks better than the women themselves did (Lurie 1953:708).

Frequently, however, women-men's superiority in the area of handiwork has been particularly stressed; handiwork, of course, demands a special talent in addition to the diligence required for women's everyday tasks. The *lhamana* were regarded as especially good potters and weavers (Parsons 1916:523; Stevenson 1904:37). Around 1900, an Acoma *kokwimu* was well known as an excellent potter (Roscoe 1988b:58), and the same held for the Laguna *kokwimu* Arroh-ah-och (1988b:59). *Nadle* outperformed women not only at everyday tasks, but also at weaving (Hill 1935:275; Matthews 1897:217, n. 33); they also competed with both sexes as extremely successful breeders of sheep (Hill 1935:275). The Pomo, Yuki, Kato, and Lassik women-men produced baskets that were at least as good as those of the women (Essene 1942: 65), and the baskets made by the Wailaki *clele* were regarded as better than those fashioned by women (Loeb 1932:93). Ponca *mixu'ga* produced the most beautiful quillwork and beadwork of the entire tribe (J. H. Howard 1965:142); the same held true of the Oglala Lakota *winkte* (Hassrick 1982:137; Mirsky 1937a:417; W. K. Powers 1977: 58; Williams 1986a:194) and also the Santee Dakota *winkta* (Landes 1968:112).

Reports of women-men's superior physical strength do not, of course, necessarily prove that the women-men actually were that much stronger than the women. First, because of the heavy jobs that had to be done, the bodily strength of Native American women must have been considerable, and should not be underestimated. Second, because the women-men had been performing feminine activities since childhood, they probably did not develop a "typical" masculine musculature.

The fact remains that Native American consultants have consistently reported women-men's superiority in women's activities, whether in terms of physical strength or other characteristics. According to Mirsky (1937a:417; see also Hassrick 1982:137), the Oglala Lakota explained the special skillfulness of the *winkte* on the basis of their access to supernatural assistance. Ethnographers, for the most part accepting the factuality of the "better woman" phenomenon, have offered a variety of explanations. Williams (1986b:59) explained that women-men were economically productive because they did not have to look after small children. However, women-men often adopted children, yet still managed to retain their economic efficiency. Williams (1986b:60) theorized that excellence in feminine skills may have been a substitute, for women-men, for "masculine" prestige earned through hunting and warfare. He (1986b:59) also theorized that socialization played a role in women-men's success: they were expected to excel, and they did. The idea that woman-man socialization may have played a part in encouraging success, particularly for *winkte,* may have some credence. However, Williams' (1986b:60) characterization of this influence as "male socialization" is less credible, as women-men were, in many cases, specifically *not* socialized as males, but as women-men. Further, the excellence of women-men in women's work has been reported from tribes in which male children underwent a specifically feminine socialization. Implicit in Williams' position is that (1) young women-men were raised as males and (2) the quest for prestige (in men's *or* women's spheres) is a specifically masculine trait.

Whitehead (1981:109) asserted that the "berdache" phenomenon—which includes the superiority aspect—functioned as a means for biological males to usurp areas of feminine prestige. Whitehead's position is similar to Williams' in that they both conceived of women-men as having a specifically masculine drive (whether biologically or socially induced) to achieve that enabled them to surpass women in their own spheres of activity. This notion finds a parallel in the following statement by a Western male-to-female transsexual interviewed by Raymond (1979):

> Genetic women cannot possess the very special courage, brilliance, sensitivity and compassion—and overview—that derives from the transsexual experience. Free from the chains of menstruation and childbearing, transsexual women are obviously far superior to Gennys [genetic women] in many ways. (Male-to-female transsexual, cited in Raymond 1979:117)

The quest for prestige was not, however, an exclusively masculine personality trait, even in the Plains region. Every gender role offered its own opportunities to acquire—and strive for—prestige. In reference to the Ojibwa, Landes (1937:121) mentioned the "woman's world, closed to men or ignored by them, with its own standards of excellence." ("Ignored by them," incidentally, is an apt characterization. Whereas a great fuss was made over every bit of a boy's progress, girls learned early on to practice modesty, and at most, to hope for official recognition from other *women.* Thus, while it is true that each sex had opportunities to strive for and achieve prestige, it also seems that in some cases masculine prestige was viewed as superior to prestige in the feminine sphere, at least by the men, and possibly also by the women; Landes 1938:10ff.) The Oglala Lakota women competed with each other in doing art crafts such as quillwork and beadwork, just as the men did with respect to deeds of heroism in warfare (Hassrick 1982:57). Organized invitational competitions were announced, and the prestige of the female victor was considerable (1982:58). Women whose parents had declared them to be "child-beloved" in a costly ceremony were similarly able to gain prestige within this status through exhibiting generosity (Mirsky 1937a:414). Consequently, women had ample opportunities to strive for public recognition in the area of feminine occupations and exhibited a great deal of ambition in that respect (see Kehoe 1983).

Particularly on the Prairies and Plains, where the woman-man status expressed the highest degree of gender ambivalence and was at the same time associated with supernatural power, it is likely that the woman-man's skillfulness at women's tasks was influenced by his/her group's expectations of superior performance (see Williams 1986b: 59f.). It was not a substitute for the prestige that could otherwise be obtained within the man's role. Whether a woman-man attempted to gain prestige in traditional masculine role domains—for example, as a warrior or a medicine-man—probably depended on his own individual personality. On the Plains, the woman-man was not required to totally extricate himself from the masculine role. What is really remarkable here is that his prestige equaled that of men who likewise possessed a special latent spiritual power and surpassed that of women who were endowed with supernatural power. Admittedly, the Double Woman visions did make women and women-men equally *wakan,* but the wide-ranging ritual tasks which were grounded in the visions fell only to the latter. Thus, the prestige quest of the Plains women-men was not a substitute for masculine prestige, but instead expressed their ambivalent gender status. They demonstrated masculine prestige-seeking behavior in the masculine role components they retained, and they exhibited feminine prestige-seeking behavior in the feminine role components they practiced. The quest for prestige was not tied to a definite gender role, but the kind of prestige attainable was. By seeking to attain both kinds of prestige at once, Plains women-men expressed their own ambivalent gender role, composed of elements of both the masculine and the feminine roles, and their likewise ambivalent gender status. This holds true of the Navajo *nadle* as well, who were associated in their culture with prosperity and carried out occupations of both sexes within the framework of a highly developed ambivalence of both role and status. If they put the main emphasis on the feminine role, then their striving for prestige was preponderantly developed within that role (e.g., weaving). By contrast, Klah stressed aspects of the masculine role and gained prestige as a renowned chanter.

Wherever women-men's gender role was less characterized by ambivalence, where they were denied the quest for masculine prestige, where they were not seen as holy persons, and where masculine prestige was not primarily defined in terms of reckless daring in military undertakings, another explanation must be sought for the women-men's special talent in women's tasks. The respect accorded to women-men in these places was often attributed to their physical strength, which is supposed to have enabled them to perform heavy women's work with relative ease and without special assistance (Coahuiltecan, Oto, Juaneño, Luiseño, Papago, Zuni). Because women-men in these groups did not retain masculine components, their actions were concentrated on aspects of the feminine gender role. This is true of the Pueblos and also most of the California groups, as well as the Papago and Mohave. In many cases, a standardized legitimization and confirmation of a woman-man in his new status was likewise absent. Here the attempt to attain perfection in feminine occupations can be accounted for as follows: in the absence of a public legitimization of his status enacted at a certain point in time, the woman-man had to legitimate his status continually, so that no doubt was cast on him or his status by the community. Conscientious performance of the feminine gender role was one means of accomplishing this. In contrast to a biological woman, the woman-man had to deny his physical maleness continually by carrying out the feminine role more perfectly than was required of a woman—just to maintain his quasi-feminine status. A woman did not have to continually legitimate her ascribed status. But a woman-man, who defined himself in the context of an achieved status as a non-man, needed a continual legitimation, especially where the entrance into the woman-man status did not take place according to a standardized form (vision, ritual, test), and where the status of woman-man was more quasi-feminine than markedly ambivalent.

But even in Native American cultures which featured a standardized entree into the woman-man status, and among which the woman-man's social role was decisively molded by ambivalence, the status of woman-man was brought to expression in daily life through a preponderantly feminine gender role. And this is independent of certain activities or occupations conceived of as masculine role components that may have been carried out by women-men. Again, the desire for continual reconfirmation of the achieved status (in the sense of Hoebel 1958:386ff.) motivated the individual to that perfection to which women-men carried out women's tasks. In these cases, women-men, in line with the cultural ideology, had to be particularly efficient in the *feminine* role. Thus, the pressure to do women's work better than the women themselves did it was ultimately just as strong for the Plains women-men, who were associated with latent spiritual power, as it was for women-men who lacked supernatural legitimation. In the Plains, women-men had to provide proof of their special kind of spiritual power by their remarkable efficiency, whereas in other regions, continued recognition of their quasi-feminine status depended on a perfect imitation of the feminine role. Everywhere in North America, however, perfection in feminine occupations served the function of continually legitimating the woman-man's special status, because the carrying out of women's work was considered to be the chief characteristic of the woman-man. For example, despite legitimation through dreams and ritual, this is also true of the Mohave, where the status of *alyha* is characterized by a highly developed nonambivalence in the required role behavior.

WOMEN-MEN'S ROLES AND STATUSES: A SUMMARY

The adoption by males of a feminine gender role resulted in their acquiring a gender status which was different from the masculine gender status ascribed to them at birth, and which usually in the literature has been termed "berdache." This gender status is characterized by an inherent gender ambivalence, regardless of whether the individual lived out a social role which was relatively more masculine, more feminine, or composed of components from both these gender roles. The feminine gender role was usually preponderant, and in most cases involved some degree of cross-dressing.

In no case did such a male receive the status of "woman." The status of "berdache," or woman-man, could be quasi-feminine if the feminine gender role was performed without any masculine role components. The characteristic ambivalence, expressed by the marked disjunction between male physique and female clothing and social role, was clearly evident to the woman-man's culture.

The terms used to designate women-men in different groups varied, classifying the "berdache" as "man-woman," half-man/half-woman, or as someone who "imitates a woman," "behaves like a woman," or who "wants to be a woman" (see Table 6). In no case did such a designation mean "woman." In most cases, the designations for women-men refer to a combination of the masculine and the feminine manifested by them. Moreover, different groups emphasized different aspects of gender role in their woman-man classifications and designations. Shoshoni-speaking groups emphasized infertility or sterility. Similarly, among the neighboring Yokuts and among the Maricopa, women-men were classified as non-men because they did not procreate. In still other groups, a physical ambivalence—intersexuality—was the cornerstone of the woman-man status. A succinct example of this are the Navajo, among whom a *nadle* apparently forfeited his status, at least temporarily, if he distanced himself from the intersexual model and by marriage became a "unisexual" being. Elsewhere, intersexuality was associated symbolically with the woman-man status, but physical intersexuality was not required. The Omaha, for example, used the term *mixu'ga* to refer both to hermaphroditic animals and to women-men (Dorsey 1894:379). Sexual ambivalence—whether physically or psychologically based—was a decisive criterion of the woman-man status (Williams 1986b:21f., 77).

Early sources, in particular, tended to associate "berdaches" primarily with same-sex relationships and cross-dressing. The preponderance of evidence suggests, however, that the cornerstone of the woman-man status was an interest in feminine activities, of which, of course, feminine clothing and sexual relations with men could be an expression. This

Table 6. Terms for Women-Men

Tribe	Term	Translation	Source
Achomawi		Men-women	S. Powers 1877:133
Acoma	*Mujerado*	"Womaned"	Hammond 1882:343
	Qo-Qoy-Mo	Effeminate person	Bandelier 1966:326
	Kokwina		Parsons 1923:272
		Men-women (?)	L. A. White 1943:325
Aleut	*Shupan*		Dall 1897:402
Arapaho	*Haxu'xan*	Rotten bone	Kroeber 1902:19
Assiniboine	*Win'yan inkenu'ze, winktan*	(see Oglala)	Lowie 1909:42
Atsugewi	*Yaawa*		Voegelin 1942:228
Bella Coola	*Sx'ints*	Hermaphrodite	McIlwraith 1948, 1:45
Cheyenne	*Heemaneh'*	Halfmen-halfwomen	Grinnell 1962, 2:39
Cocopa	*Elha*	(see Mohave)	Gifford 1933:294
Cree	*Aayahkwew*		D. G. Mandelbaum 1940:256
		Neither man nor woman, man and woman	Williams 1986b:83
Crow	*Bate*	Not man, not woman	Holder 1889:623
Chugach-Eskimo	*Aranu'tiq*	Half man, half woman(?)	Birket-Smith 1953:94
Dakota (Santee)	*Winkta*	(see Oglala Lakota)	Dorsey 1894:467; Landes 1968:57, 112
Eskimo (St. Lawrence)	*Anasik*		Murphy and Leighton 1965:89
Eyak		No good	Birket-Smith and De Laguna 1938:206
Flathead	*Ma'Kali, me'mi, tcin-mamalks*	Dress as a woman	Turney-High 1937:157
Hidatsa	*Miati*	To be impelled against one's will to act the woman	Dorsey 1894:517
	Biatti		Maximilian n.d., 2:309
Hopi	*Na'dle*	(see Navajo)	Beaglehole and Beaglehole 1935:65
	ho'va	Hermaphrodite	Stephen 1936, 1:276
Huchnom	*Iwap kuti*	(see Yuki)	Foster 1944:227
Ingalik		Woman pretender	Osgood 1958:261
Isleta	*Lhunide*		Parsons 1932:246
Juaneño	*Kwit*		Kroeber 1925:647
Kaniagmiut	*Shupan* (?)		Dall 1897:402

TABLE 6. CONTINUED

TRIBE	TERM	TRANSLATION	SOURCE
Klamath	*Tw!innaek*		Spier 1930:51
Kutenai	*Kupatke'tek*	To imitate a woman	Schaeffer 1965:218
Kwakiutl		Act like a woman	Ford 1941:130
Laguna	*Mujerado* *Kokwimu, kokwe'ma*	Man-woman (?) (see Acoma)	Hammond 1882:343; Parsons 1918:181; 1923:166, 272
Lakota (Oglala)	*Winkte*	Desirous of being women Would-be woman Hermaphrodite	Mirsky 1937a:417 W. K. Powers 1977:58 Lame Deer 1979:169
Lassik	*Murfidai*	("Hermaphrodite")	Essene 1942:65
Luiseño	*Cuit,* *Cuut*		Boscana 1846:283 R. C. White 1963:146
Maidu	*Suku*	Dog (in Wintun)	Loeb 1933:175
Mandan	*Mihdäckä*	(*Mih-hä* = woman)	Maximilian n.d., 2: 289, 290
Maricopa	*Ilyaxai'* (impolite) *Yesa'an* (polite)	(*cilyaxaig* = girlish) barren man or woman	Spier 1933:242
Miami	*Waupeengwoatar*	The White Face	Trowbridge 1938:68
Miwok	*Osabu*	(*Osa* = Woman)	Gifford 1926:333
Mohave	*Alyha*	Coward (?)	Devereux 1937:518
Mono	*Tai'up*	(transvestites, bachelors)	Gayton 1948:274
Natchez		*Chef des femmes*	Dumont de Montigny 1753:249
Navajo	*Nadle*	Being transformed	Hill 1935:273
Nomlaki	*Walusa, tohket*	Hermaphrodite, "boy who goes around with the women all the time"	Goldschmidt 1951:387
Ojibwa	*Agokwa*	Man-woman Man-woman Split testicles	Tanner 1830:105 McKenney 1972:258 Skinner 1911:151
Omaha	*Mixu'ga* *Minquga*	Instructed by the moon Hermaphrodite	Fletcher and LaFlesche 1911:132 Dorsey 1894:379
Oto	*Mixo'ge*	(see Omaha)	Whitman 1937:50
Paiute, Northern	*Tübas, t'üBáse moyo'ne, tüBázanàna* (polite) *Düba's* *Tüdayapi* *Tüvasa*	 Sterile person of either sex Dress like other sex Sterile person	Lowie 1924:283 Kelly 1932:157 Steward 1933:238 Stewart 1941:440

TABLE 6. CONTINUED

TRIBE	TERM	TRANSLATION	SOURCE
Paiute, Southern	*Tüwasawuts, maipots, onobakö, töwahawöts*	(see Northern Paiute)	Stewart 1942:352
	Maai'pots		Lowie 1924:282
Patwin	*Panaro bobum pi*	He has two (sexes)	Kroeber 1932:293
Piegan	*Ake'skassi*	Acts like a woman	Schaeffer 1965:221
Pima	*Wik'ovat*	Like a girl	Hill 1938b:339
Pomo, Northern	*Das*		Essene 1942:65
	Das	(*Da* = Woman)	Gifford 1926:333
Pomo, Southern	*T!un*		Gifford 1926:333
Ponca	*Mixu'ga*	(see Omaha)	Dorsey 1894:279
	Morphodite	Hermaphrodite	J. H. Howard 1965:78
Potawatomi	*M'netokwe*	(*Manito* plus female suffix)	Landes 1970:195
Quinault	*Keknatsa'nxwixw*	Part woman	Olson 1936:99
Salinan	*Joyas*		Fages 1984:164, 179
	Joyas (Spanish)	(Spanish: gem, jewel, but also scapegrace)	J. A. Mason 1912:164
Sauk	*I-coo-coo-a*	(see Ojibwa *Agokwa*)	Catlin 1926, 2:243
Shasta	*Gitukuwahi*		Holt 1946:317
Shoshoni (Lemhi)	*Tübasa, tenanduakia*	Sterile (*tenap* = man)	Steward 1943:385
Shoshoni (Bannock)	*Tuva'sa*	(*Vasap* = dry)	Steward 1943:385
Shoshoni (Promontory Point)	*Tubasa waip*	(*Waip* = woman)	Steward 1943:385
Shoshoni (Gosiute)	*Tuvasa*		Steward 1943:385
Shoshoni (Nevada)	*Tuyayap*		Steward 1941:353
	Tubasa'a	Half	
		Half man, half woman	
	Taŋgwu waip	Man-woman	
	Taŋgowaip	Man-woman	
	Waip: siŋwa	Half woman	
Tewa	*Kwido*		Jacobs 1983:460 (erroneously spelled "quetho")
Tlingit	*Gatxan*	Coward	De Laguna 1954:178
Tübatulabal	*Huiy*		Voegelin 1942:47
Ute (Southern)	*Tuwasawits*	(see Paiute, Shoshoni)	Lowie 1924:282
	Tuwasawuts		Stewart 1942:352
Wailaki	*Clele*		Loeb 1932:93
Winnebago	*Shiáŋge*	Eunuch, unmanly man	Lurie 1953:709

Table 6. Continued

Tribe	Term	Translation	Source
Wishram	*Ik!e'laskait*		Spier and Sapir 1930: 221
Yana	*Lo'ya*		Sapir and Spier 1943: 275
Yokuts (Kocheyali)	*Tonoo'tcim*	(same word as "undertaker")	Driver 1937:138
Yokuts (Paleuyami)	*Tono'cim*	(see Kocheyali)	Gayton 1948:46
Yokuts (Tachi)	*Tonochim* *Lokowitnono*		Kroeber 1925:500 Gayton 1948:46
Yokuts (Michahai)	*Tono'cim*		Gayton 1948:236
Yokuts (Yaudanchi)	*Tongochim*		Kroeber 1925:501
Yokuts (Waksachi)	*Tai'yap*		Gayton 1948:236
Yuki	*I-wa-musp* *Iwap-naip* *Iwop-naiip*	Man-woman Man-girl Men-girls	S. Powers 1877:132 Foster 1944:186 Kroeber 1925:180
Yuma	*Elxa'*	(see Mohave)	Forde 1931:157
Yurok	*Wergern*		Kroeber 1925:46
Zuñi	*Ko'thlama* *Lha'mana*		Stevenson 1904:37 Parsons 1916:521ff.

Note. Spelling of the terms follows largely the spelling in Roscoe (1987). Maidu: Suku *is a term that refers not only to "berdaches," but also to "other incapable men" and "immoral women" (Loeb 1933:175).* Miami: *It is possible, however, that "The White Face" is a personal name. The Winnebago provide another example of this. There, the term for women-men was* shiáŋge *(unmanly man), but Lurie's (1953:709f.) woman consultant said about the first woman-man (who is mentioned in a legend) that s/he had been the first* dejáŋgocowiŋga. Dejáŋgocowiŋga, *however, was the personal name of a certain well-known woman-man among the Winnebago.* Mohave: *Compare, however, the linguistically related term* ilyaxai' *used to refer to women-men among the Maricopa who, like the Mohave, belong to the Yuman language stock.* Ilyaxai' *means a "girlish" male.* Mono: Tai'up *refers to both women-men (both in an exclusively feminine role and in a role that combines masculine and feminine elements) and bachelors (men who are not known to have sexual intercourse with women and who are not married to women) (Gayton 1948:274).* Salinan: *Boscana (1846:284) mentioned* coyas *as a* native *term used in the coastal region. The meaning of the word is unknown.* Joyas, *therefore, may as well be the garbled Spanish version of the Salinan word* coya. Yana: *Compare Salinan* coya. *Yana and Salinan both belong to the Hokan language family (Kroeber 1925:337, 546).* Ya *in* Yana*—where the languages of women and men differed—meant "person" in the women's speech. (When a man was speaking, the word for "person" was* yana; *Kroeber 1925:337.)*

interest usually commenced in childhood, along with a rejection of masculine activities, and was frequently connected to a preference for the company of girls and women. The official entrance into the woman-man status occurred at very different points in time in individual cultures and culture areas, and in each case depended on the culturally determined manner of legitimating gender role change.

The putting on of women's clothes usually seems to have taken place at the time of entrance into the woman-man status. In cultures which particularly stressed the ambivalence of this status, a combination of men's and women's attire was worn. Occasionally, such a hybrid costume was also the expression of external influences which, to a great extent, made it impossible for women-men to cross-dress completely. The same holds true for cases in which women-men wore men's clothing exclusively. Women-men in men's clothing were found mainly in the Great Basin, where the woman-man status appeared in very unstandardized form: women-men frequently seemed like feminine males rather than women-men who exhibited the full image of a gender role change. At least some transvesting women-men, however, were also present. The connection between gender role change and cross-dressing was also little developed in parts of the Northwest Coast, where both complete gender role change and nontransvesting feminine males were likewise found (e.g., Kwakiutl). Here too, gender role change seems to have been subject to no fixed rules, and, moreover, occurred only seldom.

As adults, women-men in some cases carried out masculine activities (hunting, warfare), for which they frequently put on men's clothing. These activities were evidently not regarded as compatible with the status of woman-man, and suggest gender role *splitting* rather than an exclusive gender role change. Even in these cases, however, the main emphasis was on fulfilling the feminine gender role. This also holds true of the Navajo *nadle,* who, notwithstanding their access to both masculine and feminine spheres of work, typically pursued feminine activities.

Within the framework of gender role change, almost all aspects of the feminine role were performed by women-men. These ranged from everyday handiwork and artistic handiwork through the raising of his/her own (adoptive) or relatives' children to imitation of the female voice register, feminine forms of linguistic expression, and—in isolated instances—physiological characteristics such as menstruation, pregnancy, and childbirth, including observance of the culturally determined regulations connected with them.

Women-men often carried out specialist occupations as well. As healers/curers or "shamans," they usually did *not* practice in places where this occupation was assigned to the masculine role domain, and where their own gender status was quasi-feminine. Where they did practice, the profession of healer/curer was accessible to both sexes in about half of the cases; in an additional fourth of the cases, it was assigned primarily to women, and in a remaining fourth, it was assigned predominantly or exclusively to men. This last is true in places where women-men were active in quite special areas, for example, as field medics during military expeditions. If curers/healers were mainly female in a given group, the women-men must have embraced this task in the context of their feminine gender role. In these cultures, women-men were not considered to have more supernatural power than women. Nowhere in these North American Indian cultures were women-men necessarily healers at the same time. Finally, groups in which men and women-men were curers and ritual specialists tended to be those Plains tribes which most stressed the ambivalence of the woman-man status. However, this status corresponded more to that of a medicine *man* with specific latent spiritual power. A completely "unfeminine" latent spiritual power was expressed through specific visions and conferred on the woman-man a man's medical capabilities (treatment and care of the wounded on war parties; advising other medicine men) as well as the right to move into feminine ritual spheres. Wherever the latter occurred, however, the powers of the woman-man were regarded as superior to those of women (e.g., the Hidatsa). In other cases in which women-men were healers or medicine persons, the acquisition of supernatural power was likewise associated with vision quests that were primarily undertaken by boys and men. Nowhere, however, did such a great measure of latent spiritual power reside in the woman-man as on the Plains and in parts of the Prairies region—that is, exactly there where the vision quest was especially elaborated and significant. There, at the same time, the ambivalence of the woman-man status was most distinctive; the woman-man appeared as a male androgyne (in O'Flaherty's 1982 sense).

Tasks that are supposed to have been assigned specifically to women-men usually turn out to be components of the feminine gender role (e.g., buriers of the dead in California, Cheyenne *heemaneh'* in the Scalp Dance and Sun Dance, and Papago women-men in conferring witty-erotic names). Other tasks for which women-men were regarded as especially destined fall within the masculine gender role, as, for example, felling the tree for the central post at the Sun Dance or providing medical care for the wounded in warfare. When heavy women's tasks requiring much physical strength were involved, the woman-man's male physique alone must have seemed especially suited to executing these. In places where the women-men carried the dead or other loads, no particular latent spiritual powers were usually attributed to them. By contrast, in those cases in which they took over ritual tasks, their qualifications were based on their having access to considerable spiritual powers in both the masculine *and* feminine areas as a result of vision experiences. Thus, with the exception of the California Yuki, women-men occupied a special ritual position in the Plains area alone.

Where the women's role comprised activities involving artistic handiwork, women-men also performed this work as well, often with special commitment and great efficiency, and independently of whether their status expressed ambivalence or quasi-femininity. Even when they were entitled to privileges that continued to be denied to a woman, the women-men's daily life was usually taken up with women's tasks, which they strove to perform with special perfection. That women-men performed women's work better than the women themselves has been reported from all of the culture areas in which the status of woman-man has been found. This can be traced to several factors. On the Prairies and Plains, really outstanding achievements in this sphere were expected of women-men because they stood under the protection of female deities who had bestowed feminine skills on them, and the women-men sought to fulfill these ideologically conditioned expectations. Notwithstanding their ritual obligations, however, which fell into the masculine rather than the feminine role sphere, even here in daily life the woman-man status found expression in the performance of women's work. Thus, by his perfect execution of the feminine role, the woman-man, first of all, had to display publicly the special efficiency granted to him on the grounds of his vision experience, and second, by exercising this efficiency he continually legitimated his status. Wherever an institutionalized legitimation of gender role change and the assumption of a woman-man status were lacking, this status had to be legitimated completely by means of conscientious fulfillment of the feminine role. Such continual legitimation probably lies at the basis of the women-men's quest for perfection and feminine prestige in all pertinent Native American cultures.

Another expression of the feminine gender role is represented by the partner relationships into which women-men typically entered, most often with male partners. They mainly entered into relationships with women in groups in which the woman-man's role was not very standardized. Their relationships with men ranged from casual sexual contacts to partnerships of several or many years, all the way to permanent, monogamous bondings. Generally speaking, women-men were found as one of several wives with whom a man had formed bonds in the course of his life, often in the framework of polygynous marriages. Women-men frequently did not enter into a permanent bond of any kind, but instead lived alone or in their family of birth. In no case did women-men appear as socially isolated. Unmarried women-men for the most part had sexual contacts with numerous men, usually married and fathers of families; in other cases, the women-men's partners were young men who were still unmarried. The popularity of the women-men as sexual partners in the context of cursory sexual contacts can be explained by the fact that, on account of their feminine gender role and their nonmasculine status, they could be visited when the men's wives were not able or allowed to have sexual intercourse because of menstruation, pregnancy, or other "taboo" situations. It is, incidentally, possible that intercourse with women-men also had a function in the context of birth control, but this is difficult to prove. To classify the relationships between men and women-men as homosexual in the Western sense is not conducive to an understanding of the phenomenon within its own cultural context. The men involved did not perceive themselves to be homosexual, and they led a completely heterosexual daily life in general. The women-men likewise did not regard such relationships as homosexual, because they after all did not possess a straightforwardly unambiguous masculine gender identity, and their gender status differed from the masculine gender status of their partners. In a number of groups, homosexual relationships occurred *along* with relationships between men and women-men, and these were classified as different from the latter (see Chapter 19). A classification of sexual relationships was obviously not made on the basis of the physical sex of the participants, but rather on the basis of the respective social roles and gender statuses which they occupied. Again, classification as woman-man was not made on the basis of one's choice of sexual partners, but rather on the basis of one's inclination toward the occupations and modes of behavior of the opposite sex.

An aspect of sexual intercourse between women-men and men which has received little attention in the literature to date is the possibility of a transference of latent spiritual power by this means, analogous to a transference of power from one man to another by means of intercourse with the same woman. (This notion regarding women-men would be most likely in the Prairie and Plains regions and among the Navajo.) In accordance with his dual sexuality or dual gender, the woman-man could unite two roles within himself: that of the donor of supernatural power and the woman functioning as a medium.

In most cases, gender role change was permanent, although there exist isolated examples of situationally conditioned cross-dressing, of alternation between the statuses of man and woman-man, respectively, and of a final and decisive transition back into the masculine gender role.

The phenomenon of male gender role change is anything but unitary. The only element found among all the males cited in the literature as "berdaches" (and usually also considered as women-men by the members of their respective cultures) is a preference for women's work as opposed to men's work. All other possible components—cross-dressing, specialized occupations, the retention of masculine role aspects, the

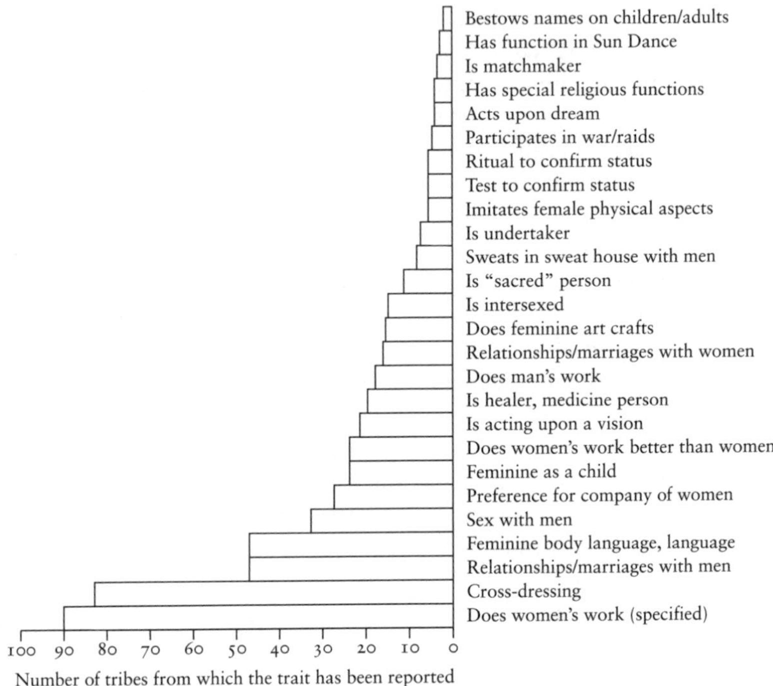

Components of the woman-man (male-bodied "berdache") role.

status as a holy or sacred person, and so on—are all added to this basic element, in each case according to the cultural organization and formulation of the woman-man status (see Figure 10).

The "berdache" phenomenon, therefore, basically comprises all those cases in which males voluntarily performed women's work within the framework of a special, culturally defined gender status. This minimal definition does more justice to the phenomenon than terms like "homosexuality" or "transvestism," which have produced bizarre effects in the literature. The designation "transvestism" itself is an infelicitous choice; even though the term literally translates as "cross-dressing," in psychiatry the term is not associated with mere cross-dressing, but instead with a special form of fetishism (see Benjamin 1966:35; Stoller 1968:179). And, in her portrayal of female-bodied *nadle,* Niethammer (1977:229) claimed that "transvestite lesbians had sex with and married both men and women"—likewise a nonsensical statement, since "lesbians" are characterized precisely by sexual relationships with *women.* With reference to females in a man's role among the Achomawi and the Atsugewi, Voegelin cited "female transvestites" only to affirm "woman's clothes" for both groups three lines later in her listing for the *Anthropological*

Records (Voegelin 1942:134). What Voegelin had before her was a partial (Atsugewi) and also a complete (Achomawi) *change of gender role*, not transvestism. Given the confusion, distortions, and misnomers that arise from such wholesale importation of Western categories and terminology, a new classification of the various kinds of gender role boundary crossing is clearly needed.

PART THREE

Gender Role Change by Females

Chapter FOURTEEN

Cross-Dressing and Mixed Gender Roles

A gender status which corresponds to that of the male "berdache," or woman-man, has been found for females in a comparatively small number of Native American cultures (see Map 6). It is remarkable, however, that gender role crossings were frequently possible for women without involving an ambivalent, nonfeminine gender status. This is above all true for the war/raiding complex, and in isolated cases also for masculine activities such as hunting or participating in certain ceremonies. "Men-women" (formerly usually referred to as "female berdaches" in the literature) should be understood as females to whom a Native American culture either explicitly attached such a gender status (referred to by a special term) that differed from the gender status of a woman (as well as from that of a man and, usually, that of a woman-man), or as females in some isolated cases for whom such a status and/or term has not been explicitly mentioned in the literature yet who exclusively performed men's work, in connection with the two most frequent other components of gender role change, cross-dressing and/or same-sex sexual relationships, and who were treated as quasi-men by the other members of the culture.

A clear-cut, definite man-woman status for females (along with a special designation) has been found among a number of Native American cultures (see Table 7), specifically, the Atsugewi (*brumaiwi,* Voegelin 1942:228); Cocopa (*warrhameh,* Gifford 1933:294); St. Lawrence Eskimo (*uktasik,* Murphy 1964:75); Ingalik ("men pretenders," no Native term given, Osgood 1958:261); Kamia (*warharmi,* Gifford 1931:79); Klamath (*tw!inna'ek* [same term as for women-men], Spier 1930:51); Maidu (*suku,* Loeb 1933:183); Maricopa (*kwiraxame',* Spier 1933:243); Mohave (*hwame,* Devereux 1937:501; *hwami,* Kroeber 1925:749); Navajo (*nadle* [same term as for women-men], Hill 1935); North-

Map 6. Female Gender Role Change and Gender Role Crossings (Not Including Women Who Went to War)

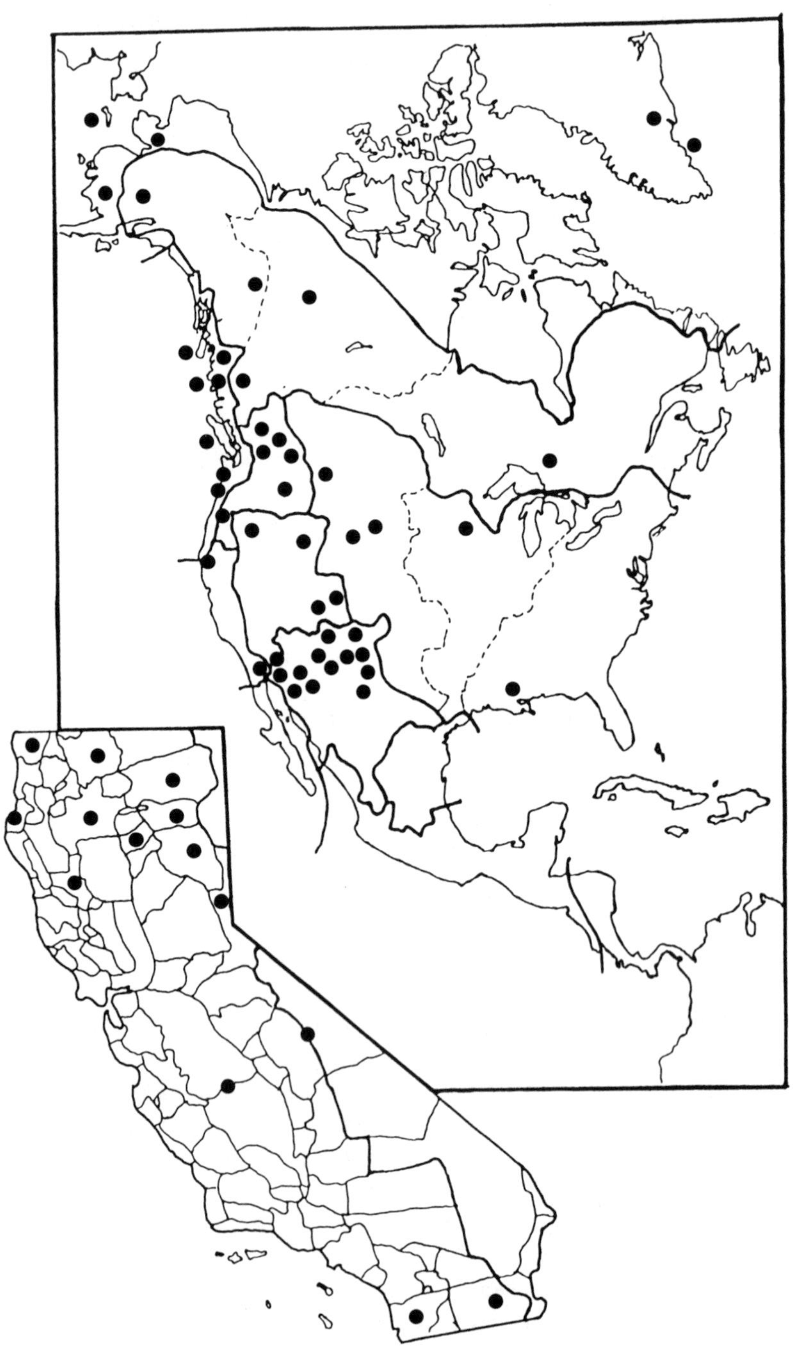

Table 7. Men-Women and "Masculine" Women (Not Including Women Who Went to War)

Tribe	Term	Source
Achomawi		Voegelin 1942:134f.
Apache (Chiricahua)		Opler 1965:111
Apache (Tonto)		Gifford 1940:66
Atsugewi	*Brumaiwi*	Voegelin 1942:134f, 228
Bella Coola		McIlwraith 1948, 1:46
Carrier		McIlwraith 1948, 1:46
Cocopa	*Warrhameh*	Gifford 1933:294
Coeur d'Alène	*St'amia* (hermaphrodite)	Ray 1932:148
Crow	Woman chief	Denig 1961:196ff.; Kurz 1937: 213f.
Dakota (Santee)		Landes 1968:49, 193
Diegueño		Drucker 1937a:27
Eskimo (Alaska)		O. T. Mason 1895:211
Eskimo (Greenland)		Kjellström 1973:180; Mirsky 1937b:83f.
Eskimo (Máhlemut)		Dall 1897:139
Eskimo (St. Lawrence)	*Uktasik*	Murphy 1964:75
Haida		McIlwraith 1948, 1:46
Haisla		McIlwraith 1948, 1:45
Hopi	*Nadle*	Beaglehole and Beaglehole 1935:65
Houma	*Femme chef*	Gravier 1959:147ff.
Ingalik	Men pretenders	Osgood 1958:262f.
Isleta		Parsons 1939b:38
Kamia	*Warharmi*	Gifford 1931:12, 79
Kaska	Females in a man's role (no native term given),	Honigmann 1954:130
	Woman chief	Crowe 1974:51
Klamath	*Tw!inna'ek*	Spier 1930:51f.
Kutenai	Manlike woman	Schaeffer 1965; Spier 1935:25ff.
Lakota (Oglala)		Mirsky 1937a:417
Lillooet		Teit 1906:267
Maidu	*Suku*	Loeb 1933:183

Table 7. Continued

Tribe	Term	Source
Maricopa	*Kwiraxame*	Spier 1933:243
Mohave	*Hwame* *Hwami*	Devereux 1937 Kroeber 1925:749
Mono (Western)		Gayton 1948:274
Navajo	*Nadle*	Hill 1935 Gifford 1940:66
Nootka		Drucker 1951:331
Ojibwa		Landes 1937:119, 121
Paiute (Northern)	*Düba's* *Moroni noho Tüvasa*	Kelly 1932:157, 158 Steward 1941:312, 353
Paiute (Southern)		Steward 1941:312
Papago		Drucker 1941:163; Gifford 1940:66, 163
Piegan	Manly-hearted woman Female "berdache" (no native term given)	Lewis 1941 Schaeffer 1965:228ff.
Pima		Hill 1938b:338ff.
Quileute (?)*		Olson 1936:99
Quinault	"man acting"	Olson 1936:99
Shasta		Voegelin 1942:134f.
Shoshoni (Lemhi)	*Tübasa, tenanduakia, waip:ü* (woman) *suŋwe* (half)	Steward 1943:338
Shoshoni (Nevada)	*Nüwüdüka* (female hunter), *taŋgowaip, taŋgowaipü*	Steward 1943:338
Sinkaietk		M. Mandelbaum 1938:119
Tewa	*Kwido*	Jacobs 1983:460 (erroneously spelled "quetho")
Thompson (?)*		Teit 1900:321
Tolowa		Barnett 1937:185; Drucker 1937b:260
Ute		Gifford 1940:66; Stewart 1942:298
Washo		Willoughby 1963:59
Wintu		Voegelin 1942:134f.
Wiyot		Driver 1939:347, 405; Elsasser 1978:159

Table 7. Continued

Tribe	Term	Source
Yana		Willoughby 1963:59
Yokuts (?)*		Gayton 1940:236
Yuki	*Musp-iwap naip* (woman man-girl)	Foster 1944:186
Yuma	*Kwe'rhame*	Forde 1931:157
Zuni	*Katsotse* (boy-girl)	Parsons 1916:525; 1939b:38

* *Information pertaining to females in a man's role in these tribes is not entirely clear.*

ern Paiute (*düba's,* Kelly 1932:157f.; *moroni noho* or *tüvasa*, Stewart 1941:405); Quinault ("man acting," no Native term given, Olson 1936:99); Lemhi Shoshoni (*waip:ü suŋwe* [half woman], Steward 1943:385); Nevada Shoshoni (*nuwüdüka, taŋgowaip, taŋgowaipü*—the latter also for male "berdaches," Steward 1941:353); Tewa (*kwido* [quetho], same term for androgynous males, Jacobs 1983:460); and Yuki (*musp-iwap-naip* [woman man-girl], Foster 1944:186). For groups from which no special designation for men-women has been handed down or recorded, the sources often cited "female berdaches" or female "transvestites," but more detailed information concerning the componential organization and formulation of the gender role and other relevant aspects is occasionally lacking. Sometimes females who definitely might be termed men-women represented, moreover, exceptional individuals who had become renowned because of eventful lives, even though an institutionalized form of female gender role change had not been established for the tribe concerned (e.g., Kutenai, Crow). In other cases, the persons described were simply "masculine" women with masculine interests who had broken out of their gender role but had not changed their gender status. Finally, females whose parents, in the absence of sons, raised them from childhood as the hunters urgently needed by the family, constitute a phenomenon that has primarily been encountered in the Arctic and Subarctic. The female equivalent of male gender role change has very seldom been found; crossing out of the gender role, however, has been more frequently reported. This raises the question of whether it was generally possible for females—but not males—to encroach on opposite-sex role domains in the absence of a formalized gender role change. It is also possible, however, that males who were not women-men actually *did* carry out feminine activities on a regular basis, but that observers did not recognize such activity; it may be that consultants often reported a somewhat idealized version of male behavior. DeMallie (1983) described a strict gender role polarization for the Oglala Lakota; M. N. Powers (1986:83), by contrast, reported that her female consultants said that men frequently lent their wives a hand with their tasks.

MEN-WOMEN AND INDEPENDENT WOMEN

As in the case of women-men, the adoption of the role of the opposite sex by men-women was not compulsorily tied to cross-dressing. Apart from complete gender role change, combinations of masculine and feminine role components in biological females have been reported. Along with complete gender role change, there sometimes existed partial gender role change. Infertile women, on the other hand, like infertile men, were in some cases subsumed under the same category (and term) as women-men and men-women, but did *not* carry out a gender role change. Finally, there were women who were striving for independence, and who for that purpose took up masculine activities, within the feminine gender status. Thus it is necessary to examine which of the females classified in the literature as "berdaches" actually occupied an institutionalized man-woman status.

FEMININE AND MIXED GENDER ROLES

Exclusively feminine activities performed by alleged "female berdaches" have been reported from only two groups. One alleged man-woman of the Southern Ute dressed like a man, but made pottery and baskets (Gifford 1940:163). Little is known otherwise about her daily tasks, but it is questionable whether her habits of dress alone sufficed for the Ute to classify her under the category of "man-woman." It is likely that Foster (1944:186) confused women-men with alleged Yuki "female berdaches" who were said to be living like women, but who had male voices and appearances.

More often, aspects of the feminine social role were enacted along with some masculine ones. Atsugewi *brumaiwi* wore women's clothes but did the tasks of both sexes (Voegelin 1942:134f.). The function of men's clothing as a sign of the ambivalent *brumaiwi* status could have been fulfilled here—if Voegelin's information is accurate—by a "false penis, made of pitch" which is said to have been worn by *brumaiwi* at the belt (1942:228). Like the *brumaiwi,* Shasta men-women wore women's clothes and performed the occupations of both sexes (1942:134f.). Also, two of the three Wintu groups queried by Voegelin asserted that female "transvestites" performed both men's and women's work, but unlike the Atsugewi and Shasta men-women, those among the Wintu apparently wore men's clothes (1942:134f.). These females, however, co-habited with men (1942:134). Apparently, their crossing out of their feminine social role and their wearing of masculine clothing was enough for the Wintu to place them within a man-woman category, even though they definitely still performed the feminine domestic activities that fell to them in the framework of the sexual division of labor.

The examples of a Tolowa woman who "purchased a wife and lived with her" and of a female shaman who exhibited "similar proclivities" (Drucker 1937b:260) show that same-sex partnerships were not necessarily accompanied by a reclassification of gender status. At least this shaman continued with her occupation, which in Tolowa society was mainly open to women and women-men (Gould 1978:134; Willoughby 1963:59f.), and which could bring considerable prosperity. Both women must have been prosperous and independent in order to raise the bride price for their wives. They were apparently not classified as men-women by the community. In this case, it is likely that the marriage was motivated less by the desire to fulfill a masculine role component than the desire to found an independent household without a husband and possibly the desire for a "lesbian" relationship (on differences between homosexual relationships in the Western sense and same-sex relationships among women-men and men-women, see Chapter 19).

According to Hill (1935:274), Navajo female-bodied *nadle* carried out the tasks of both sexes. Hill's description seems, however, to refer primarily to male-bodied and intersexual *nadle*. He did not give details concerning the componential organization and manifestation of the female-bodied *nadle* role. Similarly, Tewa *kwidos* resisted a "full adolescent socialization" in the traditional masculine or feminine role, which suggests gender role combination rather than change (Jacobs 1983:460).

Some Ojibwa women who preferred masculine occupations—probably without cross-dressing—were at the same time proficient at women's work (Landes 1937:121). Nonetheless, they did not occupy any status that would have corresponded to that of the male-bodied *agokwa*, and they therefore were not classified as men-women. Landes' conclusion that a total or partial, permanent or temporary, change of direction toward masculine occupational domains was held open to Ojibwa women by their culture, according to their personal inclinations (Landes 1937:132), is also worth considering in connection with other examples. These women appeared to be less the equivalents of the women-men present in their culture than they were individuals who crossed out of the traditional women's role without changing their gender status.

Chapter FIFTEEN

MEN-WOMEN IN MASCULINE OCCUPATIONS

Women from the most varied regions have reportedly turned completely to masculine tasks, with or without cross-dressing (see Table 8 for a summary). Although such practices varied widely across Native American cultures, several patterns are apparent.

DESIRE FOR INDEPENDENCE

In some cases, females obviously turned to men's occupations because they wanted to be independent. Sometimes, this motivation seems to have been combined with a woman's preference for living with another woman instead of a man.

Bella Coola women who performed masculine tasks were not equated with the women-men influenced by the supernatural hermaphrodite Sx'ints. Rather, these women were motivated by the desire to gain independence; in order to be "bold and independent" (McIlwraith 1948, 1:46), they had to be able to provide for themselves. This motivation probably also characterized the few Oglala Lakota women who left their group and wandered about alone, leading a "man's life" (Mirsky 1937a: 417), and also the isolated female hunters of the Santee Dakota, who—like female warriors—remained integrated within the tribe (Landes 1968:49, 139). This striving for independence is especially apparent in regard to the Eskimo female hunters of Alaska: "Sometimes we find females who refuse to accept husbands, preferring to adopt masculine manners, following the deer in the mountains, trapping and fishing for themselves" (Máhlemut Eskimo, Dall 1897:139). Particularly in the Arctic and Subarctic, where for the most part subsistence acquisition was carried out by men (see Driver and Massey 1957:427, Map 163), a woman who was unwilling to marry had to acquire masculine hunting techniques in order to survive (and in order not to be dependent on her family of birth; in Inuit society, remaining unmarried was an unwelcome social anomaly; see Kjellström 1973:33).

Among the Sinkaietk, women who did not want to marry and who preferred to feed themselves by hunting were also not classified as men-women (M. Mandelbaum 1938:119). Women were found among the Haisla who refused to take husbands, but who did not want to "have anything to do with their own sex," either; they dressed like men and made their living by hunting (McIlwraith 1948, 1:45). A striving for independence should probably be assumed here, as in similar cases among the Haida (McIlwraith 1948, 1:46).

Among the Ojibwa, there were frequently "independent" women of this kind who did not carry out a gender status change. According to Landes (1937), a considerable number of Ojibwa girls and women preferred to live alone, or with another woman, temporarily or permanently. In this group were also included women who had been widowed for a long time and who had learned masculine skills such as hunting, fishing, and trading, which they passed on to their daughters (1937: 121). They frequently retained feminine occupations in addition to their masculine ones (1937:123). This type of crossing out of the feminine gender role was open to women at any time during their lives; it was reversible, and was accepted by the community in all of its individual forms (1937:123). This role combination represented an alternative *feminine role* that was culturally acceptable.

The desire for independence—surely connected to the desire for prosperity and prestige—may also have played a significant role in those cases in which *married* women were predominantly involved in masculine occupational domains. Parsons mentioned a Mrs. Chavez from Isleta "who is an independent traveler and trader and a member of the War Society" (1939b:38). Nevertheless, this woman held no status that corresponded to that of women-men among the Pueblos: "Mannish women do not become transvestites" (1939b:38); womanish males, by contrast, undertook a complete change of both gender role and status, including cross-dressing. It is not clear from the sources whether Mrs. Chavez might have been a *widowed* woman who combined independence with ambition.

Nancy from Zuni was married, cultivated masculine interests, and danced the part of the Ko'thlama, which normally fell to a male-bodied *lhamana* (Parsons 1916:525), during the ceremonies where the masked dancers reenacted mythic episodes. She also specialized in building fireplaces (Parsons 1939b:38). She was jokingly called *"katsotse"* (boy-girl) in Zuni (1916:525), but she apparently did not hold a status corresponding to that of the *lhamana* (for a contrasting opinion regarding

Table 8. Masculine Role Aspects Taken Up by Men-Women and Women

Tribe	Occupations	Context
Achomawi	"masculine interests"	Women's clothing; live with women; some are "shamans"
Apache (Chiricahua)	"masculine interests"	Isolated cases
Bella Coola	"actions of a male"	"bold and independent"; rare occurrence
Carrier	Hunting	Men's clothing; married to man
Cocopa	Hunting, warfare	Septum pierced like men; marry women; masculine hairstyle
Coeur d'Alène	"associated with males"	Men's clothing; lives alone; example given by Ray (1932:148) possibly is an intersexual individual or hermaphrodite
Crow	Horse riding, shooting, hunting, trade, position of chief, peace mission	Striving for masculine status; woman's clothing; altogether four wives
Eskimo (Alaska)	Hunting, trapping, trade	Relationship with a woman; own household; isolated case (O. T. Mason 1895:211); disapproved of by other members of the community, who ended up destroying the women's house
Eskimo (Greenland)	Hunting seals, hunting other mammals, fishing	Raised by their parents to fulfill masculine hunter/provider role; men's clothing; treated like men
Eskimo (Máhlemut)	Hunting, trapping, fishing	"masculine manners"; unmarried
Eskimo (St. Lawrence)	Man's name, masculine clothing, pipe smoking	Medical measure to make people unrecognizable to malevolent spirits
Haisla	1. "man's work" (in general);	1. Frequent; sometimes married to men;
	2. Hunting (specifically)	2. Men's clothing; no marriage to man; no relationships with women
Houma	War, council	Isolated case; man's clothing; highly esteemed by community
Ingalik	*Kashim* (men's house), masculine social role	Men's clothing; usually unmarried; usually no relationship with women, either
Isleta	Trader, member of the War Society	Mrs. Chavez, who was married or widowed
Kaska	1. "male tasks"	1. Decision by parents to raise girl to fulfill masculine role; man's clothing; relationships with women
	2. Female chief	2. *Not* a man-woman

TABLE 8. CONTINUED

TRIBE	OCCUPATIONS	CONTEXT
Klamath	Single case: "lived like man"; single case: claimed to be a man	One married to woman; other had relationships with women and men; later ended up as "prostitute"; no men's clothing worn in either case
Kutenai	"habits and pursuits" of a man; war, hunting, guide, prophet, "shaman," peace mission	Isolated case; man's clothing; relationships with women
Métis (Canada)	Trade	Single example (Crowe 1974: 90); man's clothing; married (widowed?)
Mohave	All masculine occupations except warfare	Did not go to war; relationships with women
Navajo	All masculine occupations except hunting and warfare	All feminine occupations, too; did not hunt or go to war; relationships and sex with both men and women
Nootka	1. Men's work 2. Female war chiefs	1. Rare cases; often confounded with women who went to war but did not change gender status; 2. *Not* women-men
Ojibwa	1. Vision quest, men's work 2. "man's work"	1. Parents decided to bring up girl as a boy because there were no sons in the family; 2. In addition to women's work; wish for independence; no change of gender status
Paiute (Northern)	1. "man's work"; 2. Hunting, "acted like man"	1. In some cases man's clothing; lived with women; 2. Preferred company of men; possibly men's clothing
Paiute (Southern)	1. Single case: men's work; 2. Single case: men's work	1. Men's clothing; relationships with women; 2. Men's clothing; marriage to woman
Papago	Hunting, war, worked as cowboy	Did not marry; female cowboy around 1935
Piegan	Hunting, tending horses, war	Isolated case; power from the Sun; man's name; highly esteemed, member in the Brave Society; unmarried
Pima	"inverts," interest in men's occupations	Not clear
Quinault	Men's work	Man's name, relationships with women
Santo Domingo	Hunters' Society	No gender role change; men opposed and disapproved of the women's wish to join the society

Table 8. Continued

Tribe	Occupations	Context
Shoshoni	Hunting, men's work in general	Sometimes men's clothing; one case: married, hunted; other case: wore only man's clothing
Sinkaietk	Hunting	Refused to marry; behavior not supported by the community
Tewa	"resistance to socialization in traditional men's and women's roles"	Emphasis on combination of masculine and feminine features, "third gender"
Thompson	Behaved like men	Rare cases; men's clothing
Ute	Men's work	Men's clothing
Wintu	Men's work, not clothing	Women's clothing; lived with woman
Wiyot	Hunting	Men's clothing
Yuki	Hunting, warfare	Possibly men's clothing
Zuni	Built fireplaces; member of ko'tikili; Kachina dancer	Isolated case; not a "transvestite"; masculine; apparently also did women's work; married

Note. For references see Table 7.
Navajo*: While Hill (1935) stated that female-bodied* nadle *did not go to war, Gifford (1940:163) stated that they did, at least among the eastern Navajo.*
Wintu*: Only reported from one of the three groups investigated by Voegelin (1942:134).*

Nancy's gender status, see Roscoe 1991:28), and she did not undertake a complete gender role change. Parsons (1916:525) described her as a masculine, very capable woman, who apparently also pursued feminine occupations.

Likewise married, masculine, and active in masculine occupations was "Madame François Houle . . . a colorful Métis character . . . a strong woman, dressed in deerskins with a knife at her belt, bossing the rough-tough scowmen of the Liard River" (Crowe 1974:90). One Carrier woman wore men's clothing and was a successful hunter; she was also married (McIlwraith 1948, 1:46). She probably also filled the feminine role on the side, for it is likely that the couple had children. McIlwraith's Bella Coola consultants cited this woman as an example of the "bold and independent [women]" already mentioned (McIlwraith 1948, 1:46); but again, a form of institutionalized gender role change with assumption of a special status is very unlikely. Olson (1940:200) reported of the Haisla that "berdaches of both sexes . . . [were] fairly common." There, some females who did men's work stayed single, while others married men. They never entered into relationships with women (Olson 1940:200), and cross-dressing was not mentioned. Whether such masculine women took on a feminine role after marriage in regard to the sexual division of labor is not known. Just as little can it be determined whether the masculine work domain was chosen out of a striving for independence or out of an interest in masculine occupations.

A distinction between men-women and "independent" women becomes clearly evident in connection with the Shoshoni. A woman who went hunting and who was married to a man did not come under the category of "female berdache" (*taŋgowaipü),* but seems to have received instead a separate designation, *nuwüdüka* (see Steward 1941:353).

INSTITUTIONALIZED STATUS

Numerous females in Native American cultures who devoted themselves to men's work did so out of a desire to occupy the masculine gender role—above all in the area of subsistence; frequently, additional masculine components were included, such as cross-dressing and marriages or relationships with women. The desire for independence from a husband or interest in masculine work within the context of a marriage to a man does not appear to be of primary importance in these cases. Parallels to women-men are also found insofar as a girl's interest in masculine occupations typically was apparent in childhood, which for the most part resulted in an expanded masculine gender role and frequently in a characteristically ambivalent gender status.

Achomawi men-women kept their feminine clothing, but they performed exclusively men's work and co-habited with women (Voegelin 1942:134). Sometimes they took up the profession of "shaman," which was open to both sexes, although males were predominant (Olmstedt and Stewart 1978:232; Voegelin 1942:157ff.; Willoughby 1963:59). The female partners took over the feminine areas of the sexual/gendered division of labor. Similar relationships existed among the Wintu; in one local group, a female in women's clothing performed men's work and lived together with a woman (Voegelin 1942:134f.); her female partner must have devoted herself to the feminine spheres of activity.

As children, Ingalik "men pretenders" usually refused to learn women's skills, and their fathers looked after them and taught them men's tasks. They soon joined the boys and men in the Kashim (men's house), in connection to which they knew how to conceal female sexual characteristics during the sweat bath. As adults, they assumed the social role of a man completely, but they only rarely married women (Osgood 1958:262f.). Men-women of the Lillooet remained single, combining men's work with cross-dressing and generally behaving like the opposite sex

(Teit 1906:267). Transvesting men-women "behaving like members of the opposite sex" also seem to have existed in isolated cases among the Thompson Indians (Teit 1900:321).

Among the Paiute, Mohave, and Quinault, men-women wore men's clothes and, as in some Nevada Shoshoni groups, did men's work and married women (Devereux 1937:515; Drucker 1941:163; Kroeber 1925:749; Olson 1936:99; Steward 1941:312; Stewart 1941:405). One Quinault man-woman, moreover, bore a man's name (Olson 1936: 99). Some Paiute *moroni noho* carried out a gender role change, but remained single, just like some Shoshoni *taŋgowaipü* (Steward 1941: 353; Stewart 1941:405). A certain Northern Paiute *düba's* "acted like a man"; "she killed deer and stayed with the men all the time" (Kelly 1932:158). Cross-dressing can also be assumed here. She had in common with many women-men the preference for the companionship of the opposite sex.

Like Ingalik "men pretenders," Cocopa *warrhameh* showed an inclination to play with boys and to hunt in childhood. A "young man might love such girl, but she cared nothing for him, *wished only to become [a] man*" (Gifford 1933:294, emphasis mine). *Warrhameh* also had their septums pierced in the manner of males, wore their hair in a male style, went to war, and ultimately founded families with women (1933:294). As girls, Mohave *hwame* played with boys, refused to learn women's work, and demanded a loincloth instead of a woman's skirt (Devereux 1937:503). As adults, they were regarded as excellent providers, and they adopted masculine role components, such as the taboo against sex when their wives were menstruating or were pregnant (Devereux 1937: 515; the wives naturally did not become pregnant from the *hwame,* but rather from their former husbands or from male lovers). Allusions to their female genitals displeased them, but in contrast to *alyha,* they did not insist that their genitals be called by the analogous terms from the opposite sex (Devereux 1937:510). Papago men-women remained unmarried, hunted, and went to war. Around 1935, one man-woman worked as a cowboy in Sells (Gifford 1940:163).

In these cases as well, the man's role taken up by men-women extended beyond subsistence acquisition. They also adopted body decoration and behavioral modes which were culturally defined as masculine. War/raiding and the cowboy's profession were specifically masculine role domains and expressed masculinity to an especially high degree.

Nootka men-women primarily exhibited a preference for men's work; whether they were identical to the female war chiefs who were cited "almost invariably" to Drucker (1951:331) in answer to his question about "female transvestites" is, however, questionable. Women who went to war usually made their mark only in this one masculine domain, without striving for the total masculine role (see Chapter 17). Nootka "warrior women" went to war on account of special visions (Drucker 1951:331), whereas men-women, if they participated in acts of war at all, did so within the framework of their masculine role.

Ute men-women wore men's clothing and exclusively performed men's work (Stewart 1942:298). They seem, like women-men, to have been called *tuwasawits* (Stewart 1942:352). Since Stewart's consultants denied both masculine and feminine "homosexuality" only in regard to people who were not "berdaches," it is likely that such females paired up with female partners.

Cross-dressing and hunting also characterized the "woman man-girls" *(musp-iwap-naip)* of the Yuki (Foster 1944:186) and Wiyot men-women (Elsasser 1978:159), although in addition, the *musp-iwap-naip* went along to war and fought (Foster 1944:186). (Notice the terminology: women-men were *iwap-naip*, "man-girls"; men-women were *musp-iwap naip*, literally "female male 'berdaches.'")

A certain Klamath man-woman did not transvest, but "lived like a man" and married a woman. When this woman died after many years, the man-woman carried out the mourning ritual customary for men, and, like a man, wore a belt made of bark (which was supposed to have prevented one's back from becoming stooped). She spoke like a man and also described herself as one (Spier 1930:53). Another female behaved similarly (Spier 1930:53).

Some very few Santee Dakota females hunted bison on horseback and went on the warpath (Landes 1968:49). Whether this is a case of gender role change (and change of gender status) or feminine role alternative cannot be clearly ascertained on the basis of the sources.

ISOLATED CASES

All of the examples cited thus far have referred to Native American cultures in which women either maintained a fundamentally feminine status or undertook some form of an institutionalized gender role change. Consequently, it appears reasonable to distinguish from these, as a third group, those few females who achieved considerable renown in a man's role, even though their culture did not, as a rule, provide for a feminine gender role change—that is, there existed no institutionalized man-woman status for females which resembled that of women-men (male "berdaches").

Kutenai: Ququnak Patke, the "Manlike Woman"

Ququnak patke (Kocomenepeca), a Kutenai woman who had married a White fur trader of the Northwest Company, returned to her tribe after a year and announced that her husband had "operated upon her and thereby transformed her into a man," a deed which no Indian would be able to accomplish (Schaeffer 1965:196). She changed her name to Gone to the Spirits and claimed to possess great supernatural powers (which implied that her "transformation" also had a spiritual background). Clearly, changes such as this were uncommon in Kutenai society, at least on the part of females; the members of the tribe reacted with a complete lack of understanding, and some even believed that she had lost her mind (Schaeffer 1965:197). She put on men's clothes, began to live in a masculine role, and took a wife. Her transformation was so complete that she was often mistaken for a male, especially by Whites (Schaeffer 1965:197; Spier 1935:26f.). She spent the following years in different occupations—as a warrior, as a courier for White explorers and fur traders, as a leader of a group of traders among the Thompson Indians into the interior—and with a series of female partners (Schaeffer 1965:199ff; Spier 1935:26). She also occupied herself among the surrounding tribes as a prophet, proclaiming alternately that either gifts or diseases were being brought by her White companions (on the prophecies as predecessors of the Prophet Dance, see Schaeffer 1965:204ff. and Spier 1935:27). Fifteen years later (1825), she was heard from again; she busied herself as a healer—once again a masculine occupation (Schaeffer 1965:214). Finally, in connection with an attempt to mediate between the Flathead and the Blackfeet, she is said to have deceived the latter and to have been killed by them (Schaeffer 1965:214). The Kutenai, incidentally, seem to have overcome their initial bewilderment regarding Kocomenepeca's behavior, since one nineteenth-century chronicler wrote that the "Manlike Woman" was one of the "principal leaders" of the tribe and that supernatural powers were attributed to her (Spier 1935:36).

Gender role change which was related to the supernatural was not foreign to the Kutenai, but only when it affected males, to whom the gender status of *kupatke'tek* was available (Schaeffer 1965:218). It is probable that the successes of the Manlike Woman, who increasingly made a name for herself in a man's role, both legitimated her gender role change and validated her claim to possession of supernatural powers. For the Kutenai, however, her transformation was such a unique phenomenon that Schaeffer's (1965:195) consultants still recalled her story a hundred years later.

Woman Chief and Running Eagle

The life careers of Woman Chief (Crow) and Running Eagle (Piegan) were no less spectacular. The biographies of both women show remarkable parallels. Both began at the age of ten to twelve years to become interested in men's work, and were supported in this by their fathers (or in Woman Chief's case, her stepfather—she was a captive Gros Ventre,

Denig 1961:196; Schaeffer 1965:227). Both soon proved themselves in war; Woman Chief's war deeds were so daring that she was invited into the men's council meetings, and in the circle of heads of families there, she ranked third in a group of 160 lodges (Denig 1961:198; see also Kurz 1937:213f.). Running Eagle's first war expedition resulted in a Scalp Dance being held in her honor, and a major battle with the Pend d'Oreille brought her—as the only female in the tribe's history to be so honored—a man's name (Schaeffer 1965:228). She was also received into the Brave Society (one of the men's societies not organized into age grades; see Hartmann 1979:81f.). Both women remained unmarried. Running Eagle stayed unmarried on account of a vision in which the Sun bestowed supernatural powers on her and forbade her to marry a man (Schaeffer 1965:228). Both women lived at about the same time—around 1850 (Denig 1961:200; Schaeffer 1965:229).

The two women differed, however, in terms of their respective componential organizations and formulations of the masculine role. Along with her man's name, Running Eagle also put on men's clothing, but Woman Chief did not (Denig 1961:196; Schaeffer 1965:228). On the basis of her appearance and behavior, Kurz (1937:213) described Woman Chief as "neither savage nor warlike. . . . On the contrary . . . modest in manner and good natured rather than quick to quarrel." Running Eagle's interest in the man's role was restricted to prestige acquired in war, in which she finally met her death (Schaeffer 1965:229). For Woman Chief, though, the position she won by her earlier deeds in war was merely the springboard to altogether different spheres of activity. She strove to gain traditional masculine prestige, but within wide-ranging aspects of the masculine role: the horses which she stole on raids and the numerous hides obtained through her hunting activities made her wealthy (Denig 1961:198). To process the hides, she took a total of four wives, whom she married according to the "usual formula of Indian marriage" (1961:199). Denig, who, like Kurz, knew Woman Chief personally, commented: "Strange country this, where males assume the dress and perform the duties of females, while women turn men and mate with their own sex!" Woman Chief was also occupied as a trader. Her wealth in wives and horses, in turn, reinforced her status as chief (Denig 1961:199). Running Eagle also took in a woman who was supposed to help her in providing for the family (Schaeffer 1965:228), but not, like Woman Chief, in order to draw prestige from areas other than warlike deeds.

Such highly developed and distinctive opportunities for social advancement existed for both women primarily because they distinguished themselves in warfare. Women who went to war were no rarity among the Crow, Blackfoot, and other Plains tribes (see Lowie 1922:341, 364;

Schaeffer 1965:229). To want to make one's mark in the masculine prestige domain of warfare and raiding was regarded as thoroughly honorable for women, and not at all unseemly; their successes demonstrated the power of their medicine and their personal bravery. This warlike behavior in women did not, however, involve gender role change. Once a woman had moved up into the status of a "brave," other domains of the masculine role were also open to her, depending on her personal inclination and ability. Most of the women who went to war did not pursue these, but in isolated cases women would seize the opportunity, take up a masculine role, and achieve a quasi-masculine status in their community.

What is striking about Running Eagle and Woman Chief is the similarity of their childhood biographies to those of women-men, all the way to Running Eagle's vision experience of the (male) Sun, which legitimated her gender role change and made her a medicine woman, or holy person (Schaeffer 1965:228). It is very likely that a comparable supernatural legitimation was also attributed to Woman Chief. Thus, both women were genuine men-women, whose legitimation was culturally accepted but not institutionalized. In contrast to a woman-man, a woman did not have to undertake an official gender role change in order to gain entrance to masculine prestige domains. In terms of access to masculine domains, men-women were similar to both the women-men and the female "warrior women" of their cultures. Success as a warrior smoothed all paths to further masculine prestige, but did not compel a woman to go that way.

HOUMA: "GREATER HONOR WAS PAID TO HER . . ."

The biography of a Houma "Amazon" who died around 1700 and about whom Gravier reported reads similarly. Houma women obviously went to war, but one of them so distinguished herself that she rose to achieve the highest honors:

> Greater honor was paid to her than to the great Chief, for she occupied the 1st place in all the Councils, and, when she walked about, was always preceded by four young men, who sang and danced the Calumet to her. She was dressed as an Amazon; she painted her face and Wore her Hair like the men. (Gravier 1959:147f.)

As "femme Chef" (woman chief), she was laid to rest in the temple of the Houma (Gravier 1959:147), an honor that in the Southeast was restricted to the nobility (see Swanton 1946:718ff.). Dead commoners among the Houma were buried on scaffolds (Swanton 1946:729). Again, the "Amazon" who apparently carried out a complete gender role change and who participated in meetings of the men's council is probably an isolated case. Female chiefs were found elsewhere in the Southeast, but their status was based on inheritance, and not on war deeds (on the Chitimacha, see Swanton 1911:349; similarly, Cherokee women seem to have gained frequent admittance to the council meetings, Swanton 1946:691).

THE WISH OF THE PARENTS

Finally, some females who performed masculine tasks were raised as boys from childhood. These cases are limited to the Arctic and Subarctic regions, where meat obtained by hunting, as opposed to vegetable foodstuffs gathered by women, played the more important role in nourishment. Examples of raising girls to be boys have been reported among the Ojibwa of Canada (Landes 1937:119, 121; 1938:169ff.) and among the Kaska (Honigmann 1954:130), as well as—outside the subcontinent, but still in the context of the Inuit culture represented there—in Greenland (Kjellström 1973:180; Mirsky 1937b:83f.). The Greenland examples are included because of similar cultural elements and a similar economic situation as those of the North American Inuit.

The Inuit disapproved of gender role change initiated by a woman herself. Two such women aroused such displeasure within one particular group that, one time while they were absent hunting deer, their co-villagers unceremoniously reduced their cabin to rubble and forced them to return to the village (and back into the feminine role?) (O. T. Mason 1895:211). This suggests that feminine gender role change was supported in Arctic regions only if it served the well-being of the extended family group or band, and not if it merely resulted from a personal striving for self-sufficiency.

An example from Greenland documents this with particular clarity: In the locality of Imarsarik in Southeast Greenland, there were only five hunters available to a population of twenty-five people. In order to secure the survival of the group, some fathers—primarily in families which had no sons—taught their daughters how to kill seals from a kayak. These girls acquired a quasi-masculine status, wore men's clothing, and, if they were offered gifts, they chose "masculine" utensils such as iron arrowheads and knives (Mirsky 1937b:84). A similar example comes from Akerniaq (East Greenland), where no sons had been born into a family, and the father brought his daughters up as boys (Kjellström 1973:180). Gender role change took place in the interests of the community, and not on account of the individual's personal inclinations.

Kaska parents who saw their provision for their old age endangered by their lack of sons selected a daughter "to be like a man" (Honigmann 1954:130). The girl wore boys' clothing and usually developed into an excellent hunter; after becoming an adult, she probably took up relationships with women (1954:130). From the time she was small, she wore an amulet made of dried bear's ovaries that was supposed to prevent a pregnancy, and she always vigorously rejected male advances: "She knew that if he gets her then her luck with game will be broken" (1954:130). No doubt the amulet and the refusal of heterosexual intercourse both reflected the very realistic estimation that the girl would have been of no use to the family as a hunter if she had a child.

From time to time, Ojibwa parents who had an only child who was female raised her as a boy, and sometimes a father of girls selected his favorite daughter for this role (Landes 1937:121). She was treated as a boy in every respect and was also sent on a vision quest (1937:119). In other cases, widows who were living alone taught their daughters masculine subsistence techniques so that the family could survive (Landes 1938:169ff.). These girls occasionally later entered into marriages and adopted the standard women's role (Landes 1938:168f.). The supply situation among the Ojibwa was apparently not so problematic that they could not tolerate self-sufficient women who did men's work out of a striving for independence. Nonetheless such women—in apparent contrast to the girls who had been systematically brought up as boys—did not take on the complete social role of a man.

That which was positively valued by the Ojibwa community—the ability of a woman to maintain herself, her children, and sometimes another woman independently by means of masculine subsistence activities—would have been regarded in the Arctic as an offense against the community's rules. The grounds for such a different attitude must, partially at least, be traceable to the respective economic foundations of life. The very plausible explanation offered by Callender and Kochems (1983:445) for the lack of male "berdaches" in the Arctic—that no hunter could be dispensed with because the food supply depended to an extreme degree on this masculine activity—could be applied to any person who adopted a masculine gender role. (Müller 1989 has convincingly argued that the survival of the group, however, also depended heavily on *feminine* tasks). It goes without saying that women now and then crossed out of their gender role and killed game in order to ensure survival. Nevertheless, in general among the Inuit, the respective work spheres of the two sexes in the subsistence area were clearly separated (see Schloßer 1981:9, 25, 34 in regard to emergency crossing out of roles). Hunting by women (and men) always contributed to the survival of the group or family, not to that of the individual alone. If a woman took over the social role of a man, she would have contributed what she killed to the family or larger local group: it was exactly for this purpose that the Greenland Inuit and Kaska brought up their daughters as hunters. The members of the village in Alaska mentioned above probably did not hold the woman's gender role change itself against her, but rather the fact that she used her masculine skills for herself (and her female companion).

The Subarctic Ojibwa, by contrast, lived in more balanced nutritional circumstances, and in another cultural structure or tradition. There, males in a feminine gender role were just as possible as women in a permanent or temporary masculine role that was freely chosen and was not negatively sanctioned. Moreover, the very isolated life of the Ojibwa families during large parts of the year made it necessary for women to learn masculine subsistence activities for survival (Landes 1938:168f., 176). The latter, however, also held true for the Inuit.

The fact that these crossings out of the gender role were supported and esteemed in Ojibwa society, but not among the Inuit, for whom such crossings would not have been less functional or expedient, cannot be explained on the basis of the respective economic backgrounds alone. (The larger Inuit band-like residence units likewise split up into nuclear families in the summer in order to pursue their widespread hunting and gathering activities; Schloßer 1981:7.) Gender role change for either sex seems to have been extraordinarily uncommon among the Inuit. For North America, there exist only two reports concerning female gender role change in Inuit groups (Dall 1897:139; O. T. Mason 1895:211), and likewise only two cases of male gender role change (Chugach Eskimo, Kaniagmiut). The phenomenon has been reported only for Western Alaska, a region in which Siberian influences can be assumed. In view of the richness of the literature for all Inuit groups, the absence of reports of gender role change probably reflects an actual absence of the phenomenon rather than gaps in the sources. Müller (1989:9) merely noted that the rearing of boys as daughters was "rarer" than that of raising girls as hunters, but he did not cite any figures or examples. In some Canadian Inuit groups, male gender ambivalence occurred within the context of Arctic shamanism and complex incarnation beliefs (Goulet 1982; Saladin d'Anglure 1986, 1992). This is not strictly comparable, however, to the examples of gender role change that are under discussion in the present context.

It may be that there was an absence of institutionalized gender role change among the Inuit because, despite the sexes' different working spheres, flexibility was vital for the Inuit in order to be able to cope with emergency situations. Although the gender roles were clearly defined, they were at the same time open in everyday life (see Giffen 1930; Schloßer 1981:25f.). In fact, they were even more open than in the neighboring groups, including the Ojibwa, who were firmly anchored in their Woodland culture: there, crossings out of gender roles were only possible for women who, for one reason or another, left the community. In case of marriage, they gave up their masculine activities in order to dedicate themselves to feminine occupations—the sexual division of labor was upheld. Where the gender roles were open and flexible, however—as among the Inuit—the necessity for a gender role change probably did not exist except in cases of extreme emergency, as discussed above, since boys and girls learned both masculine and feminine skills. Giffen's work (1930) is full of examples showing that although tasks in Inuit society were assigned to one sex or the other, men or women could accomplish them if the need arose. At the same time, and in contrast to the Ojibwa approval of individualistic life paths, the Inuit expected that these skills be used for the welfare of the extended family band. The instruction of children took place with an eye to possible acute emergencies that could arise in the course of their lives. Likewise, the systematic instruction of a specific (female) child in the social role of the opposite sex occurred against the background—that is, the memory—of previous emergency situations. (Since the Inuit usually experienced a surplus of women, the need apparently seldom arose to bring boys up as girls; in any case, the occupations of *both* sexes were important for group survival, so if there was no surplus of women or girls, boys were instructed in feminine tasks; on this, see Müller 1989).

In Ojibwa society as well, socialization of females into the masculine gender role—a permanent change of gender role—occurred only in the case of *girls*. Those women who lived from masculine subsistence activities without undertaking a gender role change were adults; for most of them, this life was temporary and also voluntary, and either came to an end with marriage or was interrupted by temporary marriages (Landes 1937:121). Among the Ojibwa, masculine skills which were crucial to survival could well be used for the realization of individual strivings for self-sufficiency or (economic) independence, without—as among the Inuit—eliciting the disapproval of one's culture.

In such a context, the surplus of women that has been observed both among the Ojibwa and the Inuit is remarkable; the frequency of polygynous marriages among the former is very probably an index of this (Driver and Massey 1957:400; Kohl 1859/1970:155f.; Tanner 1830: 106). For the Inuit groups which he investigated, Kjellström (1973:126) has established an average ratio between men and women of 114:100, because female infanticide and male mortality evidently canceled each other out over the years. During childhood, according to Kjellström's (1973:124) tabulation, boys were usually in the majority, so a family was likely to have trained a son in feminine occupations. The surplus of women is particularly striking in Greenland (1973:125), and it is precisely from there that the examples concerning girls raised as boys have been reported.

One would expect Arctic and Subarctic cultures to tolerate or encourage women's hunting when the following circumstances converged: a surplus of women, male-dominated subsistence acquisition, and food shortage. Hunting by women who did not find a husband in such communities unburdened both sexes. However, the sources indicate that there were many unmarried Ojibwa women, but few unmarried Inuit women (see Kjellström 1973:33). Jenness (1947:47) mentioned an Inuit male shaman who was able to "afford" a polygynous marriage only because one of his two wives was a competent hunter. This kind of arrangement may have occurred more frequently than the sources would at first suggest. The husband would have been relieved of some of the heavy burden of subsistence acquisition (see also Giffen 1930; Müller 1989). In combination, these facts suggest that there existed a tendency toward feminine role flexibility *within* marriage in Inuit society, but *outside* of marriage in Ojibwa society. Evidently, the cause must be sought ultimately in the climatically extreme environment of the Inuit, in which a stress on group solidarity worked strongly to the disadvantage of highly individualistic persons. Because of this, living alone was usually impossible for women (and men), even if they possessed the requisite skills.

ADOPTION OF OTHER MASCULINE ROLE COMPONENTS

Like women-men, men-women also assumed additional opposite-sex role components, mainly external features that signaled the individual's masculinity to the social environment "outside." Cocopa *warrhameh* wore the masculine hairstyle, and, like boys, had their nasal septums pierced (Gifford 1933:294). The Maidu female *suku* also had the septum pierced at their initiation into the men's secret society (Loeb 1933: 183). The Houma "Amazon" painted her face in the male fashion and wore her hair like a man (Gravier 1959:149). Klamath men-women adopted masculine habits that were not further specified (Spier 1930: 53), as did the Manlike Woman of the Kutenai (Schaeffer 1965:197). Teit described Lillooet men-women (like the women-men of the same tribe) as "behaving like members of the opposite sex" (1906:267); similarly, a Paiute man-woman "acted like a man" (Kelly 1932:158), and Pima men-women were reported as "acting, talking and expressing themselves like members of the opposite sex" (Hill 1938a:339). One Klamath female-bodied *tw!inna'ek* spoke like a man (Spier 1930:53); Mohave *hwame* were tattooed like men instead of women (Devereux 1937:501). Both Lemhi Shoshoni and Thompson men-women similarly "behaved" like members of the opposite sex (Steward 1943:385; Teit 1900:321).

Isolated cases of physical anomalies were also either reported or claimed by consultants. Men-women often denied female physiological patterns, which is a parallel to the imitation of female physiological patterns by women-men (see Whitehead 1981:92). Cocopa *warrhameh* reportedly did not menstruate and had male musculature (which was probably actually acquired by doing men's tasks, Gifford 1933:294). Mohave *hwame* allegedly had no breasts and did not menstruate (Devereux 1937: 510). Paiute female-bodied *tüvasa* were regarded as infertile—"women tüvasa . . . never menstruate or have babies" (Stewart 1941:440). It is possible that some other Paiute *tüvasa* were intersexes (Stewart 1941:405 was told that some supposedly female-bodied *tüvasa* had "male organs"), although these might have been confused with feminine males, who were also, of course, classified as *tüvasa*. One Quinault man-woman is supposed to have been intersexual (Olson 1936:99), as well as a female of the Coeur d'Aléne who undertook a gender role change (Ray 1932:148). Yuma *kwe'rhame* are also said to have never menstruated, and at the same time are said to have exhibited underdeveloped secondary sexual characteristics. Some are even supposed to have been intersexual (Forde 1931:157). The Ute, on the other hand, denied anomalies of any kind (Stewart 1942:332). The Crow woman-man has been described as especially strong and masculine (Denig 1961:197; cf. Kurz 1937:213), as have those of the Alaska Eskimo (O. T. Mason 1895:211), Kaska (Honigmann 1954:130), Kutenai (Schaeffer 1965: 195), and Quinault (Olson 1936:99).

CONCLUSIONS

Gender role change by females, then, was not a unitary phenomenon. Instances of the equivalent of male "berdaches" were infrequent. In such cases, men-women assumed the masculine role in its totality, expressed by role components such as occupations, clothing, and marriages to or partnerships with women. Examples include the Ingalik, Lillooet, Paiute, Ute, Quinault, Mohave, Cocopa, Klamath, Nootka, and Yuki. In addition are those isolated, exceptional cases represented by the Crow, Piegan, and Houma, which can best be understood as extremely pronounced developments of a warrior's role that was also open to women without a gender role change.

In other cases, by contrast, the desire for independence or autonomy was the primary motivating factor behind women engaging in masculine occupations; in these instances, the women did not try to assume a masculine gender role in its entirety. Sometimes the pertinent women were married and continued to fulfill a feminine role along with the masculine activities they performed. Often, however, the sources have cited precisely the wish to remain unmarried (permanently or temporarily) as the motivation for a woman's taking up masculine occupations, especially subsistence activities.

By contrast, females who from childhood were already being raised as boys fulfilled the criteria of a female "berdache," or man-woman, status, and along with masculine subsistence activities also undertook additional masculine role components (Kaska, Greenland, partially Ojibwa).

Chapter SIXTEEN

STATUS, RELATIONSHIPS, AND ENTRANCE RITUALS OF MEN-WOMEN

SPECIALIZED OCCUPATIONS

Only a few men-women and masculine women (that is, women who encroached on masculine activities without being reclassified as men-women) practiced specialist occupations. The men-women of the Achomawi were occasionally medicine people, or healers (Voegelin 1942:134), as were also some Klamath female-bodied *tw!inna'ek* (Voegelin 1942:134) and the Manlike Woman of the Kutenai (Schaeffer 1965:214; she is surely identical with the "transvestite shamaness" of whom Turney-High 1941:128 was told). Mohave *hwame*—like women (Williams 1986b:35)—were regarded as especially efficient "shamans" (Devereux 1937:516). In Ojibwa society, independent women likewise were often engaged as curers and were consulted by both sexes in order to heal and to pass on medicinal knowledge (Landes 1937:121). When it was said about Running Eagle that she was revered as a "medicine woman" (Schaeffer 1965:222), this probably meant that she was not a curer but rather a sacred person, since she had, through fasting, received supernatural power from the Sun.

Some masculine females of the Shasta were also curers (Voegelin 1942:134). One of the two Tolowa females who took wives was a "shaman" (Drucker 1937b:260) and became prosperous and independent because of it (see Gould 1978:134). Most of the Tolowa healers were female (Drucker 1937b:258; Gould 1978:134); this also holds true for the Shasta, where women, moreover, were regarded as more able (Holt 1946:327). The question of whether men-women were healers was explicitly denied by the Northern Paiute (Kelly 1932:158; Steward 1933:311; Stewart 1941:405, with the exception of one local group), by the Ute (Stewart 1942:332), the Wintu (Voegelin 1942:134), and the Atsugewi (Voegelin 1942:134).

In regard to Klamath men-women, Voegelin's consultants cited helping at burials or digging graves (Voegelin 1942:135). The Kutenai Manlike Woman was engaged as a courier, as a guide of White fur traders, as a trader, and as a prophet (Schaeffer 1965:202ff.). Woman Chief was a trader (Denig 1961:199), and so were the Métis woman Mme Houle (Crowe 1974:90) and Mrs. Chavez from Isleta (Parsons 1939b:38).

A special case of crossing out of one's gender role in the religious sphere is found in Santo Domingo. For reasons of sickness, two women desired admission to the Society of Hunters (Shaiyaka), which specialized in prayer and rites relating to hunting game animals. The male *ch!aiañi* (the word in general designates members of the Secret Societies, Curtis 1970:130f., and also curers, Curtis 1970:173) were indignant at first: "How can women be ch!aiañi? They would have to pretend to be men when they go to sipapu and when they use the eagle-feather whips" (1970:134f.). The initiation of women into men's societies on grounds of illness was possible in Zuni (see, e.g., Parsons 1916:527, n. 2), but apparently not in Santo Domingo. The two women finally did have their way, and appeared at rituals clad, like the men, in a loincloth, and used eagle-feather whips and bear's paws "like any ch!aiañi" (1970:135). One of these women, in addition, practiced as a healer; when she demanded still more masculine privileges in the context of her membership in the Shaiyaka, these were denied her, and she "died of shame" (1970: 135). Women could cross out of their gender role only in the face of the men's resistance, and such crossing was evidently most unusual. Moreover, the women did not receive the same rights as the male *ch!aiañi.* This case thus did not involve a gender role change; the masculine role appears generally to have been rather impenetrable.

The trade in hides—in which Woman Chief specialized—was dominated by men on the Plains, although the women prepared the hides. Women as traders were the exception (see Weist 1980:264). Woman Chief and Mme Houle no doubt took up this occupation against the background of the sexual division of labor, seeking the masculine role. In addition to men's clothing, Mme Houle also adopted masculine manners in order to be accepted by the "rough-tough scowmen" with whom she worked (Crowe 1974:90); Woman Chief, "ranking as a warrior and hunter, . . . could not be brought to think of female work" (Denig 1961: 199), so she took over the trade, leaving the preparation of the hides to her wives. Parsons' (1939b:38) description suggests that the occupation of "independent traveler and trader" practiced by Mrs. Chavez also fell within the masculine role domain.

Although women also cropped up in isolated cases as guides of White traders and explorers (e.g., the Chipewyan Slave-Woman, Crowe 1974:

87; or Sacajawea [Sakakawea], H. P. Howard 1971), the Kutenai Manlike Woman clearly chose this occupation in the context of her masculine gender role; she and her female life companion turned up in early reports as a formally married Indian couple (Spier 1935:26). Her "shamanic" activity was also identified by Schaeffer (1965:214) as a masculine role component. The same holds true of her prophetic activity; the prophets of the Prophet Dance Cult and the Ghost Dance Cult that arose in the nineteenth century were generally male (see Hartmann 1979:243f.; Hultkrantz 1980:152; Spier 1935:9f., 20f.). Of course, from the very beginning, it was very important for the Manlike Woman to stress her supernatural powers. These were recognized by her own tribe only much later. She was first encountered as a "shaman" around 1825 (Schaeffer 1965:214); her first efforts as a prophet had occurred in 1811 (Schaeffer 1965:213; cf. Spier 1935:25f.). After Gone to the Spirits' transformation, the Kutenai were evidently not well disposed toward her; her brother even ridiculed her in public (Schaeffer 1965:200f.). She soon went to work for the fur traders and was active as a prophet. She was probably trying to have her supernatural powers confirmed where she was unknown. She gained her considerable high standing and esteem among the Kutenai only as a mature individual, after she had proven herself in her new gender role. Her achievements served to legitimate her transformation retroactively—after the grass had finally grown over the embarrassing experiences of the early years.

Mohave "shamans" were of both sexes (Drucker 1941:158), although according to one source, stronger powers were attributed to female ones (Williams 1986b:35). Thus, the practice of this occupation on the part of *hwame* was probably not an expression of their masculine gender role. Moreover, they shared their special qualification for the profession of "shaman" with the *women,* but not with the men. Further, the *hwame*—and not the *alyha*—were especially powerful as "shamans" (Devereux 1937:516). The latent spiritual power which, according to the Mohave view, resided in both *alyha* and *hwame,* and which has already been emphasized in connection with *alyha* "shamans," is surely of significance here. At the same time, it is notable that the status of *hwame* was less accepted than that of *alyha* (Devereux 1937:515), so it is likely that it was easier and more socially acceptable for a *hwame* to retain this feminine role component, which also offered some protection against aggression and ridicule, especially by men. (Sahaykwisa was known and feared as a "witch," and this protected her to some degree; still, she was eventually killed for that reason; Devereux 1937:525f.)

Shasta healers were preponderantly female (Holt 1946:327), so that the masculine females who were engaged in this area but who otherwise performed the everyday occupations of both sexes probably stayed within the feminine role sphere. They did not undertake a complete change of gender role (see Voegelin 1942:134f.). Among the Achomawi "shamans," men predominated slightly (Voegelin 1942:157ff.). Since men-women there did exclusively men's work (Voegelin 1942:135), their healing activity can be regarded as a masculine role component. The same holds for the Klamath female-bodied *tw!inna'ek;* they likewise performed only men's work, and they carried out a complete gender role change (without cross-dressing). Klamath "shamans" were usually men, and they were regarded as more powerful than female healers (Spier 1930:107).

In Ojibwa society, the occupation of curer was not tied to one's sex, although men did predominate. Medicine women, however, enjoyed considerable esteem (Niethammer 1985:207f.). Both masculine and "feminine" women healed and taught both sexes equally (Landes 1937:121). Since the women who performed men's work did not give up their feminine gender role (or their feminine status), they practiced as medicine *women* within the framework of the feminine gender role.

In Zuni, Nancy shared her specialist role as a builder of fireplaces with male *lhamana* and danced their role as *ko'thlama* in Kachina ceremonies (Parsons 1939b:38); along with this, however, she was married and apparently also performed women's work (see 1916:525). She did not hold a female "berdache," or man-woman, status. As a kachina-dancer, she was one of the few women who were initiated into the ko'tikili (Parsons 1916:527, n. 2.). Women were mainly initiated on account of illnesses (Parsons 1916:527, n. 2), and it is improbable that Nancy was initiated on the basis of her masculinity alone; she was probably the preferred candidate for the role of the *ko'thlama* because she was both a "girl-boy" (that is, somehow ambivalent in terms of gender) *and* a member of the ko'tikili.

In summary, men-women, like their male equivalents, engaged in certain specialist occupations within the framework of their masculine gender role. In regard to masculine females, on the other hand, whether or not they also took up masculine specialist occupations in addition to men's everyday work seems to have depended on individual inclinations. Where they were specialists, such occupations often fell within the sphere of the feminine gender role or were open to both sexes.

PARTNER RELATIONSHIPS AND SEXUALITY

Like women-men and feminine males, men-women and masculine females exhibited the entire spectrum of possible partner relationships (see

Table 9. Partner Relationships and Sexuality of Men-Women and "Masculine" Women

Tribe	With Women	Not with Women	With Men	Not with Men
Achomawi* P	Voegelin 1942: 134			
Apache (Tonto S)	Gifford 1940:163			
Atsugewi P	Voegelin 1942: 134			
Carrier P			McIlwraith 1948, 1:46	
Cocopa* P,S	Drucker 1941: 163; Gifford 1933:294			
Coeur d'Alène* P		Ray 1932:148		Ray 1932:148
Eskimo (Alaska P)	O. T. Mason 1895:211			
Eskimo (Máhlemut P)				Dall 1897:139
Haisla P		McIlwraith 1948, 2:46; Olson 1940: 200	Olson 1940:200	McIlwraith 1948, 2:46
Ingalik* S	Osgood 1958: 261	Osgood 1958:262f.		
Isleta P			Parsons 1939b:38	
Kaska* P	Honigmann 1954:130			Honigmann 1954: 130
Klamath* P, S	Spier 1930:53; Voegelin 1942: 134			
Kutenai* P, S	Schaeffer 1965: 198f.			
Lillooet* P				Teit 1906:267
Maidu* P, S		Loeb 1933:183		Loeb 1933:183
Maricopa* P	Spier 1933:243	Drucker 1941:163		
Métis P			Crowe 1974:90	
Mohave* P, S	Devereux 1937: 515; Drucker 1941:163; Kroeber 1925:740			Devereux 1937: 524ff.
Navajo* P, S	Hill 1935:276		Hill 1935:276	
Ojibwa P	Landes 1937:121		Landes 1937:121	
Paiute (Northern)* P	Stewart 1941: 405			Kelly 1932:158

TABLE 9. CONTINUED

TRIBE	WITH WOMEN	NOT WITH WOMEN	WITH MEN	NOT WITH MEN
Paiute-Southern* P	Steward 1941: 312			
Papago* P				Gifford 1940:163
Piegan* P	Schaeffer 1965: 228			Schaeffer 1965:228
Pima* P, S		Hill 1938b:339		
Quinault* P, S	Olson 1936:99			
Shasta P		Voegelin 1942:134		Voegelin 1942:134
Shoshoni* P			Steward 1941: 353	
Tewa* S,P	Jacobs 1983:460		Jacobs 1983:460	
Tolowa P	Drucker 1937b: 260			
Ute* P		Stewart 1942:332		
Wintu P	Voegelin 1942: 134		Voegelin 1942: 134	
Yuma* P	Gifford 1940:56			
Zuni P			Parsons 1916: 525; 1939b:38	

*Note. P = Partner relationship mentioned in the source(s). S = Sexual relationship mentioned in the source(s). * Man-woman with nonfeminine gender status. Examples with no asterisk refer to "masculine" women who retained their feminine gender status. Information may be contradictory for one and the same tribe because (1) different authors (and their consultants) may have disagreed about whether men-women of a given tribe had sex/relationships with women or with men; or (2) in some tribes, it was possible for men-women to enter into relationships, and have sex, with both women and men.* Ingalik: *Sometimes relationships with women, but usually not; no relationships with men, either.* Klamath: *One man-woman had intercourse with both sexes promiscuously. This was atypical, however.* Maidu: *According to Loeb (1933: 183), women "avoid"* suku *and men did not marry them.* Mohave: *According to Devereux, one* hwame *prostituted herself to men after having been raped.*

Table 9 and Map 7). Like their male counterparts, men-women usually entered into relationships with partners of the same sex, which for the most part probably also included sexual relationships. The latter, to be sure, were not always explicitly mentioned. The "berdaches" of both sexes among the Southern Tonto Apache were described to Gifford (1940:163) on the basis of sexual behavior alone: they were said to be

Map 7. Partner Relationships Entered into by Men-Women (Female "Berdaches") and Masculine Females

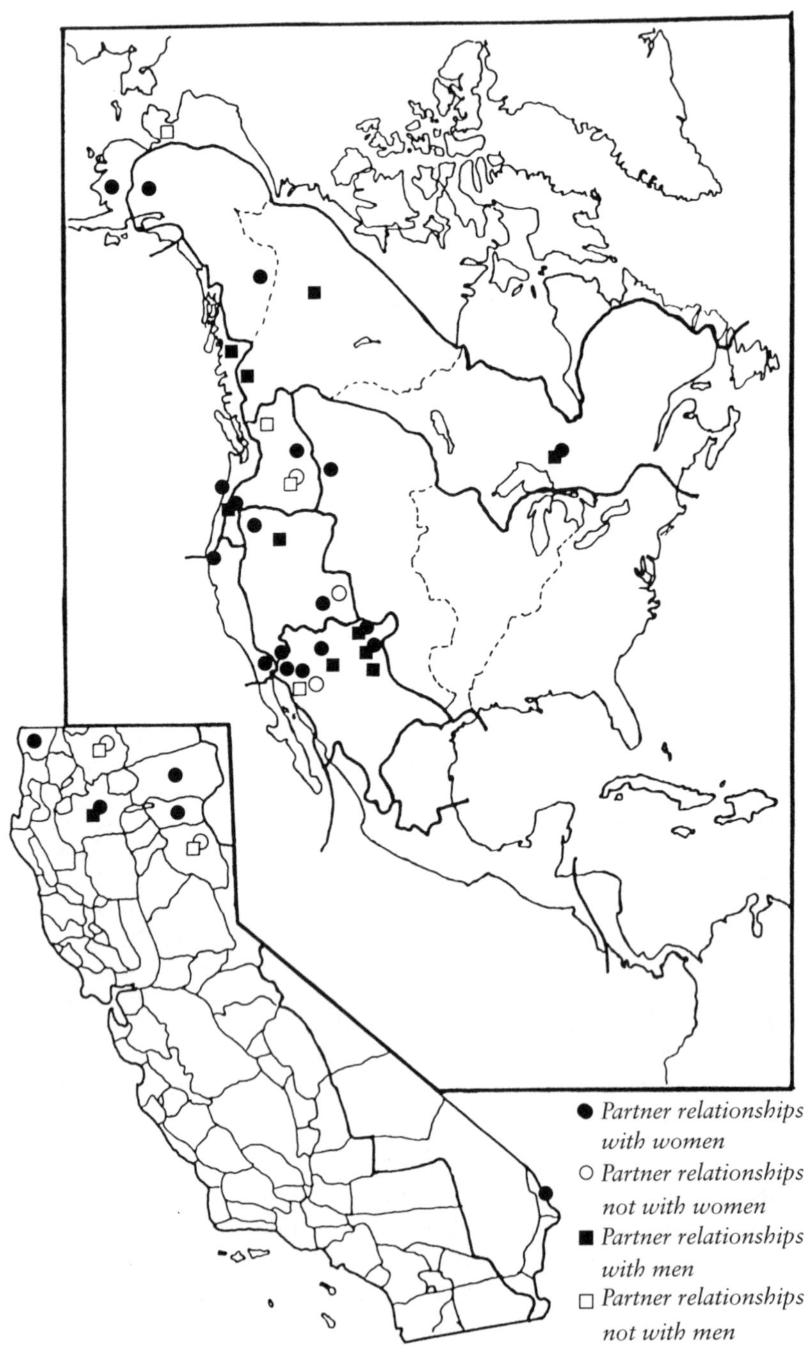

"lazy men and women who wanted to cohabit with their own sex." This statement reflects the rejection of "berdaches" that apparently was characteristic of all the Apache groups; along with the Lipan, the Southern Tonto were the only Apache among whom a "berdache" status of any kind existed at all (see Gifford 1940:66; Opler 1966:11), with one male exception, a Chiricahua woman-man who died in 1880.

In the remaining cases, the sexual aspect was secondary. Woman Chief took four wives primarily for economic reasons; in the framework of the sexual/gendered division of labor, she was ensuring the dressing and processing of the hides as a complement to her own masculine hunting activity (Denig 1961:199). Denig (1961:199) accurately stressed the relationship of this to her status as a "chief": Woman Chief entered into a polygynous marriage, just as any man in her position would have done. Whether she had sexual relations with her wives is not known. The marriages, at any rate, took place within the framework of her masculine gender role as chieftain and hunter.

Whether or not Running Eagle also married the young widow whom she took in to perform the women's work that needed to be done, Schaeffer (1965:228) did not say. Since she had already adopted the masculine gender role as a girl (1965:228), having a woman helper in Running Eagle's family should be seen as the expression of this role. By this time, Running Eagle's father had already been killed by the Crow, and she had moved up into his position as head of the family. Since her mother was ill, and since Running Eagle was a man-woman, she did what any man would have done: she did not do the feminine tasks herself, but instead she brought a woman into the house. This was possible only after the death of her father, who until that time was the head of the household. Before this, Running Eagle had to perform the necessary women's work herself for some years, irrespective of her changed gender role. From the time of her father's death onward, however, she, as a "quasi-man," was able to take over her father's position and both make use of and consolidate her man-woman status.

The Kutenai Manlike Woman had an entire series of female life companions with whom she entered into lasting relationships. That sexual relations occurred as well is evident from the rumor that she had fashioned an artificial phallus out of leather especially for this purpose (Schaeffer 1965:198). She, too, entered into alliances with women within the framework of her masculine gender role. To White observers, the Manlike Woman and her companion gave the absolutely perfect impression of an ordinary Indian married couple (Spier 1935:26).

Like *alyha*, the *hwame* among the Mohave did not woo their same-sex partners in the fashion customary for opposite-sex couples. Instead, they went up to women at dance celebrations or paid them a visit.

Hwame were regarded as excellent providers, and they liked to gossip with "other men" about the intimate details of their married lives. Nonetheless, their marriages were unstable, because men liked to use their physical strength to shut *hwame* out as rivals or to take their wives away from them (Devereux 1937:515). Sexual intercourse did take place in the marriages of the *hwame* (1937:514). If a *hwame* married a pregnant woman, she could, like a man, claim paternity of her child (according to the Mohave view, sexual intercourse with a pregnant woman changed the paternity; Devereux 1937:514). A child's membership in a descent group was not altered by the marriage of the mother to a *hwame,* but it was if the woman left her male husband for another man (1937:514; the descent groups were patrilinear and nameless, but all the women born in one of these groups carried the same name; Kroeber 1925:741). Thus, on marriage to a *hwame,* the woman's child evidently still belonged to the descent group of its biological father, not to that of the *hwame.*

Like the husbands of the *alyha,* the wives of *hwame* were often teased, so that, according to Devereux (1937:515), their marriages proved to be unstable, especially since *hwame* could not hold their own physically against male rivals. The *hwame* were also exposed to actual verbal and physical assaults, and occasionally they were even raped by men (1937:519; Devereux described the rapists as "practical jesters"; this estimation of a situation in which a drunken *hwame* was forced to have intercourse with several men seems astonishingly insensitive).

The *hwame* Sahaykwisa experienced this also. As the last of her wives ran off with a man—the one to whom this wife had been married before the alliance with Sahaykwisa—the *hwame* armed him/herself with bow and arrow and went to get her back. The man was not to be deterred: "The next time she comes I will show her what a real penis can do" (Devereux 1937:525). Devereux continued:

> The next time he ambushed her in the bushes, tore off her clothes and raped her. Then he left her in the bushes and returned to his camp. Sahaykwisa stood up and left without a word. Never again did Sahaykwisa take a wife . . . she became a drunkard and began craving men. Not seldom, when she was drunk, some men dragged her to a convenient place and farmed her out to various men, including certain Whites, at so much the intercourse. (Devereux 1937:525)

Whether it was customary or usual to break *hwame* in this way cannot be ascertained. In any event, her quasi-masculine status was less respected than the quasi-feminine one of the *alyha.*

The reason why a Klamath female-bodied *tw!inna'ek* ended as a prostitute cannot be determined. She had co-habited with older women earlier on and had described herself as a man, although—like all Klamath men-women—she did not transvest. "She is today a common prostitute, an abnormal, irascible person" (Spier 1930:53). She and her female partners are said to have been avoided by other Klamath. On the other hand, Co'pak, the second female-bodied *tw!innа'ek* of the Klamath described by Spier, married a woman in the framework of her masculine role and co-habited with her until the latter's death. She seems in no way to have been socially ostracized (1930:53). It may be that the first-mentioned man-woman was vulnerable to attack not because she lived with a woman, but because she was promiscuous ("They say of such: they have lots of partners, friends," Spier 1930:53; promiscuity or quickly changing relationships were called "*sawa'linaa*" [to live as partners], Spier 1930:53).

The co-habitation of men-women with women has also been reported from the Kaska (Honigmann 1954:130); Cocopa (marriage, Gifford 1933:294); Maricopa (marriage, Spier 1933:243); Yuma (marriage, Gifford 1931:56); Northern Paiute (co-habitation, Stewart 1941:405); and Southern Paiute (marriage, Steward 1941:312). Tewa *kwidos* of both sexes had sexual relationships with women, men, and other *kwidos* (Jacobs 1983:460). This is unusual; women-men and men-women rarely entered into relationships of this kind with each other. Callender and Kochems (1986:168) even cited the absence of sexual relations with persons of the same ambivalent gender status as a characteristic of the status of "gender-mixing," which is generally confirmed by the data.

A Quinault man-woman at the end of the nineteenth century lived with a woman and is also supposed to have had sexual relations with her (Olson 1936:99). Ingalik "men pretenders" seem to have had sexual intercourse with women occasionally, but nevertheless usually remained single (Osgood 1958:261); Osgood told of a "man pretender" who reacted in a very indignant manner when her male cousin—who allegedly took her for a man—wanted to marry her off to a woman (1958:262f.). Finally, like their male counterparts, Navajo female-bodied *nadle* could marry partners of either sex. If Hill's statements also refer to female-bodied *nadle*, these persons—like male *nadle*—had to don men's clothing if they married, and to carry out exclusively masculine tasks (Hill 1935:276). They generally had sexual intercourse with both men and women; one female-bodied *nadle* even bore a child (1935:276).

A certain Eskimo man-woman mentioned by O. T. Mason (1895:211) also sought a female partner in order to maintain the sexual division of labor. Nothing is known about the partner relationships of the Shoshoni *taŋgowaipü*. In other groups, some men-women apparently did not enter into partner relationships at all. One Ute man-woman did women's work, transvested, and did not marry (Gifford 1940:163);

other men-women seem at least to have had sexual relationships with women (Stewart 1942:226; "male or female homosexuality" was denied, "except with berdaches").

Lillooet men-women did not marry men (Teit 1906:267); nothing is known about their possible relationships with women. The only known man-woman of the Coeur D'Alène lived alone (Ray 1932:148; there is some indication that she was intersexual, called "*st'amia*" by the Coeur D'Alène). Papago men-women did not marry (Gifford 1940: 163); for Pima men-women, same-sex marriages were explicitly denied (Hill 1938b:339). By the 1930s, however, the "berdache" status there had already fallen victim to acculturation; persons who would surely have carried out a complete gender role change in earlier times had begun to represent themselves either as masculine females or feminine males (1938b:339). There and in other cases in which relationships with men were denied, it is possible that (sexual) relationships with women traditionally were a component of the masculine gender role assumed by men-women.

In contrast to men-women, masculine women frequently married men, providing that they did not prefer to live alone. A Kitimat-Haisla woman who did men's work did not want to "have anything to do" with either men or her own sex (McIlwraith 1948, 1:45); the Máhlemut huntresses/female hunters (Dall 1897:139) likewise wandered alone, as did those of the Oglala Lakota (Mirsky 1937a:417) and probably also those of the Santee Dakota (Landes 1968:193).

The data available for Maidu *suku* suggest that "*suku*" was a complex term that was used to refer to both male and female "berdaches"; among female-bodied *suku,* the term corresponded to two subcategories, one meaning "man-woman" and the other meaning "promiscuous." Loeb's report on female *suku* seems at first glance to be contradictory; he (1933:183) reported that they were treated as men and initiated as such into the men's secret society, but also that they were subjected to gang rape (or voluntary intercourse) in the dance house by all of the men present and were regarded as "prostitutes." It is likely, however, that there were actually two subcategories of female "*suku*"—those who were seen as "morally lax" and those who were seen as having a "masculine nature" (Loeb 1933:183; see Figure 11).

Men-women among the Shasta did the tasks of both sexes and lived independent lives, forming relationships with neither men nor women (Voegelin 1942:134f.). Masculine women were married to men among the Carrier (McIlwraith 1948, 1:46), among the Haisla (Olson 1940: 200), in Zuni (Parsons 1916:525), and in Isleta (Parsons 1939b:38), among the Métis in the territory of the Dogrib and Yellowknife (Crowe 1974:90), and among the Ojibwa (Landes 1937:121), although when

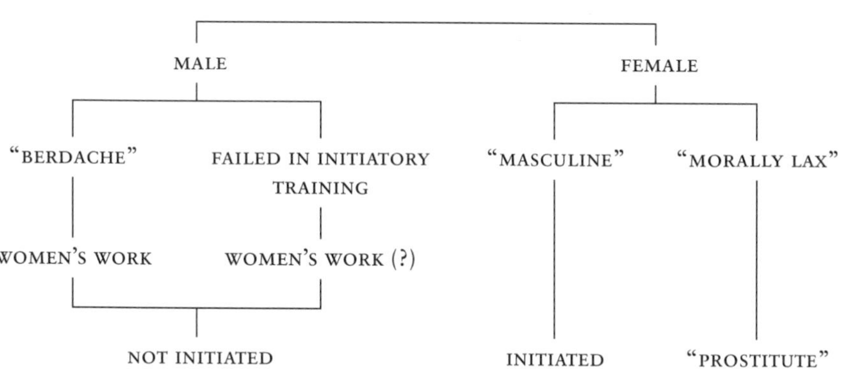

"Suku" in Maidu society.

they married, Ojibwa masculine women evidently returned to women's work. Ojibwa masculine women did men's work primarily in order to be able to live an independent, self-sufficient life between marriages or after being widowed. Women could leave their husbands if the latter physically or sexually abused them, their sisters, or their daughters (see Landes 1938:103). Some of them lived with other women (Landes 1937:121), although in such cases, it is not clear whether they divided the work according to the sexual/gendered division of labor, or whether the two women did both men's and women's tasks at the same time. Landes did not say whether this co-habitation of two women contained a sexual component as well.

In two of the three Wintu groups investigated by Voegelin (1942: 134f.), masculine females lived with men and did the tasks of both sexes. In a third local group, masculine females lived with other women and performed only masculine tasks (1942:134f.). Paradoxically, in the former two groups, it was denied that they wore women's clothes, whereas in the group where they did only men's work, they were said to wear women's garb.

All of the men-women of the Achomawi and Atsugewi lived with women, although none of them transvested. Among the Atsugewi and possibly also in one of two Achomawi local groups investigated, they did the tasks of both sexes, but among the Western Achomawi, they did only men's work (Voegelin 1942:134f.). All three groups, incidentally, exhibited a fully developed *male* gender role change, including cross-dressing and the exclusive performance of women's work (Voegelin 1942:134). The men-women did not form an exact parallel to this. In the work sphere, however, a traditional division of roles is conceivable for those cases in which the masculine female engaged only in masculine activities, and her female partner performed only feminine activities. Masculine/independent females of the Tolowa also co-habited with women; nothing is known about their day-to-day work, although one of them practiced the occupation of "shaman," which was mainly restricted to women (Drucker 1937b:260).

Men-women, therefore, for the most part maintained partner relationships with women, while masculine women—who were not classified as non-women by their cultures—in general chose male partners. Masculine women who lived in relationships with other women possibly represent an intermediate stage that comes closer to the role and status of men-women. Married masculine women must have taken up masculine occupations out of efforts toward independence and out of the desire to make the most of their individual potential. Single masculine women usually did not enter into liaisons with women, but rather made use of their skills for themselves. In contrast to men-women, they did not strive for a gender role change and a quasi-masculine gender status; this possibly explains why they did not form alliances with other women. In contrast to the promiscuity of women-men, men-women seem to have wished for, and also to have lived out, longer term relationships. The only examples of promiscuous behavior are the two cases in which men-women at first lived in relationships with women, and later—in one case allegedly on account of being raped—became side-tracked. They are said to have prostituted themselves to *men* and to have given up their man-woman status. As for the partner relationships of men-women, the same pattern holds true as that for women-men: the wish to exercise a masculine gender role stood saliently in the foreground, and sexual relationships with women were taken up in the context of this role.

CAUSES OF GENDER ROLE CHANGE

The possible motivations for a partial (masculine women) or a complete (men-women) gender role change have been discussed in earlier contexts. In contrast to men-women, who typically displayed an inclination toward gender role change as children, masculine women were encountered only as adults, after menarche and at a marriageable age (and sometimes married). The Kutenai Manlike Woman who carried out a gender role change only after her marriage (and who separated from her husband at the same time) constitutes an exception. The Kutenai, however, did not have institutionalized female gender role change. While this likewise holds for the Crow and the Piegan as well, Woman Chief and Running Eagle grew up with fathers who supported their interests in masculine occupations to an unusual degree, and as soon as they had begun to express themselves on the matter. Woman Chief's interest in masculine tasks was awakened at around the age of ten, and Running Eagle's at the age of ten or twelve (Denig 1961:196; Schaeffer 1965:227; other boyish girls, or "tomboys," among the Piegan did not grow up to be men-women, but rather so-called manly-hearted women; see O. Lewis 1941:185; and see below, Chapter 17).

Some Mohave *hwame* took up their man-woman status only after they had already given birth to a child, and the Mohave themselves suggested that such a decision may have been influenced by difficult childbirths (Devereux 1937:515). Usually, however, the development of *hwame* was similar to that of *alyha:* as early as childhood they refused to learn to do women's work and demanded to be clad in a loincloth instead of the bark skirt worn by women and girls (Devereux 1937:503). Yuma *kwe'rhame* also showed an inclination toward a gender role change in childhood (Forde 1931:157).

Female-bodied *nadle* likewise began to act like boys when they were still children, and as adults made the final and binding decision for or against their *nadle* status (Hill 1935:273). Ingalik "men-pretenders" also rejected women's clothing and activities when they were still children (Osgood 1958:262). Kaska men-women were provided with a contraceptive talisman when they were about five years old; they were apparently chosen soon after birth to fill the role of a son (Honigmann 1954:130). The training of Greenland Inuit girls as hunters and their entrance into what was probably in general a masculine gender role also began in childhood (Kjellström 1973:180; Mirsky 1937a:83f.), as did the bringing up of daughters as sons by the Ojibwa (Landes 1937:119, 121). Both Lillooet and Yuki men-women, on the other hand, did not undertake their gender role change before puberty (Foster 1944:186; Teit 1906:267). In the Achomawi view, Achomawi masculine females (who represent an intermediate case on the boundary between masculine women and women-men) were "born that way" (Voegelin 1942:228), so that their masculine behavior for the most part probably manifested itself early. Here, dreams seem to have played a significant role in the legitimation of gender role change, and above all when it was first undertaken at an adult age: "1 Pit River (Achomawi) woman, after she'd had children, dreamt to be like that" (Atsugewi consultant cited in Voegelin 1942:228).

Just as in the case of the women-men, the primary indication that a girl was a potential man-woman was her preference for the occupations of the opposite sex, often connected with a decided rejection of the tasks of her own sex. Young Cocopa *warrhameh* typically played with boys, made bows and arrows for themselves, hunted birds and rabbits, and later turned down offers of marriage (Gifford 1933:294). Woman Chief showed an interest in acquiring "manly accomplishments" (Denig 1961: 294); both Ingalik "men pretenders" and Mohave *hwame* complained about their girls' clothes and stubbornly resisted having to learn feminine skills (Devereux 1937:503; Osgood 1958:262). Running Eagle caught her father's attention by her "masculine traits" (Schaeffer 1965:227), and Yuma *kwe'rhame* played with boys' playthings (Forde 1931:157).

In regard to the various backgrounds of gender role change cited by the consultants, men-women followed the same general pattern as women-men. The Achomawi cited a dream as the legitimation for gender role change by females (Voegelin 1942:228) as well as males (1942: 134). Gender role change was usually carried out by both sexes after puberty (1942:134, 228). Since women-men and men-women among the Achomawi were regarded as "born that way" (1942:228), the dream must have merely legitimated a process of change either already manifest or latently present. The Atsugewi *brumaiwi* were also considered "born that way" (1942:228), and the Klamath female-bodied *tw!inna'ek* were as well (1942:228). (In addition, for the Achomawi and Klamath alike, Voegelin [1942:115] also mentioned the custom of turning the afterbirth inside out in order "to change sex of child." However, she did not connect this custom with gender role change.)

During puberty, Yuma *kwe'rhame* dreamed of weapons, by means of which their gender role change, which had already begun earlier, was legitimated (Forde 1931:157). Mohave *hwame* had already dreamed of their transformed gender while they were in the womb (Devereux 1937: 502). As in the case of the male *ilyaxai,* dreams were important in the gender role change of Maricopa female *kwiraxame* (Spier 1933:242).

Running Eagle cited a vision sent by the male Sun, just as women-men could appeal to the Moon Goddess (Schaeffer 1965:221, 228). Her interest in masculine occupations began early, but only after the vision experience did she adopt masculine clothing and a masculine name (1965:228). The female war chiefs of the Nootka took over this function on the basis of visions (Drucker 1951:331), although these women were "warrior women," not men-women; whether or not a supernatural legitimation was also available for the gender role change of Nootka men-women is not clear. It seems, however, that their inclination toward masculine tasks was sufficient for the adoption of the status of man-woman (Drucker 1951:331). The gender role change of the Cocopa *warrhameh* was also founded on an inclination toward masculine occupations (Gifford 1933:294).

In the case of the Kutenai man-woman, her White husband at first fulfilled the function of a supernatural helper: she told her fellow tribes people that he had changed her sex (Schaeffer 1965:196f.). However, a vision experience also seems to have taken place at the same time, because the woman claimed to possess supernatural powers and changed her name to "Gone to the Spirits" (Schaeffer 1965:197).

That the few Lillooet men-women may have legitimated their change through vision experiences is suggested by the fact that both Lillooet men-women and women-men adopted their status immediately after puberty training (Teit 1906:267). Although it is true that girls did not deliberately go on vision quests during this training, they evidently were able to receive visions (see Teit 1906:263ff.; on women with guardian spirits, see Teit 1906:286).

For the Ojibwa, Greenland Inuit, and the Kaska, supernatural legitimation did not play a role; the parents made the decision to bring their daughters up as sons (Honigmann 1954:130; Kjellström 1973:180; Landes 1937:119; Mirsky 1937b:83). As noted, such cases do not really constitute gender role *change*. Nevertheless, the Inuit female who refused to do women's tasks because she preferred masculine occupations can be considered a man-woman (O. T. Mason 1895:211).

The desire for economic independence constitutes the primary motivation for masculine women to carry out men's work. This is especially clear in the case of the Máhlemut women who refused to marry (Dall 1897:139), and likewise holds for the Sinkaietk women who were not interested in marriage (M. Mandelbaum 1938:119), as well as for temporarily or permanently single women of the Ojibwa (Landes 1937:121). There, the tasks of the opposite sex were taken on if a woman was of marriageable age and was competent in masculine occupations—above all in the area of subsistence, so that she would not have to be dependent on a husband or on her family of birth.

Two further reasons for female gender role change are found among the Yuki and the St. Lawrence Eskimo. Among the Yuki, if a girl became a man-woman, or *musp-iwap-naip,* it was considered to be a punishment for a breach of the regulations connected with the puberty ceremonies (Foster 1944:183, 186). Other penalties that such a girl could suffer included difficult childbirth or death by a lightning bolt (1944:183). If a girl did not behave as the feminine role prescribed upon entering the status of "woman," therefore, her femininity was damaged. Here, becoming a *musp-iwap-naip* was only a relative intensification of the penalty "difficult childbirth"; both phenomena are named in the same breath with death by lightning. Thus, becoming *musp-iwap-naip* theoretically would have been equal to a kind of death—probably social death. Since, however, it has been reported that *musp-iwap-naip* hunted and also fought along with the warriors in battle (Foster 1944:186), their social position cannot have been held in contempt. Thus, their "social death" was probably related to their relinquishing the role and gender of a woman, but this did not mean that they were ostracized in their resulting status and role as men-women.

By contrast, temporary gender role change served as a medicinal measure among the St. Lawrence Eskimo: in order to become invisible to malevolent spirits, a girl cut her hair short, put on boys' clothing, and began to smoke a pipe (Murphy 1964:62f.). In some cases, this change seems even to have been retained on a permanent basis (1964:63).

In all the essentials, the pattern established for their male counterparts is repeated with men-women: an upbringing by the parents as a boy in some cases, and early signs of a gender role change in the others, with or without later supernatural legitimation. With masculine women, moreover, the adoption of masculine occupations crystallized at a later point in time. The motivation for this did not lie in a primary interest in the masculine role; rather, it was based much more on the necessity to acquire masculine skills, particularly in the area of subsistence, in order to realize needs for independence. In other cases again, married women engaged in trade or pursued other masculine occupations, reflecting the individual's striving for prestige and economic improvement.

TESTS AND RITUALS

Tests and rituals were for the most part planned only for boys; the sources either did not mention such a procedure for men-women or explicitly denied it (Maricopa, Spier 1933:243; Pima, Hill 1938b:340).

Kroeber (1925:749) denied a rite of initiation for men-women among the Mohave; Devereux (1937:504), however, indicated that a ritual for *hwame* once existed. The singers who specialized in this ceremony knew songs not only for *alyha,* but also for *hwame.* The portrayals of rituals in Devereux's account refer only to *alyha.* The aged singer Ñahwera, however, reported that a dress made of bark for an *alyha* and a loincloth for a *hwame* were made in connection with the preparations for a ritual (1937:503); this clearly shows that *hwame* were also formally initiated into their new status. On the other hand, another consultant of Devereux's (1937:507) was not sure about this. The statements of an old "shaman" should be authoritative and decisive; this one had obtained his information from Kuwal, who had been married to several *alyha* and had encountered gender role change when it was still occurring. The "shaman" described the *alyha* ritual to Devereux and added: "The same ceremony is enacted for the hwame, who then dons the breech-clout" (1937:508). Thus, there once existed among the Mohave a ceremonial introduction into the *hwame* status, but it had already disappeared by the time of Kroeber and Devereux.

Chapter SEVENTEEN

WARRIOR WOMEN AND MANLY-HEARTED WOMEN

GENDER ROLE CHANGE AND GENDER ROLE BOUNDARY CROSSING

As Medicine (1983) has noted, there is a difference between gender role change and crossing out of gender role boundaries (on role variability, see Weist 1980:262f.). Female warriors were generally women who strove for masculine prestige without giving up their gender status. (For another definition of "women warriors" see McCloud 1977.) This is also true of women who crossed out of their role in other spheres (see Figure 12), and who often gained considerable esteem because of it—for example, Slave Woman (Crowe 1974:87), Sacajawea (P. Howard 1971), or Wi-ne-ma (Meacham 1876). Particularly on the Plains, the masculine prestige system represented the standard for both sexes, and it could exert such an attraction for women that—like Woman Chief and Running Eagle—they began as women who went to war and ultimately carried out a gender role change. Most women, however, did not change completely, but rather carried out warlike activities, either temporarily or in a way that otherwise was subordinated to their feminine gender role. Cheyenne women, for example, sometimes accompanied their husbands to war (Grinnell 1962, 2:44f.), as did some Choctaw women, although they themselves usually did not fight, but instead spurred on their men (Bossu 1962:164). At times they definitely did take up firearms and accompanied groups of warriors (Romans 1962:75). Many Cherokee women were regarded as "famous both in war and in council" (Swanton 1946:691). Cree women sometimes accompanied the men on raids of revenge (D. G. Mandelbaum 1940:300), and Lowie reported an esteemed "female warrior" among the Crow (1922:364), as well as another woman who, equipped with the medicine of a powerful medicine

Shoshonie Woman: Throwing the Lasso, *1867. Alfred Jacob Miller/National Archives of Canada/C-000406. © Expired.*

man, went on the warpath and came back victorious (Lowie 1922:341). There are also isolated cases in which individual Santee Dakota women could not resist the temptation to acquire a warrior's fame and glory, especially if the men in their families proved to be incompetent as warriors (Landes 1968:206f.). Spurred on by visions, some individual Ojibwa women were also successful warriors (Landes 1937:110). Some Klamath women also went to war (Spier 1930:31), and some Miami women fasted and by means of visions received the command to carry the Waubenauhkee (War Medicine Bundle). Often, such visions began to occur when a woman had lost someone close to her in war. Then, clad in women's clothing, she would lead a campaign of revenge (Trowbridge 1938:36). Visions in which they received "medicines and rituals for strength and bravery" made some Nootka women into famed war chiefs (Drucker 1951:331), and one young Ojibwa woman obtained such highly developed supernatural power from a vision that, by her deeds during a war expedition, she edged the actual leader out of his position (Landes 1937:110f.). Blackfoot women also occasionally participated in war expeditions (Schaeffer 1965:229), but usually did not carry out a gender role change. The Winnebago also had one isolated warrior woman (Lurie 1953:711; for further examples and discussion, see Niethammer 1985:233ff.). On the arrival of the Europeans, the Kaska were being led by a "powerful woman chief," who also distinguished herself in war (Crowe 1974:51).

According to the sources, thus, women from a substantial number of Native American cultures went to war. The difference between women who went to war and men-women is that the former strove for masculine prestige in a limited masculine role component and without giving up their overall feminine gender role, while the latter strove for a masculine gender role and a quasi-masculine status. Warrior women stepped or crossed out of the feminine gender role temporarily or partially, but kept their feminine role, particularly as wives and mothers. Men-women, by contrast, laid aside the feminine role in its entirety in favor of a masculine one. It is notable that merely crossing out of their own gender role was apparently not usually possible for men in those cultures that emphasized warfare and raiding, perhaps because no component of the feminine role had such absolute prestige value for both sexes as did waging war. Where warfare and/or raiding did not have such an inherent and distinctive connection with prestige, warrior women, apparently, were also absent as an institutionalized feminine role alternative.

The striving for fame in warfare and raiding was of little or no importance to the motivation of men-women. At most it was seized upon as an aspect of the masculine gender role, and then only *after* that role's other components had already been adopted. Exceptions to this are Woman Chief and Running Eagle, who were among the very few men-women in the Plains area, and for whom the adoption of a man-woman gender status was made possible at all only by the institution of "warrior women."

In the androcentric prestige system of the Plains, women could also be "masculine" without achieving deeds of warfare. An example of this are the "manly-hearted women" of the Piegan described by O. Lewis (1941). For the Piegan, prosperity and generosity had a higher prestige value than deeds of war had (O. Lewis 1941:173f.). Manly-hearted women were always married, were prosperous, and held a high social position (1941:176). They acquired their wealth both by means of their skills in executing tasks of both sexes and through inheritance and gifts (1941:178). In public they appeared self-assured, and in the domestic area independent, poised, aggressive, and sexually active (1941:181f.). They were valued by their husbands as valuable economic assets (1941:178), but also on account of their personality characteristics of aggressiveness and boldness, which were classified as "masculine" (1941:183). The men also appreciated their self-assured appearance in public, a personality trait which was otherwise regarded as unseemly for Piegan women (1941:183). Lewis concluded that women "who achieve distinction can do so only in terms of men's values," and that manly-hearted women were deviant in regard to cultural norms relating to women (1941:187). Yet Medicine (1983:271) has rightly observed that these women constituted "an anomaly in the customary view of Plains Indian women as submissive and oppressed." As Medicine has argued (in contrast to Lewis), however, the role of the manly-hearted women in Blackfoot culture was not deviant, but rather one of several possible role alternatives for women (Medicine 1983:271; see also Kehoe 1983). The role of the manly-hearted woman combined masculine and feminine role components. Fundamentally, the manly-hearted woman was considered feminine. At the same time, however, her role was strongly oriented to masculine standards. Unlike men-women, however, manly-hearted women did not give up their feminine gender role and status. Manly-hearted women cursed like the men and were said to excel in both men's and women's work, but above all they achieved perfection in women's work, and they often strove to become Chief Wife (the most influential wife, with certain privileges in a polygynous marriage), or even Sun Dance Woman (Lewis 1941:183). Thus, they differed from the masculine women of other tribes who utilized their masculine skills and personality traits to avoid the role of wife. Manly-hearted women did, however, resemble those masculine women who practiced masculine occupations, even though they were married. The status of the manly-hearted woman and of the woman who went to war in their respective Plains cultures appears to have been more firmly established culturally than the status of either men-women or of masculine women, who in actual fact moved *outside* the framework of culturally recognized role alternatives. Warrior women and manly-hearted women, therefore, had in common with male "berdaches," or women-men, the fact that their "androgyny" was culturally institutionalized.

CONCLUSIONS

In regard to gender role change by females, it should be emphasized that not all females who performed masculine tasks held a female "berdache," or man-woman, status. More frequent by far than complete gender role change was gender role *crossing*. Those who did hold the man-woman status were females who exhibited an interest in aspects of the masculine role quite early, and who over a long period of time strove to attain a quasi-masculine gender status. They usually wore men's clothing and sought female life companions. Along with masculine everyday tasks, they also assumed additional role components occasionally—for example, participation in war expeditions or in male-dominated specialist occupations.

Masculine or independent women form another group of women whose gender role differed from the usual feminine role; yet these women did not strive for a complete gender role change. Generally, such women took up masculine tasks at the earliest at marriageable age, or at an even later time in their lives. In these cases, the reason for assuming masculine role components was frequently to live independently of a man. They typically practiced masculine subsistence occupations in addition to feminine tasks—they needed both in order to survive.

Still other women took up masculine occupations even though they were married. These women were probably motivated by the desire to achieve esteem and prosperity through activities and occupations outside of their own feminine subsistence area (e.g., trade). Their motivation, however, seems to have been multilayered: enjoyment of masculine work, striving for independence within marriage, and the desire for adventure should doubtless be seen as possible motives.

A third group of females crossed over the boundaries of the feminine gender role in order to earn esteem in masculine prestige areas, and above all in warfare and/or raiding. Although different opportunities existed for men and women to attain prestige within their respective gender roles, on the Plains the area of warfare offered the greatest potential for prestige for both sexes: a successful warrior was the hero of both the men and the women. Thus, it was regarded as honorable when women also strove for this kind of prestige, and—if they proved themselves as warriors—their position in the tribe was equal to that of male warriors, even though these women did not undertake a gender role change. War honors, however, sometimes did bring them entrance into other masculine areas, for example, the tribal council. Thus, in isolated individual cases, they were able to take on a complete masculine role, as long as this was consistent with their individual ability and personality. Woman Chief and Running Eagle represent extreme examples of the (esteemed) feminine role alternative of warrior woman that was institutionalized culturally on the Plains. Nevertheless, women who went to war usually did not strive for the totality of the masculine role, and even less for independence from husband and family of birth.

The fourth and last group comprises females who were already selected by their parents as children to fulfill the function of the missing son. Although this function manifested itself primarily in the area of subsistence, such girls adopted the entire masculine role, as well as forming occasional bonds with female partners. They were therefore "genuine" men-women. In contrast to most men-women, however, they did not initiate their gender role change—their parents did. Nonetheless, it is likely that parents selected a "tomboy" to become a boy.

It is important to note that these different formations of female gender role change cannot be entirely separated from each other. There existed subtle gradations among the individual categories, and some females cannot with certainty be assigned to one category or another, particularly because more detailed information concerning the componential organization and formulation of their gender role and status is frequently lacking. It is striking, however, that more culturally approved possibilities for crossing out of their gender role existed for women than for men, and that in such cases their community did not assign an ambivalent gender status to them. The only example of males infringing on a feminine role sphere to a significant degree without having to redefine themselves as women-men are the Pueblo potters of this century: there, on account of a great demand for Southwestern Native American pottery, a traditionally feminine occupation became a standard of prestige for both sexes.

PART FOUR

The Cultural Context of Gender Role Change

Chapter EIGHTEEN

ATTITUDES TOWARD WOMEN-MEN AND MEN-WOMEN

Numerous sources address the question of the prevailing attitudes toward "berdaches" in particular Native American cultures. Frequently, however, it is unclear whether these statements reflect the opinion of the Native American consultants themselves. It may be, for example, that the consultant provided the answer he or she thought the ethnographer wanted. Or, it may be that regardless of how a consultant responded, the ethnographer distorted the response in his or her reporting of it. Further, White influence has over time had a significant negative impact on Native American attitudes toward the "berdache" phenomenon. Williams has discussed in detail the distortions that have arisen through prejudice within Anglo-American culture, the suppression of information about the "berdache" institution, and also the negative changes in the attitudes of Indian communities as a result of White acculturation (1986b; see especially Part 2, "Changes in the Berdache Tradition Since the Coming of the Europeans," and 11ff., 183ff.).

Given such unreliability, it is difficult to interpret the available information about Native American attitudes toward gender role change. As noted, according to Stewart's (1941:440) consultant, "berdaches" never existed in the tribe in question "because our Indians were good and taught their children right." In reference to the Winnebago, Lurie related that *shiáŋge* were esteemed at one time, "but . . . the Winnebago had become ashamed of the custom because the White people thought it was amusing or evil" (Lurie 1953:708). Devereux (1937:523) could not interview a wife of the *hwame* Sahaykwisa, he said, "because she resents any allusion to her homosexual venture" (Devereux's male consultants, however, had no inhibitions whatsoever about discussing the topic with him).

In the sources on the Oglala Lakota, estimations regarding *winkte* are radically divergent. Hassrick represented *winkte* as failures and as "mama's boys," feared, and not honored, but tolerated as "victims either of biological homosexuality or of parental overprotection" in a culture where even the children's games "rather definitely separated the brave boys from the sissies" (Hassrick 1989:134). Fathers are supposed to have warned their sons against getting involved with *winkte*—and if they did so anyhow, they, along with the *winkte,* would live set apart from all others among the murderers in the afterworld, and the *winkte* would "torture" them (Hassrick 1989:134). DeMallie (1983) drew a similarly pessimistic picture. This kind of negative assessment is apparent as early as Keating (1825:436); by contrast, although Lame Deer (1979:169) stated that fathers admonished their sons not to hang around *winkte*, his portrayal also expresses respect and acceptance: "To us a man is what nature, or his dreams, make him. We accept him for what he wants to be. That's up to him" (Lame Deer 1979:169). On the other hand, the judgment which an old medicine man related to the physician Thomas Lewis was extremely negative: *winkte* were "freaks," with whom the Indians had "a lot of fun"—"somebody who is like that is ashamed of himself" (T. H. Lewis 1973:312). And, according to Lewis, mothers who prematurely called off a ceremony which served to ascertain the sex of the unborn fetus would be punished by being made to give birth to a *winkte* child (1973:312).

Almost thirty years earlier, Mirsky (1937a:416f.) had portrayed the *winkte* as respected, and not as tainted with a social stigma, and the self-identified *winkte* interviewed by Williams (1986a:195ff.) at the beginning of the 1980s described themselves as well-nigh holy persons or saints. Likewise, other consultants—although in more moderate tones—have described a respected person endowed with spiritual power. Attitudes toward the *winkte* have followed a discernible historical pattern, from traditional respect, passing through the contempt traceable to acculturation, and finally a new strengthening of the *winkte* status. This renaissance is related to the new awakening of Native American self-awareness beginning in the 1970s (Williams 1986a:193ff.).

So far, at least, the gay rights movement has not played a significant role in reestablishing acceptance of women-men and men-women on the reservations. It has been important, however, to urban gay, lesbian, and otherwise "two-spirited" Native Americans (see Jacobs, Thomas, and Lang, 1997b). Also, while the reawakening of Native American self-awareness has in some places led to an appreciation of contemporary people who identify themselves as *winkte, heemaneh', nadle,* and so on, in many other places it has not had these effects. A negative attitude toward all kinds of homosexual behavior is widespread in the Indian communities both on and off the reservations. Particularly marked is a non-acceptance of women-men, who are equated with "homosexuals" (see

Lang 1995, 1997a, 1997b; Robles Juarez 1992). Moreover, while some Native American traditionalists on the reservations accept gender role change as a cherished part of their tribal culture, others claim that women-men, men-women, and the often same-sex relationships they enter into have never been part of the tribal cultures, and state that "homosexuality" is an evil that did not exist in traditional Native American cultures but was brought in by the Whites. Thus, while the examples described by Williams (1986b) of women-men being held in high esteem in contemporary Native American cultures no doubt exist, they represent only a very small fraction of the overall picture. During my fieldwork in 1992–1993, people told me many sad stories of rejection, discrimination, and sometimes even physical violence resulting from a negative attitude in the Indian communities toward alternatively gendered and gay and lesbian Native Americans.

Mirsky's (1937a) investigation reflects the traditional esteem which attached to the *winkte* and that began to disappear only in the 1940s under the force of acculturation (see Williams 1986a:193). Hassrick (1964), T. H. Lewis (1973), and (to a limited extent) Lame Deer (1979) expressed the predominant attitude, ranging from negative to ambivalent, during the years when the *winkte* institution had reached its nadir. At the time of Williams' investigation, the Native Americans' ethnic self-awareness in general, and also the self-awareness of the *winkte,* had gained strength. Potential women-men, that is, feminine or androgynous males, either turned to the traditional woman-man status in communities where this was feasible or defined their role anew within the urban contexts of the gay subculture and founded, inter alia, the organization of Gay American Indians (GAI; see Williams 1986b:201ff.). M. N. Powers' (1986:14) comment on Hassrick's presentation can be generalized to the work of some of his contemporaries: the "degree of projection is extraordinary; virtually all of his comments on sexuality . . . mirror Euro-American attitudes and concerns."

Traditionally, women-men and men-women were accepted in most Native American cultures—to some extent, even highly respected—although they could also be joked about and teased (see Table 10; this joking may have occurred partly within so-called joking relationships; Greenberg 1986; Williams 1986b:39f.). They were accepted without any especially judgmental evaluation—either positive or negative—of their gender role change by the Achomawi, Atsugewi (true only of women-men), Diegueño, Flathead, Hare, Klamath, Ingalik, Kutenai, Mandan, Maricopa, Nisenan, Nootka, Ojibwa, Paiute, Papago, Piegan, Quinault, Shasta, Shoshoni, Sinkaietk, Tübatulabal, Ute, Wailaki, Wintu, Yana, Yokuts, Yuki, and Yurok, and also in Acoma, Laguna, Isleta, and San Felipe. They were regarded as esteemed persons with special spiritual

Table 10. Attitudes Toward Women-Men, Men-Women, Feminine Males, and "Masculine" Females

Tribe	Attitude	M	F	Source
Achomawi	"regarded indifferently"	M	F	Voegelin 1942:35
Acoma	no disgrace, "protected and supported by the pueblo," "held in some sort of honor"	M		Hammond 1882:348
	"a shame"			L. A. White 1943:325
	"treat him kindly"			Bandelier 1966:326
Apache (Tonto)	"lazy men and women who want to cohabit with own sex"	M	F	Gifford 1940:163
Atsugewi	"regarded indifferently"	M		Voegelin 1942:135
	"regarded disapprovingly"		F	Voegelin 1942:135
Arapaho	"miraculous power," "could do supernatural things"	M		Kroeber 1902:19
Assiniboine	are "wakan"	M		Lowie 1909:19
Cheyenne	are "very popular"	M		Grinnell 1962, 2:39
Choctaw	"highly despised especially by the women"	M		Romans 1962:83
	"held in great contempt"			Bossu 1962:169
Chumash	"lograban de grande consideración"	M		Costansó 1984a:42
Cocopa	"apparently disliked"	M		Gifford 1933:294
Costanoan	"ostracized"	M		Harrington 1942:32
Cree	"never teased," "never made fun of"	M		D. G. Mandelbaum 1940:256
Crow	"seldom much respected by either sex"	M		Denig 1961:187
	is "his nature," protective attitude			Lowie 1912:226
	"general merriment" (Sundance)			Lowie 1935:312
	"highly regarded" because of their "many charitable acts"			Simms 1903:580
	parents try to dissuade *bate*			Simms 1903:581
	very high status, highly esteemed		F	Denig 1961:198
Dakota (Santee)	exiled from home community, very respected and popular in other community*	M		Landes 1968:31f., 57, 112
Diegueño	not "ostracized"	M	F	Drucker 1937a:46
Eskimo (Chugach)	"more skilled than ordinary persons," "lucky like twins"	M	F	Birket-Smith 1953:94
Eskimo (Alaska)	devastating attitude		F	O. T. Mason 1895:211
Eskimo (Greenland)	treated like men, abilities appreciated		F	Mirsky 1937b:84
Eskimo (St. Lawrence)	most powerful "shamans"	M		Murphy and Leighton 1965:72

Table 10. Continued

Tribe	Attitude	M	F	Source
Eyak	"despised," lived on left-over scraps	M		Birket-Smith and De Laguna 1938:206
Flathead	"decently treated," "source of fun and ridicule behind their backs," "mildly tolerated"	M		Turney-High 1937:85
Hare	attitude good-humored, joking	M		Broch 1977:98f.
Hidatsa	"feared," "respected," "avoided," "pitied," "mysterious, holy"	M		Bowers 1965:168, 236
Hopi	accepted, protected	M		Williams 1986b:52, 101
Klamath	"regarded indifferently"	M		Voegelin 1942:134
	"permitted," "scorn," "taunting"			Spier 1930:51
	"avoided" (one case)		F	Spier 1930:53
Illinois	regarded as "Manitous"	M		Marquette 1959:129
Ingalik	apparently accepted	M	F	Osgood 1958:261, 262
Isleta	accepted, popular with the boys of the village	M		Parsons 1932:246
Iroquois	"souverainement méprisés"	M		Charlevoix 1744:5
Kansa	"do not appear to be despised, or to excite disgust"	M		James 1823:129
Kutenai	crazy, ridiculed by brother; later highly esteemed (one case)		F	Schaeffer 1965:197ff.
	"good natured . . . tolerance," "rarely teased"	M		Schaeffer 1965:218
Kwakiutl	accepted, "the women like him"	M		Ford 1941:131
Laguna	(like Acoma)	M		Hammond 1882:348
Lakota (Oglala)	"freak," "ashamed of himself"	M		T. H. Lewis 1973:312
	"sacred people," "respected," "gifted persons," "joked about," "[people] never talked disrespectfully about winkte," "sacred"			Williams 1986a:193f., 195
	feared, ostracized, avoided			Hassrick 1982:135
	ambivalent attitude			Lame Deer 1979:169
	no stigma, a few are famous			Mirsky 1937a:417
	ostracized (homosexual men, not *winkte*)			Mirsky 1937a:417
Maidu	treated like men		F	Loeb 1933:183
	rather negative, apparently not very respected	M		Loeb 1933:175
Mandan	disapproved of in childhood, later accepted	M		Maximilian n.d., 2:78f.
Maricopa	"men approve," "women uneasy"	M		Spier 1933:243
Miami	"respected by both sexes"	M		Trowbridge 1938:68

Table 10. Continued

Tribe	Attitude	M	F	Source
Mohave	parents "not proud"; *alyha* and *hwame* "crazy," "cannot help it," teased	M	F	Devereux 1937:503, 518
	are sometimes raped		F	Devereux 1937:519, 525
Navajo	very highly regarded, "afforded favoritism" in childhood, "sacred," "holy"	M	F	Hill 1935:274, 278
Nisenan	"never ridiculed," "made [born] that way"	M		Beals 1933:376
Nomlaki	"childishlike"	M		Goldschmidt 1951:387
Nootka	"no belief that [they are] sexual perverts"	M		Drucker 1951:331
	"famous war chiefs"		F	Drucker 1951:331
Ojibwa	masculine abilities appreciated by community		F	Landes 1937:121
	"saints," "inspired by manitou," "never allowed privileges refused [women]"	M		Kinietz 1947:155
	accepted, welcome in people's lodges			Tanner 1830:105f.
	father tries to dissuade son from becoming a woman-man			Henry 1897:163
Omaha	"great calamity," "subject to gross actions"	M		Fletcher and La Flesche 1911:132
	"mysterious," "sacred," accepted			Dorsey 1894:378f.
Oto	"no one attempted to dissuade him," yet "neglected and scorned"	M		Irving 1835:197ff.
Paiute (Northern)	"bad luck for a man to wear woman's clothing"	M	F	Kelly 1932:158
	"funny," regarded "indifferently"	M	F	Stewart 1941:405, 440
Paiute (Southern)	regarded "indifferently," not disapproved of	M	F	Stewart 1942:298, 326
Papago	consultant "burst into laughter at the possibility"		F	Underhill 1939:187
	"scorned," "partner singled out for ridicule"	M		Drucker 1941:218
	popular among the women, esteemed, respected in the community, men sometimes tease women-men			Underhill 1936:39, 43f.
Piegan	One *akeskassi*, in his declining years, was ridiculed by the men for wearing women's clothes and doing women's work; in his earlier years, the custom was accepted	M		Schaeffer 1965:223
	"medicine woman," highly respected (one case)		F	Schaeffer 1965:228

Table 10. Continued

Tribe	Attitude	M	F	Source
Pima	strongly stigmatized, despised, "no cultural niche"	M	F	Hill 1938b:339f.
Ponca	accepted, made best quillwork and beadwork	M		J. H. Howard 1965:142
Potawatomi	respected, "extraordinary," "manitu"; traditionally accepted, taken seriously	M		Landes 1970:195, 196
Quinault	"no social stigma"	M	F	Olson 1936:99
Salinan	"grande estima"	M		Fages 1984:164
San Felipe	apparently accepted	M		Parsons 1932:247
Sauk	"contempt," "pitied" "medicine," "sacred"	M		Keating 1825:227f. Catlin 1926,2:244
Shasta	"not looked down upon," "a little queer," "not very bright"	M		Holt 1946:317
	"regarded indifferently," "born that way"			Voegelin 1942:134
	not regarded indifferently, "born that way"		F	Voegelin 1942:135
Shoshoni	"mild interest," "no disapproval"	M	F	Steward 1941:353
	"regarded indifferently"	M		Steward 1943:338
	family "kind," "helpful," "sympathetic," "outsiders . . . mock cruelly," suicides, attempts to change women-men			Shimkin 1947:298
Sinkaietk	"sometimes forced to marry"		F	M. Mandelbaum 1938:119
	"good-for-nothing"	M		Cline 1938:137
	"not frowned upon," "not powerful"			M. Mandelbaum 1938:119
Tewa	"should be raised to be what they are," respected, special potential	M	F	Jacobs 1983:460
Timucua	"considered odious"	M		Le Moyne 1875:7
Tolowa	"considered very shameful"		F	Drucker 1937b:260
Tübatulabal	"never openly ridiculed"	M		Voegelin 1938:47
Ute	"regarded indifferently," not socially restricted	M	F	Stewart 1942:298, 332
Wailaki	"bothered no one"	M		Loeb 1932:93
Winnebago	once "highly respected," "honored," nowadays people are "ashamed" of the custom	M		Lurie 1953:708
Wintu	"regarded indifferently"	M	F	Voegelin 1942:134f.
Yana	"not ridiculed"	M		Sapir and Spier 1943:275

Table 10. Continued

Tribe	Attitude	M	F	Source
Yokuts	women-men are supposed to be accepted; "freely accepted," "status no secret"	M		Gayton 1948:106, 236
Yuki	"people feel sorry for them," "not their fault"	M	F	Foster 1944:186
	respected (priests and teachers)	M		S. Powers 1877:132
Yuma	"parents ashamed of such children," "no attempt to force or suppress," have "power" ("more than ordinary men")	M		Forde 1931:157
	Yuma object strongly, "attempts to bully them into feminine ways"		F	Forde 1931:157
	no ostracism	M	F	Drucker 1937a:46
Yurok	"socially recognized," "not combated"	M		Kroeber 1925:46
Zuni	"family somewhat ashamed," "no reticence or shame"	M		Parsons 1916:523
	women tease, but welcome *lhamana*'s efficiency in work, men discourage and ridicule *lhamana*			Stevenson 1904:37, 38

Note. M = Males in a woman's role/feminine males. F = Females in a man's role/masculine females. *Santee: *The* winkta *concerned were exiled from their village because of exogamy rules, not because of ostracism or any negative attitude toward their status (see Greenberg 1986:183f.).*

powers by the Arapaho, Assiniboine, Cheyenne, Crow, Oglala Lakota, Hidatsa, Illinois, Omaha, Potawatomi, Sauk, Winnebago, Piegan, Cree, Yuma, Tewa, and, at one time, also the Yuki. They were esteemed without any explicit reference to supernatural legitimation among the Navajo, in Acoma, among the Chumash, the Santee Dakota, the Chugach Eskimo, the Greenland Eskimo (men-women), the Hopi, the Kwakiutl, and also in Zuni. In more recent times, gender role change has been disapproved of (but tolerated) in Acoma, among the Tonto Apache, among the Atsugewi men-women, among the Choctaw, the Cocopa, the Costanoan, and acculturated Oglala Lakota, and also among the Eyak, the Klamath (according to Spier 1930:51 but not according to Voegelin 1942:134), the Iroquois, the Mohave (with special reference to the *hwame*), the Nomlaki, the Maidu (probably), the Omaha (according to Fletcher and LaFlesche 1911), and also among the Oto, the Pima, the Wind River Shoshoni, the Timucua, and the Winnebago (after acculturation). Evidently, the behavior of two masculine/independent Tolowa women, whose only deviation from the feminine role consisted in marrying other women, was also disapproved of (Drucker 1937b:260). Male Tolowa women-men seem to have been accepted.

Occasionally, "berdaches" of one biological sex were more accepted than those of the other sex. Women-men were regarded indifferently among the Achomawi and Atsugewi, but female "berdaches" were regarded negatively among the latter (Voegelin 1942:134f.). Oglala Lakota *winkte* were viewed as *wakan,* whereas masculine women seeking independence were expelled from the community (Mirsky 1937a:417). Male Kutenai *kupatke'tek* were allowed to do as they wished, but the Manlike Woman was first declared insane and then ridiculed so much that she left the village (Schaeffer 1965:196ff.). It is true that she became highly respected years later, after having proved the supernatural legitimation of her behavior. Still, her adoption of masculine occupations and dress at first went beyond the comprehension of the other members of her community. Underhill's (1939:187) female consultant burst into laughter at the mere thought that there could possibly be female "berdaches," but women-men were respected and valued. Gifford's (1940:163) Papago consultants, on the other hand, did not laugh, but instead named examples of females in a man's role who hunted, who went to war, and who worked as cowboys. Sinkaietk women-men were accepted, but women who stayed single and who wanted to feed themselves by hunting were sometimes forced into marriage (M. Mandelbaum 1938:119). Yuma parents let their sons have their way if they wanted to carry out a gender role change, but they tried to force *kwe'rhame* daughters into the feminine role (Forde 1931:157). Mohave *hwame* were exposed to more cruel "pranks" by the men than were *alyha* (Devereux 1937:519). The reverse case—encouraging female, but not male, "berdaches"—is unknown; at the very most, some Inuit groups, under the pressure of economic emergencies, may constitute an exception to this. Women who went to war were highly esteemed insofar as they could prove their abilities (and their medicine) on war expeditions. Nonetheless, they did not undergo a complete gender role change.

Women and men sometimes held different attitudes toward women-men. Maricopa men approved of the gender role change of the *ilyaxai',* but women felt "uneasy" toward them (Spier 1933:243). Papago women-men were popular among the women, whereas the men apparently feared sexual contacts between their wives and women-men; nevertheless, the women regarded Shining Evening as "just like a woman. We have forgotten he is a man" (Underhill 1936:43). Zuni women encouraged *lhamana* and welcomed them as co-workers, whereas the men tried to humiliate and make fools of them (Stevenson 1904:37f.). If, however, the decision of the *lhamana* was irreversible, then any attempts to "convert" them let up, and the *lhamana* was generally accepted. The Zuni did not make fun of the *lhamana* U'k because she had carried out a change of gender role, "but because she is half-witted" (female consultant to

Parsons 1916:528) At the Sha'lako, and to the great amusement of the spectators, U'k danced both out of step and out of line because she could not remember the choreography (1916:527f.).

That parents—and especially fathers—often attempted with all means possible to dissuade their sons from undertaking a change of gender role has already been addressed. Thus, Mandan fathers used to thrash their sons on account of the latter's feminine inclinations (Maximilian n.d., 2:79); Hidatsa fathers admonished their sons to keep their hands off women's tasks, so that they did not become *miati* (Bowers 1965:132), and a certain Laguna *kokwimu,* who could not hope even for a vision, because gender role change there was not legitimized in this way, had to wait until the death of his father, who opposed any such change, until he was able—at the age of thirty—to take on the status of a *kokwimu* and put on women's clothing (Parsons 1918:181). According to some sources, Oglala Lakota fathers admonished their sons to stay away from *winkte* (Hassrick 1982:136; Lame Deer 1979:169), or mocked them as potential *winkte,* if they did not live up to their fathers' expectations with respect to the masculine role (DeMallie 1983:248). However, once the requisite legitimation (dream, vision, test) had occurred, such efforts subsided, and women-men were definitely well regarded in the pertinent tribes. At the same time, the women-men's dreams and visions released not only themselves (Williams 1986b:29) but also their families and the entire village community from the responsibility of holding them to the conventional masculine role. Nonetheless, even where the status of woman-man was connected with supernatural powers and definitely esteemed, it seems that parents themselves did not like to see their sons develop into women-men. And even in these groups, women-men were frequently the butt of jokes. Thus the esteem which attached to the status of woman-man was ambivalent.

Attempts to dissuade boys from becoming women-men in the Plains can surely also be traced to the fact that subsistence acquisition was a male-dominated occupation, and a son who switched over into the feminine gender role was lost to the family as a provider. The Plains gender hierarchy, too, certainly played a role. Most examples of attempts to deter boys from a gender role change have been reported from the Plains (Crow, Simms 1903:581; Hidatsa, Bowers 1965:105, 115; Mandan, Maximilian n.d., 2:79; Ojibwa, Henry 1897:163; Omaha, Dorsey 1894:379). On the Plains, the position of women was not as low as many sources have indicated (see Albers and Medicine 1983; Niethammer 1985:156; M. N. Powers 1986). Nevertheless, the domains of decision making, war, and hunting were dominated by males (see Weist 1980:258ff.), although the male prestige system was in principle accessible to both sexes. Women and women-men were respected, but within this system, which was dominated by male values, a gender role change by a male signified a "step down," just as crossing out of the gender role by a woman represented a "step up" (see Whitehead 1981: 86). A male who changed genders effectively withdrew from those activities which brought the highest prestige and respect: war and raiding. Nonetheless, he remained bound to another predominantly male prestige domain: latent supernatural power through visions. Even when Plains women (and women of other Native American cultures) could seek and receive visions, the vision quest was above all a component of the masculine gender role (see Weist 1980:259f.).

The attempts to forestall gender role change ended when a male received a legitimating vision, which led to social acceptance. Before such legitimation, he occupied a masculine gender status, and for someone defined as "man" (or "boy"), female personality traits were inappropriate. Once the woman-man was established in his status, his privileges and also the supernatural power attributed to him often surpassed the privileges and spiritual power of even the most esteemed women in his group. The ambivalence of his status enabled him to fill a feminine gender role and also to retain masculine privileges: the prestige acquired in warfare was for the most part denied him, but not the prestige of the medicine man—the male-bodied holy person. Where prestige based on warlike deeds was not foregrounded, serious attempts to change feminine boys were usually absent (e.g., the Great Basin, California, the Plateau, most of the Pueblos). In warlike groups in which the status of woman-man was not defined as ambivalent, but as quasi-feminine, by contrast, the esteem attaching to the woman-man status was far less pronounced or even low (e.g., Mohave, Apache, Choctaw, Cocopa, Iroquois, Oto, Wind River Shoshoni, Timucua).

In the Plains area, men-women could carry out an accepted gender role change only if they had already proven themselves as "masculine"/ "manly" in deeds of war. For independent/masculine women—as in the isolated cases of Dakota huntresses—the corresponding esteem acquired was negligible. By contrast, men-women who had been raised as boys were accepted because their status was culturally anchored: in the relevant tribes, they fulfilled the function of the male provider, which was necessary for the survival of the family. The Inuit woman who hunted only for herself and her woman life companion, on the other hand, had her house destroyed by the community (O. T. Mason 1895:211), and both women "returned to the ways of the world"—which meant the conventional feminine role. Boas, by the way, reported a parallel to this episode from a story of the Cumberland Sound Eskimo, even though the story is open ended (Boas 1901:261f.). A man once wanted to marry the sister of his wife. The two women, however, decided to leave and live by themselves. They caught and killed many caribou to live on, and built a house of stone for themselves by the sea. Finally the husband and one of his friends went in search of the women, and discovered the house they had built. After that, the wife apparently returned to live with her husband, but the story is not clear about that.

The Native American cultures of the Great Basin seem to have conceded a wide flexibility for variations on both masculine and feminine roles. Women-men, men-women, feminine males, and masculine females were allowed to do as they pleased and were not granted a special status with special responsibilities and privileges. Finally, in Northern California, the Atsugewi *brumaiwi*—who were more masculine women than men-women, and who could perform the tasks of both sexes—were disapproved of by the community (Voegelin 1942:135). The Achomawi men-women, by contrast, did exclusively men's work and were regarded with indifference (1942:135). It may be that in these cases gender role change was easier for the members of a group to comprehend and accept than role ambivalence. In addition, it was possible for men-women of the Achomawi, Mohave (Devereux 1937:502), Yuma (Forde 1931:157), Lillooet (Teit 1906:267), and Maricopa (Spier 1933:142) to appeal to a dream or vision experience as legitimation of their gender role change.

Thus, attitudes toward women-men and men-women varied across tribes as well as across time. Women-men, in particular, were traditionally revered as recipients of supernatural gifts in some tribes. In most Native American cultures outside the Prairies and Plains, however, their role was apparently much more secular. Women-men and men-women were nonetheless usually accepted, and an institutionalized alternative gender status was provided for them. Culture change has almost everywhere had adverse effects on gender role change, and the overall positive picture of the lives of contemporary "berdaches" provided, for example, by Williams (1986b) has not been confirmed by my own fieldwork. The situation of women-men, men-women, gays, and lesbians is difficult in many Indian communities on and off the reservations, and in most places institutionalized gender role change has ceased to exist. On the other hand, however, an increasing number of urban Native American gays and lesbians have come to claim the women-men and men-women as their predecessors in the tribal cultures. Thus, they argue that there were highly respected statuses for homosexual, "two-spirited" people in the tribal societies, and they use that argument to counteract homophobia in the Indian communities (see Jacobs, Thomas, and Lang 1997b; Lang, 1997a, 1997b; Robles Juarez 1992).

Chapter NINETEEN

GENDER ROLE CHANGE AND HOMOSEXUALITY

Relationships between men and women-men cannot automatically be described as homosexual in the Western sense (see Chapter 11). With the disappearance of the traditional woman-man status and the rise of the American gay/lesbian movement, some Indian males who possessed the ambivalent gender identity typical of women-men ultimately did, in fact, choose an identity as homosexuals, or gays. Others alternated between a woman-man status in the social environment of their tribe and a gay status in the urban community outside (Williams 1986b: 219ff.). Williams has pointed out, however, that by the term "gay," the Native American consultants he talked to did not necessarily refer to persons who are homosexual in the sense of the Western definition, but meant instead men who could be characterized as "not stereotypically masculine" (1986b:223). Consequently, the identity of some modern Indian gays, now as before, is more similar to that of traditional women-men than to the unambiguously masculine identity of a homosexual man.

This raises the question of whether homosexual relationships between two men identified as masculine in gender—or between two women with feminine gender identity—existed at all in the traditional Native American tribal cultures to a degree worth mentioning. This question is difficult to answer, not least because most ethnographers equated male-bodied "berdaches" with (passive) homosexuals, and did not seem to have even inquired about same-sex relationships outside of the "berdache" institution. If "berdaches" existed in a particular group, the topic of homosexuality was usually ticked off as having been dealt with. Perhaps this explains the sparseness of information on homosexual relationships.

Also, early reports about "sodomy" or "the abominable sin" do not necessarily refer to homosexual behavior between two people of the same sex and the same gender; it is likely that these describe relationships between men and women-men (e.g., Chickasaw, Romans 1962:70; Creek, Romans 1962:97). In some cases, it seems very probable that claims that nearly all the Indians of a particular tribe were addicted to "sodomy" were merely invented out of thin air, serving the purpose of representing them as especially godless and depraved in order to legitimate either the chronicler's or his military superior's goals of conquest and colonization. This pertains to statements regarding cannibalism as well. Arens wrote about the conquest of Mexico: "The outcome of the adventure was akin to genocide, but the Spaniards were able to rationalize the deed. Sometime shortly after the Conquest, it became apparent that in addition to being idolaters the Aztecs were both sodomists and cannibals" (1979:58). (In fact, the Aztecs of Mexico apparently thoroughly disapproved of homosexual behavior among women and men—and also of gender role change—even before the Conquest, and, moreover, imposed sanctions on it; Sahagún 1961:37f., 56).

In the excerpts from works of early Spanish chroniclers relating to Middle and South American cultures of the sixteenth and seventeenth centuries, collected by Guerra (1971), "sodomy" was also often cited in connection with cannibalism and idolatry. In Spanish law of the sixteenth century, sodomy—anal intercourse between men and women or between men—was an act which came directly after heresy and crimes against the person of the King (1971:221). The regularity with which sodomy turns up in the triad of godless acts committed by various tribes in the Americas prompts the speculation that such statements regarding homosexuality are suspect, above all when they are not discussed in more detail (see Figure 13). (Granzberg 1983:458 briefly pointed out the dubious nature of the sources in regard to this topic).

The information on female homosexuality is especially meager. Paula Gunn Allen (Laguna-Sioux), who has studied the lives of Native American women intensively, noted: "In my reading about American Indians, I have never read an overt account on Lesbians, and that reading has included hundreds of books and articles" (1981:67). On the basis of her analysis of the structure of Native American communities and of the role of women in traditional tribal cultures, she concluded that lesbian women must have existed, but she did not have any concrete examples: "Simple reason dictates that Lesbians did exist in tribal cultures, for they exist now" (1981:79). This lack of information is the result of an entire series of factors which applies to research not only on lesbian Indian women but also on Indian women generally: "Given American scholars' almost pathological attachment to Indian wars, horsemen of the Plains, and 'End of Trail' chiefs, I suppose we should be grateful that anything

The conquistador Nuñez de Balboa has Indian "sodomites" torn apart by his dogs in Quaregua (Panamá). (From Benzoni 1970 [1594], p. XXII.) Reproduced by permission of Reprint-Verlag Konrad Kölbl KG, © 1970.

at all has been written about Native American Women" (Green 1980: 249; see also Albers and Medicine 1983; Kehoe 1983; Weist 1983). For a long time, predominantly male ethnographers interviewed male consultants, and homosexual relationships between women in particular must have remained invisible to them, especially since the women involved were usually married. Early female ethnologists, on the other hand, were too firmly imprisoned in the moral ideas of their own time to consider female (and male) homosexual behavior. Stevenson, for example, who was good friends with the *lhamana* Wewha, and who provided detailed information in her monograph concerning a number of topics, particularly about religious ceremonies, dealt with the sexuality of *lhamana* with the following embarrassed remark: "There is a side to the life of these men which must remain untold. They never marry women, and it is understood that they seldom have any relations with them" (Stevenson 1904:38).

Homosexuality in the sense of sexual relations between two men identified as masculine exists among the modern Oglala Lakota (Williams 1986a:193, 195) and among urban Native Americans of differing tribal heritage (Williams 1986b:207ff.). It is not clear whether the Teton Lakota men who were "active homosexuals," according to Mirsky (1937a:417), were masculine partners of *winkte* or homosexual men who had sexual relationships with other men. They are said to have been called "dogs" and to have been despised. Homosexual contacts were widespread among the Flathead; Turney-High's (1937:85) information clearly does not refer to "berdaches," since he wrote that "berdaches" did not practice "homosexuality," which implies that they did not engage in any same-sex relationships. Turney-High (1937:156f.) also cited several Flathead terms in connection with homosexual relations for both sexes (see Map 8).

Homosexual behavior also seems to have occurred in Ingalik society; Osgood (1958:219) reported that this was "almost entirely"—and thus, apparently *not completely*—restricted to "berdaches." During his time, however, there existed no example of "overt homosexuality" (1958: 261). Honigmann (1954:130) observed an example of male homosexuality involving men among the Kaska. Essene (1942:30) included homosexual and heterosexual fellatio among the sexual practices of the Kato and Pomo, although again it is not clear whether sexuality between men and women-men might in fact possibly be meant here, since Essene (1942:65) equated "berdaches" and homosexuals.

Among the Kwakiutl, Mohave, and Hopi, homosexual acts were commonplace, mainly among boys (Devereux 1937:499; Ford 1941: 68; Williams 1986b:90, 188). One Hopi man, according to his autobiographical recollections, had recurrent homosexual dreams (Talayesva 1950:108, 117). A Ute man cited by Steward (1943:385), who "made beaded clothes and was homosexual but did not marry," was obviously a woman-man or a feminine male. "Casual secret homosexuality" on the part of both sexes was well known among the Yuma and was "not considered objectionable" (Forde 1931:157); the persons involved in these relationships "would resent being called elxa' or kwe'rhame" (Forde 1931:157), and thus were culturally clearly distinguished from women-men and men-women.

Among the Sanpoil, homosexual behavior occurred especially among young people of both sexes, and special terms were applied to it (*sitkspatixent' su'ta,* "homosexual contacts between men"; *sitsme'sumt' su'ta,* "lesbian relationships"; Ray 1932:148). Homosexual tendencies are said to have been punished there by beatings (Ray 1932:148). DuBois (1935:50), referring to the Wintu, wrote that homosexuality was a "recognized phenomenon" among them; but this might have meant only the feminine males of the tribe.

In regard to lesbian women—and contrary to Hassrick's (1982: 137f.) insinuations—there exists no clear-cut evidence for their occur-

Map 8. Male and Female Homosexuality

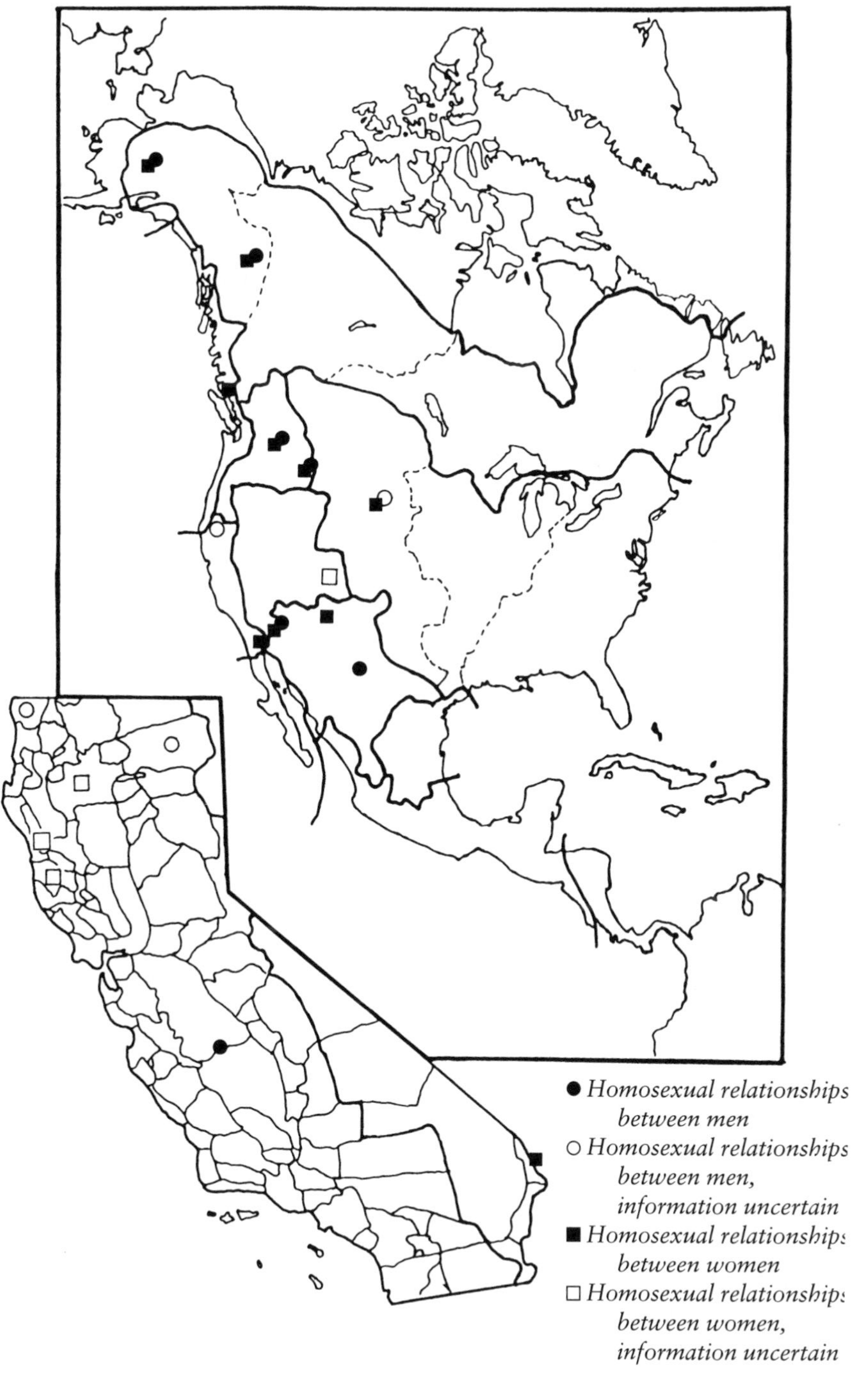

rence in Teton Lakota society (on this, see the biting, but justified, critique by M. N. Powers 1986:16f.). Women who received a vision from Anukite became excellent artisans and also became more sexually active than other women, but were not lesbians. Allen (1981) described the *koskalaka* (a term which according to her translates as "young man" or "woman who doesn't want to marry") as possibly lesbian women. Allen claimed that such women's behavior was legitimated by visions sent by Double Woman *(wiya numpa),* and that they were united by a special dance (1981:82): "They do a dance in which a rope is twined between them and coiled to form a 'rope baby' . . . two women who don't want to marry [a man] become united by the power of wiya numpa and their vision is validated." Double Woman herself has been described as "two women joined together by a rope from which dangles a baby" (DeMallie 1983:246), although in other sources the women who dream of her have not been characterized as lesbian/masculine, but rather as promiscuous and also as skillful in feminine tasks (DeMallie 1983:245; W. K. Powers 1977:58f.).

In principle, Anukite appears as the protective patroness of sexual behavior that differs from the cultural norms and of ambivalent identity ("lewd women," *winkte*). Thus, it is totally conceivable that she also called forth and/or legitimated homosexual behavior. Nevertheless, apart from Hassrick's (1982) undocumented claim, Allen's (1981) interpretation of the Double Woman Dance is the only indication of this. Particularly against the background of the assertion that Double Woman herself has been conceptualized as two women bound to each other by a rope from which a baby hangs, the dance might also be interpreted as a ritual in which women who have dreamed of this goddess personify Double Woman—without referring to a lesbian relationship. Moreover, Medicine (1993), on the grounds of her profound knowledge of Lakota culture and language, has pointed out that *koskalaka* by no means refers to lesbian women but instead to young, postpubescent males.

Osgood (1958:219) related an anecdote from the Ingalik which indicates a lesbian relationship between two girls. Female homosexuality—termed "getting on top of each other"—also existed among the Kaska (Honigmann 1954:130). Lesbian relationships have also been reported from the Yokuts (Gayton 1948:236) and likewise from the Chiricahua Apache (Opler 1965:111).

Female homosexuality—that is, sexual relations between two women as opposed to a relationship between a woman and a man-woman—was expressly denied among the Haisla (Olson 1940:200), Hopi (Beaglehole and Beaglehole 1935:65), Navajo (Stewart 1942:334, "except with berdaches"), Southern Paiute (Stewart 1942:334, "except with berdaches"), Ute (Stewart 1942:334, "except with berdaches"). Essene

(1942:52) reported an absence of "homosexuality among women" for the Kato, Lassik, and Yuki, but it is not completely clear whether by this he meant relationships between two women or between men-women and women.

A classification with lesbian women instead of with men-women is also conceivable in the case of the two Tolowa females who married women, but who apparently did not do men's work (Drucker 1937b: 260), and possibly also in the case of the Achomawi women who did the tasks of both sexes, who did not cross-dress, and who co-habited with other women (Voegelin 1942:134f.). In the case of feminine males and masculine females who entered into same-sex partnerships, the issue of whether or not the desire for a homosexual relationship was sometimes a motive for adopting the tasks of the opposite sex—so that the sexual division of labor was preserved in the framework of such a relationship—cannot be ascertained on the basis of the source materials.

Williams (1986b:81f.) has indicated that the very close emotional and romantic friendships which are common in many tribes between two persons of the same sex are not identical with homosexual relationships, but they may well include at least a homoerotic component. Williams (1986b:91) added to this a personal communication from Omer C. Stewart: "My impression is that the American Indians were fairly unconcerned one way or the other regarding homosexual behavior." Williams (1986b:91) and Allen (1981:80ff.) both concluded that in Native American cultures, the strongest emotional bonds were those to persons of one's own sex. An individual spent the greater part of his or her time with those people, in any event. In light of the very strong emotional component of these often formally sealed friendships, they can at least be termed "homoerotic." An even better term might be "homoemotional."

Among many of the cultures investigated in connection with this study, such intimate friendships have been indicated—especially among males: the Cree (*niwitcewahakan,* "he with whom I go about," D. G. Mandelbaum 1940:244; these young men also used to delouse each other in turn like lovers, Mandelbaum 1940:209); the Crow (*i'rapa'-tuE,* "comrades"; among women *hi'raawe',* "female companion," Lowie 1912:212); the Santee Dakota (Riggs 1893:196, *koda,* "an arrangement of giving themselves to each other, of the David and Jonathan kind. . . . This arrangement was often a real affection . . . often lasting to old age"); the Hopi (Beaglehole and Beaglehole 1935:65, *na.sin-wamu'* or *na.mi'nim,* "partners," "children or adults of the same sex"); the Kansa (James 1823:115, permanent bonding, "continuing often throughout life"); Maricopa (Spier 1933:331, *mataxcuva'k,* contains the root *matat-mig,* "married"; "They were more than friends: What one did, the other did"); Skidi Pawnee (Dorsey and Murie 1940:107, "formally recognized type of friendship" for young men and women); Ingalik (Osgood 1958:222, "special friends").

Open homosexuality between two men and two women, therefore, is seldom encountered in the sources. Nonetheless, if "casual and secret" homosexual relationships such as those described for the Yuma were carried on and treated with the same discretion in other tribes as well, then it is possible that homosexual behavior among men and women occurred more frequently than the sources suggest. Among the Yuma as well as in other Native American cultures, partners in such relationships were probably wedded in heterosexual marriages, and from the outside appeared to lead fully "normal" and—above all for ethnographers—inconspicuous lives.

Chapter TWENTY

Gender Role Change in Native American Oral Traditions

▼

Within both religious and secular spheres, many Native American cultures have expressed ideas about an "androgynous" human potentiality. This may be expressed through a union of the respective male and female principles in a single individual, one who, by being both "a man and a woman," attains completeness (see Laski 1959:26, 65, 88, 150 passim on the Tewa). The idea of androgyny is also expressed by "berdaches" and hermaphrodites, who unite both sexes within themselves. Thus far, the focus has mainly been on ethnographic data; here, the emphasis is on how gender role change—and sometimes homosexuality—appears in the oral traditions ("mythologies") of North American Indian cultures. With some exceptions, these stories can be organized into three categories:

1. Stories in which supernatural beings appear as hermaphrodites or women-men/men-women.
2. Stories of the trickster cycle, in which the trickster disguises himself in women's clothing in order to play a trick on some person.
3. Stories which describe homosexual relationships.

Many Native Americans resent their oral traditions being referred to as "myths" because this implies that these traditions are thought by White researchers to be less "true" than, for example, the Western biblical traditions. The word *story* is used here for lack of an agreed-upon alternative and with the understanding that narratives, whatever they may be called, carry cultural significance.

SUPERNATURAL "BERDACHES" AND HERMAPHRODITES

The hermaphrodite Sx'ints is among the very numerous supernatural beings of the Bella Coola. In the Land Above, he watches over and plays with the daughters of a series of deities. Primarily, he protects them from Sxaiaxwax, a malevolent being who is out to seduce girls. Sx'ints frequently also goes around on the earth and is recognized by humans by his peculiarly nasal voice (McIlwraith 1948, 1:45; 2:179). He has masculine as well as feminine characteristics (McIlwraith 1948, 2:179). Sx'ints influences women-men and men-women "in some mysterious way," which McIlwraith (1948, 1:45) did not explain further. Episodes from his life are portrayed in several dances which emphasize his function as the successful protector of the supernatural maidens from the lascivious Sxaiaxwax (McIlwraith 1948, 2:147f., 179). The mask of Sx'ints was illustrated in Boas (1900; see Figure 14 of the present work). In addition, Sx'ints belonged to the crew of the canoe in which, on account of a dream, Winwi'na—a kind of culture hero—convenes numerous animals in order to make a journey with them to the Land of the Salmon. On arriving there, each animal kidnaps a male and a female of each of the different kinds of salmon and takes them to the canoe. They return home after they have first visited a place where enormous quantities of very different kinds of berries are growing. Sx'ints gathers some berries of each kind. After they have returned to the Bella Coola, they throw the salmon into the sea, and Winwi'na tells each kind of salmon when in the annual cycle it should arrive where the Bella Coola live. He also scatters the berries gathered by Sx'ints and instructs them to ripen at certain seasons of the year (Boas 1900:40). This story is likewise reenacted in a dance which includes a song describing Sx'ints (whose "mythical name" is ala'ya'o; Boas 1900:40; McIlwraith 1948, 2:188) and his exploits in the Land Above (McIlwraith 1948, 2:184f.).

Associations between women-men/men-women and twins are encountered among a number of tribes. Chugach *aranu'tiq* are said to be "lucky like twins" (Birket-Smith 1953:94). According to Lame Deer, *winkte* are twins merged into one person (Lame Deer 1979:169). The Navajo apparently also regarded twins as well as *nadle* as fortune bringing (Bailey 1950:94f.; see also O'Flaherty 1982:287f., 296 on twins as androgynes).

A supernatural female *warharmi* and two male twins appear among the Kamia as culture heroes: the three bring seedlings of cultivated plants to the Kamia (Gifford 1931:12). In addition, they bring weapons of war (1931:80), although the weapons apparently are more associated with the male twins, whereas the seedlings are more associated with the *warharmi* (1931:80). The culture heroes are sent out by the god Mastamho

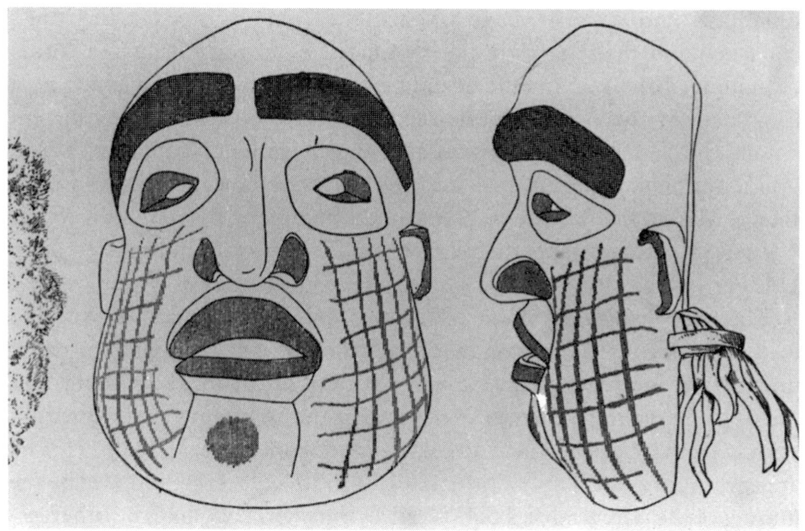

Mask of the hermaphrodite Sx'ints, Bella Coola. (From Boas 1900, Table XI, Fig. 10.) Courtesy Department of Library Services, American Museum of Natural History.

(1931:77). This deity resides on the mountain Wikami; the twins are regarded as "sons" of the *warharmi* (who did not, however, bear them; Gifford 1931:79).

The culturally related Mohave lack a supernatural *alyha* or *hwame;* however, the god Matavilye determines before his death that *alyha* and *hwame* will come into existence:

> Ever since the world began at the magic mountain Avi-kwame it was said that there would be transvestites . . . [Matavilye] is on his death-bed and people are all around him. He tells them that their lives would be different, and some of them would turn into transvestites. (Devereux 1937:503)

Matavilye is the equivalent of Pukumat, the "dying God" of the Kamia (see Gifford 1931:76f.). Wikami, Awi-kwame, Avialyxa (Maricopa, Spier 1933:242), and the Yuma mountain (which is likewise called Avi-kwame) are related through their names in the Yuman languages. Avi-alyxa in the Maricopa language means "berdache mountain" (1933:242); this is the mountain in which a supernatural woman-man lives. Prospective Maricopa *yesaa'n* (women-men) dream of it (1933:242). Wi-kami, or alternately Avikwame, apparently means "*hwame*-mountain"; it is possible that this points to a tradition (which is not handed down in the sources) of a supernatural (female) "berdache" residing inside a mountain among the Mohave and also the Yuma. Moreover, the Maricopa believed that not only the mountain Avialyxa, but also a Yuma mountain of the same name are alike inhabited by a "berdache"; this, too, suggests that similar ideas regarding *their* Avialyxa were current among the Yuma. The two mountains played gambling games with each other, and depending on which of the two supernatural beings lost, either a Maricopa male or a Yuma male became a woman-man (Spier 1933:242). "As one sees them in dreams, the two mountains are young girls" (1933:242).

The oral traditions of the Zuni also exhibit supernatural women-men and androgynes. A'wonawil'ona, "the supreme life-giving bisexual power, who is referred to as He-She, the symbol and initiator of life, and life itself, pervading all space" turns up at the beginning of the creation story related by Stevenson (1904:22), but does not appear again. He/she appears more as an abstract principle of a completeness symbolized by the uniting of the potentialities of both sexes than as a deity like the other, essentially more concrete, supernatural beings of the Zuni. Bunzel pointed out that Stevenson erred in her interpretation of A'wonawil'ona as a "bisexual deity." A'wonawil'ona is not one deity, but rather is a collective term for supernatural beings who influence the lives of people—for example, Sun, Earth, Maize (corn), prey animals, war gods—"These are called a'wona wil'ona, 'the ones who hold our roads'" (Bunzel 1932:486). If people in Zuni are asked whether a'wona wil'ona is a man or a woman, according to Bunzel (1932:486, n. 12), "they say, 'Both, of course', since it refers to a great class of supernaturals"; since the supernatural beings which constitute A'wonawil'ona are male as well as female, this concept naturally comprises both sexes, too.

It is questionable whether Kor'kokshi, the only supernatural woman-man, is actually comparable to the earthly *lhamana,* even if his coerced feminization (*only* by means of clothing) was regarded as the "first instance of a god or man appearing in woman's dress" (Stevenson 1904:37, n. a). In Zuni, cross-dressing put the seal on entrance into the status of *lhamana,* but this status was nevertheless primarily defined by a male's preference for feminine, as opposed to masculine, occupations. Kor'kokshi is the first-born of the incestuous union of the siblings Si'wulutsi'wa and Si'wulutsitsa (who later become the deities A'wan tätchu and Ko'mokätsi and the parents of the Kok'ko [anthropomorphic deities, "kachina"]). Of the sibling-couple's ten children, Kor'kokshi is "normal in all respects," while "the other nine children did not possess the seeds of procreation" (1904:32f.; according to Cushing, cited in Parsons 1916:524, however, the first-born child is a "woman in fullness of contour, but a man in stature and brawn"—a hermaphrodite). When the A'shiwi (Zuni) and the Kok'ko, during their wanderings after their ascent from the lower worlds to the surface of the earth, come upon the Kia'nakwe, another group of deities who are led by the fierce Chakwena, who is associated with wild animals, the Kia'nakwe take four of the Kok'ko prisoner, among them Kor'kokshi: "Kor'kokshi, the firstborn, was so angry and unmanageable that Ku'yapälitsa [the Chakwena] had him dressed in female attire previous to the dance, saying to him: 'You will now perhaps be less angry'" (Stevenson 1904:37). Kor'koshi, therefore, is not depicted as a *lhamana*, but instead is forced into women's clothes because of his wildness. Furthermore, as a *class* of deities personified in the mask dances, the Kor'kokshi are not ambivalent in terms of gender (see Stevenson 1904:47, 104, 141f.).

It is possible that Kor'kokshi's forced transvesting is provisional in nature and situationally conditioned in the context of the dance, in which the temporarily victorious (hunting) Chakwena makes the defeated (horticultural) Kok'ko perform. Only then, in the dance reenactment of this particular episode from the origin story, does Kor'kokshi also appear as *ko'thlama* in women's clothes. None of the male and female Kor'kokshi of other dances are *ko'thlama,* even if men take over the role of the female deities (see, e.g., Stevenson 1904:104, 145): since women were not in general initiated into the *ko'tikili,* men—and not *lhamana*—inevitably had to portray the goddesses. It was natural that a *lhamana* portrayed the transvesting Kor'kokshi in the dance reenactment of this episode, but even this apparently was not imperative. Notwithstanding her/his gender role change, the *lhamana* counted as a male who occupied an ambivalent gender status (see Parsons 1916:528). In contrast to other kachina dancers, who put on women's clothing only in the context of dances, the *lhamana* permanently embodied the male in women's clothes into whom Kor'kokshi had temporarily been made.

Hermaphrodites played a significant role in the creation stories of the Navajo. The first-born offspring of First Man and First Woman are hermaphrodite *(nadle)* twins (Matthews 1897:70)—a male and a female androgyne (O'Flaherty 1982:286)—who are infertile; the additional four pairs of twins born afterward, however, were fertile and were not intersexual. The two *nadle* invent pottery making and the woven water bottle (Matthews 1897:70). When the men and women split up after quarreling, the *nadle* go with the men, after First Man first has sent for them:

> They came, covered with meal, for they had been grinding corn. 'What have you that you made yourselves?' he asked. 'We have each two milling-stones, and we have cups and bowls and baskets and many other things', they answered. 'Then take these all along with you', he ordered, 'and join us to cross the stream.' (Matthews 1897:72)

Here, both *nadle* appear as perfect *male* androgynes in a woman's role, equipped with all the requisite working utensils. Thanks to the *nadle,* the men are later able to maintain the sexual division of labor. They live in affluence because the "order" of the sexual/gendered division of labor remains preserved. The women, however, live in such "chaos," or disorder, because the masculine component is lacking in their lives, that they finally have to give in (Matthews 1897:73). At the same time, one of the *nadle*—the female androgyne—is the first human being to die. Two hunters ultimately find her/him "seated by the side of the river, in the fourth world, combing her hair" (Matthews 1897:78; several versions of this origin story exist which differ slightly from each other; see Reichard 1950:140, 433f.; on the association of the female androgyne with death, see O'Flaherty 1982:286).

The origin of the *nadle* lies in the third of a total of five worlds. In the origin story, both the Holy People (the supernatural beings) and the ancestors of the Navajo ascend from one lower world to the next, until they finally arrive in the fifth, uppermost world, which is the surface of the earth. In the third world, First Man resolves that marriage and exogamy, "the legitimacy of the hermaphrodite's life," and also the office of chief, shall exist (Reichard 1950:434). According to O'Bryan (1956: 5), the two *nadle* are called Turquoise Hermaphrodite (or Turquoise Boy, Ashon nutli') and White Shell Hermaphrodite, alias White Shell Girl. In the version of the story related by this author, Ashon nutli'—the male androgyne—also goes with the men during the separation of the sexes, "ground the corn and cooked the food" (1956:7); the consultant added: "Nadle means that which changes. Ashon nutli', or nadle, the Turquoise Hermaphrodite, was the first man to change, or become, as a woman" (1956:7, n. 30): on the occasion of the separation of men and women, he goes from his undifferentiated hermaphroditic state over into the feminine role. Afterward, during the further ascent through the lower worlds, he seems to change once again back into the undifferentiated androgynous form (see O'Bryan 1956:9f.). Later, Turquoise Boy, as the male First Boy, becomes the Sun-Carrier. And as First Girl (the two are, after all, the first-born children of First Man and First Woman), White Shell Girl steps into a great, white mussel shell, which becomes the Moon (1956:15). As the price of their journey across the firmament, the two require that death shall come into the world (1956:18). Thus, the first hermaphrodites of the origin story at last go over into a thoroughly straightforward and unambivalent gender state. In Navajo religion, apparently, both the Sun and the Moon deities are male (Reichard 1950: 451, 470ff.). In the Pueblos, however, the Sun appears to be associated generally with the masculine principle, and the Moon with the feminine; maybe the association in the origin story of the Moon with the female

White Shell Girl reflects the ideas of their Pueblo neighbors. (For another interpretation of this story, see Williams 1986b:19f.)

Reichard (1950:386ff.) described be'gotchidí, "One-Who-Grabs-Breasts," as the youngest son of the Sun God. (His blond hair and blue eyes probably symbolize the Sun; see Reichard 1950:387, 389.) Be'gotchidí is "a transvestite and the first pottery-maker" (1950:387); in many respects, he is a "nadle," "one who changes," since he can change his form just as he likes—"rainbow, wind, sand, water, or anything else" (1950:387): "He got his name because he would make himself invisible, then sneak up on young girls to touch their breasts as he shouted 'be'go', be'go'" (Reichard 1950:387; see also Hill 1938a:99). He allows himself similar kinds of fun with hunters, and also with couples who are having sexual intercourse. Even the Holy People are not safe from his tricks (Reichard 1950:387f.). Along with the Sun God, he is regarded as the creator of both wild and domesticated animals, which at the same time are entrusted to his care (1950:387f.). He appears in another story as the generous giver of all kinds of domesticated animals (1950:388). Navajo who wanted a good horse for themselves sang some songs for be'gotchidí and then could be certain of obtaining such a horse (1950:389).

In many aspects, be'gotchidí appears as a supernatural equivalent of the earthly *nadle:* bisexual and infertile, but at the same time uninhibited and unconventional in sexual matters, he is associated with both feminine and masculine areas (e.g., pottery making as well as wild and domesticated animals). At the same time, as lord of the animals—above all, the domesticated animals—he is connected with wealth and prosperity. Hill (1935:279) indicated that Klah embellished b'egotchidí's position in the Navajo pantheon, a finding that Reichard (1950:142) essentially confirmed. Nevertheless, these associations of be'gotchidí are not only found in stories which Klah told (see Reichard 1950:386ff.). As noted, Klah was himself a *nadle* (see also Reichard 1944:21ff.).

The oral traditions of the Nootka tell of malevolent woman-man-beings. Of the ten *haqwo'lum*—supernatural beings with very long hair—two were male, but nonetheless they turned up in women's clothes. If you came across all ten of them, it meant good fortune, but if you met only the supernatural women-men, the result was mental illness (Drucker 1951:324f.).

THE TRICKSTER CYCLE

Cross-dressing episodes are encountered in the context of the trickster cycle and also other stories of, for example, the Arapaho, Assiniboine, Fox, Maricopa, Menomini, and Sinkaietk, as well as the Eskimo of Cumberland Sound and Hudson Bay, although the latter did not have the institution of gender role change.

The Assiniboine trickster Sitconski wanders around in his daughter's clothes, marries a young man, and simulates a pregnancy. The husband sees through the trick, but Sitconski escapes: "Turning around to his husband's sister, mentulam suam demonstravit" (he displayed his male member; Lowie 1909:125). In a Sinkaietk story, Coyote transforms himself into a girl in order to win the chieftain Cougar and his immense food supply for himself, which he succeeds in doing, although here also the fraud is finally seen through. Moreover, he constantly has to evade consummation of the marriage, because only the upper half of his body has been transformed—"the rest was like Coyote" (Cline et al. 1938:232f.).

While disguised in a woman's clothes, Nihançan, the culture hero of the Arapaho, marries Mountain Lion and feigns childbirth (Kroeber 1902:19). In a story told by the Fox, Wisakä transforms himself into a gloriously beautiful girl in order to get even with his friend Turtle, who has scolded him on account of his constant squandering away of his gambling winnings. By doing so, Wisakä chooses the surest way of doing it, since Turtle is always after the women: as a woman, he steals his adversary's medicine bag, then transforms himself back into Wisakä, and finally throws Turtle into a pond, ordering him to become the animal "Turtle" (Jones 1907:315). An almost identical story is found among the Menomini (Skinner and Satterlee 1915:263ff.).

The Menomini also know an almost identically worded variant of the Assiniboine story, in which Trickster humiliates an arrogant chieftain's son by first having sexual intercourse with him with the aid of an artificial vulva. He then feigns a pregnancy and finally throws the "now putrid flesh that he has used as a vulva" into his face (Skinner and Satterlee 1915:303).

Widely distributed among the cultures on the Prairies is the episode in which the trickster/culture hero transforms himself into an old medicine woman who is on the way to heal Trickster's brother, who has been wounded and carried off by the gods of the world below. In this disguise, he gets into the malevolent deities' home unrecognized and avenges his brother (e.g., Menomini, Skinner and Satterlee 1915:261; Fox, Jones 1907:355f.). In a Maricopa story episode, Coyote also takes on the form of an old woman in order to avenge—and to revive—his brother (Spier 1933:363).

In these cases, the transformation is tied to a specific situation and takes place for a very concrete purpose. Trickster does not strive for any permanent change of gender role, but, usually at the end of the story, he instead triumphantly reveals himself as a man. As a man in women's clothes, he deceives and punishes opponents. That this temporary gender role change on the part of Trickster is at least regarded as similar to the women-men's permanent change is shown by the following comment of a Sinkaietk consultant: Coyote is said to have "announced that there would be such [i.e., women-men] when he left Cougar's house, where he had masqueraded as a woman" (M. Mandelbaum 1938:119).

OTHER EXAMPLES

Just as the rare cases of female gender role change among the Inuit were born of necessity, so also is, in a story, the transformation of an old woman who, along with her granddaughter, is abandoned and left behind by the community. In order to be able to feed herself and the girl, the old woman transforms herself into a man—including male genitals—and at the same time, fashions dogs and hunting equipment from parts of her body. She marries the girl and impregnates her. When a "real" man turns up, the old woman drops dead from shame, but only after she has transformed herself back into an old woman (Boas 1901: 249, 323ff.).

The same two Inuit groups (Hudson Bay and Cumberland Sound) tell the story of a shaman who is emasculated in connection with a hunting accident and immediately transforms himself into a woman. If his fellow humans insinuate that he actually is not a woman, he strips off the skin from his face, so that the person opposite drops dead from the horrible sight. Finally, with the aid of a cunning ruse, he is put to death by the villagers (Boas 1901:250f., 325f.). This is probably a variation of the story motif of a powerful but malevolent shaman. At the same time, it suggests that the villagers disapproved of the change of gender role.

In a Sinkaietk story, a woman feigns her own death and lets herself be buried by her daughters (whom she had created out of salmon roe) and—disguised as a young man—returns to them. Lacking male genitals, she uses a pestle hammer in order to have sexual intercourse with the young girls. The girls become skeptical when they wake up the next morning "very swollen in [their] genitals." They tickle the "man" until "he" reveals himself to be their foster mother, and then they kill "him" by tickling him until he dies (Hill-Tout 1905:185ff.). Here also—just as in the trickster episodes—a concrete goal lies at the basis of the gender role change (in this case, incestuous desires).

LESBIAN LOVE

The Michahai Yokuts told of seven young wives who were actually homosexual. They kept their husbands away from them by consuming excessive quantities of onions, and they searched for a way to escape from married life once and for all. Finally, they fasted for six full days and then made their way to a big cliff. Only the youngest of them decided to remain behind, and she changed herself into a rock. The others got onto ropes of eagle down, which rose into the air carrying the women; these women became the Pleiades. Their husbands followed them in the same manner, but even on the firmament the women still did not want their husbands to come near them, so the men became the constellation of Taurus (Gayton and Newman 1940:35; see also Gayton 1948:236). Variants of this story in which the homosexuality of the women is not so explicitly stated are also found among the Waksachi, Choinimni, Wobunuch, and Patwisha bands of the Yokuts.

Lesbian love is also described in a Fox story: two girls refuse to marry. Their two suitors secretly follow them when they go into the woods to peel and collect tree bark, and find them just as they are undressing. "And to their amazement the girls began to lie with each other!" Caught in the act, the girls beg the men not to betray them: "We have done it under the influence of some unknown being." However, one of the girls is pregnant by her female lover, and bears a child—"the child was like a soft-shell turtle" (Jones 1907:151ff.).

A similar Assiniboine story also tells of lesbian love: a woman and her sister-in-law run away together, and the woman's husband tracks down the two women and their child. The child "looked like a football. It had no bones in its body, because a woman had begotten it." The husband kills both the child and his wife (Lowie 1909:223). Just as in the Fox case, the story is moralizing and points to a negative and disparaging evaluation of female homosexuality. Even more straightforward is a story in which two women are satisfying each other with a wooden stick. A man comes along, catching them in the act and frightening them so that the stick breaks in two and the ends remain stuck in the women's vaginas. The man then "rescues" or saves them in this manner: he "four times . . . raised their legs, when he shot an arrow into each of the split pieces of wood and extracted them" (Lowie 1909:224f.). The symbolism of this act, in the context of which the man shoots arrows into the vaginas in order to eliminate the consequences of the unsuccessful lesbian act, is plain enough.

THE ORIGIN OF WOMEN-MEN

The origin of women-men (but not men-women) is related in stories of the Pima, Oto, Winnebago, and Crow. In one Crow story, Coyote's wife and the malevolent female deity Red Woman determine the affairs of the world, and among other things (through a mistake in the creation of men and women), determine the existence of *bate* (Lowie 1918:28f.). In the origin stories of the Oto, *mixo'ge* are associated with a particular descent group, in which they turn up for the first time (Whitman 1937:22, 29, 50). Finally, a Pima story puts the blame on the Papago that women-men also occurred in their own (Pima) tribe (Hill 1938b:339). According to one Winnebago story, the first woman-man among them was a Sioux chieftain whom they had captured and forced into women's clothing (Lurie 1953:710). Nevertheless, men made to wear women's clothes for purposes of humiliation are everywhere (including among the Winnebago) distinguished from women-men (see Lurie 1953:711; on the existence of the woman-man institution simultaneously with the coerced cross-dressing of cowardly warriors, or in the context of joking relationships, see also Lowie 1909:69 [Assiniboine]; D. G. Mandelbaum 1940:296 [Cree]; Hassrick 1982:135 [Teton Lakota]; Landes 1968: 122ff. and 207 [Santee Dakota, as a joke]; Bossu 1962:82 [Illinois]; Olson 1936:97 [Quinault, as a joke]).

One Mandan story offers a legitimation of the status of *mihdäckä:* a warrior tries to force a *mihdäckä* to adopt the masculine role and ultimately shoots and kills him. The *mihdäckä* turns himself into a heap of stones. "Since then, no one wants to meddle in this affair, which is believed to have been established and protected by higher powers" (Maximilian n.d., 2:79, translation J.L.V.).

In some cases, therefore, one encounters supernatural beings who are women-men, men-women, or hermaphrodites. Within the pantheon, they have for the most part little significance, but can represent a supernatural, mythical legitimation of a gender role change carried out by human beings. This also seems to be true of cross-dressing episodes in the trickster cycle, although in the cycle the gender role change is situationally conditioned, and takes place only temporarily in the context of a prank carried out by the trickster. The temporary sexual ambivalence also fits in well with the otherwise ambivalent character traits of the trickster (see O'Flaherty 1982:286f.) and should be seen against the background of them. In regard to the moral of portrayals of male and female gender role change in the oral traditions, one cannot help thinking of O'Flaherty's (1982:235f., 286, 335f.) compelling distinction between positive male and negative female androgynes. Episodes in the oral traditions regarding female gender role change and female homosexuality mostly represent these modes of behavior as unsuitable, improper, and abnormal. In these stories, gender role change is also undertaken for a specific purpose (emergency; incestuous desires). Lesbian intercourse is "punished" by the conception and birth of a monster—or a man appears as the phallic liberator of two women who have placed themselves in jeopardy through lesbian intercourse.

Chapter TWENTY-ONE

CONCLUSION

Against the background of a wider cultural context, gender role change in Native American cultures proves not to be a unitary phenomenon, but rather a means of expressing an array of possibilities for varying the gender role which forms the cultural norm for either females or males. Following Roscoe (1987, 1988a:217), these possibilities can be termed *alternative gender roles*. Not all alternative gender roles necessarily involve an alternative *gender status*—women-men and men-women have a characteristically ambivalent masculine-feminine gender status. At the same time, the fulfillment of alternative gender roles sometimes brought with it different consequences for males than for females. In the present book, four kinds of alternative gender roles can be ascertained on the basis of the data:

1. *Crossing out of the gender role*: the infringement on role areas of the opposite sex without giving up either one's own gender role or one's own gender status. Examples of this are the warrior women of the Plains, the manly-hearted women of the Piegan, the (crude) basket-weaving men of some Northern California tribes, and modern Pueblo potters.
2. *Gender role mixing*: a permanent adoption of role components of the opposite sex to a greater extent with partial giving up of one's own gender role. This can lead to a redefinition of one's gender status as ambivalent. Examples are Ojibwa women who lived alone permanently (and whose gender status did not change) and Plains women-men (whose gender status did change).
3. *Gender role change*: the total adoption of the social role of the opposite sex, accompanied by giving up the gender role to which one is entitled on the basis of one's biological sex. Under these circumstances, a male's gender status always

changes, but a female's does not necessarily change. Examples are most of the California women-men, as well as men-women of the Mohave, Cocopa, and Ute; the independent women of the Bella Coola, Santee Dakota, and Carrier did not change their gender status.

4. *Gender role splitting*: living out both masculine and feminine role components alternately over time, whereby the roles are not mixed, but rather are kept separate. Examples are males who adopt a women's role in everyday life, but who nevertheless sometimes pursue masculine occupations while dressed in men's clothing (e.g., hunting, warfare). The exclusively male representatives of this group are classified as women-men within their respective cultures and therefore hold an ambivalent gender status.

The transitional zones between these gender role alternatives are fluid, especially those between crossing out of one's gender role and gender role mixing. Apparently, males in particular were allowed by their culture(s) to cross out of their gender roles only to a certain degree without having to redefine their gender status (see Essene 1942:65; Parsons 1939b:38).

By contrast, females in many places were able to participate in masculine role domains without having to change their gender status from feminine/woman to quasi-masculine or nonfeminine—that is, without having to become female "berdaches," or men-women. Their physiological functions (i.e., menstruation), therefore, can hardly be the cause of there having been fewer female "berdaches" than male ones, as Whitehead (1981) argued, since those bodily functions did not actually prevent women from participation even in the particularly masculine prestige-related activity of warfare. Instead, it seems that the female "berdache" status—particularly in the Prairies and Plains region—was not at all required, precisely because aspects of the masculine gender role were already accessible to women. However, the reverse situation did not hold: a woman who possessed the necessary personal prerequisites, and very possibly a legitimating vision as well, could go to war, but a man could not begin to distinguish himself in beadwork or in basket weaving, for example, without redefining himself as a non-man (i.e., as a "berdache," or woman-man). It was just exactly on the Prairies and Plains where women-men were found almost exclusively; the few men-women were isolated cases that emerged from the warrior woman tradition (e.g., Woman Chief, Running Eagle). This must be related to the fact that, although two separate prestige domains existed for the respective sexes, the male system stressing bravery, reckless daring, and deeds of war had become the standard for *both* sexes. Even prestige within the feminine sphere was often expressed in terms of the masculine one (see Landes

1938:180; O. Lewis 1941; Weist 1980:158ff.). Nevertheless, there was no possibility of acquiring prestige that was equally valid for both sexes and that belonged to the *feminine* gender role. This is in contrast to the Pueblos, where, as a traditional feminine sphere of work, pottery making, in particular, became attractive not only for women-men in earlier times, but also for men in the present century. Wherever, therefore, a significant domain of either gender role became the standard of prestige for both sexes, an encroachment into this role sphere was possible without the adoption of an ambivalent gender status, as, for example, the entry into the war complex by Plains women, or the entry into the production of ceramics by Pueblo men.

Whitehead's (1981:109) explanation of the "berdache" phenomenon as an attempt on the part of men to usurp feminine prestige areas in addition to their own is, finally, not convincing. Whitehead's characterization of a literal battle of the sexes, especially on the Plains, has been placed in doubt by more recent research (see DeMallie 1983: Kehoe 1983; M. N. Powers 1986). However, in view of the dominant male prestige system, Whitehead's interpretation seems valid to the extent that the choice of a feminine gender role probably meant a drop in social status for a male (1981:86; cf. Williams 1986b:66f.). The available data suggest that the woman-man in such situations lost access to potential prestige in the central area of warfare, but he/she did retain another important masculine role component that brought with it considerable prestige: latent spiritual potential, legitimated by visions. Thus his gender role change did not necessarily constitute failure in the warrior's role. Rather, his new status meant that he was the recipient of gifts from supernatural beings: the adoption of women's clothing, activities, and mannerisms expressed a special kind of thoroughly masculine personal medicine, acquired in the masculine way (vision quest). At the same time, this personal medicine is connected ideologically to the woman-man's superiority over women: on account of his latent spiritual potential, he was regarded as excellent in all feminine occupations and possessed privileges (primarily of a ritual nature) which were withheld even from women with significant latent spiritual potential.

The sexual ambivalence of the woman-man status is most striking on the Plains, and it is no wonder that women-men in this region did not strive either for the feminine gender role in its totality or even for an imitation of female bodily functions. Gender role change there was legitimated within the structures of a component of the masculine role—the vision quest. From then on, the woman-man's gender status was clearly nonmasculine, but it was nonetheless also nonfeminine: it represented a combination of both gender statuses. On the Plains, too, it is evident that women-men's excellence in feminine occupations did not result from their attempt to usurp the women's areas of prestige: in the context of a system of prestige molded exclusively by males, feminine prestige would have been without interest. Rather, the woman-man's motivation to perform perfectly derived from two sources: (1) from social expectations that women-men would, on account of their greater spiritual power, surpass women, and (2) from the need for a constant relegitimation of his ambivalent status in view of his masculine physical form and biological functions.

According to the data, it was not primarily the desire for feminine prestige as a substitute for masculine prestige that made prospective women-men conspicuous as children, but rather the desire to exchange the masculine *gender role* for the feminine one, expressed by an interest in feminine everyday activities. In addition to this, the women-men's perfection in feminine occupational spheres appeared not only on the Plains, where male prestige was stressed, but also in many other regions; regarding the Plains cultures, the interpretation that male-bodied "berdaches" had to compensate for the loss of opportunities to acquire masculine prestige by gaining feminine prestige is at least possible, even though it is not convincing, as has been repeatedly pointed out above. The "berdache" phenomenon, however, was also found in regions in which a masculine warrior ideal was not the standard for both sexes. And outside of the Plains, there were usually no privileges inherent in the status of woman-man which were comparable to masculine privileges, and visions were often sought by members of both sexes.

Almost everywhere, gender role change seems to have required some kind of legitimation. On the Prairies and Plains, and also on the Plateau, this purpose was served primarily by standardized visions, and in the Southwest and parts of California, standardized dreams. Sometimes, in addition, a "test" served as the final opportunity for a decision and as the final, decisive legitimation.

West of the Prairies and Plains, as well as in the Arctic and Subarctic regions, there were noticeably more men-women or women who mainly pursued masculine subsistence activities on a long-term or permanent basis. The quest for masculine prestige usually did not play a significant role because the pertinent cultures did not share the warrior ideal of the Prairies and Plains tribes. (Even the potlatch system of the Northwest Coast should not be seen as a masculine prestige system because it drew in and involved entire extended family bands, including the women.) It is clear from the case examples that the motivations of such women often lay in a striving for independence and that an unmarried woman had to master masculine subsistence techniques in order to survive.

A characteristic of the "berdaches" of both sexes is a marked interest in occupations and activities of the opposite sex which was already manifest in childhood. By contrast, "independent" or masculine women—mainly in the Subarctic, the Arctic, and also parts of the Northwest Coast—typically engaged in masculine occupations and activities out of economic necessity. Further, these masculine activities were generally first taken up at an adult age because either the husband or the family of birth was absent as the provider within a male-dominated subsistence economy. Such cases did not involve a reclassification of these women as men-women.

In the true sense of the definition, men-women, or "female berdaches," were rare, and have been found, first, where visions or dreams legitimated the behavioral modes of *both* sexes (the Plateau, Southwest, parts of California), and second, where sons were lacking in a male-dominated subsistence economy, and girls were therefore raised as boys (Subarctic, Arctic).

In contrast to women-men, no latent spiritual potential of a specific kind was usually attributed to men-women. Moreover, in the oral traditions, female androgynes are regarded as morally reprehensible; women-men, by contrast, are portrayed as amusing at worst, and divine at best, which supports O'Flaherty's (1982:235ff., 285f., 333f.) assertion that the female androgyne is in general judged negatively, and the male androgyne is judged positively. There existed, in their respective tribes, no female counterparts either to the wealth-bringing *nadle,* who were generally described as either male-bodied or as male androgynes, or to the spiritually potent *winkte.* Such a different evaluation of masculine and feminine gender role change is most likely to be found in groups which construed the woman-man as endowed with supernatural powers, and his gender status as distinctively ambivalent.

Numerous Native American cultures did not ascribe any spiritual component to the woman-man or man-woman status, and therefore did not regard the male-bodied "berdache" as a supernaturally endowed person on account of his gender ambivalence. This is especially true of those regions in which men-women were also found (California, the Great Basin, the Plateau, the Northwest coast). As early as 1934, Benedict had already established that the majority of the North American "berdaches" were not as distinctively associated with the supernatural as the Siberian "soft men" (Benedict 1949:243).

When, in the western part of the subcontinent, women-men practiced as "shamans," this occupation was probably a feminine role component that was not considered to be related to the ambivalent gender status. Therefore, gender status and gender role in these cases were *quasi-feminine,* but nevertheless ambivalent. This ambivalence of status is revealed both in the designations for women-men and in certain masculine privileges sometimes retained by them (e.g., use of the sweat house, which is the men's club house). In these cases, what was usually of decisive influence for the execution of a change of gender role (by males or females) was not some spiritual experience, but rather merely an inclination to the occupations and behavioral modes of the opposite sex; attempts to force a child into the role of her/his anatomical sex were absent. The legitimation of the gender role change here consisted primarily in the perfect fulfillment of the adopted gender role. The gender role components of one's own sex were put aside, and role components of the opposite sex were taken on, all the way to physiological processes: males imitated pregnancy and birth; females denied their menstruation. Among the Mohave—from whom originates the only example of women-men taking on female physiological patterns—dreams and a formal initiation into the *alyha* status still did not suffice to legitimate that status. Culturally, *alyha* were not construed as androgynes like the women-men of the Plains, but rather as quasi-women.

Occasionally, persons were also integrated into the status of woman-man or man-woman who were ambivalent (nonmasculine or nonfeminine), not on account of a discrepancy between their physical sex and their gender role, but rather for anatomical or physiological reasons. Some groups classified women-men and men-women with men and women who were sterile: neither women-men nor men-women procreated in those cultures (e.g., because they only entered into same-sex relationships). This is likewise true of intersexes ("hermaphrodites"), whom the Navajo made the standard of sexual ambivalence. For example, if "someone who pretends to be *nadle*"—a physically unambiguous woman-man—became sexually unambiguous (and able to procreate) through marriage to a woman, then he apparently lost at least part of his *nadle* status, which was based on the infertility and the ambivalence of the hermaphrodite. In other cases, the (anatomically not ambivalent) woman-man was the standard for the culturally defined status into which intersexes could be integrated, because their sexual ambivalence was apparently equated with the psychic-physical ambivalence of the woman-man.

Contrary to a long-standing and widespread misconception, the woman-man/man-woman status is not a matter of institutionalized homosexuality. Overall, the evidence suggests that although same-sex relationships may be characteristic of many women-men and men-women, this type of relationship is not as central an element as interest in the activities and occupations of the opposite sex. Homosexuality has often been mistakenly understood as identical with femininity in men or masculinity in women. This equation is a characteristic of Anglo-American (and European) culture, which, in assigning gender membership, attaches a priority to the choice of sexual partners as opposed to activities (see Callender and Kochems 1986:176). Thus in Western culture homosexual men are classified as "feminine" or at least as nonmasculine (and sometimes even classify themselves this way) because they choose same-sex partners. Similarly, men who in Anglo-American (and European) culture demonstrate an interest in feminine role components are often classified as homosexual. However, homosexuality—as well as gender—is a cultural construct (see McIntosh 1972).

In Western culture, homosexuals are defined as persons who enter into partner relationships with humans of the same biological sex, whereby the two partners change neither their gender statuses nor their gender roles. The partner relationships of women-men and men-women, however, differed from the Western model. Women-men took up relationships with men as a component of their feminine gender role, and men who maintained sexual relationships with women-men filled a masculine gender role in daily life, including a heterosexual sex life. Within the framework of these relationships, the woman-man was seen as nonmasculine (and also saw himself as such), and his partner was seen as masculine. The same holds true of the partner relationships of men-women. Within systems of multiple genders, the woman-man and man-woman always belong to a gender that is different from his or her partner's gender. This holds true for those cases where, for example, women-men entered into sexual relationships with men, as well as for those cases where women-men formed relationships with women. Both the man's and the woman's gender differed from that of the woman-man. Thus, regardless of whether women-men and men-women entered into relationships with women or men, these relationships were always culturally constructed and viewed as *hetero-gender* (Lang, 1997b; Tietz 1996). A survey of the sources shows that in Native American tribal cultures, all kinds of hetero-gender relationships were usually condoned and, in one way or another, institutionalized (man and woman, woman and man, man and woman-man, man-woman and woman), whereas homo-gender relationships were not (man and man, woman and woman, woman-man and woman-man, man-woman and man-woman). Relationships between women-men and men and men-women and women seem to have been viewed as quasi-heterosexual, given the different genders involved and the fact that such couples usually expressed the same sexual/gendered division of labor as that found among heterosexual couples consisting of a woman and a man. Thus, it is worth noting that, despite the ambivalence of the women-men's and men-women's gender status, institutionalized gender variance apparently did *not* challenge either the cultural normativity of heterosexual marriage or the notion that certain activities are appropriate for men and others for women within the gendered division of labor.

While the sexuality and sexual orientation of the women-men are frequently discussed in the literature, hardly anyone has asked what might motivate a man to take a woman-man for his spouse. The partners of women-men in same-sex relationships have been described as men who otherwise have relationships with women, either within polygynous marriages where the woman-man is one of the wives or within alternating relationships where the man has various wives in the course of his lifetime, including woman-man wives. Sexual attraction may very well have played a role, without, however, resulting in a classification of the man as "homosexual" or "bisexual" on the grounds of his attraction to both women and women-men (see Williams 1986b:112ff.). Even though some (hetero-gender) sexual relationships were culturally institutionalized while others (homo-gender) were not—sometimes even being viewed as socially undesirable—people in Native American cultures were not put into different categories according to their sexual behavior.

Apart from attraction, several more pragmatic aspects may have made a woman-man a desirable partner for a man. On account of menstruation, pregnancy, or taboos connected with hunting and warfare, sexual intercourse was frequently forbidden to marital partners. Women-men, by contrast, were always available without restrictions as suitable sex partners. They filled a feminine gender role, and they held a quasi-feminine or at least a nonmasculine gender status, but they were not subject to the same physiological restrictions (such as seclusion during menstruation) as women. Moreover, because extramarital relations between men and women could result in harsh sanctions for both parties concerned, while intercourse with women-men did not, the woman-man's function as a quasi-feminine partner for married or still unmarried men is certainly not to be underestimated. In addition, it is to be assumed that intercourse with women-men possibly also played a role in connection with birth control.

Particularly in places where a special supernatural latent potential was ascribed to women-men, it is possible that a man could share in this supernatural potential by having intercourse with a woman-man, analogous to the transmission of such potential from one man to another by means of intercourse with the same woman (see Kehoe 1981, Roscoe 1987:166): the woman-man united in one person the spiritual powers of a medicine man and mediator. Hermaphrodites among the Navajo, on the other hand, were regarded as lucky, and at the same time, it was believed that ritual knowledge—and therefore, certainly also the *nadle*'s lucky potential—could be transmitted during sexual intercourse. It is likely that this function of intercourse with women-men occurred in places where latent supernatural power was attributed to women-men on account of their sexual ambivalence. Their function as "ersatz women," however, should be generally accurate; and the promiscuity often attributed to women-men can possibly be explained on this basis. This promiscuity was absent among men-women in regard to female partners. Men-women often entered into formal marriages with women.

Homosexual relationships according to the Western definition have been encountered only rarely in Native American cultures, or they at least were not recorded by the ethnographers. They are indeed to be found in more recent times, under the influence of Western culture, but they are distinguished by the Native Americans themselves from same-sex relationships with "berdaches" (Williams 1986a, 1986b). Now as before, the main characteristic of both women-men and men-women is their inclination to participate in the activities and the companionship of the opposite sex, and not the desire for sexual relations with members of their own sex.

Interest in the role of the opposite sex does not necessarily include the desire to adopt the gender status or even gender category of that sex—that is, to *become* a member of the opposite sex. This differentiates women-men and men-women from most transsexuals in Western culture: a polarization into masculine and feminine gender status does not tolerate any ambivalence. Consequently, any gender ambivalence in Western culture is under significant pressure to conform to the masculine or feminine role. In extreme cases, the subjectively felt divergence of physique and personality leads to bringing the anatomically "wrong" sex in line with the subjectively felt "right" sex (and the corresponding gender status) by surgical means. Where an ambivalent gender status is available for the expression of an ambivalent identity, there arises neither the subjective feeling of being a personality imprisoned in the "wrong" body nor the desire for a physical adaptation to the opposite biological sex by means of surgical removal of the primary and secondary sex characteristics. In no case has self-castration, for example, been reported of women-men. The feeling that there is a discrepancy between one's physique and one's psyche can come into being only against the background of two polarized gender statuses. In the few cases in which autobiographical information from women-men is available (Williams 1986a, 1986b), an ambivalent and nonmasculine—but also not purely feminine—gender identity is revealed. This is also confirmed by my own fieldwork data. This ambivalent identity can be lived out within the framework of the woman-man/man-woman status. Despite all the ambivalence, this status was *expressed* everywhere by conscientious fulfillment of the feminine (or, in the case of men-women, the masculine) gender role, most often including—outside of the purely occupational area—the imitation of characteristics culturally defined as typically masculine or feminine. Cross-dressing and sexual relations with persons of the genetically or anatomically same sex were not an indispensable component of the woman-man's and man-woman's role, even though these apparently were traditionally found in most Native American societies.

The most positive descriptions of the attitudes of individual cultures toward male-bodied "berdaches" have come from self-identified contemporary women-men (Williams 1986a, 1986b). Non-"berdaches" usually expressed themselves more reticently and guardedly. Overall, the sources suggest an ambivalent attitude that combines sympathy or amusement with respect for the individual who has undertaken a gender role change. Decidedly negative judgments can almost always be traced to external influences in the context of the process of acculturation. Women-men generally enjoyed higher esteem than men-women, above all where the women-men were regarded as spiritually powerful. Even in these cases, however, there were occasional attempts, mainly by male community members, to avert the process of gender role change on the part of a boy. These attempts lasted until the boy was able to enter the status of woman-man officially through some type of legitimating device (vision, test, cross-dressing, decision at puberty, etc.). After that, both the woman-man and the community were relieved equally of the responsibility for the gender role change (see Williams 1986b:30).

Where women-men fulfilled specialist tasks, these were generally not restricted to them, but rather were occupations that could belong either to the masculine or to the feminine gender role. Whether or not women-men engaged in "masculine" or "feminine" specialist occupations depended on whether, in any given group, the woman-man status was defined as ambivalent or as quasi-feminine. If women-men practiced as healers (often termed "shamans" in the literature), this specialty usually either belonged to their adopted (women's) role or was accessible to both sexes, particularly when the woman-man status was defined as quasi-feminine (e.g., California, the Great Basin, the Plateau). If, as on the Plains, their status was highly ambivalent, then they often fulfilled functions which fell within the role domain of male medicine men. In the extreme, cross-dressing merely appeared as the expression of personal medicine or special power bestowed upon the individual by a supernatural being, without involving a gender role change or change of gender status (e.g., the Piegan Four Bears). As healers, men-women (female "berdaches") practiced within the scope of their masculine role; in contrast to this, independent or masculine women, who otherwise infringed on masculine occupational domains, did so within the framework of their feminine gender role and gender status (e.g., Ojibwa, Shasta).

Although the categories of woman-man and man-woman were culturally established role alternatives wherever gender role change was institutionalized in Native American cultures, it seems that their roles did not constitute "alternative roles" in the sense that they contained elements that were not already part of the culturally defined woman's and man's roles. In general, the woman-man's social role was modeled after the woman's, and the man-woman's role after the man's role. Thus, regardless of any gender mixing that might have occurred, such as among those tribes where women-men's spiritual power resembled that of the men rather than that of the women (but where the woman-man role was nevertheless characterized by excellence in women's work), one might ask whether the institution of gender role change and gender mixing really shook the foundations of gender polarity. On the other hand, however, gender role change does show that gender and gender role are not inevitably tied to biological sex, and it thus creates cultural recognition and acceptance for people whose gender identity and occupational preferences are in contrast to the gender role usually assigned to their physical sex within their culture. Thus, the roles of woman-man and man-woman in a sense do provide true alternatives to the standard masculine and feminine roles. When it comes to assigning gender, occupational preferences outweigh physical sex. At the same time, however, physical sex is not completely irrelevant when it comes to classifying a person in terms of gender. While a male could become a woman-man and a female a man-woman, it was not possible for males to become women, or for females to become men.

Within the framework of the componential organization and manifestation of their gender role, women-men have frequently been characterized as superior to women in all things. Nowhere, apparently, were women-men perceived to be superior to the *men* of their respective cultures on account of their ambivalence, and nowhere were men-women regarded as especially excellent quasi-men. Where women-men did not retain components of the masculine role or male privileges, they could, in any event, only compete with the women. Even in an ambivalent gender role, their status in such cases usually contained sufficient femininity to preclude competition with male medicine men or even with warriors. Since their status was ambivalent, they were able—as were women—to distance themselves from masculine prestige activities without being held in contempt because of it. Notwithstanding their non-masculine status, however, both women and women-men were free to prove themselves within the masculine prestige system: some women-men and women by all means did go to war. To be classified under the category "woman" or "woman-man" ("non-man") was humiliating only for a male who defined himself as masculine. Consequently, the forced cross-dressing of cowardly warriors should not be equated with the woman-man institution, nor does it in principle point to a low status for women-men (or women). Nevertheless, such forced cross-dressing does make it clear that males in particular—and above all, males in cultures with a warrior-oriented masculine prestige system—absolutely had, at some point in their lives, to decide clearly for either a masculine or a nonmasculine status. In such cultures, this problem did not arise for the women because masculine prestige domains were accessible to non-men.

Within the range of alternative gender roles, gender role change certainly represents the most extreme form, compared with the possibility of varying one's gender role by discarding some of one's own role components and adding role components of the opposite sex. Furthermore, in many places, male dominance, whether in the area of prestige or of subsistence, made crossing out of gender roles easier (and possibly more attractive) for women than for men, who, in many groups, were more readily able to change than to cross out of their gender roles, at least if their interest in feminine tasks went beyond lending their female fellow family members a hand when needed.

Gender role change proves to be neither an institutionalized form of homosexual behavior nor a humiliating alternative for persons who failed to attain the role ideals predetermined by their culture. Rather, it demonstrates the possibilities of exchanging, combining, and crossing out of gender roles according to individual personality structures; thus it is the total componential organization and manifestation of the role, and not merely the choice of sexual partners, that determines the gender status of a person and that person's place in the culture. Women-men and men-women are not classified as "homosexuals" in Native American cultures, but rather as people who occupy a certain gender status in combination with a culturally determined gender role alternative. Further, the nonambivalent gender status of their partners was not called into question, since it was not based on the choice of sexual partners, but instead on other components of the gender role. Such a construction of gender status also leads to an acceptance of sexual relations between anatomically same-sex partners. The cultural institutionalization found in some Native American cultures of a variety of gender role alternatives, instead of two rigid gender roles, furthermore, makes possible a considerable degree of freedom for the individual in the componential organization and formulation of a role which corresponds to his or her personal inclinations and abilities. On the basis of this institutionalization of gender role alternatives, males and females, who in such a manner cross out of the conventional role for their sex, are not defined as deviant, but rather experience acceptance, and frequently even a considerable degree of esteem and respect.

References

Alarcón, Hernando. 1565. Relazione della navigatione & scoperta che fece il capitano Fernando Alarchone per ordine dello illustrissimo Signor Don Antonio Mendozza, vice Re della nuova Spagna data in Colima, porto della nuova Spagna. In *Navigationi et Viaggi* . . . , ed. Gio. Battista Ramusio, 3:363–371. Venice: De Giunti.

Albers, Patricia, and Beatrice Medicine, eds. 1983. *The Hidden Half: Studies of Plains Indian Women.* Washington, D.C.: University Press of America.

Allen, Paula Gunn. 1981. Lesbians in American Indian Culture. *Conditions* 7:67–87.

———. 1986. *The Sacred Hoop: Recovering the Feminine in American Indian Traditions.* Boston: Beacon Press.

Angelino, H., and C. L. Shedd. 1955. A Note on Berdache. *American Anthropologist* 57(1):121–126.

Anguksuaq (Richard LaFortune). 1993. Commentary. On papers read in the session "The 'North American Berdache' Revisited Empirically and Theoretically" at the 92nd Annual Meeting of the American Anthropological Association, Washington, D.C.

Arens, W. 1979. *The Man-Eating Myth.* New York: Oxford University Press.

Arizona Highways. 1974. *Arizona Highways* 50(5) (Special issue, "Southwestern Pottery Today").

Bailey, Flora L. 1950. Some Sex Beliefs and Practices in a Navaho Community. *Papers of the Peabody Museum of American Archaeology and Ethnology* 40(2), 1–108.

Bancroft, Hubert Howe. 1874. *The Native Races of the Pacific States of North America.* Vol. 1. New York: D. Appleton.

Bandelier, Adolph E. 1966. *The Southwestern Journals of Adolph E. Bandelier 1880–1882*, ed. Charles H. Lange and Caroll L. Riley. Albuquerque: University of New Mexico Press.

Barnett, H. G. 1937. Culture Element Distributions 7: Oregon Coast. *Anthropological Records* 1(3), 155–204.

———. 1955. The Coast Salish of British Columbia. *University of Oregon Monographs, Studies in Anthropology* 4, 1–320.

BAUMANN, HERMANN. 1950. Der kultische Geschlechtswechsel bei Naturvölkern. *Zeitschrift für Sexual forschung* 1, 259–297.

———. 1955. *Das doppelte Geschlecht: Studien zur Bisexualität in Ritus und Mythos.* Berlin: Reimer.

BEAGLEHOLE, ERNEST, AND PEARL BEAGLEHOLE. 1935. Hopi of the Second Mesa. *Memoirs of the American Anthropological Association* 44, 1–65.

BEALS, RALPH. 1933. Ethnology of the Nisenan. *University of California Publications in American Archaeology and Ethnology* 31(6), 335–414.

BENEDICT, RUTH F. 1922. The Vision in Plains Culture. *American Anthropologist* 24(1): 1–23.

———. 1923. The Concept of the Guardian Spirit in North America. *Memoirs of the American Anthropological Association* 29, 1–97.

———. 1934. Anthropology and the Abnormal. *Journal of General Psychology* 10: 59–82.

———. 1949. *Patterns of Culture.* New York: Mentor Books.

BENJAMIN, HARRY. 1966. *The Transsexual Phenomenon.* New York: The Julian Press. Original edition 1934.

BENZONI, GIROLAMO. 1970. Neue und gründliche Historien von dem niederländischen Indien . . durch Girolamo Benzoni [1594]. In *Collectiones peregrinationum in Indiam Orientalem et Indiam Occidentalem. America. Deutsch (1590–1634).* Munich: Kölbl. Original edition, Frankfurt am Main: Bry.

BIRKET-SMITH, KAJ. 1953. The Chugach Eskimo. *Nationalmuseets Skrifter, Etnografisk Roekke 6.* Copenhagen: Nationalmuseets publikationsfond.

BIRKET-SMITH, KAJ, AND FREDERICA DE LAGUNA. 1938. *The Eyak Indians of the Copper River Delta, Alaska.* Copenhagen: Levin and Munksgaard.

BLACKWOOD, EVELYN. 1984. Sexuality and Gender in Certain Native American Tribes: The Case of Cross-Gender Females. *Signs: Journal of Women in Culture and Society* 10: 1–42.

———. 1993. Commentary. On papers read in the session "The 'North American Berdache' Revisited Empirically and Theoretically" at the 92nd Annual Meeting of the American Anthropological Association, Washington, D.C.

———., ed. 1986. *The Many Faces of Homosexuality: Anthropological Approaches to Homosexual Behavior.* New York: Harrington Park Press. Originally published as *Journal of Homosexuality* 11(3/4), 1985.

BLEIBTREU-EHRENBERG, GISELA. 1970. Homosexualität und Transvestition im Schamanismus. *Anthropos* 65: 189–228.

———. 1984. *Der Weibmann: Kultischer Geschlechtswechsel im Schamanismus.* Frankfurt am Main: Fischer.

Boas, Franz. 1900. The Mythology of the Bella Coola Indians. *Memoirs of the American Museum of Natural History* 2(2) (Publications of the Jesup North Pacific Expedition I). New York: American Museum of Natural History.

———. 1901. The Eskimo of Baffin Land and Hudson Bay. *Bulletin of the American Museum of Natural History* 15(1/2):1–570.

Bogoraz, Vladimir G. 1907. The Chukchee. *Memoirs of the American Museum of Natural History* 11. Vol. 2 (Publications of the Jesup North Pacific Expedition VII). New York: American Museum of Natural History.

Boscana, Geronimo. 1846. *Chinigchinich: A Historical Account of the Origin, Customs, and Traditions of the Indians at the Missionary Establishment of San Juan Capistrano, Alta California.* New York: Wiley and Putnam.

Bossu, Jean Bernard. 1962. *Jean Bernard Bossu's Travels in the Interior of North America, 1751–1762,* ed. and trans. Seymour Feiler. Norman: University of Oklahoma Press.

Bowers, Alfred. 1950. *Mandan Social and Ceremonial Organization.* Chicago: University of Chicago Press.

———. 1965. Hidatsa Social and Ceremonial Organization. *Bulletin, Bureau of American Ethnology,* no. 194.

Broch, Harald Beyer. 1977. A Note on Berdache Among the Hare Indians of Northwestern Canada. *Western Canadian Journal of Anthropology* 7(3):95–101.

Broude, Gwen. 1981. The Cultural Management of Sexuality. In *The Handbook of Cross-Cultural Human Development,* ed. Robert Munroe, Ruth Munroe, and J. Whiting, 623–673. New York: Garland STMP Press.

Brown, Dee. 1974. *Begrabt mein Herz an der Biegung des Flusses.* Munich: Knaur.

Bry, Theodor de, ed. 1970. *Collectiones peregrinationum in Indiam Orientalem et Indiam Occidentalem. America. Deutsch. (1590–1634).* Munich: Kölbl. Original edition, Frankfurt am Main: Bry.

Bullough, Vern. 1976. *Sexual Variance in Society and History.* New York: Wiley.

Bunzel, Ruth. 1929. *The Pueblo Potter: A Study of Creative Imagination in Primitive Art.* New York: Columbia University Press.

———. 1932. Introduction to Zuni Ceremonialism. *Annual Report, Bureau of American Ethnology* 47:467–544.

Burchard, Johann M. 1961. Struktur und Soziologie des Transvestismus und Transsexualismus. *Beiträge zur Sexualforschung* 21:1–69.

Burns, Randy. 1988. Preface. In *Living the Spirit: A Gay American Indian Anthology,* ed. Gay American Indians and Will Roscoe, 1–5. New York: St. Martin's Press.

Cabeza de Vaca, Alvar Nuñez. 1555. *La relacion y comentarios del gouernador Aluar nuñez Cabeça de vaca, de lo acaescido en las dos jornadas que hizo a las Indias.* Valladolid.

Callender, Charles, and Lee Kochems. 1983. The North American Berdache. *Current Anthropology* 24:443–470.

———. 1986. Men and Not-Men: Male Gender-Mixing Statuses and Homosexuality. In *The Many Faces of Homosexuality: Anthropological Approaches to Homosexual Behavior,* ed. Evelyn Blackwood, 165–178. New York: Harrington Park Press.

Carrier, Joseph M. 1986. Foreword. In *The Many Faces of Homosexuality: Anthropological Approaches to Homosexual Behavior,* ed. Evelyn Blackwood, xi–xii. New York: Harrington Park Press.

Catlin, George. 1926. *North American Indians.* 2 Vols. Edinburgh: John Grant.

———. 1973. *Letters and Notes on the Manners, Customs, and Condition of the North American Indians.* 2 Vols. New York: Dover.

Charlevoix, Pierre François Xavier de. 1744. *Journal d'un Voyage fait par ordre du roi dans l'Amérique Septentrionale.* Vol. 6. Paris: Rollin Fils.

Cline, Walter. 1938. Religion and World View. In *The Sinkaietk or Southern Okanagon of Washington,* ed. Leslie Spier, 131–182. General Series in Anthropology 6 (Contributions From the Laboratory of Anthropology 2). Menasha, Wis.: George Banta Publishing.

Cline, Walter, R. Commons, M. Mandelbaum, R. H. Post, and L. W. Walters. 1938. Tales. In *The Sinkaietk or Southern Okanagon of Washington,* ed. Leslie Spier, 195–249. General Series in Anthropology 6 (Contributions From the Laboratory of Anthropology 2). Menasha, Wis.: George Banta Publishing.

Costansó, Miguel. 1984a. Diario Histórico de los Viajes de Mar y Tierra hechos al Norte de California. In *Gaspar de Portolá: Crónicas del Descubrimiento de la Alta California 1769,* ed. A. Cano Sánchez et al., 29–50. Barcelona: Publications i edicions de la Universitat de Barcelona.

———. 1984b. Diario del Viage de tierra hecho al Norte de la California . . . (1769). In *Gaspar de Portolá: Crónicas del Descubrimiento de la Alta California 1769,* ed. A. Cano Sánchez et al., 53–137. Barcelona: Publications i edicions de la Universitat de Barcelona.

Coues, Elliott, ed. 1897. *New Light on the Early History of the Greater Northwest: The Manuscript Journals of Alexander Henry and of David Thompson 1799–1814*. Vol. 1. New York: Francis P. Harper.

Crowe, K. J. 1974. *A History of the Aboriginal Peoples of Northern Canada*. Montreal: McGill-Queen's University Press.

Curtis, Edward S. 1970. *The North American Indian*. Vol. 16. New York: Johnson Reprint Corporation.

Curtis Graybill, Florence, and Victor Boesen. 1979. *Ein Denkmal für die Indianer: Edward Sheriff Curtis und sein photographisches Werk über die Indianer Nordamerikas 1907–1930*. Munich: C. H. Beck.

Dall, William H. 1897. *Alaska and Its Resources*. Boston: Lee and Shepart.

D'Andrade, Roy G. 1966. Sex Differences and Cultural Institutions. In *The Development of Sex Differences*, ed. Eleanor E. Maccoby, 174–204. Stanford, Calif.: Stanford University Press.

Dannecker, Martin, and Reimut Reiche. 1974. *Der gewöhnliche Homosexuelle: Eine soziologische Untersuchung über männliche Homosexuelle in der Bundesrepublik*. Frankfurt am Main: Fischer.

Datan, Nancy. 1983. Comment. (On Callender and Kochems 1983). *Current Anthropology* 24(4):458.

Dekker, Rudolf, and Lotte van der Pol. 1990. *Frauen in Männerkleidern*. Berlin: Wagenbach.

De Laguna, Frederica. 1954. Tlingit Ideas About the Individual. *Southwestern Journal of Anthropology* 10:172–191.

Deloria, Ella. 1978. *Dakota Texts*. Vermillion: University of South Dakota.

DeMallie, Raymond. 1983. Male and Female in Traditional Lakota Culture. In *The Hidden Half: Studies of Plains Indian Women*, ed. Patricia Albers and Beatrice Medicine, 237–266. Washington, D.C.: University Press of America.

Denig, Edwin T. 1961. *Five Indian Tribes of the Upper Missouri*, ed. John C. Ewers. Norman: University of Oklahoma Press.

Devereux, George. 1937. Homosexuality Among the Mohave Indians. *Human Biology* 9:498–527.

———. 1951. Mohave Indian Verbal and Motor Profanity. *Psychoanalysis and the Social Sciences* 2:99–127.

Dixon, Roland B. 1905. The Northern Maidu. *Bulletin of the American Museum of Natural History* 17(3).

Dorsey, George A., and James R. Murie. 1940. Notes on Skidi Pawnee Society. *Anthropological Series, Field Museum of Natural History* 27(2), 67–119.

Dorsey, James Owen. 1894. A Study of Siouan Cults. *Annual Report, Bureau of American Ethnology* 11, 351–544.

Douglas, Mary. 1988. *Reinheit und Gefährdung.* Frankfurt am Main: Suhrkamp. Original edition, *Purity and Danger,* 1966.

Downie, D. C., and D. J. Hally. 1961. A Cross-Cultural Study of Male Transvestism and Sex-Role Differentiation. Unpublished manuscript, Dartmouth College.

Driver, Harold E. 1937. Culture Element Distributions 6: Southern Sierra Nevada. *Anthropological Records* 1(2):53–154.

———. 1939. Culture Element Distributions 10: Northwest California. *Anthropological Records* 1(6):297–433.

———. 1941. Culture Element Distributions 16: Girls' Puberty Rites in Western North America. *Anthropological Records* 6(2):21–90.

———. 1961. *Indians of North America.* Chicago: University of Chicago Press.

Driver, Harold E., and William C. Massey. 1957. Comparative Studies of North American Indians. *Transactions of the American Philosophical Society,* n.s. 47(2):165–456.

Drucker, Philip. 1937a. Culture Element Distributions 5: Southern California. *Anthropological Records* 1(1):1–52.

———. 1937b. The Tolowa and Their Southwest Oregon Kin. *University of California Publications in American Archaeology and Ethnology* 36(4):221–299.

———. 1941. Culture Element Distributions 12: Yuman-Piman. *Anthropological Records* 6(3):91–230.

———. 1951. The Northern and Central Nootkan Tribes. *Bulletin, Bureau of American Ethnology,* no. 144.

———. 1963. *Indians of the Northwest Coast.* New York: Natural History Press. Original edition 1955.

Du Bois, Cora. 1935. Wintu Ethnography. *University of California Publications in American Archaeology and Ethnology* 36(1): 1–148.

Dumont de Montigny. 1753. *Mémoires Historiques sur la Louisiane,* ed. Le Mascrier. Vol. 1. Paris: C. J. B. Bauche.

Eliade, Mircea. 1975. *Schamanismus und archaische Ekstasetechnik.* Frankfurt am Main: Suhrkamp.

Elsasser, Albert B. 1978. Wiyot. In *Handbook of North American Indians, Vol. 8: California,* ed. Robert F. Heizer, 155–163. New York: Smithsonian Institution.

Erikson, Erik H. 1949. Childhood and Tradition in Two American Indian Tribes. In *Personality in Nature, Society, and Culture,* ed. Clyde Kluckhohn and H. A. Murray, 176–203. New York: Alfred A. Knopf. Originally published in *Psychoanalytical Study of the Child* 1(1945):319–350.

ESSENE, FRANK. 1942. Culture Element Distributions 20: Round Valley. *Anthropological Records* 8(1):1–97.

EVANS-PRITCHARD, E. E. 1970. Sexual Inversion Among the Azande. *American Anthropologist* 72:1428–1434.

FAGES, PEDRO. 1984. Continuación y suplemento a los dos impresos que de orn. de este superior han corrido . . . (1769). In *Gaspar de Portolá: Cronicas del Descubrimiento de la Alta California 1769*, ed. A. Cano Sanchez et al., 175–193. Barcelona: Publications i edicions de la Universitat de Barcelona.

FAHEY, JOHN. 1974. *The Flathead Indians.* Norman: University of Oklahoma Press.

FEWKES, J. WALTER. 1892. A Few Tusayan Pictographs. *American Anthropologist* 5:9–26.

FINDEISEN, HANS. 1957. *Schamanentum.* Stuttgart: Kohlhammer.

FIOCCHETTO, ROSANNA. 1988. Rom für Frauen. In *Italien der Frauen*, ed. Monika Savier and Rosanna Fiocchetto, 211–216. Munich: Frauenoffensive.

FIRE, JOHN (see Lame Deer).

FLETCHER, ALICE, AND FRANCIS LA FLESCHE. 1911. The Omaha Tribe. *Annual Report, Bureau of American Ethnology* 27:15–672.

FORD, CLELLAN S. 1941. *Smoke From Their Fires: The Life of a Kwakiutl Chief.* New Haven, Conn.: Yale University Press.

FORD, CLELLAN S., AND FRANK BEACH. 1968. *Formen der Sexualität.* Hamburg: Rowohlt. Original edition, *Patterns of Sexual Behavior,* 1954.

FORDE, C. DARYLL. 1931. Ethnography of the Yuma Indians. *University of California Publications in American Archaeology and Ethnology* 28(4):83–278.

FORGEY, DONALD E. 1975. The Institution of Berdache Among the North American Plains Indians. *Journal of Sex Research* 11:1–15.

FOSTER, GEORGE A. 1944. A Summary of Yuki Culture. *Anthropological Records* 5(3):155–244.

FULTON, ROBERT, AND STEVEN W. ANDERSON. 1992. The Amerindian "Man-Woman": Gender, Liminality, and Cultural Continuity. *Current Anthropology* 33:603–610.

GAY AMERICAN INDIANS AND WILL ROSCOE, eds. 1988. *Living the Spirit: A Gay American Indian Anthology.* New York: St. Martin's Press.

GAYTON, ANNA H. 1948. Yokuts and Western Mono Ethnography. *Anthropological Records* 10(1/2):1–302.

GAYTON, ANNA H., AND STANLEY S. NEWMAN. 1940. Yokuts and Western Mono Myths. *Anthropological Records* 5(1):1–109.

Gerhards, Eva. 1980. *Blackfoot-Indianer.* Innsbruck: Pinguin-Verlag and Frankfurt am Main: Umschau-Verlag.

Giffen, Naomi M. 1930. *The Roles of Men and Women in Eskimo Culture.* Chicago: University of Chicago Press.

Gifford, E. W. 1926. Clear Lake Pomo Society. *University of California Publications in American Archaeology and Ethnology* 18(2): 287–390.

———. 1931. The Kamia of Imperial Valley. *Bulletin, Bureau of American Ethnology,* no. 97.

———. 1932.The Norfolk Mono. *University of California Publications in American Archaeology and Ethnology* 31(2):15–65.

———. 1933. The Cocopa. *University of California Publications in American Archaeology and Ethnology* 31(5):257–333.

———. 1940. Culture Element Distributions 12: Apache-Pueblo. *Anthropological Records* 4(1):1–207.

Goddard, Pliny Earle. 1919. Notes on the Sun Dance of the Cree in Alberta. *Anthropological Papers, American Museum of Natural History* 16(4):295–310.

Goldman, Irving. 1937. The Zuni Indians of New Mexico. In *Cooperation and Competition Among Primitive People,* ed. Margaret Mead, 313–353. New York: McGraw-Hill.

Goldschmidt, Walter. 1951. Nomlaki Ethnography. *University of California Publications in American Archaeology and Ethnology* 42(4):303–443.

Gould, Richard A. 1978. Tolowa. In *Handbook of North American Indians, Vol. 8: California,* ed. Robert F. Heizer, 128–136. New York: Smithsonian Institution.

Goulet, Jean-Guy. 1982. Religious Dualism Among Athapaskan Catholics. *Canadian Journal of Anthropology/Revue Canadienne d'Anthropologie* 3(1):1–18.

Granzberg, Gary. 1983. Comment. (On Callender and Kochems 1983.) *Current Anthropology* 24(4):458.

Gravier, Jacques. 1959. Relation ou Journal du voyage du Père Gravier de la Compagnie de Jesus en 1700. In *The Jesuit Relations and Allied Documents,* ed. Reuben G. Thwaites, 65:100–179. New York: Pageant.

Gray, J. P., and Jane E. Ellington. 1984. Institutionalized Male Transvestism, the Couvade, and Homosexual Behavior. *Ethos* 12(1):54–63.

Green, Rayna. 1980. Native American Women. *Signs: Journal of Women in Culture and Society* 6(2):248–267.

Green, Richard. 1974. *Sexual Identity Conflict in Children and Adults.* New York: Basic Books.

———. 1979. Psychological Influences on Sexual Identity. In *Human Sexuality: A Comparative and Developmental Perspective,* ed. Herant A. Katchadourian, 115–133. Berkeley and Los Angeles: University of California Press.

———. 1987. *The "Sissy Boy Syndrome" and the Development of Homosexuality.* New Haven, Conn.: Yale University Press.

GREEN, RICHARD, AND JOHN MONEY. 1969. *Transsexualism and Sex Reassignment.* Baltimore: Johns Hopkins University Press.

GREENBERG, DAVID F. 1986. Why Was the Berdache Ridiculed? In *The Many Faces of Homosexuality: Anthropological Approaches to Homosexual Behavior,* ed. Evelyn Blackwood, 179–190. New York: Harrington Park Press.

———. 1988. *The Construction of Homosexuality.* Chicago: University of Chicago Press.

GRINNELL, GEORGE B. 1962. *The Cheyenne Indians.* 2 Vols. New York: Cooper Square.

GUERRA, FRANCISCO. 1971. *The Pre-Columbian Mind: A Study into the Aberrant Nature of Sexual Drives, Drugs Affecting Behavior, and the Attitude Towards Life and Death, with a Survey of Psychotherapy, in Pre-Columbian America.* New York: Seminar Press.

HALL, CLYDE (LEMHI SHOSHONI). 1992. Interview by Sabine Lang. Tape recording, April 22.

———. 1993. Commentary. On papers read in the session, "The 'North American Berdache' Revisited Empirically and Theoretically" at the 92nd Annual Meeting of the American Anthropological Association, Washington, D.C.

HAMBURGER, CHRISTIAN. 1954a. Intersexualität. In *Mensch, Geschlecht, Gesellschaft,* ed. Hans Giese and A. Willy, 816–825. Frankfurt am Main: Zühlsdorf.

———. 1954b. Vermännlichung und Verweiblichung. In *Mensch, Geschlecht, Gesellschaft,* ed. Hans Giese and A. Willy, 826–830. Frankfurt am Main: Zühlsdorf.

HAMMES, MANFRED. 1981. *Die Amazonen: Vom Mutterrecht und der Erfindung des gebärenden Mannes.* Frankfurt am Main: Fischer.

HAMMOND, WILLIAM A. 1882. The Disease of the Scythians (Morbus Feminarum) and Certain Analogous Conditions. *American Journal of Neurology and Psychiatry* 1(3):339–355.

———. 1891. *Sexuelle Impotenz beim männlichen und weiblichen Geschlecht.* 2d ed. Berlin: Hugo Steinitz. Original edition, 1887, *Sexual Impotence in the Male and Female,* Detroit: George S. Davis.

HARRINGTON, JOHN P. 1942. Culture Element Distributions 19: Central California Coast. *Anthropological Records* 7(1):1–46.

Hartmann, Horst. 1979. *Die Plains- und Prärieindianer Nordamerikas.* 2d ed. Berlin: Museum für Völkerkunde.

Hassrick, Royal. 1982. *Das Buch der Sioux.* Cologne: Diederichs.

———. 1989. *The Sioux: Life and Customs of a Warrior Society.* 8th ed. Norman: University of Oklahoma Press.

Hauser, G. A. 1961. Testikuläre Femininisierung. In *Die Intersexualität,* ed. Claus Overzier, 261–282. Stuttgart: Thieme.

Heizer, Robert F., ed. 1978. *Handbook of North American Indians. Vol. 8: California.* New York: Smithsonian Institution.

Hennepin, R. P. Ludov. 1699. *Neue Entdeckung vieler sehr grossen Landschaften in America zwischen Neu-Mexico und dem Eyß-Meer gelegen . . .* Translated into German by M. J. G. Langen C.Th. Bremen: Gottfried Saurmann.

———. 1902. Relación de la América Septentrional. In *Colección de libros raros y curiosos que tratan de América,* ed. Carlos de Sigüenza y Gongora. Vol. 20. Madrid: Pedraza.

Henry, Alexander (see Coues, Elliott, ed., 1897).

Herodotus. 1971. *Historien.* Stuttgart: Kröner.

Hester, Thomas R. 1978. Salinan. In *Handbook of North American Indians, Vol. 8: California,* ed. Robert F. Heizer, 500–504. New York: Smithsonian Institution.

Hill, Willard W. 1935. The Status of the Hermaphrodite and Transvestite in Navaho Culture. *American Anthropologist* 37:273–279.

———. 1938a. The Agricultural and Hunting Methods of the Navaho Indians. *Yale University Publications in Anthropology* 18:1–194.

———. 1938b. Note on the Pima Berdache. *American Anthropologist* 40:338–340.

Hill-Tout, Charles. 1905. Report on the Ethnology of the StlatlumH of British Columbia. *Journal of the Royal Anthropological Institute of Great Britain and Ireland* 35:126–218.

Hirschfeld, Magnus. 1914. *Die Homosexualität des Mannes und des Weibes.* Berlin: Louis Marcus.

Hoebel, E. Adamson. 1958. *Man in the Primitive World: An Introduction to Anthropology.* 2d ed. New York: McGraw Hill. Original edition 1949.

———. 1960. *The Cheyennes: Indians of the Great Plains.* New York: Holt, Rinehart and Winston.

Holder, A. B. 1889. The Bote: Description of a Peculiar Sexual Perversion Found Among the North American Indians. *The New York Medical Journal,* n.s. 575, 50(3):623–625.

Holt, Catharine. 1946. Shasta Ethnography. *Anthropological Records* 3(4):299–349.

HONIGMANN, JOHN J. 1954. The Kaska Indians: An Ethnographic Reconstruction. *Yale Publications in Anthropology* 51:1–163.

HOWARD, HAROLD P. 1971. *Sacajawea*. Norman: University of Oklahoma Press.

HOWARD, JAMES H. 1965. The Ponca Tribe. *Bulletin, Bureau of American Ethnology*, no. 195.

HULTCRANTZ, ÅKE. 1980. *The Religions of the American Indians*. Berkeley and Los Angeles: University of California Press.

HUNTER, DAVID, AND PHILIP WHITTEN. 1976. *Encyclopedia of Anthropology*. New York: Harper and Row.

IRVING, JOHN T. 1835. *Indian Sketches Taken During an Expedition to the Pawnee and Other Tribes of American Indians*. Vol. 1. London: John Murray.

———. 1838. *Indianische Skizzen*. Trans. F. Reichmeister. Leipzig. Reprint 1974: Cologne: German-American Pioneer Society.

JACOBS, SUE-ELLEN. 1968. Berdache: A Brief Review of the Literature. *Colorado Anthropologist* 1:25–40.

———. 1983. Comment (On Callender and Kochems 1983). *Current Anthropology* 24(4):459–460.

JACOBS, SUE-ELLEN, AND JASON CROMWELL. 1992. Visions and Revisions of Reality: Reflections on Sex, Sexuality, Gender, and Gender Variance. *Journal of Homosexuality* 23(4):43–69.

JACOBS, SUE-ELLEN, AND WESLEY THOMAS. 1994. Native American Two-Spirits. *Anthropology Newsletter* 35(8):7.

JACOBS, SUE-ELLEN, WESLEY THOMAS, AND SABINE LANG. 1997a. Introduction. In *Two-Spirit People: Native American Gender Identity, Sexuality, and Spirituality*, ed. Sue-Ellen Jacobs, Wesley Thomas, and Sabine Lang, 1–18. Urbana: University of Illinois Press.

———, eds. 1997b. *Two-Spirit People: Native American Gender Identity, Sexuality, and Spirituality*. Urbana: University of Illinois Press.

JAMES, EDWIN. 1823. *Account of an Expedition to the Rocky Mountains in the Years 1819 and '20, by order of the Hon. J. C. Calhoun, Sec'y of War: Under the Command of Major Stephen H. Long*. Vol. 1. Philadelphia: H. C. Corey and I. Lea. Reprint 1966: Ann Arbor, University Microfilms Inc., March of America Facsimile Series No. 65.

JENNESS, DIAMOND. 1947. *Schneehütten-Völkchen*. Wiesbaden: Herta Hartmannsheim.

JONES, WILLIAM. 1907. Fox Texts. *Publications of the American Ethnological Society* 1:1–383.

KALWEIT, HOLGER, ed. and trans. 1983. *Frank Hamilton Cushing: Ein weißer Indianer—Mein Leben mit den Zuni*. Olten-Freiburg: Walter-Verlag.

Kardiner, Abram. 1945. *The Psychological Frontiers of Society.* New York: Columbia University Press.

Karsch-Haack, Ferdinand. 1911. *Das gleichgeschlechtliche Leben der Naturvölker.* Munich: Reinhardt.

Katz, Jonathan. 1985. *Gay American History: Lesbians and Gay Men in the U.S.A.* New York: Harper and Row. Original edition 1976, New York: Crowell.

Keating, William H. 1825. *Narrative of an expedition to the source of St. Peter's River, Lake Winnipeek, Lake of the Woods, etc., etc., performed in the year 1823 under the command of Stephen H. Long, Major U.S.T.E.* Vol. 1. London: Geo. B. Whittacker.

Kehoe, Alice B. 1981. The Function of Ceremonial Sexual Intercourse Among the Northern Plains Indians. *Plains Anthropologist* 15: 99–103.

———. 1983. The Shackles of Tradition. In *The Hidden Half: Studies of Plains Indian Women,* ed. Patricia Albers and Beatrice Medicine, 53–76. Washington, D.C.: University Press of America.

———. 1992. *North American Indians: A Comprehensive Account.* 2d ed. Englewood Cliffs, N.J.: Prentice-Hall.

Kellogg, Louise Phelps. 1917. *Early Narratives of the Northwest.* New York: Scribner.

Kelly, Isabel T. 1932. Ethnography of the Surprise Valley Paiute. *University of California Publications in American Archaeology and Ethnology* 31(3):67–210.

———. 1939. Southern Paiute Shamanism. *Anthropological Records* 2(4):151–167.

Kenny, Maurice. 1988. Tinselled Bucks: A Historical Study of Indian Homosexuality. In *Living the Spirit: A Gay American Indian Anthology,* ed. Gay American Indians and Will Roscoe, 15–31. New York: St. Martin's Press.

Kessler, Suzanne J., and Wendy McKenna. 1977. *Gender: An Ethnomethodological Approach.* New York: Wiley.

Kiev, Ari. 1964. The Study of Folk Psychiatry. In *Magic, Faith, and Healing: Studies in Primitive Psychiatry,* ed. Ari Kiev, 3–35. New York: The Free Press of Glencoe.

Kinietz, W. Vernon. 1947. Chippewa Village: The Story of Katikitegon. *Cranbrook Institute of Science Bulletin* 25:1–259.

Kjellström, Rolf. 1973. *Eskimo Marriage: An Account of Traditional Eskimo Courtship and Marriage.* Lund, Sweden: Nordiska museets Handlingar.

Kohl, Johann Georg. 1859. *Kitschi-Gami Oder Erzählungen vom Obern See.* Bremen: Schünemann. Reprint 1970: Akademische Druck- und Verlagsanstalt Graz.

KROEBER, ALFRED L. 1902. The Arapaho. *Bulletin, American Museum of Natural History* 18:1–454.

———. 1925. Handbook of the Indians of California. *Bulletin, Bureau of American Ethnology,* no. 78.

———. 1932. The Patwin and Their Neighbors. *University of California Publications in American Archaeology and Ethnology* 29(4): 253–428.

———. 1940. Psychosis or Social Sanction. *Character and Personality* 8:204–215.

KURZ, FRIEDRICH RUDOLPH. 1937. Journal of Rudolph Friedrich Kurz (1846–1852). *Bulletin, Bureau of American Ethnology,* no. 115.

LAFITEAU, FATHER JOSEPH FRANÇOIS. 1974. *Customs of the American Indians Compared With the Customs of Primitive Tribes,* ed. William F. Fenton and Elizabeth L. Moore. Vol. 1. Toronto: The Champlain Society. Original French edition 1727.

LAME DEER [FIRE, JOHN], AND RICHARD ERDOES. 1979. *Tahca Ushte, Medizinmann der Sioux.* Munich: List.

LANDES, RUTH. 1937. The Ojibwa of Canada. In *Cooperation and Competition Among Primitive People,* ed. Margaret Mead, 87–126. New York: McGraw-Hill.

———. 1938. *The Ojibwa Woman.* New York: Columbia University Press.

———. 1968. *The Mystic Lake Sioux.* Madison: University of Wisconsin Press.

———. 1970. *The Prairie Potawatomi.* Madison: University of Wisconsin Press.

LANG, SABINE. 1990. *Männer als Frauen, Frauen als Männer: Geschlechtsrollenwechsel bei den Indianern Nordamerikas.* Hamburg: Wayasbah.

———. 1994. "Two-Spirit People": Gender Variance, Homosexualität und Identitätsfindung bei IndianerInnen Nordamerikas. *Kea* 7: 69–86.

———. 1995. Two-Spirit People: Geschlechterkonstruktionen und homosexuelle Identitäten in indigenen Kulturen Nordamerikas. *Zeitschrift für Sexualforschung* 8(4):295–328.

———. 1996. Travelling Woman: Conducting a Fieldwork Project on Gender Variance and Homosexuality Among North American Indians. In *Out in the Field: Reflections of Lesbian and Gay Anthropologists,* ed. Ellen Lewin and William Leap, 86–107. Urbana: University of Illinois Press.

———. 1997a. Various Kinds of Two-Spirit People: Gender Variance and Homosexuality in Native American Communities. In *Two-Spirit People: Native American Gender Identity, Sexuality, and*

Spirituality, ed. Sue-Ellen Jacobs, Wesley Thomas, and Sabine Lang, 100–118. Urbana: University of Illinois Press.

———. 1997b. Wer oder was ist eigentlich homosexuell? Reflexionen über Gender Variance, Homosexualität und Feldforschung in indigenen Kulturen Nordamerikas. In *Intersexions: Feministische Anthropologie zu Geschlecht, Kultur und Sexualität,* ed. Gerlinde Schein and Sabine Strasser, 67–109. Vienna: Milena.

Laski, Vera. 1959. Seeking Life. *Memoirs of the American Folk-Lore Society* 50:1–176.

Le Moyne du Morgues, Jacques. 1875. *Narrative of Le Moyne, an Artist who accompanied the French Expedition to Florida under Laudonnière, 1564,* trans. Frederick B. Perkins. Boston: James R. Osgood.

———. 1970. Warhafftige Abconterfaytung der Wilden in America / so daselbst erstlichen lebendigerweise abgerissen / von Jacob Le Moyne / oder Morges genannt [1603]. In *Collectiones peregrinationum in Indiam Orientalem et Indiam Occidentalem. America. Deutsch* (1590–1634). Munich: Kölbl. Original edition, Frankfurt am Main: Bry.

Le Vine, Robert A. 1973. *Culture, Behavior and Personality.* London: Hutchinson.

Lewis, Oscar. 1941. Manly-Hearted Women Among the Northern Piegan. *American Anthropologist* 43:173–187.

Lewis, Thomas H. 1973. Oglala (Sioux) Concepts of Homosexuality and the Determinants of Sexual Identification. *Journal of the American Medical Association* 25(3):312–313.

Liette, Pierre. 1962. Memoir of Pierre Liette on the Illinois Country. In *The Western Country in the Seventeenth Century,* ed. Milo Quaife. New York: Citadel.

Lindig, Wolfgang, and Mark Münzel. 1976. *Die Indianer: Kulturen und Geschichte der Indianer Nord-, Mittel und Südamerikas.* Munich: Wilhelm Fink.

Linton, Ralph. 1936. *The Study of Man.* New York: D. Appleton-Century Company.

Loeb, E. M. 1932. The Western Kuksu Cult. *University of California Publications in American Archaeology and Ethnology* 33(1):1–137.

———. 1933. The Eastern Kuksu Cult. *University of California Publications in American Archaeology and Ethnology* 33(2):139–231.

Lowie, Robert H. 1909. The Assiniboine. *Anthropological Papers, American Museum of Natural History* 4(1):1–270.

———. 1912. Crow Social Life. *Anthropological Papers, American Museum of Natural History* 9:181–248.

———. 1915. The Sun Dance of the Crow Indians. *Anthropological Papers, American Museum of Natural History* 16(1):1–50.

———. 1918. Myths and Traditions of the Crow Indians. *Anthropological Papers, American Museum of Natural History* 25(1):1–308.

———. 1919. Sun Dance of the Shoshoni, Ute and Hidatsa. *Anthropological Papers, American Museum of Natural History* 16(5):387–431.

———. 1922. The Religion of the Crow Indians. *Anthropological Papers, American Museum of Natural History* 25(2):309–444.

———. 1924. Notes on Shoshonean Ethnography. *Anthropological Papers, American Museum of Natural History* 20(3):185–324.

———. 1935. *The Crow Indians.* New York: Farrar and Rinehart.

Luria, Zella. 1979. Psychosocial Determinants of Gender Identity, Role, and Orientation. In *Human Sexuality: A Comparative and Developmental Perspective,* ed. Herant A. Katchadourian, 163–193. Berkeley: University of California Press.

Lurie, Nancy O. 1953. Winnebago Berdache. *American Anthropologist* 55(5):708–712.

MacCormack, Carol P. 1980. Nature, Culture and Gender: A Critique. In *Nature, Culture and Gender,* ed. Carol P. MacCormack and Marilyn Strathern, 1–24. New York: Cambridge University Press.

MacCormack, Carol P., and Marilyn Strathern, eds. 1980. *Nature, Culture and Gender.* New York: Cambridge University Press.

Mandelbaum, David G. 1940. The Plains Cree. *Anthropological Papers, American Museum of Natural History* 37(2):155–316.

Mandelbaum, May. 1938. The Individual Life-Cycle. In *The Sinkaietk or Southern Okanagon of Washington,* ed. Leslie Spier, 101–130. General Series in Anthropology 6 (Contributions from the Laboratory of Anthropology 2). Menasha, Wis.: George Banta Publishing.

Marquette, Jacques. 1959. Le premier Voyage q'a fait Le P. Marquette vers le nouveau Mexico & comment s'en est formé le dessin (1674). In *The Jesuit Relations and Allied Documents,* ed. Reuben G. Thwaites, 59:86–163. New York: Pageant.

Martin, M. Kay, and Barbara Voorhies. 1975. *Female of the Species.* New York: Columbia University Press.

Mason, J. Alden. 1912. The Ethnography of the Salinan Indians. *University of California Publications in American Archaeology and Ethnology* 10(4):97–240.

Mason, Otis T. 1895. *Woman's Share in Primitive Cultures.* New York: Macmillan.

Matthews, Washington. 1897. Navaho Legends. *Memoirs of the American Folk-Lore Society,* no. 5.

Maximilian, Prinz zu Wied. n.d. *Reise in das innere Nordamerika* [1832–1834]. 2 Vols. Koblenz: Rhenania. Original edition 1839–1841, Coblenz: J. Hölscher.

McCloud, Janet. 1977. A Tribute to Native Warrior Women. *Akwesasne Notes* 9(3):27.

McIlwraith, T. F. 1948. *The Bella Coola Indians.* 2 Vols. Toronto: University of Toronto Press.

McIntosh, Mary. 1972. The Homosexual Role. In *The Social Dimension of Human Sexuality,* ed. Robert R. Bell and Michael Gordon, 176–188. Boston: Little, Brown.

McKenney, Thomas L. 1972. *Sketches of a tour to the lakes, of the character and customs of the Chippeway Indians, and of incidents connected with the treaty of Fond du Lac.* Barre, Mass.: Imprint Society. Original edition, Baltimore: Fielding Lucas, 1827.

Meacham, A. B. 1876. *Wi-ne-ma (The Woman Chief) and her People.* Hartford, Conn.: American Publishing.

Mead, Margaret. 1932. *The Changing Culture of an Indian Tribe.* New York: Columbia University Press.

———. 1961. Cultural Determinants of Sexual Behavior. In *Sex and Internal Secretions,* ed. W. C. Young, 1433–1479. Baltimore: Williams and Wilkins.

———. 1970. *Geschlecht und Temperament in drei primitiven Gesellschaften.* Munich: Deutscher Taschenbuch-Verlag.

Medicine, Beatrice. 1983. "Warrior Women"—Sex Role Alternatives for Plains Indian Women. In *The Hidden Half: Studies of Plains Indian Women,* ed. Patricia Albers and Beatrice Medicine, 267–280. Washington, D.C.: University Press of America.

———. 1993. Commentary. On papers read in the session "The 'North American Berdache' Revisited Empirically and Theoretically" at the 92nd Annual Meeting of the American Anthropological Association, Washington, D.C.

Midnight Sun. 1988. Sex/Gender Systems in Native North America. In *Living the Spirit: A Gay American Indian Anthology,* ed. Gay American Indians and Will Roscoe, 32–47. New York: St. Martin's Press.

Miller, Alfred Jacob. 1975. *Braves and Buffalo: Plains Indian Life in 1837. Water-Colors of Alfred J. Miller With Descriptive Notes by the Artist.* Intro. Michael Bell. Toronto: University of Toronto Press.

MILLER, JAY. 1974. The Delaware as Women: A Symbolic Solution. *American Ethnologist* 1: 507–514.

———. 1982. People, Berdaches and Left-Handed Bears: Human Variation in Native America. *Journal of Anthropological Research* 3: 274–288.

MILLER, WICK. 1972. Newe Natekwinappeh: Shoshoni Stories and Dictionary. *University of Utah Anthropological Papers* 94:1–172.

MINTURN, L., M. GROSSE, AND S. HAIDER. 1969. Cultural Patterning of Sexual Beliefs and Behavior. *Ethnology* 8:301–318.

MIRSKY, JANET. 1937a. The Dakota. In *Cooperation and Competition Among Primitive People,* ed. Margaret Mead, 382–427. New York: McGraw-Hill.

———. 1937b. The Eskimo of Greenland. In *Cooperation and Competition Among Primitive People,* ed. Margaret Mead, 51–86. New York: McGraw-Hill.

MONEY, JOHN, AND ANKE EHRHARDT. 1972. *Man and Woman, Boy and Girl: The Differentiation and Dimorphism of Gender Identity From Conception to Maturity.* Baltimore: Johns Hopkins University Press.

MÜLLER, ERNST WILHELM. 1989. Geschlechterrollen bei den Inuit (Eskimo): Wandel im hohen Norden und in der wissenschaftlichen Darstellung. *Saeculum* 40(1):1–14.

MUNROE, ROBERT L. 1980. Male Transvestism and the Couvade: A Psycho-Cultural Analysis. *Ethos* 8(1):49–59.

MUNROE, ROBERT L., AND RUTH MUNROE. 1977. Male Transvestism and Subsistence Economy. *Journal of Social Psychology* 103: 307–308.

———. 1987. *Samoan Time Allocation.* New Haven, Conn.: HRAF Press.

MUNROE, ROBERT L., RUTH MUNROE, AND J. W. M. WHITING, eds. 1981. *The Handbook of Cross-Cultural Human Development.* New York: Garland STMP Press.

MUNROE, ROBERT L., J. W. M. WHITING, AND D. J. HALLY. 1969. Institutionalized Male Transvestism and Sex Distinctions. *American Anthropologist* 71(1):87–91.

MURPHY, JANE M. 1964. Psychotherapeutic Aspects of Shamanism. In *Magic, Faith, and Healing: Studies in Primitive Psychiatry,* ed. Ari Kiev, 53–83. New York: The Free Press of Glencoe.

MURPHY, JANE M., AND ALEXANDER LEIGHTON. 1965. Native Concepts of Psychiatric Disorder. In *Approaches to Cross-Cultural Psychiatry,* ed. Jane M. Murphy and Alexander Leighton, 64–107. Ithaca, N.Y.: Cornell University Press.

NANDA, SERENA. 1986. The Hijras of India: Cultural and Individual

Dimensions of an Institutionalized Third Gender Role. In *The Many Faces of Homosexuality: Anthropological Approaches to Homosexual Behavior,* ed. Evelyn Blackwood, 35–54. New York: Harrington Park Press.

Newcomb, W. W., Jr. 1961. *The Indians of Texas From Prehistoric to Modern Times.* Austin: University of Texas Press.

Niethammer, Carolyn. 1985. *Töchter der Erde: Legende und Wirklichkeit der Indianerinnen.* Bornheim-Merten: Lamuv.

O'Bryan, Aileen. 1956. The Dìné: Origin Myths of the Navaho Indians. *Bulletin, Bureau of American Ethnology,* no. 163.

O'Flaherty, Wendy D. 1982. *Women, Androgynes, and other Mystical Beasts.* Chicago: University of Chicago Press.

Ohlmarks, Åke. 1939. *Studien zum Problem des Schamanismus.* Lund, Sweden: C. W. K. Gleerup.

Olmstedt, D. L., and Stewart, Omer C. 1978. Achumawi. In *Handbook of North American Indians, Vol. 8: California,* ed. Robert F. Heizer, 225–235. New York: Smithsonian Institution.

Olson, Ronald L. 1936. The Quinault Indians. *University of Washington Publications in Anthropology* 6(1):1–194.

———. 1940. The Social Organization of the Haisla of British Columbia. *Anthropological Records* 2(5):169–200.

Opler, Marvin K. 1965. Anthropology and Cross-Cultural Aspects of Homosexuality. In *Sexual Inversion,* ed. Judd Marmor, 108–123. New York: Basic Books.

Ortner, Sherry B. 1974. Is Female to Male as Nature Is to Culture? In *Woman, Culture and Society,* ed. Michelle Z. Rosaldo and Louise Lamphere, 67–87. Stanford, Calif.: Stanford University Press.

Osgood, Cornelius. 1940. Ingalik Material Culture. *Yale University Publications in Anthropology* 22:1–500.

———. 1958. Ingalik Social Culture. *Yale University Publications in Anthropology* 53:1–289.

Overzier, Claus. 1961a. Echter Agonadismus. In *Die Intersexualität,* ed. Claus Overzier, 348–352. Stuttgart: Thieme.

———. 1961b. Hermaphroditismus verus. In *Die Intersexualität,* ed. Claus Overzier, 188–240. Stuttgart: Thieme.

———. 1961c. Pseudohermaphroditismus. In *Die Intersexualität,* ed. Claus Overzier, 241–260. Stuttgart: Thieme.

———, ed. 1961d. *Die Intersexualität.* Stuttgart: Thieme.

Overzier, Claus, and K. Hoffmann. 1961. Tumoren mit heterosexueller Aktivität. In *Die Intersexualität,* ed. Claus Overzier, 409–462. Stuttgart: Thieme.

PARSONS, ELSIE CLEWS. 1916. The Zuni λa'mana. *American Anthropologist* 18:521–528.

———. 1918. Notes on Acoma and Laguna. *American Anthropologist* 20:162–186.

———. 1923. Laguna Genealogies. *Anthropological Papers, American Museum of Natural History* 19(5):133–292.

———. 1932. Isleta, New Mexico. *Annual Report, Bureau of American Ethnology* 47:193–466.

———. 1939a. The Last Zuni Transvestite. *American Anthropologist* 41(2):338–340.

———. 1939b. *Pueblo Indian Religion.* Vol. 1. Chicago: University of Chicago Press.

PAULY, IRA F. 1974. Female Transsexualism: Parts I and II. *Archives of Sexual Behavior* 3(6):487–526.

PFÄFFLIN, FRIEDEMANN. 1987. Letter to the author in answer to questions relating to genital atrophies described by Hammond (1882, 1891).

POWERS, STEPHEN. 1877. Tribes of California. *U.S. Geographical and Geological Survey of the Rocky Mountains Region, Contributions to North American Ethnology 3*. Washington, D.C.: U.S. Government Printing Office.

POWERS, MARLA N. 1986. *Oglala Women: Myth, Ritual, and Reality.* Chicago: University of Chicago Press.

POWERS, WILLIAM K. 1977. *Oglala Religion.* Lincoln: University of Nebraska Press.

PYTLIK, ANNA. 1983. Weibliche Homosexualität aus "ethnologischer Sicht": Ein Überblick. Master's thesis, University of Tübingen, Institut für Ethnologie.

RANKE-GRAVES, ROBERT VON. 1960. *Griechische Mythologie: Quellen und Deutung.* 2 Vols. Reinbek: Rowohlt.

RANKE-HEINEMANN, UTA. 1988. *Eunuchen für das Himmelreich: Katholische Kirche und Sexualität.* Hamburg: Hoffmann und Campe.

RAY, VERNE F. 1932. The Sanpoil and Nespelem: Salishan Peoples of Northeastern Washington. *University of Washington Publications in Anthropology* 5:1–237.

———. 1963. *Primitive Pragmatists: The Modoc Indians of Northern California.* Seattle: University of Washington Press.

RAYMOND, JANICE G. 1979. *The Transsexual Empire.* Boston: The Women's Press/Beacon Press.

REICHARD, GLADYS A. 1928. Social Life of the Navaho Indians With Some Attention to Minor Ceremonies. *Columbia University Contributions to Anthropology* 7:1–239.

———. 1944. Individualism and Mythological Style. *Journal of American Folk-Lore* 57:16–25.

———. 1950. *Navaho Religion: A Study in Symbolism.* The Bollingen Series XVIII. Princeton: Princeton University Press.

Riggs, Stephen R. 1893. Dakota Grammar, Texts, and Ethnography. *U.S. Geographical and Geological Survey of the Rocky Mountains Region, Contributions to North American Ethnology* 9. Washington, D.C.: U.S. Government Printing Office.

Robles Juarez, Jennifer. 1992. Tribes and Tribulations. *The Advocate* 616:40–43.

Romans, Bernard. 1962. *A Concise Natural History of East and West Florida (1775).* Gainesville: University of Florida Press.

Roscoe, Will. 1987. Bibliography of Berdache and Alternative Gender Roles Among North American Indians. *Journal of Homosexuality* 14(3/4):81–171.

———. 1988a. North American Tribes with Berdache and Alternative Gender Roles. In *Living the Spirit: A Gay American Indian Anthology,* ed. Gay American Indians and Will Roscoe, 217–222. New York: St. Martin's Press.

———. 1988b. Strange Country This: Images of Berdaches and Warrior Women. In *Living the Spirit: A Gay American Indian Anthology,* ed. Gay American Indians and Will Roscoe, 48–76. New York: St. Martin's Press.

———.1991. *The Zuni Man-Woman.* Albuquerque: University of New Mexico Press.

———. 1994. How to Become a Berdache: Toward a Unified Analysis of Gender Diversity. In *Third Sex, Third Gender: Beyond Sexual Dimorphism in Culture and History,* ed. Gilbert Herdt, 329–372. New York: Zone Books.

Sahagún, Fray Bernardino de. 1961. *General History of the Things of New Spain (Florentine Codex).* Part XI, Book 10, "The People." Trans., with notes and illustrations, Arthur J. O. Anderson and Charles E. Dibble. Albuquerque: School of American Research.

Saladin d'Anglure, Bernard. 1986. Du foetus au chamane: la construction d'un "troisième sexe" inuit. *Études Inuit/Inuit Studies* 10(1/2):25–113.

———. 1992. Le "Troisième" sexe. *Recherche* 245:836–844.

Sapir, Edward, and Leslie Spier. 1943. Notes on the Culture of the Yana. *Anthropological Records* 3(3):239–297.

Savier, Monika, and Rosanna Fiocchetto, eds. 1988. *Italien der Frauen.* Munich: Frauenoffensive.

Schaeffer, Claude E. 1965. The Kutenai Female Berdache. *Ethnohistory* 12(3):193–236.

SCHERER, JOHANNA COHAN. 1975. *Indianer: Photodokumente über das Leben der nordamerikanischen Indianer, 1847–1929, aus der Sammlung der Smithsonian Indtitution.* Rüschlikon: Albert Müller.

SCHICKETANZ, RENATE ET AL. 1989. *Auf der Suche nach meiner Identität: Transsexuelle in der Gesellschaft.* Tutzinger Materialie No. 60. Tutzing, Germany: Evangelische Akademie.

SCHLOSSER, ROSEMARIE. 1981. Die geschlechtliche Arbeitsteilung bei den Zentral-Eskimo. Graduate Seminar Paper, University of Hamburg.

SCHNARCH, BRIAN. 1992. Neither Men nor Women: Berdache—A Case for Non-Dichotomous Gender Construction. *Anthropologica* 34: 105–121.

SCHWAB, GUSTAV. 1986. *Die schönsten Sagen des Klassischen Altertums.* Stuttgart: Reclam.

SHIMKIN, DIMITRI B. 1947. Childhood and Development Among the Wind River Shoshone. *Anthropological Records* 5(5):289–325.

SIGNORINI, ITALO. 1972. Transvestism and Institutionalized Homosexuality in North America. *Atti del XL Congreso Internazionale degli Americanisti,* 2:153–163.

SIMMS, S. C. 1903. Crow Indian Hermaphrodite. *American Anthropologist* 5:580–581.

SKINNER, ALANSON. 1911. Notes on the Eastern Cree and Northern Saulteaux. *Anthropological Papers, American Museum of Natural History* 9(1):1–177.

———. 1913. Social Life and Ceremonial Bundles of the Menomini Indians. *Anthropological Papers, American Museum of Natural History* 13(1):1–165.

———. 1919a. Notes on the Sun Dance of the Sisseton Dakota. *Anthropological Papers, American Museum of Natural History* 16(4):381–385.

———. 1919b. The Sun Dance of the Plains Cree. *Anthropological Papers, American Museum of Natural History* 16(4):287–293.

———. 1919c. The Sun Dance of the Plains-Ojibway. *Anthropological Papers, American Museum of Natural History* 16(4):311–316.

SKINNER, ALANSON, AND JOHN V. SATTERLEE. 1915. Folklore of the Menomini Indians. *Anthropological Papers, American Museum of Natural History* 13(3):217–546.

SPIER, LESLIE. 1921a. Notes on the Kiowa Sun Dance. *Anthropological Papers, American Museum of Natural History* 16(6):433–450.

———. 1921b. The Sun Dance of the Plains Indians: Its Development and Diffusion. *Anthropological Papers, American Museum of Natural History* 16(7):451–527.

———. 1930. Klamath Ethnography. *University of California Publications in American Archaeology and Ethnology* 30(1):1–338.

———. 1933. *Yuman Tribes of the Gila River.* Chicago: University of Chicago Press.

———. 1935. *The Prophet Dance of the Northwest and Its Derivatives: The Source of the Ghost Dance.* General Series in Anthropology 1. Menasha, Wis.: George Banta Publishing.

———, ed. 1938. *The Sinkaietk or Southern Okanagon of Washington.* General Series in Anthropology 6 (Contributions From the Laboratory of Anthropology 2). Menasha, Wis.: George Banta Publishing.

SPIER, LESLIE, AND EDWARD SAPIR. 1930. Wishram Ethnography. *University of Washington Publications in Anthropology* 3(3):153–299.

SPINDEN, HERBERT J. 1908. The Nez Percé Indians. *Memoirs of the American Anthropological Association* 2(3):165–274.

STEPHEN, ALEXANDER M. 1936. *The Hopi Journals of Alexander M. Stephen,* ed. Elsie Clews Parsons. 2 Vols. New York: Columbia University Press.

STEVENSON, MATHILDA COXE. 1904. The Zuñi Indians: Their Mythology, Esoteric Societies, and Ceremonies. *Annual Report, Bureau of American Ethnology* 23:1–634.

STEWARD, JULIAN H. 1933. Ethnology of the Owens Valley Paiute. *University of California Publications in American Archaeology and Ethnology* 33(3):233–350.

———. 1941. Culture Element Distributions 13: Nevada Shoshone. *Anthropological Records* 4(2):209–359.

———. 1943. Culture Element Distributions 23: Northern and Gosiute Shoshoni. *Anthropological Records* 8(3):263–392.

STEWART, OMER C. 1941. Culture Element Distributions 14: Northern Paiute. *Anthropological Records* 4(3):361–446.

———. 1942. Culture Element Distributions 18: Ute-Southern Paiute. *Anthropological Records* 6(4):231–356.

———. 1960. Homosexuality Among the American Indians and Other Native Peoples of the World. *Mattachine Review* 6(1):9–15; 6(2):13–19.

STOLLER, ROBERT. 1968. *Sex and Gender: On the Development of Masculinity and Femininity.* New York: Science House.

SWANTON, JOHN. 1911. Indian Tribes of the Lower Missisippi Valley and Adjacent Coast of the Gulf of Mexico. *Bulletin, Bureau of American Ethnology,* no. 43.

———. 1946. The Indians of the Southeastern United States. *Bulletin, Bureau of American Ethnology,* no. 137.

TALAYESVA, DON C. 1950. *Sun Chief: The Autobiography of a Hopi Indian,* ed. Leo W. Simmons. New Haven, Conn.: Yale University Press.

TANNER, JOHN. 1830. *Narrative of the Captivity and Adventures of John Tanner,* ed. Edwin James. New York: Garvil.

TEIT, JAMES. 1900. *The Thompson Indians of British Columbia. Memoirs of the American Museum of Natural History,* 2(4) (Publications of the Jesup North Pacific Expedition I). New York: American Museum of Natural History.

———. 1906. *The Lillooet Indians. Memoirs of the American Museum of Natural History,* 4(5) (Publications of the Jesup North Pacific Expedition II, Part 5). New York: American Museum of Natural History.

———. 1930. The Salishan Tribes of the Western Plateau. *Annual Report, Bureau of American Ethnology* 45:23–396.

THAYER, JAMES S. 1980. The Berdache of the Northern Plains: A Socioreligious Perspective. *Journal of Anthropological Research* 36: 287–293.

THOMAS, WESLEY. 1997. Navajo Cultural Constructions of Gender and Sexuality. In *Two-Spirit People: Native American Gender Identity, Sexuality, and Spirituality,* ed. Sue-Ellen Jacobs, Wesley Thomas, and Sabine Lang, 156–173. Urbana: University of Illinois Press.

TIETZ, LÜDER. 1996. Moderne Rückbezüge auf Geschlechtsrollen indianischer Kulturen. Master's thesis, Universität Hamburg, Institut für Ethnologie.

TREXLER, RICHARD C. 1995. *Sex and Conquest. Gendered Violence, Political Order, and the European Conquest of the Americas.* Ithaca and New York: Cornell University Press.

TROWBRIDGE, CHARLES C. 1938. Meearmeear Traditions, ed. Vernon Kinietz. *Occasional Contributions From the Museum of Anthropology of the University of Michigan* 7:1–91.

TURNEY-HIGH, HARRY HOLBERT. 1937. The Flathead Indians of Montana. *Memoirs of the American Anthropological Association* 48: 1–161.

UNDERHILL, RUTH. 1936. The Autobiography of a Papago Woman. *Memoirs of the American Anthropological Association* 46:1–64.

———. 1939. Social Organization of the Papago Indians. *Columbia University Contributions to Anthropology* 30.

———. 1956. *The Navahos.* Norman: University of Oklahoma Press.

VOEGELIN, ERMINIE W. 1938. Tübatulabal Ethnography. *Anthropological Records* 2(1):1–90.

———. 1942. Culture Element Distributions 20: Northwest California. *Anthropological Records* 7(2):47–251.

Walker, James R. 1917. The Sun Dance and Other Ceremonies of the Oglala Division of the Teton Dakota. *Anthropological Papers, American Museum of Natural History* 16(2):51–221.

———. 1980. *Lakota Belief and Ritual,* ed. Raymond DeMallie and Elaine A. Jahner. Lincoln: University of Nebraska Press.

Wallace, William J. 1978a. Northern Valley Yokuts. In *Handbook of North American Indians, Vol. 8: California,* ed. Robert F. Heizer, 462–470. New York: Smithsonian Institution.

———. 1978b. Southern Valley Yokuts. In *Handbook of North American Indians, Vol. 8: California,* ed. Robert F. Heizer, 448–461. New York: Smithsonian Institution.

Wallis, Wilson D. 1919. The Sun Dance of the Canadian Dakota. *Anthropological Papers, American Museum of Natural History* 16(4):317–380.

Walter, Hubert. 1978. *Sexual- und Entwicklungsbiologie des Menschen.* Stuttgart: Thieme.

Waltrip, Bob. 1985. Elmer Gage: American Indian. In *Gay American History: Lesbians and Gay Men in the U.S.A.,* ed. Jonathan Katz, 327–332. New York: Harper and Row. Originally published in *ONE* (1965) 13:6–10.

Weist, Katherine M. 1980. Plains Indian Women: An Assessment. In *Anthropology on the Great Plains,* ed. W. Raymond Wood, and Margot Liberty, 255–271. Lincoln: University of Nebraska Press.

———. 1983. Beasts of Burden and Menial Slaves: Nineteenth Century Observations of Northern Plains Indian Women. In *The Hidden Half: Studies of Plains Indian Women,* ed. Patricia Albers and Beatrice Medicine, 29–52. Washington, D.C.: University Press of America.

Werner, Dennis. 1979. A Cross-Cultural Perspective on Theory and Research on Male Homosexuality. *Journal of Homosexuality* 4:345–362.

White, Leslie A. 1943. New Material From Acoma. *Bulletin, Bureau of American Ethnology;* no. 136:301–359.

White, Raymond C. 1963. Luiseño Social Organization. *University of California Publications in American Archaeology and Ethnology* 8(2):91–194.

Whitehead, Harriet. 1981. The Bow and the Burden-Strap: A New Look at Institutionalized Homosexuality in Native America. In *Sexual Meanings: The Cultural Construction of Gender and Sexuality,* ed. Sherry B. Ortner and Harriet Whitehead, 80–115. Cambridge: Cambridge University Press.

Whitman, William. 1937. The Oto. *Columbia University Contributions to Anthropology* 28:1–132.

Williams, Walter L. 1986a. Persistence and Change in the Berdache Tradition Among Contemporary Lakota Indians. In *The Many Faces of Homosexuality: Anthropological Approaches to Homosexual Behavior,* ed. Evelyn Blackwood, 191–200. New York: Harrington Park Press.

———. 1986b. *The Spirit and the Flesh: Sexual Diversity in American Indian Culture.* Boston: Beacon Press.

Willoughby, Nona Christensen. 1963. Division of Labor Among the Indians of California. *University of California Archaeological Survey, Records* 60:7–79.

Wissler, Clark. 1918. The Sun Dance of the Blackfoot Indians. *Anthropological Papers, American Museum of Natural History* 16(3):223–270.

INDEX

Page numbers in italics refer to illustrations